Critical Realism and Housing Research

Critical Realism and Housing Research pushes debate forward, arguing that a new ontological perspective is required to address fundamental issues in housing and comparative research. Since the nineteenth century various housing solutions have evolved, such as sprawling Australian home ownership and compact Dutch social rental housing. This phenomenon cannot be adequately explained with simple descriptions of key events, politics and housing outcomes.

Lawson proposes that we turn to critical realism for the solution. From this perspective the causal tendencies of complex, open and structured housing phenomena are highlighted. With this insight we are able to extract the key social arrangements which promote different housing solutions from the historical case studies. Social arrangements which are found to influence alternative pathways in housing history concern the property rights, circuit of savings and investment, as well as labour and welfare relations. As they develop differently over time and space they affect where, when and how housing solutions develop.

This book is clearly organised into three parts: the first evaluates ontological and methodological alternatives for comparative housing research; the second provides two historical case studies inspired by critical realist ontology and the third and final part compares the causal tendencies that explain diverging housing pathways in Australia and the Netherlands.

Dr Julie M Lawson is Guest Researcher with the Amsterdam Metropolitan Institute for International Development Studies (AMIDSt). She has examined housing issues across five continents and countless cities concerning their approach to social housing, home ownership and housing finance.

Critical Realism: Interventions

Edited by Margaret Archer, Roy Bhaskar,
Andrew Collier, Nick Hostettler, Tony Lawson
and Alan Norrie

Critical realism is one of the most influential new developments in the philosophy of science and in the social sciences, providing a powerful alternative to positivism and postmodernism. This series will explore the critical realist position in philosophy and across the social sciences.

Critical Realism
Essential readings
Edited by Margaret Archer, Roy Bhaskar, Andrew Collier,
Tony Lawson and Alan Norrie

The Possibility of Naturalism
3rd edition
A philosophical critique of the contemporary human sciences
Roy Bhaskar

Being and Worth
Andrew Collier

Quantum Theory and the Flight from Realism
Philosophical responses to quantum mechanics
Christopher Norris

From East to West
Odyssey of a Soul
Roy Bhaskar

Realism and Racism
Concepts of race in sociological research
Bob Carter

Rational Choice Theory
Resisting colonisation
Edited by Margaret Archer and Jonathan Q Tritter

Explaining Society
Critical realism in the social sciences
Berth Danermark, Mats Ekström, Jan Ch Karlsson and
Liselotte Jakobsen

Critical Realism and Marxism
Edited by Andrew Brown, Steve Fleetwood and John Michael Roberts

Critical Realism in Economics
Edited by Steve Fleetwood

Realist Perspectives on Management and Organisations
Edited by Stephen Ackroyd and Steve Fleetwood

After International Relations
Critical realism and the (re)construction of world politics
Heikki Patomaki

Capitalism and Citizenship
The impossible partnership
Kathryn Dean

Philosophy of Language and the Challenge to Scientific Realism
Christopher Norris

Transcendence
Critical realism and God
Margaret S Archer, Andrew Collier and Douglas V Porpora

Critical Realist Applications in Organisation and Management Studies
Edited by Steve Fleetwood and Stephen Ackroyd

Making Realism Work
Realist social theory and empirical research
Edited by Bob Carter and Caroline New

Also published by Routledge

Routledge Studies in Critical Realism
Edited by Margaret Archer, Roy Bhaskar, Andrew Collier,
Nick Hostettler, Tony Lawson and Alan Norrie

1. **Marxism and Realism**
   A materialistic application of realism in the social science
   Sean Creaven

2. **Beyond Relativism**
   Raymond Boudon, cognitive rationality and critical realism
   Cynthia Lins Hamlin

3. **Education Policy and Realist Social Theory**
   Primary teachers, child-centred philosophy and the new managerialism
   Robert Wilmott

4. **Hegemony**
   A realist analysis
   Jonathan Joseph

5. **Realism and Sociology**
   Anti-foundationalism, ontology and social research
   Justin Cruickshank

6. **Critical Realism**
   The difference it makes
   Edited by Justin Cruickshank

7. **Critical Realism and Composition Theory**
   Donald Judd

8. **On Christian Belief**
   A defence of a cognitive conception of religious belief in a
   Christian context
   Andrew Collier

9. **In Defence of Objectivity and Other Essays**
   Andrew Collier

10. **Realism Discourse and Deconstruction**
    Edited by Jonathan Joseph and John Michael Roberts

11. **Critical Realism, Post-positivism and the Possibility of Knowledge**
    Ruth Groff

12. **Defending Objectivity**
    Essays in honour of Andrew Collier
    Edited by Margaret S Archer and William Outhwaite

Critical Realism and Housing Research

Julie M Lawson

Routledge
Taylor & Francis Group

LONDON AND NEW YORK

First published 2006
by Routledge
2 Park Square, Milton Park, Abingdon, Oxon OX14 4RN

Simultaneously published in the USA and Canada
by Routledge
270 Madison Ave, New York, NY 10016

*Routledge is an imprint of the Taylor & Francis Group,
an informa business*

© 2006 Julie M Lawson

Typeset in Times New Roman by
Newgen Imaging Systems (P) Ltd, Chennai, India
Printed and bound in Great Britain by
Biddles Ltd, King's Lynn

British Library Cataloguing in Publication Data
A catalogue record for this book is available from the British Library

Library of Congress Cataloging in Publication Data
A catalog record for this book has been requested

ISBN10: 0–415–40549–1
ISBN13: 978–0–415–40549–2

For Margot and Leo – international housing adventurers

Contents

Figures

Tables

Acknowledgements

This book is dedicated to the memory of my father, Ian Craig Lawson, a critical thinker who stood apart from the mainstream and will be remembered by those who knew him for having extraordinary insight into ordinary things.

I was very fortunate to have the support of my growing family in the routines required to prepare this book, especially when I was burning the midnight oil during the final drafts with baby Leo on the way and little Margot on my lap. Sincere thanks go to Jacques van de Ven and Willem Salet – major players in guiding the completion of this book who believed in my capacity, even when I didn't, and in the project. Thanks also go to David Evers, Pieter Terhorst and Jan van der Schaar for reading and commenting on earlier drafts and friends Vivienne and Gary Milligan, Lianne van Duinen, Ralph Ploeger, Michael Alexander, Luis Arribas Sandonis, Leonie Janssen-Jansen and Stefan Metaal for making the journey academically stimulating and pleasurable. Many thanks to all my other colleagues and friends at the Amsterdam Study Centre for the Metropolitan Environment (AME), now the Amsterdam Institute for International Development Studies and the Netherlands Graduate School for Urban Research (NETHUR) and to mentors further afield: Pete Somerville, Bo Bengtsson, Chris Allen, Andrew Sayer and Tony Lawson, whose commentary along the way provided much momentum for continuing to write and review the text.

With thanks,
Julie Lawson
Seoul, 2005

1   Introduction

Waiting for the lights to turn on a hot summer afternoon, I look across five lanes of bitumen to the shimmering car park surrounding Chadstone, the cathedral of all shopping centres in suburban Melbourne. Adjacent are a variety of single storey brick veneer homes, set back in leafy green gardens, Venetian blinds drawn, inevitably awaiting demolition with the next wave of retail expansion. Beyond their corrugated roofs, lies a carpet of 1960s suburbia extending to the hazy distant hills some twenty kilometres away. It's green again and I jockey for position amongst my commuting companions.

How different this seems to my other life in the Netherlands, of cycling on a cold wintry morning through the centre of Leiden, weaving amongst the cars to catch the train to Amsterdam and the metro to the University. I overtake congested highways from the comfort of the train, passing numerous, compact towns and villages, of neat uniform houses and high rise flats. Large expanses of green surround them, of fenceless farmland and strategically planted willow trees. How different indeed, but why?

1.1   What's so special about housing?

And so began my journey into comparative housing provision a number of years ago, an adventure which led me to write this book and explore the fascinating terrain of international housing studies. Beyond superficial curiosity, there remain many reasons to embark on academic expedition into this open and underdeveloped field.

Housing is an object that embodies many cross-cutting and complex social, economic and cultural relationships. These relationships underpin and are influenced by the process of producing, allocating and exchanging dwellings as well as the consumption of housing services. In all, housing is a unique and concrete expression of broader social arrangements such as property relations, institutions for saving and borrowing capital and of work and welfare in and beyond the home. Given these differences in broader social relations, housing demands have been answered in a variety of ways to varying degrees of adequacy. Two case studies will examine the generative links between these arrangements and their housing 'solutions'.

Housing is not only complex and embedded in broader social arrangements but also differs from other goods in important ways. First, there is no substitute for housing, it is essential for adequate living conditions and beyond, for the reproduction of labour power. Second, unlike other items that can be purchased via one-off payment, housing under capitalist conditions is an expensive good and payments must be stretched over time. The high cost of housing relative to income stems from its constituent land, labour and material costs. For this reason, regardless of tenure, long-term credit vehicles and/or taxation arrangements tend to underpin the housing purchases of owner occupants and landlords. Third, time exposes both credit providers and borrowers to risks. Throughout the duration of the mortgage any number of contingencies may intervene threatening repayment capacity. Divorce, sickness, death are all individualised events that can affect capacity to repay. Freeway and airport extensions, rezoning, and other environmental factors may also reduce the value of the property and threaten the security offered by the property's value to credit providers. Risk-reducing mechanisms are often built into mortgage schemes and form part of the architecture of provision.

Despite these important common characteristics, few housing systems are alike. Resting upon the social arrangements of property, capital and labour relations, operating under diverse contingent conditions, different countries have answered their housing question in different ways. The generation of different solutions is the focus of this study, within the broader field of housing studies and the disciplines of social science.

As indicated by the impressions earlier, both forms of provision are fundamentally and observably different. In the Dutch case, social housing has played a significant economic, political and social role for more than a century. In this country, publicly regulated private corporations provide social rental housing to low- and middle-income earners in numerous compact towns and cities. Government-backed loans and more recently direct capital market loans have financed this form of provision. The use and development of land has involved a high degree of municipal intervention, promoting the development of affordable social housing within reach of employment opportunities. Rents levels and increases have been centrally regulated and their payment subsidised. In contrast, social housing is a minor and residual housing option for Australian households in a network of provision dominated by the tenure of home ownership. Property rights are highly commodified and the market is monopolised by private land and construction companies. Until recently a protected circuit of capital regulated the volume of credit available for mortgage finance, which was secured by public mortgage guarantee fund to improve access to credit amongst low- to middle-income purchasers. Today, most Australians live in a small number of sprawling coastal cities. Detached dwellings, with a front and back yard, dominate low-density, land-use segregated and car-dependent residential communities.

1.2   What this book is about

This book contributes towards an explanation of two divergent housing trajectories, which have evolved since the nineteenth century until the end of the twentieth century. Whilst the Australian city has been dominated by sprawling home ownership, the Netherlands provides a contrastive case, where social housing has played a significant role in the development of compact towns and cities. The research focuses upon the historical and spatial definition of postulated generative social relations, namely, those concerning property rights, saving and investment and finally, labour and welfare relations. It aims to test the empirical plausibility of the argument that the contingent definition of these relationships has played a key causal role in the formation, path dependency, crises and reformation of these very different housing solutions. Despite the influential and integral role of these relationships in each structure of housing provision, a combined examination of these interacting relationships has rarely been the focus of comparative housing explanations. This book argues why these relationships are causally significant and offers two tentative geo-historical case studies.

Beyond the substantive, the arguments presented throughout this thesis also concern issues of a methodological nature. The ontology of critical realism is explained and justified, an *abductive* and *retroductive* methodology is introduced and a comparative strategy lain forth. Further, previous research examining different housing systems has employed a range of ontological approaches and notions of causality and these are critically reviewed in this book. A conceptual argument is provided concerning the focus and level of comparison. Whilst some readers may consider that the first part of this book is pitched at a relatively high level of abstraction, this does not imply that the arguments contained are of no practical or social significance – on the contrary. For the way we perceive and research social phenomena matters to every day life, as exemplified by the following paragraphs.

1.2.1 'Truth', plausible explanation and utility

First, the goal of realist research is *explanation* – utilising a comprehensive and defensible conception of what is real and compatible modes of reasoning, with the goal of revealing empirically feasible explanatory causal mechanisms. Unlike other scientific approaches, realism not only acknowledges the existence of socially constructed experience (multiple meanings, actors' interpretations), but also actual physical and non-physical conditions, actual events and influential social relations (such as organisational hierarchy, tenancy, employee relations – regardless of actor consciousness). Further, it uses specific modes of inference to abstract the necessary and contingent relations of explanatory relevance from other accidental circumstances via intensive case study research, using contrastive questioning and counterfactual thinking.

Since the postmodernist (PM) turn in social science, some researchers[1] consider the search for truth as unfashionable, egotistical and even undesirable. Multiple interpretations are given equal merit and the supposedly objective researcher is unable to make judgements of their relative explanatory value. Critical realist researchers are disturbed by the 'modest' relativism of the PM critique. They are *critical* of both lay thought and action and, where these and resulting actions are falsely based, consider that such 'beliefs and actions should be changed' (Sayer, 2000: 19). Further, realists maintain strong criticisms of the apparent ethical neutrality of some PM research: its restrained contribution to real social knowledge and apparent lack of concern for *contributing towards answers* to identified social problems.

Conversely, critical realists are openly committed to and strive for *progress in explanation*. This naturally implies a commitment to seek the truth that can explain social phenomena. Nevertheless, they remain modest about reaching such truth goals and use conditional adjectives, such as partial, fallible and contestable, to describe their conclusions. In sum, critical realists endeavour to provide empirically feasible and competitive explanations for phenomena of social relevance and concern.

In this study, the concept of truth is a very humble and fallible one. Applying an explicit ontology and using a defensible set of ideas and concepts, two cases concerning the development of housing systems in Australia and the Netherlands are reexamined via a process of abduction and retroduction. This process aims to offer tentative, contestable explanations for further research and development.

Explanations for disturbing social problems such as racial conflict, drug abuse or homelessness are not an end in themselves. Rather, plausible explanations provide an important stepping stone for sound and feasible strategies for action. If one can better understand the processes generating social problems, such as those mentioned earlier, it is surely appropriate to argue for more relevant strategies addressing the generative causes rather than merely tempering the symptoms. Certainly, such action transfers the researcher into an explicitly normative and political world, yet for critical realists this is no unholy alliance with non-science. It demands conscientious commitment to a clear and justified standpoint based on normative theory. For this second reason the term 'critical' is often coupled with realism.[2]

The ethical or normative standpoint of this book is rather straightforward and comes to the fore in the final chapter. It embraces a concern for social equity[3] (as distinct notions of freedom or choice) and a desire for a more just city (Fainstein, 2000) as revealed by the distribution of housing-related risks (inappropriate, insecure, unaffordable housing) across a spectrum of household types and incomes. These risks emanate from dynamic relations underpinning shifting modes of housing provision, as illustrated by the case study research. Following historical analysis, Chapter 8 highlights how certain tendencies are influencing the allocation of these risks. Real risks are concentrated amongst those households with fewer and less secure monetary resources, and have emerged from important changes affecting property, savings and investment and labour and welfare relations. For this reason, policy makers concerned about the distribution of risks amongst society's households must address the cumulative influence of any changes to these key relations. Once again, it is neither sufficient nor effective to be concerned about the symptoms of housing problems without appreciating the generative causes.

1.2.2   *Generalisation and abstraction*

In addition to the positions taken earlier concerning the notion of reality, fallible truth and normative stance, is yet another important argument of realist approach to science. This stance concerns universality and generalisation. Until the 1980s, notions of objectivity were highly valued amongst social sciences such as economics, political science and sociology, facilitating grand theories, validated by findings of similar patterns promoting universal conclusions. Studies emphasising the subjective, unique or dissimilar were of little importance. The tide has since partially turned, drawn back by a range of arguments emanating from academic movements such as postmodernism, critical realism and institutional economics. It is no longer adequate to merely recite Marx's laws of capitalism, any more than the mantra of neo-classical economics, to explain real social issues.

Realists have been amongst this vanguard, criticising traditional research benchmarks such as breadth, sample size and representation. For them, generalisation is not about empirical regularities. Given their commitment to search for generative causes amongst structured, complex and open social phenomena, realists promote the use of intensive case study methods rather than extensive searches for statistical correlations amongst multiple cases. For any explanation to be reached, the historical evolution of both necessary and contingent relations and their packaging must be plausibly conceptualised, empirically tested and revised.

The concept of generalisation has recently become a hot topic in critical realist discussions. A number of view points have been put forward trying to define the limits of generalisation and related topics' universality and prediction (see, Næss 2004, forthcoming; Danermark *et al.*, 2002; Sayer, 1982, 1984, 2000). This debate continues today and is best accessed via the *Journal of Critical Realism and the Critical Realist* discussion groups active on the web.

A vital implication of this study, which compares divergent forms of housing provision, could promote a more sensitive appreciation of the locally defined, but universally relevant, generative relations of property, savings and investment, and welfare and labour in producing different housing options. Every system of housing provision, from tribal settlements to company condominiums, involves some form of these relations. The key is to appreciate how they have been defined and packaged in locally coherent, albeit unstable, ways. Thus, comparison is considered powerful when the reasons for difference are compared rather than event-level outcomes. This concept of comparing causal mechanisms is discussed in Chapter 3 and specifically section 3.6.

Ignoring generative causal mechanisms can be a costly misadventure when introducing new housing policies or programmes. Indeed, too often supra-international organisations fail to appreciate the generative significance of locally defined necessary and contingent relations. The development and implementation of housing programmes by agencies such as the World Bank and UNCHS (Habitat) could be more effective where they incorporate a local appreciation of matters[4] such as the role of the tribal chief in managing multi-generational land transfers, the methods used by villagers to store collective savings and the cultural and economic norms binding households together. Further, were contingent conditions taken into account, such as the stability of settlements in conflict areas, local experience with money lenders and security of labour conditions, even more relevant and sustainable housing strategies could be developed. For example, unsuccessful home loan programmes in isolated South African settlements overlooked the causal significance of the existing property market and lack of income-generating opportunities. An appreciation of these factors could have avoided the speculative sale of new housing allotments by first recipients, and their migration to squatter settlements on the edge of existing cities in search of an income.

This book contends that geo-historical research, inspired by a critical realist approach and mode of reasoning, can promote a more comprehensive appreciation of housing problems. Yet beyond this ontological and epistemological foundation, equal significance must go to an adequate conceptualisation of the phenomenon itself, as endeavoured in Chapters 4 to 8.

1.3   Key debates and sources of inspiration

Important issues that had to be addressed in this study included: what was the nature of housing provision in each case, what were its essential features, dynamics and dependencies, and how has change in provision been brought about?

Big questions and given the complex nature of housing provision as an object of study, no one discipline can provide all the conceptual apparatus required to investigate and explain them. With this in mind, preparatory research has purposefully crossed academic boundaries and inter-disciplinarianism has been embraced. To some degree the book is sympathetic to the call for post-disciplinary research whose primary focus is defined by the object of study itself. Thus, whilst formerly a student of planning and policy studies, I have searched for inspiration amongst the works of urban historians, sociologists, geographers, political scientists and economists. To this end the arguments of Sayer (2000) and Danermark (2002) have been persuasive.

Of course, the research issues pertaining to the object of study relate to much larger debates, which are also addressed in this book. These debates concern the relative powers of structure and agency, the postmodernist challenge to structuralism and its counter critique, the problems of comparative method in multi-country research, the basis of comparison, testing divergence and convergence or searching for differences and similarities, and last but by no means least, the nature of causality in social phenomena.

In the early days of this research, a polarised debate between postmodernists and post-structuralists and positivists and structuralists continued to simmer but had failed to reach satisfactory conclusion. For some researchers, this meant the end of scientific progress and enduring relativism, whilst for others it was a silent cold war between the quantitative and qualitative minded. Polarisation was not only divisive but also destructive. An alternative, justified stance had to be taken for a resolution to be found.

For this reason, a purposeful choice was made amongst numerous, more dominant, alternatives in the philosophy of science. This approach has since inspired and steered the course of this research. The choice for a critical realist

(CR) theory of ontology, or way of viewing the social (and natural) realm, has provided clear guidelines for this research concerning the nature of structure and agency, causality and change, and aided the process of conceptualisation.

Over this time, CR has been a catalyst for theoretical developments amongst a number of disciplines, including economics, sociology, international relations and legal studies, generating more than 20 books, a new journal of CR, conferences and countless articles, in the past decade. It is arguable, but of course disputed, that CR goes some way towards resolving the debate between social constructivists and structuralists, whilst respecting the positive contribution of both. It offers profound critique of both positivism and postmodernism and a new look at the nature of causality, emphasising the importance of concrete case study research and the, albeit 'fallible', struggle for truth.

Such ontology has driven the search for causal mechanisms of change in two historical case studies and focused the definition of necessary and contingent relations of provision. Beyond philosophy, this has taken the research into the too-often divided realms of history, sociology, economics, political science and geography. Concepts concerning the nature and influence of property rights and how they influence the development of space have been drawn from political and economic geography. An appreciation of the generative role of financial relations has been gained from literature on banking and housing economics. Comparative welfare studies have also investigated the relationship between housing consumption and welfare outcomes. The notion of coherence in forms of provision has emerged from regulation theory and political economy. A plethora of debates within and related to housing studies concerning risk, convergence, divergence and comparative methodology has also played a stimulating role.

These sources of inspiration have provided a conceptual sounding board for developing a theory of housing provision and dynamics. In addition, a wealth of historical biography provided a rich source for retroductive analysis and reinterpretation.

Last but by no means least, an important source of feedback on written work and motivation to continue have been my colleagues at the Amsterdam Metropolitan Institute for International Development Studies (AMIDSt formerly AME) at the University of Amsterdam, and a network of interested researchers in Sweden, Australia and the United Kingdom. Their insights and challenges have had a direct impact on my own thinking. Versions of all chapters were presented at various European Network for Housing Research (ENHR), Young Housing Researchers (YHR) and International Association of Critical Realism (IACR) conferences and workshops. Where more feedback was required, colleagues from the AME organised several international workshops in Amsterdam namely Comparative Methodology 1999, Critical Realism 2000 and Explanatory History 2001. All presented papers have subsequently been revised for this publication. A version of Chapter 3 has been published (Lawson, 2001c) and components of Chapters 2 and 6 have inspired published commentary (with Metaal, 2001; on Brandsen, 2001; and on Somerville and Bengtsson, 2002).

1.4   Structure of this book

In this book, readers will find three distinct but related parts addressing relevant ontological and methodological issues; providing empirical evidence via historical case study research; and finally, contributing to explanation in comparative housing studies and policy research. There is also a short glossary, a list of recommended reading and extensive appendices relating to differing explanatory approaches and empirical case study details at the end of the book.

1.4.1   Part I: Ontology, methodology and conceptual issues

The book's chosen ontological perspective is outlined and justified in Chapter 2. Following critique of dominant positivist and interpretivist ontological alternatives, this chapter argues for the application of an emerging perspective in social science and housing studies, that of critical realism. This perspective is the cumulative outcome of presentations and lively discussions which have arisen during meetings of the Institutional Theme Group of AME, methodology workshops of AME and NETHUR, the 1999 YHR meeting and the Housing and Social Theory and Housing Processes Working Groups of the ENHR. The work of Norman Blaikie (1993), Andrew Sayer (1982, 2000), Tony Lawson (1997) and Roy Bhaskar (1975, 1979) has also been of formative influence.

Building upon critical realist ontology, Chapter 3 argues for and outlines a specific epistemological and comparative methodology. It proposes a process of theory postulation and testing of causal clusters of key, contingently defined relations that may account for divergent patterns of tenure and urban forms in the Netherlands and Australia. These clusters are examined during periods of coherence and crisis, generating change in forms of housing provision. This chapter was presented as a paper at an International Workshop on Comparative Methodology organised by AME researchers with NETHUR (1999) and later published in Housing and the Built Environment (Lawson, 2001a).

In Chapters 4 and 5 we 'carve up' the object of study, dynamic and different networks of housing provision, and propose a particular conceptualisation of how networks change over space and time. Again, the explanatory approach builds on the ontology of critical realism (Bhaskar, 1979; Outhwaite, 1998; Sayer, 1992, 2000) with comparison conducted at the level of postulated causal mechanisms (Harré, 1976) generating divergence and change in forms of housing provision (Lawson, 2001d). Further, different ways of perceiving and explaining forms of provision and change are provided and the preferred concepts are distilled. These selected explanatory concepts include emergent necessary relations; contingency and agency; networks of housing provision; risk and trust; and structural coherence, crises and reformation. Importantly, a series of arguments is made for the focus upon property, investment and savings, and labour and welfare relations underpinning forms of housing provision. This is elaborated and synthesised to form a postulated causal mechanism of divergence and change. A version of this chapter was presented to the international workshop 'Approaches to Explaining Urban Development Pathways – theoretical frontiers in Geography and Social Science', organised by AME researchers, with NETHUR.

1.4.2   Part II: Divergent housing solutions – the case study evidence

The ideas and concepts outlined in the previous chapters are applied via abductive historical analysis of two long-term trajectories of housing provision. This process involves the reinterpretation and recontextualisation of existing housing histories, focusing upon the definition and packaging of key relations in the property, investment and savings, labour and welfare spheres and their contingent economic, political and social contexts.

The first of the two cases examines the development of home ownership in Australia since the mid-nineteenth century to the end of the twentieth century and is presented in Chapter 6. This chapter provides an analysis of this dynamic coherence under different conditions, during periods of emergence, acceleration, deceleration and decline of the Australian housing 'solution' (Berry, 1998). For each phase an attempt is made to explain the housing and urban development outcomes mediated by the key relations of provision and the existing housing outcomes that sustain them. This chapter is based on analysis of existing empirical data and additional fieldwork conducted in early 2000 and was presented to the ENHR Young Housing Researchers workshop in Gävle, June 2000.

The second case study, presented in Chapter 7, concerns the Dutch solution of social housing provision and examines evidence for the unique 'packaging' of property, investment and savings, labour and welfare relations, which has underpinned this form of provision in the Netherlands. A further outcome of this chapter has been a series of articles and research papers discussed with the Institutional Theme Group of the AME, in Rooilijn (in the Dutch language with Stefan Metaal, March 2001) and presented to the Housing Imaginations Conference, Housing Studies Association, Cardiff, September 2001.

1.4.3   Part III: Analysis, insights and implications

The final section, comprising the concluding Chapter 8, is dedicated to contrasting and comparing the underlying causal mechanisms, which have generated two divergent housing solutions in Australia and the Netherlands. It also brings forth a number of theoretical and substantive conclusions. These include the abstraction of core interdependencies of housing provision and the importance of path dependency and cumulative causation in meeting new challenges and contingencies. The final section is dedicated to postulating future housing scenarios with a focus on the shifting distribution of risk between households, government and industry.

Part I

Ontology, methodology and conceptual issues

2 Ontology matters

2.1 Introduction

Many times over the past few years I have been struck by the lack of attention given to ontological issues by 'young researchers' of international housing research networks. New PhD students, fresh from their masters graduation, were giving little or no critical thought to the nature of their research object in various presentations and debates. Amongst more experienced researchers, ontology and epistemology were long forgotten terms, buried deep in their mental archives and considered of no practical consequence to their research. Implicitly and without critical reflection, important choices were literally being made 'in the dark' concerning the composition, structure and dynamics of housing problems.

Nevertheless, these important philosophical issues have not left the stage of housing research and remain a focus for debate. Indeed, they have surfaced in the form of a simmering methodological debate, which has divided comparative housing and urban researchers (Ball, 1986, 1988; Ball and Harloe, 1992; Bourne, 1986; Harloe, 1991; Harloe and Martens, 1983; Kemeny, 1987, 1992, Kemeny, 2001; Kemeny and Lowe, 1998; Lawson, 2001d; Lundqvist, 1989, 1991; Oxley, 1991; Pickvance, 1986; Pickvance, 2001; Somerville, 1994; Somerville and Bengtsson, 2002; Van Vliet, 1990). The dispute surrounds the ontological perspective of research: the nature of housing systems, the differences between them and why they change over time.

For two tense days in the autumn of 2001, members of the UK Housing Studies Association assembled in Cardiff to discuss new ideas, concepts and theories. The organiser planned to create a climate of creativity, resurrect the spirit of C. Wright Mills (1959) and ignite the scientific imagination. There was electricity in the grand auditorium during the closing session of the Housing Studies Association conference. Far from collaboration, many sat stunned, arms crossed in the auditorium, some licking their intellectual wounds, others victoriously arrogant. Why was there partition rather than collaboration?

The answer partly lies in the basis for division amongst housing researchers: their ontological and epistemological approach. The tension and division experienced on that day in Cardiff was merely a superficial expression of unresolved scientific debate. On the one side were interpretivists, postmodernists, social constructionists and relativists. This group, once shrouded in intimidating jargon and mystique, was suddenly accused of a lack of scientific development, policy critique and self-indulgence. Yet it wasn't the law-seeking positivists, modernists and empiricists who were calling foul. A new group had entered the stage from the wings, demanding more scientific rigour, but of a different kind. This new group of scholars from political science, sociology, urban and housing studies included Professors Hopper, Somerville, Bengtsson and researcher Chris Allen, who launched their criticisms from a new vantage point, that of critical realism.

This chapter asserts the value of making a justified and explicit ontological choice at an early stage of any research endeavour. It takes a closer look at the forgotten fundamentals of housing studies, the competing ontological and epistemological bases, and puts forward a preliminary case for research informed by a critical realist approach. This case is further elaborated in Chapters 3 and 4.

2.2 Ontology as the basis of perception

Ontology concerns ideas about the nature of reality: its composition and causal powers. There are many different ontological theories. For an explanation and reading guide to the different ontological approaches used in the social sciences, the book by Norman Blaikie (1993) is outstandingly comprehensive. It was developed over many years when teaching research methodology to postgraduate students.

Specific to the realm of housing studies, Somerville (1994) compares the different ontological approaches that can underlie explanations of housing policy. He challenges policy researchers to justify their own ontological perspective and subsequently apply coherent research strategies. This chapter continues in this vein.

Debates and indeed misunderstandings in housing research often arise because housing systems can be *perceived* and therefore analysed from a range of positions. Indeed, different assumptions concerning conceptualisation, legitimate data sources and methods, as well as theories and approaches to comparability of housing systems have led researchers along distinct epistemological paths, leading to very different descriptions, evaluations and explanations.

From the earliest stages of the research, an explicit or implicit choice is made amongst divergent ontological pathways. This chapter attempts to clarify ontological alternatives and promote a particular approach.

The following sections are dedicated to a critical review of two divergent alternatives and outline a preferred middle path. The potential and pitfalls of positivist and interpretivist approaches are discussed and the basic tenets of critical realism are outlined.

2.2.1 Ontological differences

Positivism assumes a particular theory concerning the nature of reality, which has implications for the way it is studied and the kind of data that can be analysed. Positivist ontology perceives the world as all that is observable. Classical positivism adopts a naturalist perspective, which asserts that the same logic and methods used in the natural sciences can be applied to social science. Subsequently, social science should adopt deductive logic when analysing empirically observable objects. Positivists strive to find patterns of observable behaviour towards the development of predictive theories. Such researchers promote the testing of hypotheses to develop laws that can predict patterns between concrete events (Neutze, 1981). Such theories contribute towards universal laws with general application, which can be empirically verified.

Examples of societal 'laws' include notions of the 'natural state' of objects such as human nature, markets and the role of government. There are many different types of such theories related to housing studies, including generalisations about the nature of housing tenure, predictions of housing need, laws of 'good practice' and the convergence of national welfare states or their parallel evolution along predetermined phases.

For housing researchers, such as Oxley (1991, 1996), whilst housing systems are perceived as a complex of social relations, they are expressed in terms of directly observable and measurable variables. For this reason, Oxley considers that the relations of housing provision can be statistically analysed, and this analysis can contribute towards *general explanations* of differences between national housing systems. He goes on to promote (1991: 66–77) a specific scientific approach, involving the testing of hypotheses that are policy-specific and value free. In particular, he contends that such an approach should *not* employ theoretically deterministic categories and concepts, but rather, use familiar policy descriptors. In this way, the researcher's assumptions are tested against statistical relationships derived from uniform categories of quantifiable, cross-national data. Oxley (1991, 1996: 22) contends that abstraction from empirical evidence, in the form of statistical relationships, can provide explanations for differences and similarities in national housing systems.

Oxley's ontological persuasion is easily abstracted from these explicit comments. He maintains a flat or experiential view of housing reality, which only exists in terms of observable, measurable events. His emphasis upon hypothesis testing, observable, measured events and the search for statistical regularity places his approach squarely in the positivist camp.

Beyond this view of observable reality, other housing researchers stress the existence of structures of housing provision (Ball, 1986, 1988; Ball and Harloe, 1992); critique the presence of a dominant constructivist ideology (Kemeny, 1983, 1992; Winter, 1994); or search for underlying causal mechanisms of difference and change in housing systems (Basset and Short, 1980; Dickens *et al.*, 1985).

Positivism, which seeks universal laws deduced from observable, measurable and quantifiable events, can be juxtaposed against the anti-naturalist, subject-orientated perspective of interpretivism. This approach to social science has evolved to provide an alternative definition of not only scientific practice but also social reality. This perspective maintains that reality is defined by the meanings given by its inhabitants, rather than any objective, independent researcher.

Social constructivism and interpretivism are diametrically opposed to a positivist view of reality. Both have profound implications for the social sciences. Far from the deductive, predictable and observable world defined by positivism, such theorists interpret the hidden meanings underlying social action, which are defined by the social actors themselves and construct the world they live in. Social reality is therefore multiple and subjective, rather than singularly defined by the expert observer. The behaviour of social actors is influenced by the unobservable meanings they ascribe to their reality. In this manner, intepretivism has the potential to empower the subject in the researcher's field by listening to and directly recording people's experience of reality. Such a process should not be filtered by the researcher's pre-determined response categories, only to be further aggregated and correlated with selected variables in order to test a pre-defined model of reality.

Interpretivists try to understand social reality through the everyday explanations, common sense and attributions employed by social actors. Unlike the natural realm, it is possible for the social scientists to engage with their subject through spoken language and/or interpret their historical accounts of social life. For the interpretivist, these communications may reveal explanations for social phenomena. A wide range of data sources can be utilised, especially of qualitative nature, in the search for differing perspectives, meanings and attributions.

The difference between these and other scientific approaches stems from their 'world view' or ontology. This has a profound influence upon the theory of what is real, the logic of the research process, the selected research strategy and ultimately the results obtained.

2.2.2   The problems with positivist and the potential of constructivist approaches

One can perceive positivism and interpretivism as lying at opposite ends of the ontological spectrum. Like any polarised positions they are liable to critique from the middle field.

The arguments against the use of positivist–naturalist doctrine in social science are strong and numerous. Karl Popper made many of these arguments in the 1960s and 1970s. They have been rehearsed many times since the dominance of modernist social science between the 1930s and 1960s. Popper's arguments are outlined once again later, this time drawing upon Blaikie's contemporary interpretation (1993: 17–21).

First, many critics have argued that the subject matter of the social sciences is essentially different from natural sciences. Social life is more complex and involves the behaviour of intelligent human beings. Capable human beings learn their behaviour from their own experience and the culture of their social group.

Second, a social group is not comprised of independent parts, which can be isolated and examined in a vacuum. Society is composed of complex, interacting relationships; far from being isolated entities, human beings adopt socially and materially constructed patterns of behaviour and are influenced by social groups.

This behaviour develops unevenly over time and space, and in response to changing historical and cultural circumstances. Therefore the laws (event regularities) of positivism cannot universally apply; patterns of behaviour can be changed by human action, which is both socially constructed, materially constrained and changes over time and space.

Third, and related to the earlier points, the naturalist application of experimental method to human behaviour is artificial (often excluding explanatory causal conditions) and overly simple, denying the complex and transformative nature of social life. Regularities or patterns in social behaviour are fundamentally different from universal laws. Humans can think and learn and therefore don't necessarily behave the same way in response to controlled situations. Controlled experimentation, to prove or disprove universal laws, is therefore inappropriate for the study of social phenomena.

Fourth, no researcher is completely objective, detached or disinterested in the subject or outcome of his or her own research. Implicit values and prejudice influence what is studied and how it is perceived. Deductive prediction promotes this subjectivity, as it involves the anticipation of defined results, potentially influencing the design of the experiment and even the behaviour of the subject. The notion of scientific objectivity and controlled experimentation is therefore questionable in science generally.

Reacting to the criticisms of modernist and positivist science, contemporary social researchers tend to acknowledge the influence of understanding, meaning and power upon a variety of social phenomena. They challenge positivism's narrow conception of reality, applying a variety of epistemological strategies when analysing qualitative and quantitative data.

In addition to the criticisms mentioned earlier, critical realists are primarily opposed to the ontological assumptions of positivism and its epistemological implications. Whilst positivists view the world as being comprised of discrete and observable events (Blaikie, 1993: 94), critical realists argue for more structured ontology comprising the overlapping domains of experience, events, and necessary and contingent relations. Causal mechanisms may or may not be observable; they have emergent powers and generate tendencies for certain events to occur. Positivists seek to find empirical regularities through observation and experiment, towards the discovery of scientific laws. For the realist, causal mechanisms can emerge from any one or a combination of these domains. That is, reasons can be causes, material conditions and or embedded social relationships. This conception differs markedly from the X and leads to the Y version of constant conjunctures of events (Bhaskar, 1978 in Blaikie, 1993: 61; Danermark *et al.*, 2002; Lawson, 1997: 17–23).

The ontological position and epistemological process of critical realist research rest selectively between naturalist positivism and postmodern social constructivism. They do not seek to strive for experimental conditions of closure, which ignore the open, contingent-laden context of reality, to produce regular outcomes and make law-like generalisations. They also reject strongly the socially constructed world of multiple realities, which is sceptical of any kind of knowledge claims or scientific progress (Sayer, 2000: 3).

As with positivism, there are numerous and important criticisms of the interpretivist approach, which are summarised in the following paragraphs. These criticisms concern the level of consciousness held by actors; the implicitness of the researchers' own critique; the disregard for institutional structures and material resources; the limits placed on causality; unintended consequences of action; and existence of structures of conflict and social change (Blaikie, 1993: 110–112; Sayer, 2000).

Interpretivists stress the importance of lay accounts and rationale for their actions and are bound to them. Yet such actors may not always be able to rationalise their actions. Indeed, many actions are routine and taken for granted. An interpretive approach is of little use when actors cannot reason why they act in particular ways (Giddens, 1984: 282 in Blaikie, 1993: 111) or when their motivations are hidden or 'false'.

Unlike positivists who stress observed events, interpretivists stress the causal importance of meaning. Strong social constructivists extend this position, ignoring the importance of changing material conditions influencing not only meaning itself, but also people's very actions (Sayer, 2000: 6). What both positions ignore is the existence of social structure with causal emergent powers operating under influential contingent conditions. Such structures cannot be 'discovered' by impressions of observable events or multiple experiences of events.

Further, strong social constructivists cannot acknowledge or make use of the wealth of theoretical research concerning the existence of influential social relations, social structures, interests and power (Rex, 1974: 50 in Blaikie, 1993: 111). These social structures may be hidden from the consciousness of the social actor, and therefore s/he is unable to articulate them as a source of motivation. It is one step to apply for social security in order to pay the rent, and quite another to articulate the related, broader processes of wage levels and housing costs within the capitalist economy.

Finally, there is growing concern that strong social constructivism is inherently conservative as it is not concerned with conflict and possible sources of social change (Fay, 1975: 83–84 in Blaikie, 1993: 112). Suspicious of knowledge claims and the struggle for truth, such researchers are satisfied with documenting multiple realities and assume they are equally true (Sayer, 2000: 69).

Despite the criticisms, positivist notions of science still dominate certain areas of social science (especially econometrics, demography, psychology and subsections of geography) and strong social constructionism has taken a stable foothold in ethnography, sociology and cultural studies.

2.3   Introducing critical realism as an alternative to positivism and interpretivism

A clear and justifiable ontology and coherent epistemology are required in order to avoid stumbling blindly through past events in housing histories, categorised data and multiple meanings. This section outlines the potential of critical realism towards explanations of social phenomena.

What is critical realism? CR is an ontology that challenges the researcher's view that only that which is observable is what exists. It promotes active acknowledgement of the structured, open and dynamic nature of the object or phenomenon for explanation – important causal dimensions that may or may not be directly observed or recorded. For critical realists, the social world and its spatial organisation are perceived as something that is experienced differently by different actors. Reality comprises events (and non-events) or 'actuality' that may or may not be experienced or recorded, and further, is influenced by emergent possibly unobservable relations with a tendency to produce certain outcomes under certain contingent conditions. Given this complex, structured reality, the explanation requires more than actors' accounts or record-keepers' notes. It must engage the critical imagination to abstract geo-historical internal relations that form causal mechanisms operating in the context of contingently related conditions.

Critical realism promotes the consideration of underlying social relations and causal mechanisms generating social practices, ideological constructs and perceived phenomena. From such a perspective, housing is perceived as a complex of dynamic, underlying and interrelated social relations. These relations are the essence of provision, the necessities that operate in the context of influential contingent conditions. In later chapters, these essences are postulated and refined via concrete, empirical research.

The implications of CR can be profound, especially where dominant practice persuades naïve researchers that all that exists can be recorded and that regularities found amongst aggregated data sets provide certain proof of causality and thus explanatory truth. CR offers no such claims, but challenges researchers to understand the complex, dynamic and structured nature of their object of study, in order to postulate, refine and offer *practically adequate explanations* for continuing critique and development.

Rather than impose theoretical concepts, the conceptual process closely interacts *with the object of study*, to postulate appropriate ideas and concepts with the potential to abstract complex, interacting dimensions from accidental circumstances, towards a more adequate theory of explanation (Sayer, 2000). The abduction process can draw upon existing theories to sharpen the focus of abstraction and avoid drowning in empirical detail. Abstraction can be aided by selective adaptation of a number of meta-theories and concepts, which may include for example: the structure of housing provision thesis, the commodification continuum, and the welfare continuum and labour-housing costs thesis, etc. Dutch social science has generated its own body of explanatory concepts including the corporate passive welfare state thesis, pillarisation and the division of welfare responsibilities, the role of housing providers in social control and suppressing labour costs.[1] Ultimately, middle range theoretical explanations must plausibly theorise the object of study, thus not merely 'fit' the data but competitively provide the most adequate explanation.

Critical realist ontology forces researchers to reject an observable and recordable view of social events and address the interconnections between forces generating housing forms in their contingent context. For example, CR explicitly informs

Anglo developments in regulation theory (Jessop, 1990). This theory is based on an understanding of the interdependence of political/economic processes, which differ over time and space. Under different regimes of accumulation distinctive political, economic and cultural practices combine to ensure growth, forming a mode of regulation. Realism provides the ontological justification for the open, conflicting nature of regulatory mechanisms – in which structural relations are always dependent upon contingency, leading to different forms of capitalism over time and space. Well beyond regulation theory, CR has illuminated explanations for the variable success of government programmes, helped to explain uneven health impacts and distinguish real causes from mere associations in gendered organisational hierarchies.

Indeed, there is a wide and growing body of work and debate concerning contemporary critical realism. For the purpose of this research, the following view of ontology is based upon the early work of the philosopher Roy Bhaskar (1975, 1979) and social theorist and geographer Andrew Sayer (1992, 2000).

Contrary to positivist ontological conception, reality is not merely observable, but comprises several interconnected domains: the empirical, actual and the real. *Empirical* experience is the observable domain, whilst the *actual* domain of reality comprises possibly unobservable events. These events are generated by *real* underlying mechanisms or structures, which tend to have influence in favourable circumstances (Bhaskar, 1975).

The following Figure 2.1 illustrates Bhaskar's (1975) conception of everyday experience, social practices, ideological discourse and underlying real relations: Bhaskar explains his schema as follows: real relations (A) generate phenomenological forms (B), which are reflected in ideological discourse (C) that sustain every day practices (D). The vertical line represents the everyday consciousness, which may be visible or conceivable to individuals (Bhaskar, 1975: 89).

The positivist remains fixed upon everyday, observable practices, which are ordered by the objective researcher for convenient statistical analysis (Oxley, 1991, 1996). Interpretivists are more likely to be focused upon meanings

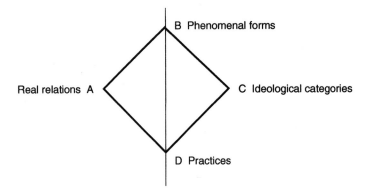

Figure 2.1 Bhaskar's concept of ideology, phenomenon, relations and practices.

expressed through discourse, and therefore place ideology in a more decisive role (Kemeny, 1992: 86).

However, realism contends that causal mechanisms can comprise not only practices and meanings but also social relations; together these overlapping domains of reality can shape social phenomena. Ideology and institutionalised social practices are important, but alone merely represent the locally mediated expression of underlying networks of social relations. Thus, the aim of the realist researcher is to discover the necessary and contingent causal relations of housing systems in order to explain difference and change in housing phenomena (Dickens *et al.*, 1985; Keat and Urry, 1982: 27–28).

2.3.1 *Difference and change in housing systems*

Integral to one's ontological perspective is the treatment of change in social phenomena. Again, there is considerable debate over the *nature of change* in housing systems. This debate has several facets concerning the source of change, its application and direction.

Few housing researchers contend that change is a random process. Some propose specific combinations of *causal factors* centring on class struggle (Dickens, *et al.*, 1985), ideological hegemony (Kemeny, 1992) or politics and institutions (Ludqvist, 1989). Other researchers argue for specific causes or combine a more flexible range of influential factors (Boelhouwer and Heijden, 1992; Harloe, 1987).

There are also debates surrounding the *universality* of causal processes (Pickvance, 1986). Are the same causes responsible for change everywhere, or are causes specific to time and place? The *direction* of change is also a source of controversy. Change may be viewed as a 'natural' evolution towards convergence (Donnison and Ungerson, 1982), a general movement from regimes of Fordism to post-Fordism (Boyer, 1986; Lipietz, 1986), or developmental phases along the bumpy road of capitalism (Castells, 1977).

Inspired by realist ontology, housing systems can be considered to be generated by the interaction of necessary and contingent social relations. From this perspective, it is not feasible to conceive that cross-national housing systems are being drawn along the same developmental path, or converging towards a singular state. There is simply no ontological basis for this type of explanation. Housing systems can only be explained by reference to their necessary social relations, which are *contingently embedded in time and space*.

A more evaluative discussion on causality and change in housing research and a preferred concept is provided in Chapter 4 concerning housing theory.

2.4 Methodological strategies for realist research

The search for generative mechanisms: the way of acting or operating of a structured phenomena requires an account of how these mechanisms or tendencies work, derived from intensive, rather than extensive concrete research. Yet, mechanisms *tend* to generate events that may or may not occur, be observed or recorded by the researcher. Further, such mechanisms may not produce outcomes at all but be impeded by other countervailing tendencies. Thus the realist's goal, given the complex, open and structured nature of the social realm, is to tease out the *tendencies* at work. Tendencies, of course, differ from universal laws deduced from the constant conjunction of events.

If critical realist explanation doesn't involve deduction or induction, what then? Two modes of inference form the backbone of realist inspired methodology: *abduction and retroduction*. Very briefly, *abduction* involves the interpretation and recontextualisation of the phenomena to be explained, using a competitively plausible set of explanatory ideas and concepts to produce a new interpretation. It will be argued that specific attention can fruitfully be given to the definition and allocation of property rights, the dynamic system of savings and investment, as well as labour and welfare relations at the levels of the household, workplace, and community, religious and/or state institutions, which have had a generative influence upon the form of housing provision over space and time. Reaching beyond the field of urban and housing studies, critical use can be made of the conceptual tools of temporally and spatially defined perceptions of social and economic risk and the organisation of trust (6, 1998; Allen and Sprigings, 1999; Hutson and Liddiard, 1994; Lawson, 2000). This process is outlined in detail and implemented in Chapters 3–7. *Retroduction* follows abduction, moving from this new description to abstract the tendencies that cannot be directly observed, using thought processes such as contrastive and counterfactual questioning. The results of this approach are to be found at the case study conclusions of Chapters 6 and 7 and in their comparison in Chapter 8.

This Chapter merely promotes the adoption of critical realist ontology to historical explanation in housing studies, which requires a structured ontology and employs a process of abduction and retroduction. It has argued that such an approach can provide a more fruitful pathway to progress in causal explanation – but no 'royal road to truth' (Sayer, 2003). CR acknowledges and promotes an understanding of the influence of temporally and spatially specific ideas and practices around housing provision and importantly, recognises the existence of emergent real relations that may have generated these ideologies and practices. However, CR is merely a new starting point, an ontological alternative to positivism and strong social constructivism, providing a more fruitful basis for theoretical explanation. *It is not a theory of housing divergence.* This requires a process of abduction and retroduction, via intensive historical research to understand the connected relations generating dominant ideas and housing events. Much of the latter empirical work has been done; it is now time for the causal explanation to progress.

3 Methodology and comparative research[1]

3.1 Introduction

International comparisons of housing and urban phenomena are undertaken for a variety of reasons. These include policy development, problem evaluation, the testing of explanatory theories or the development of new ones. The purpose of comparative research should correspond with the type of conclusions sought: describing, evaluating, suggesting actions or explaining the topic of interest. Some studies may demand a combination of aims and outcomes: for example, that the research be both evaluative and action-orientated.

Whilst the purpose of comparative research may be easy to define or discern, the *ontology* and *epistemological process* tend to be far less explicit. The attractiveness and curiosity of international research on housing and urban phenomena often overshadow the difficulties of tackling more complex issues such as the focus of comparison, rationale for case selection, the time period to be analysed, the uniqueness of institutions and their path dependency. The purpose of this comparative study is the development of not only a new explanatory theory of difference for housing provision, but also a fresh, new application of a specific ontological theory and epistemological approach.

Epistemology refers to the theory of knowledge. It concerns the conditions, possibilities, nature and limits of knowledge (Blaikie, 1993: 6; Danermark *et al.*, 2002: 206). This is clearly linked and builds upon any theory of reality or ontology. This chapter argues for a specific epistemological approach to comparative explanation, which is compatible with critical realist ontology, as promoted in Chapter 2.

At the methodological level, there are a number of coherent 'packages' of ontology and epistemology that can help clarify the comparative research strategy. These include positivist deduction, interpretive abstraction, and realist abduction and retroduction. Conscious selection of such a package is important, as the choice determines the object or level of comparison. The focus and subsequent comparative analysis of cases may rest upon observable regularities, patterns of behaviour or events, socially constructed meanings, underlying social relations or causal mechanisms. Together, the purpose, desired outcome, logic and object of research will shape the entire design of the cross-national comparative research strategy.

Employing the chosen ontology and methodology of realist abduction and retroduction requires the development of a clear, albeit preliminary *conceptualisation* of the endogenous relations relevant to the phenomenon under investigation and an appreciation of the exogenous relations, often described as *context*. This chapter provides an initial sketch of such a concept, whilst a more elaborate version is promoted in Chapters 4 and 5.

Difference and change in housing solutions are often simply explained as differences in context. But what is *context*, what are the endogenous and exogenous relations of housing provision and how can they influence difference and change? To answer these questions, much needs to be known about the underlying relations, embedded institutions, development pathways and influential conditions affecting particular forms of housing provision. Towards this end, important questions include: what does the housing solution necessarily comprise, what are the underlying relations between agents producing and reproducing it, what institutions sustain the phenomenon and what can bring about change?

Following this introduction, section 3.2 will discuss ways to approach the comparison of two long established housing *solutions* represented by different housing tenures and urban forms in Australia and the Netherlands during the twentieth century. The term housing *solution* refers to the coherent fit between social relations underpinning a housing system and the practical solutions and outcomes produced.[2] It is contended that housing solutions in Australia and the Netherlands have emerged from the fundamentally different packaging of property, investment and savings, and labour and welfare relations, which have promoted distinctive housing choices and living environments. Most Australian households aspire to home ownership and reside in large, low-density cities. In the Netherlands, until recent years, social rental housing has been the dominant tenure in relatively numerous compact towns and cities.

Section 3.3 builds upon the ontology of critical realism and the corresponding epistemology of *abduction and retroduction*. The basic tenets of critical realism are further outlined: structured reality, necessary and contingent relations, clusters of causal mechanisms. To understand the observable world it is considered necessary to postulate and empirically validate the kind of necessary and contingent relations that underlie, and tend to influence, actual events, experiences and outcomes of housing solutions over time.

To bring the necessary and contingent relations 'to the surface' and identify the causal mechanisms at work, additional concepts concerning agency must be employed. Towards this end, section 3.4 critically reviews the notions of risk and trust in housing studies more generally and a preferred concept of agency is distilled. This contributes to an emerging debate in housing studies concerning *risk* and demonstrates how the concept relates to the finance, land development, construction, exchange and consumption of housing, within the shifting boundaries of the welfare state and the increasingly global political economy. It is considered that risk perception emerges from the dynamic interactions of relations underlying a housing system as well as threats or opportunities that lie 'outside' the housing system. In the context of uneven power resources, housing agents compete or collaborate to establish norms, policies, contracts and laws. These conventions can be perceived as the organisation of trust to minimise perceived risks in the housing system. The organisation of trust may be sustained or undermined by the open and dynamic nature of housing solutions. In subsequent chapters, an historical view of housing-related risks is taken in the two countries, Australia and the Netherlands, which enables consideration of the extent to which the concept of risk provides a vehicle for understanding two very different housing 'solutions'.

In section 3.5, we move beyond abstract concepts to consider more concretely the role risk and trust play in housing-related actions. Building on the concept of *clusters of necessary and contingent relations* underlying urban form and housing tenure, a number of important social relations, those of property rights, savings and investment, and labour and welfare, are further examined. It is contended that the state plays an integral, mediating and contested role in the definition of these relations and their structural coherence in generating actual housing solutions. For this reason, understanding the institutionalised role, relations and resources of the state is also an integral part of any explanation.

Finally, section 3.6 summarises a number of issues associated with comparative research, the level of comparison and the problem of time and space, and stresses the need for a strategy that compares clusters of causal mechanisms rather than events or experiences of them. This approach will inform the selection of the two case studies: the Netherlands and Australia. It is contended that each case provides a good illustration of the significance of defining and packaging property, finance and welfare relations *differently* upon housing tenure and urban form. Comparison within these case studies, during periods of crises, adaptation and coherence, demonstrates the sustainability and change of different clusters under dynamic political, economic and cultural conditions.

3.2 Conceptualising housing solutions

Despite similar economic and demographic trends (Donnison, 1967; Donnison and Ungerson, 1982), housing solutions in many Western industrialised capitalist countries have fundamentally diverged (Boelhouwer and Heijden, 1992; Doling, 1997; Golland, 1998; Kemeny and Lowe, 1998). To analyse divergence, various approaches have been developed to compare housing systems and explain important differences between them.

Often implicit and difficult to expose, divergent research strategies can stem from quite incompatible ontological and epistemological foundations. Differing perceptions of how a housing system works and different modes of logic and justification have led to the employment of different categories, foci, frameworks and typologies for analysing housing systems.

More explicit and comprehensive descriptive tools include the *chain of provision* framework developed and applied by Ambrose (1991, 1994) which emphasises the wide variety of state, private and voluntary configuration of agents engaged in the interconnected stages of housing promotion, investment, construction, allocation and maintenance (Ambrose, 1991: 41; Doling 1997: 50). Similarly, the *structure of housing provision* (SHP) thesis (Ball, 1986, 1988; Ball and Harloe, 1992) provides a meta-tool to explore diversity of housing solutions. Ball stresses the need to identify the social agents involved in the production, allocation, consumption and reproduction of housing (Ball, 1986: 160) and their inter-linkages (Ball, 1988: 29). Sensitivity to these unique relationships helps the researcher to understand difference. Boelhouwer and Heijden (1992) have developed a more concrete model outlining numerous background factors which may influence the structure of the housing market in different countries. Lundqvist (1990) has also put forward a useful scheme categorising the variety of interventions employed by governments to influence household income and dwelling costs.

In contrast to Ambrose and Ball, who stress the unique nature of housing networks, various typologies of housing systems have also been developed as a basis for testing theories concerning the driving forces influencing different housing systems. These include the liberal–corporatist–social democratic typology and the evaluative comparison of Barlow and Duncan (1994) and Golland (1998) and Lundqvist's theories of the 'political–ideological and structural–institutional' relations underpinning market–state mixes in housing policy (1989, 1991). Country-specific theories, from a variety of perspectives, also try to explain the development and change of specific housing outcomes.[3]

There are important similarities in contemporary comparative approaches: most stress the relational, multi-dimensional quality of housing phenomena, the inter-connectedness of housing systems with other non-housing phenomena, and the dynamic and shifting nature of housing systems. Debate is most divisive concerning the appropriate level of comparison, relative causal powers of particular relations in a housing system, the direction of change and the universality of explanatory theories.

The remainder of this chapter seeks to contribute towards this debate by returning to the ontological and epistemological basis of housing solutions. What do we need to examine to explain difference and what type of evidence would provide an empirically plausible explanation? Categorising variables across nations can provide stimulating descriptions but cannot explain difference. Further, typologies (or ideal types, contrastive tools) of housing systems may reduce the researcher's sensitivity to the unique configuration of social relations underlying national housing solutions and their uneven application across regions and localities. It will be argued that explanation of difference and change requires a deeper level of analysis of the causal mechanisms underlying housing outcomes over history and geography.

3.2.1   *The prospects and limitations of the structure of housing provision approach*

Over the past decade, a simmering methodological debate has divided a number of comparative housing and urban researchers.[4] Ball (1998, 1988) remains one of the most fervent critics of comparative research, arguing that it is descriptive, shallow, policy focused and unable to explain housing in terms of wider economic structures and uneven power relations. His sharpest criticisms have been directed towards the liberal–interventionist view, which pervades some comparative housing research. Such research is considered to focus upon consumption dimensions between tenants and the state, ignoring the relations of production and treating state intervention as a mere deviation from normal market relations (1988: 21–22).

In contrast, Ball promotes the structure of housing provision approach (SHP) which assumes, in the first instance, that housing systems are 'an historically given process of providing and reproducing the physical entity, housing'. He recommends that researchers focus on the social agents essential to the process of housing provision and the relations that exist between them (1986: 158).

SHP has been developed and defended by Ball and Harloe since the mid-1980s as a tool for the explanation and comparison of housing systems (Ball, 1986, 1988; Ball and Harloe, 1992). However, SHP is a meta-tool. It does not theorise or generalise the type of relations that may exist in a housing system, other than to suggest the examination of broad economic relations such as the extraction of surplus value through exchange and production, and the reproduction of labour power through consumption of certain forms of housing. Nor does SHP stress how differences are established between or within housing systems. Finally, the SHP approach does not provide a clear epistemology or clues to help distinguish cause from association in 'context'.

To build upon the ontological foundations of Ball (1986, 1988, with Harloe, 1992) and address the methodological deficiencies of SHP, this chapter reinterprets and elaborates their approach, using critical realist ontology and retroductive epistemology. It is argued that particular clusters of social relations can become 'packaged' or temporarily locked together in coherent, albeit conflicting, ways. This structural coherence tends to differentiate actual housing solutions *at the base*.

Ball tends to downplay the role of the state (1988) and emphasise the economic relations of production. Whilst these relations are important, this research assumes that the state plays an integral role in regulating such economic relations. Indeed, the relations of property, finance and welfare play a fundamental role in defining housing solutions. Their establishment and development is by no means a 'natural', given or random process, but one mediated by the state (Jessop, 1990). The state itself is subject to the uneven, often conflicting power relations that are concretised in the fiscal, territorial and democratic rules of the state (Terhorst and Van de Ven, 1997) and expressed (or suppressed) via informal norms, ideologies, processes and practices (Lukes, 1974; Saunders, 1983).

3.3 Realist concepts – an introduction

This section elaborates the ontology of necessary relations, contingent relations, clusters of causal mechanisms and the epistemology of retroduction, which are to be applied to the subsequent study of change and difference in housing solutions.

3.3.1   Necessary and contingent relations

To begin, explanations of housing systems informed by the philosophy of critical realism, are

> concerned in a significant way with identifying social structures and conditions which govern, facilitate, or in some way produce, actual social events and states of affairs of interest.
>
> (Lawson, T. 1997: 192)

Necessary relations inform our understanding of the relationships between agents in a housing solution. Different necessary relations bind tenants to landlords, landowners to purchasers, borrowers to lenders and commissioners of projects to builders. Many comparative studies implicitly assume that relations between agents in housing systems are the same across different countries. This is clearly not the case. We cannot, for example, apply the same definition of tenancy to analyse housing consumption in different countries (Barlow and Duncan, 1988; Marcuse, 1994).

Necessary relations are *not* fixed behavioural laws or predictors of events. They do not exist as isolated atoms in a laboratory. There are no standard definitions of necessary relations applicable to all time and space. This is not a deficiency but the recognition of the 'open and ontologically stratified structure of reality (both natural and social) outside the experimental laboratory' (Steinmetz, 1998: 174). Necessary relations are actualised in the context of other sets of interacting contingent relations. For this reason, concrete historical case study research is an integral part of the explanatory process.

Contingent relations are circumstantial relations that intersect with necessary relations to divert their 'necessary outcome'. Contingent relations may impede, mute, stifle and even extinguish the necessary relationships of a network. They are always present in open, interactive systems. In this way, necessary relations can only be regarded as causal in a limited sense. They generate tendencies and probabilities but cannot directly generate specific events or experiences of them. For this reason, contingency is a very important notion for examining difference in housing solutions. With their many multi-dimensional relationships, the production, exchange and consumption of housing are highly vulnerable to changes in contingent conditions. Many different, often unanticipated actions, events and relations may influence internal dynamics of provision, and indeed have a cumulative effect on entire systems of provision.

For these reasons, the housing solutions can be understood to be highly dependant upon other networks of provision such as the finance, labour and property sectors. For example, the level of housing production is sensitive to the availability of credit, which at any given time may be diverted to more lucrative forms of investment. It is also sensitive to increased labour and material costs, and of course changes in household income.

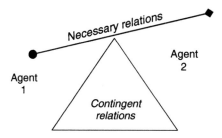

Figure 3.1 The interaction of necessary and contingent relations.

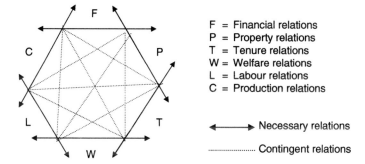

Figure 3.2 Cluster of necessary relations in their contingent conditions.

Figure 3.1 illustrates the basic idea; necessary relations are defined in the context of contingent relations. Thus, relations between agents 1 and 2 are subject to contingent conditions.

3.3.2   *Clusters of causal mechanisms*

In combination, necessary and contingent relations provide the foundations for explaining particular relationships underlying housing solutions. As stated, relations can only be isolated in thought, existing in real life in the context of other necessary and contingent relations. Their combined interaction forms a *cluster of causal relations* with the capacity to influence broader housing processes and events. Causal clusters underpin conventions that enable or constrain housing outcomes such as property rights, the system of credit provision, development promotion and production, dwelling allocation and consumption.

Figure 3.2 illustrates the type of necessary and contingent relations in a housing solution, which may interact to form dynamic clusters of causal mechanisms.

From a realist vantage point, illustrated by Figure 3.2, SHP is redefined as a *cluster of social relations* that can be postulated and empirically tested and revised. Clusters of social relations, such as those influencing property development, investment and consumption, interact with one another to influence housing solutions. Differences within such a cluster may be able to explain key differences in actual housing outcomes. The key to comparison, therefore, is to postulate, revise and contrast clusters of causal mechanisms in different case studies towards an explanation of difference.

3.3.3 Postulating causal mechanisms – the process of abduction and retroduction

As stressed throughout this chapter, every ontological perspective implies a corresponding epistemology or theory of knowledge. Preferably this theory should be explicitly introduced, justified and rigorously followed, enabling the researcher to confidently say, this is how I reached these conclusions. However, logical coherence cannot be taken for granted (Lawson T, 1997). Methodology is often hidden amongst research findings or explicitly avoided, with the results justifying the means.

In contrast with positivist comparative strategies, realist-inspired explanatory research does not begin with international comparisons between categories of constructed variables because this process cannot *explain* difference. Such a strategy is merely a fishing expedition, which reduces sound reasoning to the accidental discovery of correlations. Alternatively, explanation informed by realist ontology tries to postulate and reveal the underlying causal mechanisms of change and difference through strategic, historical case study research. Any subsequent international comparison contrasts these underlying causal mechanisms, rather than observable events or experiences.

Whilst housing outcomes are often observable and even measurable, their underlying causal mechanisms are not. Indeed, analysing the traces emitted by underlying causal mechanisms will not lead directly to their exposure. Because of the open, contingent nature of housing solutions, there is no direct link between mechanism and outcome – cause and event. Thus, the link must be postulated and tested in a continual and spiralling process known as *abduction* and *retroduction* (Blaikie, 1993; Danermark *et al.*, 2002; Harré, 1976; Keat and Urry, 1975; Lawson, 1997; Steinmetz, 1998), towards empirically competitive explanations (Bhaskar, 1993; Sayer, 2000).

Realist *abduction* and *retroduction* is not new; it currently provides a springboard for research and debate within a variety of social scientific disciplines including geography (Banai, 1995; Dickens *et al.*, 1985; Sayer, 1985; Terhorst and Van de Ven, 1997), sociology (Jessop, 1990; Keat and Urry, 1975; New, 1995; Outhwaite, 1987; Pawson and Tilley, 1998; Sayer, 1984, 2000; Steinmetz, 1998) and economics (Collier, 1994; Fleetwood, 1999b; Lawson T, 1997, 1999a). *Abduction* involves the contestable postulation of ideas and concepts relevant to the object of study and their use in interpreting and recontextualising phenomena, in order to produce a new description for analysis. Realist abduction has been used to generate new interpretations, which have been analysed to explain differences in the spatial form of cities (Terhorst and Van de Ven, 1997), differences in housing policy between nations and regions (Dickens *et al.*, 1985) and provide reasons for the success of social programmes (Pawson and Tilley, 1998). Further, it has stimulated alternative perspectives and criticisms, such as the critique of mainstream neo-classical economics (Lawson T, 1997) and rigid positivism or postmodernism in social history (Steinmeitz, 1998).

Blaikie (1993: 162–169) and Lawson (T, 1997) summarise the *retroductive* strategy by drawing upon the writings of Harré (1961), Bhaskar (1979) and Keat and Urry (1975). First, researchers should aim to discover the relevant structures and mechanisms that explain observable phenomena and regularities. Critical analysis of everyday conceptions of reality should lead to the postulation of these (perhaps unacknowledged) structures and mechanisms (Lawson T, 1997: 196). Examining actual empirical consequences should test these ideas and concepts of causal mechanisms. Finally, the model should be continuously tested and revised until it 'fits' these consequences.

3.4 Risk and the organisation of trust

So far a generic metaphorical model, depicting a cluster of necessary relations and contingent conditions, has been put forward in Figure 3.2. Yet this model is highly abstract and cannot account for tendencies in specific housing solutions. It certainly cannot explain day-to-day decisions or micro interactions. Assuming causal mechanisms can help to define the 'realm of the possible' in *actual* housing solutions, *clues to their existence* can be found in the realm of experience and perception via intensive case study research. Towards this end, this section elaborates critical realism's definition of the experience and event dimensions of reality by introducing the concepts of *risk and trust*.

The study of risk and risk assessment is a growing field that has emerged from particular branches of economics, behavioural psychology and is related (although not necessarily so) to rational choice theory (RCT). The notion of 'risk' has been applied to a diverse range of substantive fields including organisational decision-making, financial management, marketing, health policy and environmental assessment. The contribution of risk researchers varies from self-assured calculation of objective risk to discursive debates on its social construction (Johnson and Covello, 1987). The realm of research also varies significantly. Risk has been applied to shifts across western society (the transition from modernity to radical modernity) and within household relations, as well as shifts in the global money market. Risk is also viewed as being differentially perceived between different actors, professions, groups, classes and cultures; and must be historically and spatially defined.

3.4.1 The use of risk in housing studies

The concept of risk has entered the field of housing studies, particularly in the United Kingdom where home purchasers experienced a major economic downturn generating unemployment, falling house prices, negative equity and a jump in mortgage defaults, leading to housing-related poverty. The following section outlines and evaluates the various notions of risk and trust that appear in this primarily British housing literature.

These notions concern:

- constantly shifting definition of risk
- risks vary throughout one's housing career
- risks are multiple and unevenly allocated
- information about risks varies between agents and limits 'perfectly rational' decision making
- sources of risk and our ability to control them differ
- allocation of risk and the asymmetric organisation of trust
- measures to protect households against risk and their differentiation by tenure
- risk as a basis for understanding social change.

Housing risks are constantly shifting

A basic definition of risk, chance or 'odds' concerns the perception of potentialities, which may positively or negatively influence the achievement of desired goals. This perception may be based on experience and evidence – however complete, accurate or otherwise. Take for example the capital gains estimated on the speculative purchase of a home. The size of a financial gain may be subject to the extension of a nearby freeway, off-site investments in the surrounding neighbourhood and confidence amongst potential purchasers of an inflating housing market.

In this vein, Croft considers housing risks as complex and multiple, unevenly distributed and dynamic (2001: 738–742). Her preferred definition of risk in housing studies is one that embraces the changing nature of risk, the different perceptions of uncertainty and their potential consequences. Risk is not appreciated in a uniform manner, nor is it only experienced as a threat but may offer positive opportunities. Further, when uncertainties crystallise into consequences they too may bear further implications.

Risks vary throughout one's housing career

The simplest application of risk to the realm of housing studies concerns the potential threats to the achievement of an individually desired housing career or ladder. Traditionally, life course risk analysis has focussed upon the choices households actually make and their demographic and socio-economic character-istics. Actual events, available resources and perceived opportunities or risks may influence steps down or 'along' the ladder, or indeed 'falling off', leading to displacement or homelessness.

In Western capitalist societies, most households pay for their housing services in some form. Payment implies that the ability to consume largely depends upon one's financial resources. Such resources are strongly related to income as defined by the households' position in the paid labour market, the number of dependents, living and lifestyle expenses, and any provisions derived from a welfare system emergent from family, community, private or government relations. Transfer payments or subsidies from the state to the individual, such as rental allowances and the ability to deduct interest from taxable income, may assist in the ability to pay for housing costs. In the case of home purchase, payments for housing services may relate to a schedule of mortgage payments to a financial institution and vary according to the purchase price, the duration of the loan and changes in the interest rate. The level of payments made by renters to their landlord is less often dependent on the original purchase or cost price of the dwelling and is often more related to the market position of tenants and possibly subject to the conditions laid down in a rental agreement. Nevertheless, in both cases the capacity to pay for housing services is largely determined by one's income (Terhorst and Van de Ven, 1988: 23).

At certain life stages or circumstances, the risk of income loss, causing housing stress or even homelessness, may heighten. According to research in Australia and the United Kingdom, the risk of mortgage default is enhanced when a home purchaser experiences periods of unstable employment, has a single/part-time or casual income, becomes divorced or must provide for a high number of dependants. Vulnerability may increase when caring for the young, taking the first steps from the parental home, during unemployment, when divorced, elderly or disabled. It may also occur at certain stages of the business cycle when housing costs may rise beyond capacity to pay. Further, the level of mortgage arrears is also important, as well as factors such as high loan to value ratios, unexpectedly high mortgage interest rates and regional market variations.

Multiple perspectives and experience of risk

As suggested earlier, risks influencing decisions about the consumption of housing are embedded in time and space. Beyond consumption, different types of risks and risk-averting behaviour may also influence other aspects of housing provision: namely, the finance, production and allocation of dwellings. Towards this end, it is helpful to view housing as being embedded in a solution of connected, reinforcing and/or conflicting relationships involving actors operating in a specific environment and time. From this perspective it can be appreciated that different agents involved in various dimensions of housing provision will be subject to their different, dynamic and uneven interpretations of relevant risks.

Institutions offering mortgage finance to home purchasers face the risk of mortgage arrears and eventual non-payment of the borrowed sum. This risk may be reduced where the land title, a cash deposit or other valuable assets are committed as security. Borrowers can be required to privately insure their capacity to pay. Further, governments may establish guarantee funds to reduce potential risks to financial institutions of lending to lower-income households.

The estimation of opportunities and threats plays a cumulative role influencing the actions and inactions of agents. Consider the role the estimation of risk plays in the family plans of home purchasers, investment strategies of housing associations, election campaigns (including housing manifestos) of political parties, lending criteria of financial institutions and the design of instruments by mortgage guarantee funds.

The calculation of risk may not be informed by adequate information or 'hard facts', but rather by estimation, impressions and even ignorance. The study by Gruis (2002) examines the increasing importance of financial continuity amongst Dutch housing associations and argues the need for a more informed rational decision making based on the collection and interpretation of data. The necessity for financial self-reliance requires associations to actively protect their income stream (rental, investment revenue) in a way that anticipates market developments and likely expenditure, maximises yield from investments and minimises vacancies. This necessity has stimulated interest in the risk assessment processes associated with asset management for housing associations.

Yet, according to 6 (1998), risk perception is not perfectly *rational*, but culturally defined. Certain risk cultures evolve which may be risk accepting or minimising. These cultures have been categorised by 6 (1998) as individualistic, fatalistic, isolated, hierarchical or egalitarian. Different risk cultures may pervade political ideology and influence the policies and actions of executive government. Meen (1994 in 6, 1998) elaborates the kinds of risk policy makers may consider, directed towards specific housing outcomes such as individual well-being, community safety and the housing industry. Further, political parties may view certain policy statements or actions as being more risky than others, in terms of legitimacy and electoral support.

Risk and rational decision-making

The emergence of norms and institutions based on notions of risk and trust has been explained from an individualist, rational choice and exchange perspective, which derives from neo-classical economics (Olson, 1965) and behavioural psychology (Simmel, 1955).

Rational choice theory implies that members of a group, community or society act individually or collectively in order to maximise their own personal utility (Somerville, 1999). People compulsively make decisions, in a competitive environment, which maximise their desired value and potential rewards. Collective choices are made to minimise individual costs and maximise group advantage, spreading costs more thinly amongst group members (Ostrom, 1990). The common resource pool over which struggles occur defines the context of choice and value. In this way rational choice theory, with its maximisation of value, minimisation of cost and context-defined value, aims to explain the social relations guiding individual and collective behaviour.

Terhorst and Van de Ven (1997) and Somerville (1999) elaborate several key themes in the rational choice approach: the need for boundaries excluding and including people in the group, establishing members' right of access to resources, their obligatory contributions and preventing free rider access. Rights and obligations may reinforce uneven access to power resources, where weaker members of a group have less to offer the collective pool of resources and therefore suffer from diminished access. Sharing of costs may redistribute some benefits to weaker members, where this collective action reduces individual costs. Co-operative action, the distribution of resources and performance of certain duties, is established when reciprocal individual benefits are clear to participating members.

Societal forms can be considered to be a cumulative outcome of rational individual and collective choices. This perspective has prompted complex construction of behavioural models, applying ideas from game, exchange and strategic interaction theories (Jary and Jary, 1991). Such theories have come under severe criticism from critical realist sociologists. They argue that the material and social context is very important in making day to day, cummulative and sometimes path dependent choices (or non-choices). They argue that 'rational actors' are treated in isolation, aggregated and thereby stripped of influential contexts in which they operate (Tritter and Archer, 2000).

Does the use of risk in housing research assume perfect or bounded rationality? No, according to Somerville and Bengtsson (2002) who demonstrate the application of rational action theory to the field of housing studies which

> assumes that actors operate on the basis of 'thin' rationality, where the context of their action has a crucial effect on the decision and choices that they make.
>
> (2002: 23)

Source of risk, severity and the degree of control

The housing sector is vulnerable to influences outside its immediate or core network of operations. Changes in interest rates, rising land, building and labour costs as well as unemployment all hold indirect but important implications for housing provision. The actions of individuals within the finance, property and labour markets may hold important ramifications for the definition of various influential dimensions contributing towards a housing solution. According to Croft (2001), risk may emanate from the individual agents themselves, their partners for action, the actions of contingent others or cumulative actions of externally related agents, as well as natural events influencing all or some relevant agents.

According to Perri 6 (1998), the source and severity of risk can be categorised and allocated according to two intersecting continuums. These continuums concern the depth of risk, describing how acute or chronic risk is, and the breadth of risk, in terms of its systematic or individual impact. The power to secure oneself against the different types of risk, including those that are acute and individual, varies between different agents in the housing network over time. Importantly, agents do not have uniform powers and resources to control the circumstances influencing housing-related risk and thereby ensure the certainty of outcomes. For example, the risk of a tenant's eviction may be minimised during a slack rental market, whilst a tighter housing market may permit the landlord to raise rents without generating vacancies.

Indeed, the perception of risk also relates to the degree of control over important contingent circumstances. These include market conditions, institutional conventions, income levels and security, personal relations, health and the availability of social protection (Ford *et al.*, 2001). Housing choices may be made on the basis of the perceived availability of resources such as a stable, sufficient and secure income, the provision of which may be beyond the control of individuals, whilst being of great personal significance. Indeed, opportunities in the labour market, interest rate policy, social welfare provisions and fiscal rules all provide a source of personal risk and opportunity but are largely beyond the control of individual agents.

Allocation of risk and the asymmetric organisation of trust

A common theme throughout risk-related housing research concerns the distribution of risk via state/market institutions and the individual (employment, class, gender, ethnicity, life course).

In particular, an important aspect of research on home purchase concerns the movement of financial risk from the collective to the individual via promotion of home ownership, withdrawal of state mortgage protection schemes, compulsory mortgage insurance and mortgage guarantee funds (Croft, 2001: 737). It is argued that risks have been accumulating amongst housing consumers in the context of increasing deregulation of labour markets, polarisation of incomes, reliance upon part time and temporary work, relationship breakdown and reduced role of government in mortgage relief, dwelling allocation and social housing provision (Ford *et al.*, 2001).

An important related phenomenon is termed the ideological 'individualisation of risk', which demands self-sufficiency and responsibility for managing one's own housing needs and risks and less dependence upon universal, redistributive state-centred strategies. Social insurance, which may guard against housing-related risks, is also shifting towards user paid pension contributions, and away from collectively funded and redistributed social provisions. Further, the increasing use of market-based allocation of housing services, rather than queuing based upon other 'social' criteria, is becoming the norm in many countries (Croft, 2001). An argument has also emerged that home ownership is a form of private social insurance (Castles, 1994; Taylor-Gooby *et al.*, 1999). Taylor-Gooby *et al.* (1999) argue that the shifting of risk management, from the public sector towards private organisations, actually erodes personal security.

The response to risk, which plays a role in defining the careers, strategies, policies, regulations and instruments developed by individuals and organisations, involves efforts to avert negative risks – and thereby maximise trust. Thus the two concepts of risk and trust can be integrally related. Yet, the capacity and ability to avert risks is far from uniform.

Responsibility for risk minimisation and tenure differences

The three points mentioned earlier, concerning the rationality, source and allocation of risk lead us to the question concerning responsibility for housing risks. To what extent can housing agents be held responsible for the actualisation of risks beyond their control and expectations? For example, if the risk of unemployment rests in the hands of corporate directors beholden to shareholder interests in another country, who should be responsible for insuring against the potential loss of income, which may lead to mortgage default? Currently, the borrower may be required to pay a mortgage protection premium to insure against the eventuality of unemployment. Yet this insurance protects the banks and not the borrower (Ford *et al.*, 2001). In a few countries, the state may intervene to address mortgage payment shortfalls, albeit for a limited period or amount, before eventual foreclosure. This contrasts with the situation of renters who may receive generous rental subsidies over unlimited periods of time.

Risk as social theory

The concept of risk has also entered broader discussions on social theory in housing studies. The 'risk society thesis', as postulated by sociologists Giddens and Beck claims that greater uncertainty, flexibility and change in social and economic relationships (in the workplace, home and social networks) are shifting risks along new societal lines. As societies modernise, old processes are subject to increasing scrutiny and modification. Traditions fall rapidly by the wayside, old structures and collective institutions recede. Risks, both natural and manufactured, accumulate differentially. The post-traditional society sees risk as emanating from human interventions in the natural world through technology, which may mitigate or generate risks. These risks are difficult to control and expert opinion on strategies to avert them is divided. Overloaded with information, the laypersons' trust in experts is undermined, eroding the influence of rational reasoning and increasing reliance upon individualised solutions focusing on safety and preventative life strategies, promoting the rolling back of collective welfare state (Taylor-Gooby *et al.*, 1999: 179). This post-traditional 'risk society' provides more space for individualisation and personal strategy making – and indeed personal *risk* taking. However, *increased and uneven awareness of risk and limited choices* distributes social vulnerability in different ways and risks are accumulating amongst the lower socio-economic classes.

The risk society thesis has emerged in property and housing studies (6, 1998; Allen, 2000; Berry and Dalton, 2000; Ford *et al.*, 2001; Guy and Harris, 1997; Winter and Stone, 1998) concerning shifts in social vulnerability, policy decision making and property investment. Ford *et al.* (2001) conditionally apply the thesis to examine how risks associated with home ownership have been inserted into individual agency and broader psychosocial change. Using the risk society thesis as a sensitising framework brings agency and identity to the foreground when examining the process of change. Via extensive empirical research, they examine low-income home ownership in the context of an increasingly complex and uncertain economic environment. Globalisation, deregulation of financial markets, flexibility and insecurity of labour, housing market recession and the rolling back of welfare state support all have important consequences which are both quantitatively and qualitatively examined (Ford *et al.*, 2001: 6).

3.4.2   The preferred concept of risk

Within this growing realm of risk-related housing studies, it is possible to link the concept of *risk* to the generation of divergent housing solutions.

Agents in the housing network make decisions in an open and dynamic environment. Different agents in the housing process perceive risks relating, but not limited, to the necessary relations to which they are bound. Contingent relations pose perceived risks, which threaten the stability of relations between agents. Decisions to save, build, buy, rent or invest are all made (or not made) in the context of contingent relations. Ever-changing contingent conditions imply that perceived risks also change over time and space. According to Schillmeier 'competent actors perceive (mis-) interpret and construct their world in relation to the changing socio-political context' (1999: 174).

To reduce their exposure to risk, agents may co-operate or compete to establish norms, processes, policies and laws that provide certainty and security in housing contracts and transactions. Risks are neither uniform nor responded to in the same manner. Indeed we can find important differences in norms, institutions and contracts affecting land development, housing finance and the consumption of housing services in different housing solutions.

Housing is unique because it involves long-term contracts to finance. As mentioned in the very beginning of Chapter 1, housing is expensive, payments are stretched over time and time exposes both borrowers and creditors to risk. Risk-reducing mechanisms are often built into mortgage schemes and form part of the architecture of provision.

The following example of tenant–landlord relations illustrates the notion of risk and how these risks may be averted (for some) by the organisation of trust. A tenant's capacity to pay her rent, in exchange for the landlord's accommodation, is threatened by her loss of income. She may sign a contract, which she assumes will protect her from eviction under such circumstances, or ensure she has access to adequate unemployment insurance. Alternatively, the landlord may be able to extract payment of rent from her remaining assets and employ his right of eviction. The norms of tenancy and credit are embodied in dominant ideologies, written down in codes of conduct, policies and legislation. These forms of risk-reducing measures are conceived to be the *organisation of trust* that develops over time and space. Once again, the basic idea is outlined in abstract terms in Figure 3.3.

This figure is an abstraction from complex reality. In complex, multi-dimensional social life there are many different examples of perceived risks that influence actor's agency. Generically, the organisation of trust can be said to be an outcome of power struggles between agents within the housing network; these interactions become regularised and institutionalised, momentarily fixed in time and space. Such institutions or conventions reduce the chance of unanticipated behaviour and promote a sense of trust. Trust enables a certain assembly of social relations to stabilise and form an actualised housing solution. Long-term solutions comprise a pattern of norms, dominant ideas, processes and organisational structures, which underpin a form of housing provision.

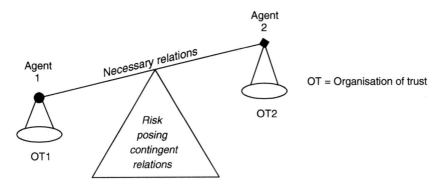

Figure 3.3 Risk and the organisation of trust.

3.5   The concepts applied to housing solutions

This section is devoted to the elaboration of Figures 3.1–3.3. It further defines the types of social relations that may contribute to housing solutions, as well as the type of risks agents perceive and the trust-enhancing norms, processes and organisational outcomes that may emerge over time.

3.5.1   Social relations in the housing solution

The following paragraphs explore the definition of three necessary relations of provision, property, investment and consumption, in order to demonstrate how they can be differently defined under diverse contingent conditions, emitting a variety of risks for different agents. Further, trust can also be organised and established in a variety of ways. Examples of risk-reducing norms, dominant ideologies and organisational strategies, which may emerge, are also provided. Later, in Chapter 5, it will be argued that these relations and their definition should form a key causal cluster differentiating forms of housing provision.

Property relations can be perceived as abstract social relations between people, rather than concrete things, which define the liberties, benefits and costs associated with the ownership and exchange of scarce, useable goods. Property relations imply norms of behaviour between people with respect to ownership, trespass, usage, capturing the benefits from that usage, as well as the right to alter the property or transfer it to another party. In Western societies, such relations are commonly expressed in law and enforced by legal authority (Pejovich, 1990: 27).

The *property relations* underpinning the residential development of a city, region or nation play an important role in the form and distribution of housing outcomes (Badcock, 1984). They define the rights of possession, use or development, and may specify how the rewards or costs of occupation, use, or exchange should be allocated. A number of contingent relations may influence the actualisation of property relations between owners of land and residential developers. These are listed as follows.

Contingent relations influencing the definition of property rights may include:

- location of land, accessibility to end users, existence of related infrastructure;
- land tenure: leasehold or freehold;
- certainty and flexibility of land-use or zoning rights: relative value of existing and potential uses;
- cost of developing land, availability of materials, suitability for development;
- costs associated with land holding: taxes, levies, maintenance or transferring property rights;
- exclusivity of land title: undisputed ownership or threat of repossession;
- land value: inflating, stable or deflating;
- competition, collaboration or monopoly position of landowners or purchasers;
- a secure, long-term method of financing purchase and
- capacity to repay the loan, the prospects of return and rising land value.

Risk-reducing strategies employed by relevant actors may include:

- clear system of land survey, legally enforceable system of ownership, undisputed occupation rights;
- right of compulsory purchase or repossession to meet 'public interest' goals;
- laws permitting the collection of betterment tax on unearned increment in property values;
- efficient and cost-effective system for transferring ownership;
- price regulation and compensation based on former usage;
- state-subsidised infrastructure provision;
- land-use planning clearly defined, long-term and protective of property values;
- monopoly selling or buying strategies and
- maximising formal and informal influence upon land-use defining agents.

Whilst fundamental to the system of housing provision, property relations do not exclusively define housing tenure and urban form. The *financial relations* of housing provision also play an integral and influential role in housing outcomes. Housing is costly to produce. Developers and purchasers of housing, whether they are voluntary, private or state institutions, often require the use of *borrowed capital* to purchase land and materials, or the labour required in order to complete, maintain or refurbish a particular dwelling. In return for capital, the lender or investors (joint venture partners, governments, public banks, retail banks, foreign banks, building societies, merchant banks, insurance companies and pension funds) will require a defined schedule of instalments or dividends. A wide range of contingent relations, as indicated here, defines the actual processes of housing credit provision.

Contingent relations influencing the definition of financial relations may include:

- interest rate conditions;
- existence of lenders offering favourable terms and conditions;
- competition, collaboration or monopolisation of credit providers for particular segments of the housing market;
- lending criteria, portfolio policies, services offered and territory of operation (including 'red lining');
- risk-return ratio of housing investment relative to other forms of investment, which influence the volume of credit available;
- desired liquidity and mobility of investment;
- perceived credit worthiness of borrower, existence of desired security;
- existence of a range of financial products providing borrowers with a competitive choice and
- degree of integration of lenders with other components of the housing network such as mortgage lending, land banking, infrastructure investment, residential construction, retail development, etc.

Risk-reducing strategies employed by relevant actors may include:

- fixed interest rates, monetarist policies, interest rate subsidies;
- techniques for assessing credit risk and risk-avoiding conventions;
- promotion of certain financial management norms, values, processes and standards;
- promotion of practices supportive of maximising of property values and rents;
- right of repossession over the property or other assets of the borrower;
- demanding an equity share in the development or defined share of the profits;
- security funds to protect investors from defaulting borrowers;
- government policy regulating the system of credit provision;
- cross-national treaties defining borrowing limits of governments;
- subsidies to channel investment into particular sectors;
- mutually reinforcing lending strategies, land banking or company directorships and
- establishment of savings clubs and building societies.

The way housing is 'consumed' not only relates to property rights or investment mechanisms, but also to the system of labour relations and welfare provisions affecting the consumption of housing services, which emerges over a long period of time (Castles, 1994, 1998; Kemeny, 1992; Therborn, 1989). Family members, social networks, the wider community, as well as private, voluntary or state institutions may provide housing assistance (Kemeny, 1992). As indicated here, a wide range of contingent, exogenous relations may influence the system of labour and welfare and ultimately housing consumption.

Contingent relations influencing the definition of labour and welfare relations may include:

- economic value of skills possessed by members of household as determined by the labour market or prescribed by the state;
- gender relations within a household allocating participation in paid work;
- economic relations within the household and wider community networks;
- existing labour-market norms, including discrimination against older men, migrants or married women in times of job scarcity;
- informal or formal support services, such as affordable or free child-care;
- economic policies of government regulating job growth, wage levels: such trade-offs and conditions that influence the ability of households to consume certain housing services;
- role of labour organisations in promoting certain forms of housing production and services;
- system of social security, which may or may not cover ongoing housing expenses following retirement from the paid workforce and
- role of welfare organisations in diverting collective resources to or away from housing-related support.

Risk-reducing strategies employed by relevant actors may include:

- wage indexation, agreements and more general accords to regulate income levels and working conditions
- income transfers to maintain a certain level of purchasing power amongst households
- housing allowances to assist payment of housing costs
- rent regulations to reduce or sustain a certain level of housing costs and
- income and life insurance.

The earlier selection of relations, *property, financial and welfare*, as well as their contingencies and risk-reducing strategies, should not be perceived as an exclusive, isolated or fixed set of relations. Nevertheless, in Chapter 5 a more elaborate argument will be made as to why these and not others should be the focus. Further, as stressed in the previous section, clusters of conflicting necessary and contingent relations underlie urban form, the organisation of housing production and the type of housing services consumed. These relations interact with one another in a way that is causally significant and therefore, they cannot be conceived in isolation. Finally, as illustrated earlier, the state plays an integral and contested role in the definition of these relations. For this reason, analysing the role of the state is an important element for explaining change and difference in housing systems.

3.6 Comparing housing solutions

As stressed throughout this chapter, a well-developed ontology of housing systems provides an important foundation for explaining differences between them. Combined with a defined logic for gaining further understanding of housing systems, a coherent methodological package should also inform the data collection and analysis strategy. Two relevant issues are considered in section 3.6.1 and 3.6.2: the level of comparison and the problem of time and space.

3.6.1 The level of comparison

Informed by critical realism, forms of housing are perceived in terms of experienced reality, actual housing institutions and underlying social relations which form causal clusters of generative necessary and contingent relations.

A comparison of experiences or perceptions can be a useful starting point for a more comprehensive explanation. Such studies try to account for differences by analysing the formative constraints influencing perception. Yet, such a comparison will only highlight differences and cannot explain them.

At present, 'event level' analysis dominates cross-national housing research: comparing policies, regulatory mechanisms, allowances, investment levels and management models. Given the pragmatic aims of government-commissioned research, often with tight time-lines, such research can lead to isolated descriptions of current policies rather than comprehensive explanations for the differences between them.[5]

More explanatory research should promote the comparison of underlying causal mechanisms that generate differences between housing systems (Dickens *et al.*, 1985; Harloe, 1987, 1995; Terhorst and Van de Ven, 1997; Therborn, 1989) and indeed understand why policy transfusions, from one country to another, are often rejected by the host.

3.6.2 The problem of time and space

Any period of history chosen at random reveals uncertainties, and the modern age is decidedly no exception. Society is more complex than ever before, and is constantly in motion.

(Klien, 1975: viii)

More reflective academic studies[6] have established a clear trend away from static, atomistic policy comparisons towards more contextualised, historical approaches, which aim to explain difference in housing systems (Bourne, 1990). However, comparative explanation through analysis of event chronologies continues to be problematic. Whilst researchers have recognised the significance of events and their explanation in context, the treatment of time remains somewhat of a puzzle.

The answer lies, once again, in the level of comparison. It is considered helpful to postulate a feasible preliminary model of causal relations, which uniquely underlie each case for comparison. The packaging (and repackaging) of causal relations tends to emerge over a long period of time. Retroductively, this package should be postulated, tested and revised to capture the multi-causal, contingency basis of housing solutions (Steinmetz, 1998: 174) in time and space. Once a model of causality sufficiently explains empirical reality in a single case, comparison can be made at the level of causal mechanisms with other cases. This process prompts the researcher to define what is distinctive about each country and, in particular, explain why differences have emerged.

Thus, comparison over time is a process that occurs within, rather than between, the case studies. It enables the researcher to define the clustering of necessary relations, the role of contingent conditions and the direction and nature of change. Comparing patterns of housing events or housing histories, such as policy developments, population growth or house prices, is illuminating when the reasons for difference or change have also been analysed.

4 Alternative theories for the composition and dynamics of housing provision

4.1 Introduction

Housing is a very complex object to study and there are many different ways to perceive modes of provision. This chapter provides a critical review of existing ontological frameworks for perceiving housing and its many, multi-faceted dimensions.

As outlined in Chapter 2, ontology refers to the nature of reality and how it is to be perceived: in this case the nature of the social world with specific reference to housing provision. Critical realism (CR) is a philosophy of science with a particular ontological perspective. This entails a structured notion of reality with related, overlapping domains of real (mechanisms), actual (events) and empirical (experience).

The following discussion concerns a purposeful selection of perspectives in housing studies that fall within one or more of these ontological domains. Some perspectives locate the reality of housing provision wholly within the realm of actors' perceptions (strong social constructionism), others stress the significance of officially recorded and observed quantitative or qualitative events (econometrics, historical biography). There are also perspectives that stress the significance of potentially unobservable social structures (structures of housing provision). Often, ontological perspectives in housing studies implicitly incorporate several domains of reality (experience, events and mechanisms), as identified by CR.

To begin, it is helpful to recall the multiple meanings housing holds for different, often conflicting, agents involved in provision: the households, land developers, financiers, producers and multiple government agencies, which all have roles to play. For households, a dwelling may provide shelter, a sanctuary or sense of 'home'. Access may imply a bundle of rights and responsibilities and ownership a symbol of social difference, or source of economic burden. Other agents clearly hold different perspectives: as capital investment, rental return, a form of social control or solution to social demands.

Given these different often-conflicting perspectives, what is the most appropriate and comprehensive way to view forms of housing provision? The next section moves from subjective, singular perceptions of provision to consider the contribution of sociology, geography, economics and political science towards an ontology of housing provision and change.

4.2   Competing housing ontologies

The following selective description moves across a continuum of competing housing ontologies, from those that are strongly agency oriented, to those in the more structuralist camp. This is a useful way of ordering what can appear to be a random selection of approaches. It enables the reader to distinguish between 'flat' and 'deep' ontological alternatives: those that reduce reality to empirical data sets, or emphasise the role of actors, institutions, and more durable and pervasive social structures. A summary is provided in tabular form following a short discussion.

I begin with perspectives which place actors in the driving seat of housing provision. *Social constructionism* emerged during the 1980s to counter functionalist structural theory. Just as conventional pluralism was dismissed as in the 1970s, structuralism has now fallen out of favour for several reasons: its tendency towards theory determinism, diminution of individuals to dopes, and inability to explain difference and change. A postmodernist and post-structuralist turn now dominates theoretical developments and social constructionism, with its actor centredness, has taken centre stage (Sayer, 2000).

Social constructionists take lay perceptions of housing very seriously. They consider that everyday concepts provide the basis for many (housing) related actions (Blaikie, 1993: 177). Strong social constructionists claim that housing reality only exists at the level of experience and that it is not necessary to look beyond this reality as perceived by actors (Brandsen, 2001; Winter, 1994). Weaker social constructionists acknowledge the importance of meaning and identity in shaping actions, but also look outside the realm of subjective perception, to examine the material and socially constructed influences shaping agency (Kemeny, 1983).

There are a number of housing ontologies that try to bring various institutions and market processes into the realm of view (Ambrose, 1991; Boelhouwer and Heiden, 1992; Oxley and Smith, 1996). Of these, Ambrose's Chain of Housing Provision (CHP) highlights the variety of organisations involved in different phases of housing provision and the political, economic and social forces that influence them (Ambrose, 1991, 1994; Barlow and Duncan, 1994; Doling 1997). This approach is very useful in placing housing in a wider context and recognising the different interests involved throughout provision. Linked housing phases or tasks include development promotion, investment, construction, allocation, maintenance and redevelopment. Any one of these tasks may be undertaken by private (for profit or non-profit) or public agents. Their actions are subject to effective demand and need, influenced by levels of savings and spending, cultural and demographic factors and statutory responsibilities. A diagram illustrating the CHP approach is provided in Appendix 1.

However, Ambrose's holistic scheme is neither complete nor objective. Market interactions only seem to appear in the allocation phase. Land transactions, defined by property rights and market conditions, are left out altogether. The scheme also implies that democratically elected public sector agencies are more responsive to need, whilst other providers, only to effective demand (see Appendix 1a for an elaboration). This could promote a rather uncritical and oversimplified conception of state–market relations and responsibilities, which other housing ontologies have tried to overcome (esp. Marcuse, 1986). Doling (1997) emphasises particular links in Ambrose's chain of provision, connecting the phases of 'land development' and 'building materials' with 'construction' and 'finance'. Yet the problem still remains that processes in the chain seem to 'float' and the real relations that bind them remain vague. An elaboration of Doling (1997) is provided in Appendix 1b.

There are a number of researchers who try to explain differences in state–market relations affecting housing provision by placing housing agents in their specific *political* contexts. Notable amongst these is Lundqvist (1992), who examines different forms of market intervention in housing provision under various political coalitions and institutional settings. According to his theory, market-weak political parties use their power resources (constituencies) to move the boundaries of state–market relations in their favour, promoting non-market, public interventions in the housing market to reduce consumption costs. Lundqvist's typology of state interventions is illustrated in Appendix 2. The actions of such parties are influenced by their perception of other actors in a competitive political environment or institutional setting, the direction and extent of past housing policy and tenure forms, and the policy networks (public bureaucracy and organised private interests) which support them. Whilst Lundqvist's power resource–institutional theory is an advance on benevolent perceptions of the state (Marcuse, 1986), it is blinkered by the boundaries of his own discipline of political science, blocking out other important dimensions of explanation, namely the *economic* relations of housing provision.

Unlike Lundqvist's model of political resources, econometric models examine market interactions of aggregated categories of individuals, based on numerous assumptions concerning consumer choice, market and sub-market characteristics. The notion of a housing market or sub-market (Paris, 1993) implies more than the mere interaction of buyers and sellers, but a mechanism for the production and distribution of housing. However, often crude theoretical assumptions are embellished in market models, such as rational choice or equilibrium theory, and adopted as essential market attributes (for a critique see Barlow and Duncan 1994; Maclennan, 1982; Paris, 1993; Whitehead, 1974). The contrast between perfect markets and market failure is amplified, promoting the removal of regulation impeding open competition, in order to maximise available 'choice', usually based on one's capacity to pay. There is also a danger that markets are treated as closed systems, cut off from other market segments and downplaying their unpredictable contingent conditions. Depending on the quality of the data and of the model itself, market transactions (i.e. interactions between people) may become overly aggregated and generalised, isolated from relative social and material contexts and this submerge important socio-spatial differences (contrast Leuvensteijn and Koning, 2000 with Lawson T, 1997).

In contrast to traditional, econometric models, housing provision can also be perceived as a system of economic interactions embedded in an institutional setting (Ball, 1998; Bengs and Rönka, 1994; Boléat, 1985; Whitehead, 1974). This setting can be defined in many different ways: as a set of norms or conventions as in behavioural theory; or rules guiding actors, as in game theory; a coherence of rules, actors and ideologies as in regime theory; or interacting modes of capital accumulation and social regulation, as in regulation theory. The main thrusts of these approaches are their move away from simplistic notions of rational choice, equilibrium, closed and 'free' markets towards an acknowledgement of the importance of environment in shaping housing-related interactions. In other words, markets are not free but socially constructed, emerging from important power relations and contingent conditions and enacted by agents with different and conflicting (not always rational) interests. A good example of the social and material construction of housing markets is the empirical study by Bengs and Rönka (1994), which highlights the degree of vertical or horizontal integration between companies involved in different phases of provision, that is, land development, housing construction and mortgage provision, generating monopolistic tendencies in Finnish housing provision.

The argument that space mediates broader economic and social process (such as de-industrialisation and globalisation) prompted a number of local and regional studies in the United Kingdom and Scandinavia during the 1980s. Difference in forms of housing provision also emerged as an important theme of debate in urban and housing studies (Barlow and Duncan, 1994; Dickens *et al.*, 1985; Elander *et al.*, 1991). Various theories of explanation emerged and are elaborated upon in the following section under the themes: welfare regime shifts, crisis model, generative mechanisms and regulation theory.

Moving along our ontological continuum towards more structural ontological perspectives, we find a number of housing approaches that stress particular social relations shaping forms of housing provision. In capitalist societies, some aspects of housing production, exchange and consumption may become highly commodified, whilst others remain decommodified. Exploitation of surplus value may occur within land transactions; whilst securing development rights; employing labour and materials; in the exchange of dwellings; and ongoing house maintenance. Further, consumption of certain forms of housing may demand participation in the paid labour market and (re)enforce certain modes of domestic labour exploitation (i.e. unpaid, gendered and unevenly shared). The Structure of Provision approach (Ball, 1983; Ball, 1998; Ball and Harloe, 1992) provides a meta-framework, but no universal theory, to promote more comprehensive analysis of relevant social relations when examining different forms of housing provision. A diagram illustrating application of the SHP approach to home ownership in Britain is provided in Appendix 3.

Along similar lines, a strong urban political economy stream has emerged in housing studies, focusing upon the social relations of housing provision, and providing explanations for differences in various countries (Ball, 1983; Barlow and Duncan, 1994; Berry, 1983b, 1994; Stillwell, 1986; Watson and Austerberry, 1986).

4.2.1 Summary of ontological alternatives for perceiving forms of housing provision

Table 4.1 provides a concise summary of a number of different ways to perceive housing provision, as promoted by key authors in the field. Of course, there are numerous ways to categorise their approaches. Yet as the focus of this book has thus far been on ontological differences, their work has been ordered along a continuum beginning with 'flatter' individual agency orientated world views and ends with 'deeper' more structurally orientated ones. Housing researchers have produced work across various and numerous points along this ontological spectrum and indeed, over time many have shifted their position. For this reason, the content of each category is by no means complete but open to revision and substantial expansion. As a final qualification, this simplistic ordering device is by no means intended to address all the different dimensions and complexities of housing approaches; it is certainly fallible and open for welcome debate. Its main purpose is to demonstrate that there are substantial differences in ontological approaches and that the choice made has significant consequences for what is studied.

4.2.2 A critical review of ontological alternatives

The earlier discussion outlined a number of different ways to perceive the provision of housing, ordered from agency to more structuralist approaches. It is now time to make an explicit and justified selection of useful concepts to be adopted and refined for the purposes of explaining difference and change in divergent forms of housing provision.

First and foremost, this selection is made from the ontological position of critical realism (CR) as outlined in Chapter 2 and briefly in the beginning of this chapter. This ontological approach demands that housing be considered as a complex object, structured by the experience of agents whose (in) actions are influenced by socially and materially contingent contexts, past events in housing history and constrained by more durable social relations pervading forms of provision.

A number of ways of perceiving housing provision clearly fall outside this ontological approach, namely, ontological approaches which narrowly confine housing reality to the perception of actors, empirical data sets, organisational charts or official policy history. These ontological perspectives are too 'flat', *reducing complex structured reality* to observable, recorded and experienced 'facts', ignoring the possibility of influences 'beyond view'.

Strong social constructivism, which places much emphasis upon the perception and actions of actors, is also at odds with a critical realist approach. The perception of housing consumers, producers and policy makers is indeed socially constructed but also materially constrained. A person may think of his home as a castle, but

Table 4.1 Ontological alternatives concerning the key dimensions of housing provision

Housing research streams	How is housing perceived	Main proponents
Postmodernism and multiple realities	Traditional social science is challenged by arguing that there is no uniform reality. 'Modern' society is replaced by a fragmented 'Postmodern' world, which has multiple realities and meanings. Thus housing provision is a social construction to be analysed through the deconstruction of multiple and shifting symbols and discourses	Soja, 1989; Watson and Gibson, 1995; Michael and Pile, 1993
Political, cultural and economic meaning of housing action	Focuses on the subjective understanding of housing ascribed by different class (social), status (economic) and party (political) groups, which influence their rational and motivational actions. There is a focus on the meaning of tenure in determining class, status or party membership and its influence upon rational, value-based, emotional or habitual social action	Weber, 1968; Winter, 1994; Rex and Moore, 1967; Saunders, 1979
Social construction of housing knowledge and institutions	Emphasises the geo-historical origin and subjective understanding of housing institutions (rather than their material construction). Harloe, for example, emphasises the shifting perception of mass social housing in reproducing systems of housing provision. Kemeny examines the reinforcing relationship between ideology and housing policy promoting home ownership	Harloe, 1994; Kemeny, 1983; Brandsen, 2000
Econometric models	Models of market interactions of individuals, based on numerous assumptions concerning demand and supply of housing. Often a neo-classical ideal is compared with actual market failure, leading to recommendations to remove impediments to perfect competition. Different assumptions may inform models: rational choice; acknowledging the role of consumer aspirations; specific norms and institutions in market interactions	Leuvensteijn and Koning, 2000; Hakford and Matysiak, 1997; Fulpen, 1985; Maclennan, 1982
State market mixes	This approach focuses attention on forms of public and private intervention in various aspects of housing finance, production and consumption. Lundqvist provides a taxonomy of intervention alternatives. He then	Lundqvist, 1989, 1992; Barlow and Duncan, 1994

Agency ←————————————————————————→

Structure ↓

Approach	Description	References
	examines the power resources of market-weak and market-strong constituencies and their representative parties, influencing collective and privatised forms of welfare	
Chain of provision	Focuses upon the accountability, powers and motivations of private, public and voluntary sectors in the housing process. This process comprises promotion, investment, construction, allocation and management phases of housing provision interacting with land, labour, finance and subsidy and wider socio-economic conditions. Examines the channelling of subsidies up and down each stage of provision and their distributional outcomes in different countries over time	Ambrose, 1991, 1994; Ambrose et al., 1998; Doling, 1997
Housing as a system of economic and institutional relations	This approach stresses the spatial and temporal embeddedness of institutional relations, open market structures and shifting regulatory environments influencing the provision of housing. The main thrust of all these approaches is to move away from simplistic notions of rational choice, equilibrium, closed and 'free' markets, to acknowledge the importance of environment in shaping housing-related interactions	Priemus, 1983; Murie et al., 1976; Bengs and Rönkä, 1994; Oxley and Smith, 1996; Whitehead, 1974; and Boléat, 1985
Spatial differences	Rather than focus on national models of housing provision, these researchers seek explanations for differences in housing in the mediation of global, national and local influences	Gregory and Urry, 1985; Elander et al., 1991; Dickens et al., 1985
Social relations and structures of housing provision	Focuses upon the social relations influencing housing provision, acknowledging the ideological and material circumstances, which influence the structure of housing provision over time and space. This approach combines an understanding of social relations with the social agents involved in production, allocation, consumption and reproduction of housing. See Appendix 3	Dickens et al., 1985; Ball, 1998; Ball and Harloe, 1992; Ball, 1983; Berry, 1983 1998; Harloe, 1995, Harloe and Martens, 1983

in reality it maybe something quite different, and it is the role of the researcher to appreciate this. In Sayer's direct words,

> [o]f course knowledge and social phenomena are socially constructed; but that doesn't mean external phenomena (including existing material social constructions) cannot influence our interpretations. Nor does acknowledging that we are studying social constructions mean that many social phenomena cannot have a structural integrity that limits and enables what they can do; in other words recognizing their socially constructed character is not a licence for a kind of voluntarism.
>
> (2000: 91 referring to Malik, 1996)

Nevertheless, researchers are also bound by their own limited perceptions of reality. Often the available data becomes 'larger than life' – and life rather less convincing. Take, for example, Income Panel Data used to econometrically test the famous 'Oswald' thesis, which argues that homeowners are less mobile and flexible, in employment terms, than renters (van Leuvensteijn and Koning, 2000). Little mention is made of significant and complex economic and social relationships that may affect labour mobility outside the realm of the single breadwinner.[1] As the data analysed simply didn't cover these potentially important dimensions, a more comprehensive explanation could not be given. Such research may require more intensive qualitative case study research investigating carefully conceived social relationships, rather than the continuous search for regularity within extensive aggregated data sets.

Other forms of categorisation and representation may also oversimplify housing reality. Organisational charts, such as those produced by Oxley and Smith (1996) and Priemus (1983, 1992), quickly portray complex organisational relations in certain aspects of housing provision. Unfortunately, they tend to be rather static, date quickly and give little insight to the dynamic nature of power relations between agents (financial dependence, territory of influence, form of allegiance) or their materially or socially constructed context (market conditions, ideological hegemony, etc.). Nevertheless, a series of such charts would be preferable, highlighting the fluid interaction between various actors in their power-charged institutional setting, subject to underlying social relations (Hayward, 1992).

However, several approaches outlined in section 4.2 can be integrated to provide a more comprehensive housing ontology. At the agency end of the spectrum, the notion of weak social constructionism (Sayer, 2000) can help explain actors' agency in housing provision. This concept recognises the influence (but not determinism) of meaning and dominant ideologies that influence the *perception of different housing actors* (Harloe and Kemeny) in their material and socially constructed contexts.

Towards more institutional approaches, the power resources concept of Lundqvist recognises uneven *position of different actors* in housing provision (Lundqvist). It draws attention to the power of certain types of coalitions that may form to promote more commodified or decommodifed forms of provision.

Further, a more comprehensive account would emerge from a synthesis and elaboration of Ambrose' chain of provision and Ball's structure of housing provision. These ontological frameworks highlight the different and related elements of housing provision, each subject to its own institutional network, competing ideologies, economic relations and power coalitions.

Finally, there are no universal laws guiding housing provision over time and space. This does not imply that influential social structures do not exist (Ball). Rather, concrete research is required to define key generative social relations of housing provision (Dickens *et al.*), such as property (Berry), finance (Boléat) and labour (Sommerville, Hamnett) as they emerge over time and space.

4.3 Why do housing systems change?

Building on the selected concepts for perceiving housing provision, this section critically reviews different explanations for *change in forms of housing provision*. Once again change, and explanation of its causes, are evaluated from the chosen ontological perspective of CR. A number of 'middle-range' notions of causality are introduced and summarised in tabular form. At the end of this section, arguments for a particular 'middle-range' notion of causality are put forward.

Critical realists perceive change and causality in a specific way:

> The conception of causal relations as tendencies, grounded in the interactions of generative mechanisms; these interactions may or may not produce events which in turn may or may not be observed... the realist conception of explanation involves the postulation of explanatory mechanisms and the attempt to demonstrate their existence.
>
> (Outhwaite, 1998: 282)

The tentative 'may or may not' notion of causality stems from the realist conception of society and sub-components such as networks of housing provision, as open, dynamic and changing (Lawson, 1998: 149). We cannot predict with certainty what will happen tomorrow, as there are so many contingencies that can mediate actual events. Sayer (2000: 13–17) makes this point clearly. Given the structured nature of reality (experience, events and real relations) the relationship between cause and effect is not a direct one, but mediated by contingent conditions that may impede, block or exaggerate an effect. Thus, the discovery of (partial) empirical regularities (correlations) provides no proof of causality, especially in an open and contingency-laden system.[2] The search for causality involves the exposure of necessary relations forming underlying causal mechanisms, which begins with the following contrastive and counterfactual questions:

1 What does this form of housing provision (A) presuppose (B)?
2 Can this form of housing provision (A) exist without the above (B)?
3 How does change in (B) relate to a change in the state of (A), given the open, interactive nature of housing provision?

4 Does the postulated causal mechanism (B) provide an empirically adequate explanation?

5 What is the relative explanatory power of the postulated causal mechanism (B) compared with other competing hypothesis (C, D)?

(Adapted from Sayer, 2000: 16; Lawson T, 1998: 149–160)

Thus the challenge is to reveal the pervasive social relations and their contingencies of generative significance to diverging forms of housing provision.

4.3.1   Competing notions of causality in forms of housing provision

Critical realism offers a specific notion of causality, pitched at the ontological level of 'being'. There are many other 'middle-range' definitions of causality, relevant to explanations of change in housing provision and a selection is outlined later. Not all of these are compatible with or adaptable to the realist approach and their relative merits are discussed following the summary table.

Once again the selection is loosely ordered according to the agency–structure continuum, as applied in section 4.1. This enables the reader to distinguish between more superficial (flat) or comprehensive (deep) ontologies, which may be implicit in any notion of causality.

We begin with Random Utility Theory, which perceives human agency as the making of choices between alternatives on the basis of observed and unobserved attributes, differences in tastes between the decision makers, and uncertainty or lack of information. Little is theorised about the referents of these choices, that is, the material and socially constructed world that lies outside the individual. Institutions shaping choices are left out in a world perceived as a cumulative outcome of random choices. Such theories are most commonly applied in studies concerning consumer behaviour in the housing market or housing demand (Maclennan, 1982). Given a range of choices, housing consumers are assumed to make optimising decisions. The outcome of these decisions stimulates supply to meet demand. Changes in forms of housing provision, such as rising rates of home ownership, are explained as a calculated outcome of cumulative consumer preference.

More complex theories of human agency include Chaos theory, poetically defined by Young as follows:

> In the world of actual, living, thinking and acting human beings, Chaos theory opens up space for human agency in ways not possible in either God-hewn worlds or in clock-like models of social life. Chaos theory provides empirical grounding for an exercise of human agency in which infinite variety, plurality of centers, and the variability of postmodern sensibility most comfortably rests.
>
> (Young, 1992: 1)

So what does Chaos theory imply when explaining change in systems of housing provision? According to this theory of change, the significance of human agency varies according to the degree of order and disorder. Windows of opportunity for agency open during periods of flux or disorder.[3] During such times key agents such as policy makers, banks, angry tenants and bankrupt owners may fill available space for action and expand their scope for human agency, to push for new rules and processes that contribute towards a 'new order' in housing provision.

In contrast, Rational Choice theory (RCT) paints a more purposeful, linear picture of social causality. The emergence of norms and institutions based on notions of risk and trust has been explained from an individualist, rational choice and exchange perspective that derives from neo-classical economics (Olson, 1965) and behavioural psychology (Simmel, 1955).

RCT implies that members of a group, community or society act individually or collectively in order to maximise their own personal utility (Somerville, 2000). People compulsively make decisions in a competitive environment that maximise their desired value and potential rewards. Collective choices are made to minimise individual costs and maximise group advantage, spreading costs more thinly across a group of members (Ostrom, 1990). The common resource pool over which struggles occur defines the context of choice and value. In this way RCT aims to explain the rules guiding individual and collective behaviour. This theory perceives forms of housing provision as the cumulative outcome of rational individual and collective choice. RCT has prompted complex construction of behavioural models, applying ideas from game, exchange, transaction cost and strategic interaction theories (Jary and Jary, 1991).

The concepts of risk and trust have been strongly associated with RCT (but not necessarily so) particularly in studies of organisational and inter-firm behaviour. To minimise the transaction costs between agents engaged in an exchange process, certain norms, rules and processes evolve, such as contracts and standard forms of payment, suiting certain markets and technological resources and minimising the 'expense and risk of unwanted outcomes' (Ball, 1998).

Trust is also a concept that has been applied to macro- as well as micro-political, cultural and economic phenomena. Tied to a social system of role expectations, trust is said to be the lubricant of social exchange at the 'outer limits of social systems'. Trust concerns the partners' ability to *perform as expected*, reliably, without opportunistic defection. Co-operative dependence will occur when two or more partners believe that opportunistic behaviour is unlikely to occur, based on perceived propensity for abuse and the incentives for opportunistic behaviour (Nooteboom, 1995: 12). Erosion of trust *necessitates the development* of codes of behaviour, formalised monitoring, extensive, coercive contracts and penalty systems. According to this group of causal concepts, the interaction of risk-reducing strategies and trust-enhancing norms cumulatively builds the institutions underpinning different forms of housing provision.

Both concepts, risk and trust, have recently entered the field of sociology. Most notable contributions have been made by Beck (1992) on contemporary, uncertain and dynamic 'risk society', Beck, Giddens and Lash (1994/5) on reflexive modernisation and Fukyama (1995) on cross-national assessment of the role of trust, cultural values and social capital upon economic performance. The risk society thesis has also emerged in property and housing studies (6, 1998; sf. Allen and Sprigings, 1999; Berry and Dalton, 2000; Guy and Harris, 1997 as elaborated in Chapter 3) concerning shifts in social vulnerability, policy decision making and property investment.

Moving away from agent-oriented explanations of causality, corporate and managerial theories stress the uneven power relations between housing agents involved in housing provision. In addition to capitalist interests, agents of the state such as local government officers, urban planners, tenant managers, real estate agents and other housing professionals mediate the distribution of housing resources (information, access, privileges) making their mark upon the form and outcomes of the housing network (Dunleavy, 1981; Pahl, 1975; Saunders, 1983; Simmie, 1981).

Specific characteristics of housing have been elevated to causal significance. Housing tenure, perceived as the bundle of rights and responsibilities, is considered by some researchers to influence one's power resources and position within social and economic structures. The resulting 'housing classes' debate, concerning the significance of tenure, remains unresolved in housing studies (Barlow and Duncan, 1988; Forrest, 1983; Marcuse, 1994; Rex and Moore, 1967; Saunders 1983; Winter, 1994).

Another unresolved theoretical debate concerns the role of the state and its relative autonomy from capitalist relations of housing production, exchange and allocation. In many policy related studies, there has been a tendency to perceive the state as an independent, benevolent and more recently, as a meddling agent. Alternative explanations emphasise the embeddedness of the state within broader social and economic structures (Jessop, 1990; Kemeny, 1983; Lundqvist, 1990; Marcuse, 1986; Stillwell, 1986).

A key difference between structural and actor-centred explanations is the claim by the former that objects and events are embedded in key social relations. Such theories focus upon the definition of specific social relations in housing provision and the role of the state. These include the relations of savings and investment, the exploitation of land, materials and labour relations in the formal work place and their (gendered) reproduction in the home, as well as circuits of capital accumulation throughout the production, consumption and exchange process. Nevertheless, agents produce and reproduce relations, and thus their behaviour remains integral to causal explanation.

'Relationists' argue that particular, context-defined sets of social relations cumulatively form different types of causal chains, which can explain divergence in forms of housing provision. These causal chains or mechanisms, in combination with contingent relations and other necessary relations, help to explain the nature and development of housing-related events and experiences (Dickens *et al.*, 1985; Jessop, 1990; Sayer, 1984, 2000). According to Ball *et al.*,

> The determination of changes in housing provision is a complex historical process whose explanation can only be investigated through detailed empirical analysis.
>
> (1988: 32)

Accordingly, the search for generalised, universal state roles is futile, given their contingent definition over time and space. The theoretical challenge is to define the causal mechanisms generating difference through concrete case study research.

> Recognition that social forms (like housing provision) and their causes can only be understood in the particular does not mean that we should reject any identification of structural mechanisms. This would leave us in the fake world of volunteerism, where people do what ever they independently happen to think of next, as though no other people or society had ever existed... a world of myriad assorted and apparently random events.
>
> (Dickens *et al.*, 1985: 2)

One of the few, published realist-inspired explanations of variability and change in housing structures was provided more than 20 years ago by Dickens, Duncan, Goodwin and Gray (1985). Their research compared case studies existing under different national housing systems in Britain and Sweden. It examined the local contingencies which surround and interact with forms of housing provision such as the tradition and role of organised labour and government, the level of class-consciousness and the regime of private capital. This strategic historical approach promoted consideration of contingent relations such as the financial markets, the building process, labour relations and the system of land ownership.

Yet the ontological assumptions of Dickens *et al.*'s (1985) comparative endeavour are far from overt. Only in the epilogue is a realist-inspired approach to comparative housing research explicitly promoted, focusing upon the key social relations of labour and property upon the role of the state in housing. In this section, Dickens contends that differences between housing systems result from the effect of *local contingencies* upon these relations. Unfortunately for housing researchers, Dickens has since moved away from the field of housing studies.

Moving on towards more structural approaches, concepts arising from political economy can assist the conceptualisation of causality in dynamic and divergent housing systems. Harvey (1978b in Berry, 1983) considers the process of urban (and housing) development as being contradictory and conflict ridden. As no overarching strategy orchestrates competitive, monopolistic and uneven development, it is punctuated by crises in the process of capital accumulation (Berry, 1983). At the local level, different forms of capital accumulation falter in crises. In this faltering drive to accumulate, new structural solutions are eventually found, albeit mediated by broader forces and contingent conditions (Berry, 1983; Harvey, 1973; Wright, 1978).

According to regulation theory, which emerged from political economy, urban development should not be viewed in functional economic terms, but as an interaction between *modes of social regulation* (MSR) and *regimes of capital accumulation* (RCA). The urban development process, which encompasses the provision of housing, is regarded as internally contradictory, lurching from periods of crises to structural coherence. The reasons for the sustained provision of housing existence lie in the interaction between MSRs and RCAs, generating spatial unevenness and change in forms of housing provision. Yet once again, any theory of explanation for specific forms of housing provision must be concretely derived via intensive geo-historical research (Chouinard, 1990; Florida and Feldman, 1988; Goodwin, 2001; Painter and Goodwin, 1995).

Developments in welfare theory force housing researchers to consider the wider social relations influencing forms of housing provision, and examine the different role housing plays in the reproduction of labour power. In recent years, various explanations for convergence, divergence and change in welfare states have been put forward (Esping-Andersen, 1996; Kemeny, 1992; Taylor-Gooby, 1991, 1991a). Kemeny (1992) has specifically argued for an extension of this theoretical work to the realm of housing and the integration of a more inclusive definition of 'welfare' (beyond income transfers) towards his concept of 'residence'.

A number of policy scientists, welfare economists and sociologists have examined the link between welfare and housing. A good example is the work of Castles (1997, 1997a) who considers the role Australian home ownership plays in providing horizontal, life cycle social security, and influencing national systems of welfare as well as the levels of expenditure on pensions. Retrenchment of the welfare state has been another focus for housing researchers, especially in England (Forrest and Murie, 1988; Taylor-Gooby *et al.*, 1999) where the role of municipal housing and local government has been drastically curtailed. At a cross-national scale, Barlow and Duncan (1994) compare welfare regimes across Western Europe whilst Kleinman (1996) examines the relationships binding forms of housing provision to welfare and the state in Britain, Germany and France.

Closely related is the multi-faceted cross-national debate concerning the *convergence of welfare systems*, including trajectories in systems of housing provision.[4] Here it is contended that countries progress through similar phases of economic development and corresponding state roles, during which certain forms of housing policy temporarily dominate (Burns and Grebler, 1977; Donnison, 1967). This approach has been tested and criticised for its functionalism, vague notion of causality and insensitivity to difference and divergence (Ball, 1988; Doling, 1997; Kemeny, 1992; Kemeny and Lowe, 1998; Kleinman, 1996).

4.3.2   Summary of alternatives for perceiving causality in housing provision

Table 4.2 summarises the very different notions of *causality*, which have been applied to explain difference and change in forms of housing provision. Once again, this is not an exhaustive compilation. Rather it demonstrates how ontology and the roots of causality interact to generate different types of theories for explaining or understanding the dynamics of and differences in forms of housing provision.

4.3.3 A critical review of causal explanatory approaches

Having summarised various notions of causality implicit in explanations of housing systems, it is now time to critically evaluate these alternative positions from the preferred ontological perspective of critical realism.

Causal explanation, rather than prediction, is the aim of realist research (Haralambos and Holborn, 1991: 761). Experiences and patterns of events are considered to represent indirect traces of causal mechanisms (Bhaskar, 1975 in Blaikie, 1993: 59). The aim is to reveal the causal mechanisms at work, which have influenced the formation of divergent networks of housing provision, and compare these mechanisms in order to explain differences in provision.

From this perspective a number of notions of causality can be rejected: chaos theory, random choice, rational choice theory, personal utility and public choice models – which place little or no emphasis upon the material or socially con-structed context of 'choice' making, or the interaction of structure with agency.

In the previous section, we selected a specific number of ontological 'devices' to perceive forms of housing provision. These concepts are coherent with realist ontology as they permit recognition of interacting dimensions of reality: empiri-cal experience, actual events and real relations, thereby acknowledging the com-plexity and openness of housing provision.

There are a number of theories that focus on particular sets of social relations, for example; tenure, labour or state-capital. Whilst these theories acknowledge the generative influence of important social relations in housing provision, they tend to provide only partial explanations for change, narrowed to the selection of 'isolated' relations. Nor do they provide a theory of why particular relations should be isolated for analysis. Further, there are overly structural accounts of change in housing provision, which leave little or no room for agency, conflict, crises or contingency. Change is regarded as an inevitable outcome of shifting modes of capital accumulation. These overly functionalist accounts neglect the mediat-ing role of agents and institutions, their bounded rationality and path-dependent behaviour.

Subsequently, any notion of causality builds upon the selection of preferred ontological concepts detailed in section 4.1. These were:

- weak social constructionism recognising the influence (but not determinism) of meaning and dominant ideologies that influence the *perception of different housing actors* in their material and socially constructed contexts;
- the uneven *position of different actors* in housing provision and their coalitions that may form to promote more commodified or decommodifed forms of provision;
- the different and related elements of housing provision, each subject to its own *institutional network, competing ideologies, economic relations and power coalitions* and
- the importance of revealing *key generative social relations* of housing provision such as property, finance and labour as they emerge over time and space.

Table 4.2 The 'roots' of causality in divergent forms of housing provision

Agency	'Roots' of causality	Causality in housing networks	Illustrative proponents
←	Human agency, chaos theory and random choice	Chaos theory rejects linear, structural and modernist thinking and emphasises human agency. It perceives structure as being neither loose nor tight, but always dynamic. Random utility theory explains human agency as choices between alternatives made on the basis of observed and unobserved attributes of alternatives, differences in tastes between the decision makers and uncertainty or lack of information	Young, 1992; Briassoulis, 2000
	Rational choice theory, personal utility and public choice models	The actions of housing agents are guided by rational choice (Elster, 1989), towards the achievement of maximum personal utility. Thus individual consumers, producers, financiers of housing make choices that optimise their own outcomes	Olson, 1965; Elster, 1986; Somerville, 1999; Dieleman, 1996a
	Risk and trust in social transactions	Developments in housing policy are perceived in the context of a post-traditional 'risk society', of greater uncertainty, flexibility and change in social and economic relationships. In transaction theory (TT) agents minimise risks according to their own goals and power resources. Trust concerns the partners' ability to *perform transactions as expected*, reliably, without opportunistic defection	For a more sociological application, see Beck *et al.*, 1994/5: 6, 1998; Allen, 2000; Fukuyama, 1995; TT: Nooteboom, 1995
	The influence of multiple agents upon housing provision	Corporate and managerial theories acknowledge the uneven power relations between housing agents. In addition to capitalist interests, agents of the state such as local government officers, urban planners, tenant managers, real estate agents and other housing professionals mediate the distribution of housing resources (information, access, privileges) and thus, the outcomes of the housing network	Saunders, 1983; Pahl, 1975; Simmie, 1981; Dunleavy, 1981
	The relationship between structure and agency	Housing is the mediated outcome of individual choice (agency) and of the rules and resources external to them (structure). Each defines the other, with neither structure nor agency having law-like dominance	Giddens, 1976, 1982, 1984; Jyrkämä, 2000; Winter, 1994

The influence of tenure, as a causal power, in social structures	These researchers have examined the importance of housing tenure, perceived as the bundle of rights and responsibilities, influencing one's power resources, social position and influence within social and economic structures	Rex and Moore, 1967; Saunders, 1982, 1983; Forrest, 1983; Barlow and Duncan, 1988; Marcuse, 1994; Murie et al., 1976
The mediated role of the state	Within housing studies, there has been a tendency to perceive the state as an independent, benevolent or even meddling agent. Alternative explanations emphasise broader social and economic structures	Jessop, 1990; Marcuse, 1986; Kemeny, 1983; Lundqvist, 1989, 1992; Stilwell, 1986
The political economy of state, capital and civil society	Political economists focus upon the institutionalised circuits of savings and investment in the provision of housing, distribution of capital accumulation and exchange, and the exploitation of land rent and labour relations in geo-historically embedded systems of housing provision	Harvey, 1978b; Ball, 1983, 1986; Barlow and Duncan, 1994; Ball and Harloe, 1992; Harloe, 1987, 1995
Labour and gender relations	The nature of work, its location, activity, income and security, influences the nature of housing services consumed. Housing consumption is influenced by the organisation of paid work, access to credit and the separation of home from the workplace – often unequally affecting men and women	Allen and Hammett, 1991; Randolf, 1991; Hayden, 1981; Allport, 1983; Fincher and Nieuwenhuysen, 1998
Generative mechanisms	The dynamic interaction of necessary and contingent relations at the real, actual and empirical domains of reality generates causal chains or tendencies, which over time interact with other contingent relations to generate divergence in housing provision	Sayer, 1984, 2000; Dickens et al., 1985
Crises, coherence, social regulation and modes of capital accumulation	The urban development process is regarded as internally contradictory, lurching from periods of crises to structural coherence. Continued existence lies in the interaction between regimes of capital accumulation and the 'regulation' of society, leading to spatial unevenness and change in forms of housing provision	Jessop, 1990; Wright, 1978; Berry, 1983, 1998; Chouinard, 1990; Goodwin, 2001; Florida and Feldman, 1988
Phases of economic and welfare development	Relates the institutional development of the welfare state to the form of housing provision. Debate surrounds the extent to which the logic of capitalism and industrialism influences welfare state development and as a consequence, forms of housing provision	Donnison, 1967; Donnison and Ungerson, 1982; Harloe, 1987; Burns and Grebler, 1977; Esping-Andersen, 1990; Barlow and Duncan, 1994; Castles 1997

Structure →

Adopting a particular notion of causality underlying housing change extends these ontological assumptions. Drawing upon the discussion in Chapter 3 and section 4.2, it is considered that within the realm of experience:

- housing agents are influenced by their uneven, filtered and bounded perception of risk and trust in complex housing interactions, in their material and socially constructed contexts;
- depending on the power resources and contingent conditions influencing the actions of individual and collective agents, cumulative housing transactions evolve to influence the norms, processes and institutions of housing provision and
- repeated, path-dependent interactions may form an institutional architecture, of laws, administrative processes and bureaucracies, which may evolve to consolidate a particular form of provision.

Yet this is not a one-way process or agent 'determinism'.

- This institutional hierarchy tends to be stable when it is coherent with the package of underlying or generative social relations, which are essential to the housing provision process.
- However, due to the open, crises-prone nature of capitalist housing relations, stability and coherence are temporary conditions. Indeed, even though they are more durable, key relations are also subject to exogenous or contingent relations.

It will be argued in Chapter 5 that the architecture of housing provision is particularly vulnerable to shifts in the foundation stones: the property relations, the circuit of investment and savings, and labour and welfare relations. Crises of provision may occur when one or more of these essential relations change too quickly for agents and institutions to adapt. This crisis of provision is only overcome when adaptive processes are established and a new phase of provision in the trajectory of a housing solution evolves.

In the following chapter, this complex, multidimensional notion of ontology and causality is further elaborated via text and diagrams to cover the key components of a postulate of provision and change in housing networks:

1   necessary relations of property, savings and investment, welfare and labour and their emergent properties;
2   contingency in housing provision;
3   agency and the concept of risk;
4   trust and embeddedness;
5   structural coherence, path dependency and institutional 'fix'; and finally
6   crises and adaptation.

5 Postulating an explanation for housing divergence

A common aspect of all critical realist research is the priority given to conceptualization and abstraction, for how we 'carve up' and define our objects of study tends to set the fate of any subsequent research. Realists seek substantial connections among phenomena rather than formal associations of regularities. In explaining associations, they seek to distinguish what must be the case from what merely can be the case. Explanation of the social world also requires an attentiveness to its stratification, to emergent powers arising from certain relationships, and to the ways in which the operation of causal mechanisms depends on the constraining and enabling effects of contexts. Realists also recognize the concept-dependency of social phenomena and the need to interpret meaningful actions, though since reasons can be causes this is not something separate from or alternative to causal explanation.

(Sayer, 2000: 27)

5.1 Introduction

In this chapter we 'carve up' the object of study, dynamic and different networks of housing provision, and propose a particular conceptualisation of how networks change and diverge over space and time. This postulate will be employed and revised via two subsequent case studies in Australia and the Netherlands.

A number of explanatory concepts have been distilled and developed from earlier discussions. These concepts include necessary relations and their emergent powers; contingent conditions, risk, trust and agency; embeddedness and path dependency; structural coherence, crises and reformation. They are elaborated and synthesised to form a postulated causal mechanism of divergence and change.

This postulate will be empirically tested and further developed via intensive case study research in Chapters 6 and 7 and sharpened via counterfactual thinking and contrastive questioning in Chapter 8, towards the development of an empirically feasible explanation of divergence and change for continuing critique and development.

5.2 Proposed housing ontology and definition of concepts

How can we decide which processes are necessary for particular outcomes, which are contingent, and which are irrelevant? How can we create appropriate cut off points for investigation, or allocate particular causal claims to particular levels of generality? A set of tools is needed – not just theoretical interpretations but also an epistemological apparatus to help us link structure and agency, concept and measurement.

(Dickens *et al.*, 1985: 246)

It has been contended in Chapter 3 and section 4.3.3 that a particular cluster of social relations holds emergent powers and can become 'packaged' or temporarily locked together in coherent albeit inherently crises-prone ways. This structural coherence tends to differentiate actual housing networks *at the base*. Forms of housing provision can be differentiated by the definition and packaging of key social relations concerning property, investment and savings, and labour and welfare. The following sections provide a series of arguments for the selection of these key relations.

5.2.1 *Necessary relations*

There are many different types of housing indicators, which attempt to capture and interpret various dimensions of housing provision.[1] Indeed, it is easy to drown in a sea of qualitative and quantitative detail of various housing outcomes. Yet if we are interested in the long-term development of housing solutions, we must confine our empirical search to uncover traces of the causal mechanisms generating *divergence and change* in open, complex networks of provision. Towards this end, rather than fishing in the sea of historical detail and official data sets for possible clues, it is far more efficient to strategically 'zero in' on the key causal aspects of housing provision. Following a realist theory of ontology as outlined in the preceding chapters, causality can be found in the contingent definition of emergent necessary relations. Yet, to guide this search we need some sort of theory of what these emergent relations are.

As indicated in Chapter 3, housing provision is subject to contradictions and conflicts between fractions of capital, expressed via the interactions between private landowners, house builders, building workers, financial institutions, specialist professionals involved in buying, selling and hiring accommodation, and finally owner occupiers, renters and the state. Each of these actors strategically intervenes at one or more stages of housing provision. Ball states that

the nature of its intervention and the responses by others to that intervention are the key determinants to the present day owner-occupation provision and its problems.

(Ball, 1983: 18)

What does Ball mean by 'intervention' and 'key determinants'? He later goes on to make a number of causal claims concerning the structure of housing provision abstracted from empirical research in Britain. To guide our search for the causal mechanisms generating divergence in forms of housing provision in Australia and the Netherlands, it will be argued that there are key emergent relations essential to both forms of housing provision, which have been very differently defined over time and space. How these relations have been contingently defined is of causal significance. The following paragraphs concern the selection of these emergent relations.

5.2.2 *Property rights and the exploitation of land and buildings*

How any society regards and manages property, and particularly the ownership of land, is a central defining element, which helps to distinguish the collective value system underpinning the institutions of government and policy forma-tions. Whilst property rights and relations underpin class structure, the property system also functions as a profoundly important – though often under-rated – mechanism for the transfer of public and private wealth within society.

(Badcock, 1994: 425)

For the purposes of this research, we define abstract property relations as the distribution of rights between agents engaged in the occupation, ownership, exploitation and exchange of land and, or buildings. These rights, however defined, are considered one of the founding institutions of the urban development process, and indeed the network of housing provision. All forms of housing consume space (not just at the ground level!) and thus land is an inevitable, integral component of housing provision.

Land is a peculiar commodity in that: it cannot be done without as all activity must occupy a space; it is fixed geographically, and unlike other capital goods cannot be moved around; although many site attributes or improvements can be modified, the land itself, in being consumed, has a definite permanency and indestructibility.

(Badcock, 1984: 208)

Real property rights influence the rights of access, exploitation and transfer of land. Urban laws, policies and practices clarify rights of ownership, occupation, usage and taxation. These rights and responsibilities are important because they influence the nature of investment in the built environment. As suggested later, property rights emit signals picked up by conscious actors operating in the land market, influencing their perception of risk and consequent actions.

Property rights are at the heart of the incentive structures of market economies. They determine who bears the risk and who gains or loses from transactions. In so doing they spur worthwhile investment, encourage careful monitoring and supervision, promote work effort, and create a constituency for enforceable contracts.

(World Bank Report, 1993: 48–49)

The actual nature and origin of these incentive structures are often overlooked, especially by supra-national organisations. World Bank housing economist Renaud promotes the development of property relations that clarify traditional, 'informal' property rights and support the development of land via sound urban planning and primary infrastructure provision. Accordingly, with proper land registration, land-use control and basic services in place, secure lending can occur, and in WB terms, 'enable markets to work' (Renaud, 1999: 768).

Yet, the power resources to act upon 'incentive structures' are unevenly distributed, and the subject of intense normative debate. Indeed, the actual (rather than idealised) distribution of property rights, perceived risks and responsibilities may promote or impede flows of capital into land and housing development. Private property rights, characteristics of the land market and the control of associated costs of development influence patterns of investment: long term, speculative and short term.

Power in the property process strongly relates to one's position in the land and housing market: a tenant in a tight rental market, an overburdened home purchaser desperately trying to sell, a small land holder in the path of a proposed freeway, privileged public agency or monopoly land purchaser.

> There is, in real life, a world of difference between the property rights attached to my 'quarter-acre' block and those attached, say, to the thousands of hectares owned by a speculator, finance company, insurance company, etc. My ownership of my quarter-acre block, in practice, gives me the right to occupy it for my own use (shelter, etc.) for as long as I choose, with a fair amount of psychological security, and to pass it on to my children. It does not give me the opportunity to profit and to exploit others. But if I owned several properties, or several hundred thousand hectares, then the right attached to that ownership are precisely the rights to profit, to exploit the labour of others.
>
> (Berry, 1983b: 127)

Existing social structures surrounding land tenure, tribal, collective or capitalist, are of causal significance. In advanced capitalist economies, home ownership tends to be associated with land markets characterised by commodified, freehold tenure, but this is by no means universal.[2] According to Ball,

> [o]wner occupation needs the free, rapid and unquestionable transfer of small land plots and single dwellings without which it is exceedingly difficult to borrow on the security of a property.
>
> (1983: 29)

Where leasehold is the norm, lease market conditions, the pattern of rent reviews and related provisions must be acceptable to the financial institutions from which credit is obtained (Cadman *et al.*, 1991).

But why are property rights of relevance to housing finance? As mentioned earlier, land is an essential, unavoidable component of housing provision. Obviously, housing is spatially located and where durable materials and workmanship have been utilised, a relatively permanent object. Property rights affect the value of that land upon which the house rests and vice versa, the value of the dwelling influences land value. The method of property valuation and the exchange process are interlinked, affecting the transferral of assets and the security offered to investors and lenders. Value can be determined in a number of ways: by government; the 'open' market; defined by the interaction of buyers and sellers; income value (also sustainable mortgage) which may be based on the rent stream, operating costs and discounting factors; or reproduction value, based on the cost of 'bricks and mortar' reconstruction (ECE, 1998: 6). Together, the definition of property rights (exclusivity, use, exploitation rights and transferability) and the structure of the land market (including nature of internal and external competition) influence the exploitable value of land, house prices and thus, the extraction of surplus value under commodified housing relations.

Of relevance to this study is the explicit recognition that land value influences the relative attractiveness of residential investment and the potential for the extraction of surplus value. Thus, not only forms of land tenure, but land market conditions play a key role influencing the behaviour of a range of actors including land developers and financial institutions. Indeed, market conditions in particular areas may promote or impede levels of investment. These conditions are not only affected by the ebb and flow of demand but are also significantly structured by the actions of the state. Consider the significance of *rent freezing* upon the value of rental dwellings, the importance of *expropriation rights* on property in the path of a new freeway and conversely, the imposition of a *betterment tax* where basic infrastructure is provided to Greenfield sites.

Where no barriers exist, investment may flow into areas perceived to offer relatively less risk and greater return on investment. In a negative scenario, market perceptions may become institutionalised, leading to declining investments and the practice of red lining: blockading investment, accelerating levels of deterioration and causing 'urban blight' in existing residential areas. Institutional barriers may also exist in the public sector, land-use plans may prohibit housing development in some areas and specify certain densities and housing standards in others. Capital gains and inheritance of property may also be taxed. As mentioned earlier, the definition of property rights, process of land registration and exchange are also influential state functions. Together, these actions influence the value of land and the perceived risks to housing investors.

Property rights influence incentive structures in another important way. Real property can offer a form of collateral, to be pledged by the borrower to ensure the fulfilment of obligations in the event of repayment difficulties and loan default. Throughout the duration of the mortgage, any number of unpredictable events may occur preventing payment of interest and principal as required by the mortgage contract. Small parcels of land, of sufficient size to accommodate a single homeowner, provide a disposable, tangible asset that can be pledged as debt security. The threat of repossession of such an asset, so intimately entwined with the dwelling that rests upon it, reenforces the borrower's obligations under the mortgage contract. Land also provides a convenient hedge against inflation. Thus, lenders tend to have a 'natural' interest in the value of the pledged collateral and may monitor any maintenance and alterations to the property that in turn may influence its capital and operational value. Indeed, in the case of rental housing, the value of the dwelling partially depends on its capacity to generate rental revenue. In a competitive market, the landlord must ensure a reasonable rent to quality ratio in order to minimise vacancies and maintain a steady rental income. Other transferable assets such as stocks, bonds and insurance policies may also be pledged as security. However, mortgage providers often prefer registered land title where this is expected to increase in value; indeed, any less secure asset may hinder the financing process.[3]

In sum, property relations are emergent social relations of great relevance to the development of housing solutions, embodying and distributing power between different groups in society, influencing investment patterns and, important for this study, modes of housing consumption.

5.2.3   Savings, borrowings and the circulation of investment in housing

At a European housing conference in 1996 (Nunspeet, the Netherlands), World Bank economist Renaud provoked his audience by claiming that cities were merely built the way they were financed. With aerial images of informal (incremental, self-built), private (diversified, professional, competitive) and socially financed housing (large-scale, standardised, monotonous), he declared that 'private' finance was the answer for developing countries to promote appropriate forms of urban development. Renaud later published his bold claim in Urban Studies (1999) but did not explain why different channels of finance necessarily produced such different urban forms and tenures. Little mention was made of the property and labour relations underpinning financial transactions, influencing the capacity of households to pay for housing. Indeed, his generalising claims underestimated the multi-causal nature of housing development.

Nevertheless, the relationship between savers, borrowers and the role of financial institutions is crucial because

> [t]he major activities in housing, house buying and house building, are, due to the high price of housing in relation to other goods bought by a consumer and the structure of the construction industry, heavily dependent upon the cost and availability of finance.
>
> (Hadjimatheou, 1976: 1)

As suggested earlier, the mortgage instrument plays a crucial role in capitalist housing relations – regardless of tenure. Houses are expensive to produce and thus relatively costly to consume. Whilst a house is generally bought from a vendor in a *one-off cash payment*, this swift transaction typically requires the arrangement of a long-term credit vehicle by the purchaser. In most circumstances, when a landlord or owner occupant purchases a dwelling, he/she purchases with borrowed investment capital in the form of a mortgage instrument. Repayments are made according to a fixed schedule of payments of principal and interest over a long period of time, possibly subject to variation. On the other hand, ongoing payments for *housing (occupation) services* vary by tenure and are subject to either individual income in the case of private home purchase, or pooled capacity to pay in the case of rental. The following two simple diagrams abstract the circuits of mortgage capital and payment for housing services in different housing tenures (Terhorst and Van der Ven, 1983). In Figure 5.1, mortage finance is used to finance the landlords' purchase of rental housing.

In multiple family dwellings (e.g. blocks of apartments), revenue relates to a series of renters and is not tied to the capacity of any one household. Such rents may be based on a variety of models including *cost rent, rent pooling and market rents*. Exploitation of dwellings based on the principle of cost rent requires the payment of rents equal to the cost of building, owning, maintaining and managing the dwellings. Strictly applied, where accommodation is rented according to cost price, the demanded sum may decline every year as the remaining loan principal reduces. Thus, the rent for old buildings would be much lower than for new ones. Yet this scenario, based on *historic cost price*, will not cover the *replacement cost* of the dwelling – which under inflationary conditions will always be higher than historic costs. For this reason, cost rent must be dynamic, increasing every year with the inflating cost of replacement. However, in certain market conditions, tenants may be free to move to similar quality older buildings, leaving newer, more costly ones vacant. In such a system, governments may intervene to provide *subsidies to permit the payment of project-specific cost rents*, especially in the early phase of the mortgage via a number of instruments on both the supply and demand side. Subsidies on the supply side may reduce the amount of credit required, and limit cost rents to those affordable for tenants. These include securitisation of loans to lower the interest demanded, paying the difference between market and below-market interest rates, providing grants reducing the cost of land development and construction or topping up the exploitation

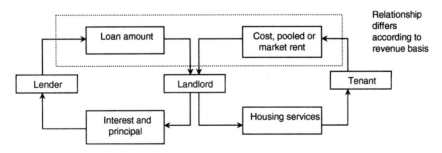

Figure 5.1 Abstraction of capital flows in rental housing (adapted from Terhorst and Van der Ven, 1983: 23).

account when shortfalls occur. On the demand side, renters may be assisted to pay cost rents via allowances for rents in specific housing projects (thus tied to their cost-rent profile).

A variation of cost renting is *cost-rent pooling*. For larger landlords, rents may be pooled across a range of buildings to enable harmonisation between old and new buildings. Rents may also be subject to government allowances or regulation. In such cases, the problem of differential cost rent is hidden from the renter, but the risk may remain for the landlord depending on his or her position in the rental market (Kemeny, 1981: 19).

However, in many cases we find that rents do not relate to the cost of financing building, owning, maintaining and operating dwellings. In an 'open' rental market, rents are set by the imperfect operation of the rental market, where tenants compete for dwellings of different types, quality and location. This rent-setting scenario is radically different from those mentioned earlier, as there is no immediate relationship between the costs incurred by the landlord and the actual profits of exploitation.

Market rents are defined by institutional constraints, market structure and the ebb and flow of effective demand and supply. The landlord anticipates that market rents are sufficient to cover the cost of finance, operation and maintenance and generate sufficient surplus revenue. In this scenario, new rental buildings may be risky loss makers in the early phase of the mortgage but potentially generate surpluses in the mature phase of the mortgage, making 'mature' rental properties more profitable. To reduce the risk of loss, larger landlords try to include a range of mortgage maturities in their investment portfolio. Landlords may also demand state assistance in the early years of the mortgage to cover any exploitation deficit, or even lobby for a system of housing allowances to permit full cost payment of rental revenue.

Typically, homeowners finance their purchase with home loan mortgage capital. However, in some countries the proportion of loaned capital is relatively low due to the savings strategies of extended family members, inheritance and dowry norms (as in India) and the distribution of resources between siblings (such as Korea's first sons). In Figure 5.2, a simplified version of mortgage-financed ownership and the consumption of housing services has been teased from each other. In this way, we can see that homeowners are both investors and consumers. This is often a surprise to many owners unconscious of this division. Nevertheless, rental 'income' is the subject of much debate amongst housing economists. Is housing a capital good or consumption good, and thus, how should it be taxed? Fictitious income from the rent of the dwelling, as distinct from outgoings associated with mortgage payments and maintenance, may be treated as income and thus liable for taxation. As these 'imputed rents' are fictitious, the taxes they attract are often unpopular and tend to be set at a low level. For this reason, home ownership is often found to be more affordable than renting in the long term.

As mentioned, the initial purchase of the home tends to occur in one swift transaction, financed by borrowed capital. Few purchasers have the ready cash for

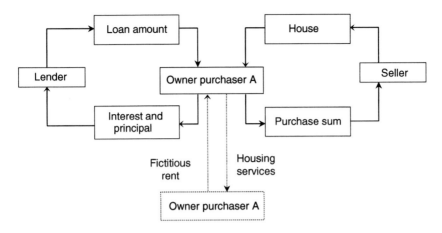

Figure 5.2 Abstraction of capital flows in owner-occupied housing (adapted from Terhorst and Van der Ven, 1983: 25).

such a large transaction and therefore must enter a mortgage contract with a lending institution, using the property as security and repay borrowed funds over a maximum period of 20–30 years. Long-term loans are typically necessary as the amount of the loan tends to be several times the annual income of the borrower. In this way payments of principal and interest can be spread over time (Boléat, 1985). Unlike rental investment, the term of the loan for individual ownership must be limited to the life expectancy and earning prospects of the *owner occupant*.[4]

Following initial purchase, there is no relationship between the amount of credit borrowed and the fluctuating value of the property. If the value of the house increases payments remain the same. Payments *may* be fixed according to the schedule agreed with the lender for a period up to 30 years. This schedule provides certainty to the owner occupant regarding his or her long-term, often declining housing costs – especially where interest rates are fixed for longer periods. However, variable interest rates imply that repayments vary over time, increasing dramatically with singular percentage point rises. By the end of the loan term, housing costs are minimal. In contrast, tenants do not have this certainty as their housing costs may fluctuate according to the rent demanded (be it cost rent or market rent) and rarely reduce over time. In recent years a vast range of mortgage products have evolved, transforming borrowers into dual investors (in housing and shares), increasing the risks considerably.[5]

As with rental housing, a range of *subsidies* may be provided affecting both the supply and demand of owner-occupied dwellings. On the supply side, various subsidies and regulations may affect *production costs* by influencing the cost of land, materials, building methods, and quality standards. Further, intervention may also occur in the financing of dwellings via regulation of mortgages, interest rates, interest rate subsidies, and the securitisation of loans. *Purchase* may be assisted via the supporting wage levels and conditions, favourable income tax rules permitting deduction of interest paid and minimal imputed rent taxes as well as simple 'starters' grants.

Figures 5.1 and 5.2 provide high-level abstractions of actual forms of housing finance and do not situate flows of housing capital within the wider context of saving and investments or the *capital markets*. Indeed, the housing sub-circuit is one of many that exist in the capital markets. This circuit provides an important link in the chain of housing provision, which is embedded in the broader financial, fiscal and legal infrastructure of specific banking laws, contracts, regulations, subsidy and accounting systems. In turn these are also linked to conditions in the world economy, as well as the nation's exchange rate, monetary and credit policy.

Moving 'down' from this level of abstraction of tenure-related capital circuits, we can consider the interplay between institutions involved in financing housing provision. The following paragraphs and Figures 5.3 and 5.4 deal with the different institutional routes and sources of investment in mortgages, the different forms of mortgage instruments, interest policies and the importance of real property as collateral securing mortgage obligations.

Most importantly, the housing finance system is influenced by the capacity of people to save, to deposit these savings and express effective demand. This

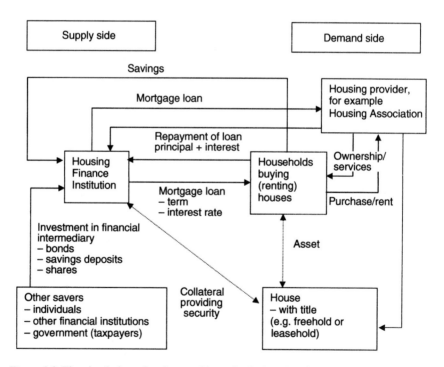

Figure 5.3 The circulation of savings and loans in the housing finance system (Baragalho and Lindfield, 2000).

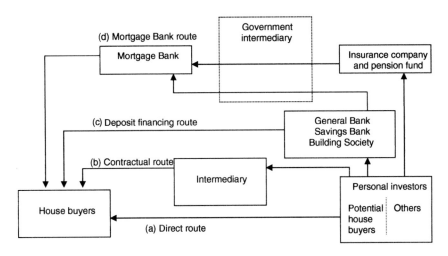

Figure 5.4 Routes for channelling savings into home finance (Boléat, 1985).

process of linking savers to borrowers is called 'intermediation'. Figure 5.3 addresses this link and portrays the housing finance system as an intermediary between a wide variety of savers and specific borrowers of housing finance (Baharoglu and Lindfield, 2000; Boléat, 1985). Ideal typically, savers place their money in bank accounts or mutual funds (unit trusts) and those institutions either provide long-term loans to house buyers directly (e.g. building societies) or lend to, buy bonds of, or buy shares in specialist mortgage providers that in turn provide mortgages. Finance for housing production may be issued in a variety of forms: as a grant, subordinated loan, mortgage or equity share holding. For loans, the level of principal and interest may be fixed or vary for a defined term (Haffner *et al.*, 1997). The conditions of credit may require a down payment or collateral for security, payment for insurance against defaults and a reliable guarantor (Boelhouwer, 1993). The investor may demand particular forms of marketable development, building processes and standards, or the minimum rent level and even specify the desired profile of eligible tenants.

Figure 5.3 is merely one conceptualisation demonstrating the link between savings, investors, property rights and housing purchase. In everyday reality, intermediation occurs via many different institutional routes, linking different types of savers to different types of purchasers. Savings, for housing purposes, may be channelled through various types of financial institutions (in the organi-sational sense) that concentrate on different fields and interests. These institutions include investors, commercial and savings banks, pension funds and insurance companies, building societies, mortgage banks and government agencies (Boelhouwer, 1997a; Boléat, 1985; Lomax, 1994).

Financial institutions seek compatible and balanced blend of savings (at call, fixed term, specific savings policy) and investments. For example, some institutions seek long-term, risk free, low return investments, whilst others pursue flexible, short-term, high return opportunities. This is because the financial institution's own source of investment (property, bonds, shares, futures) will cause it to be vulnerable to a range of non-housing concerns. The immediate environment may also influence investment behaviour. This environment may comprise competing investors or pricing cartels (sf. Bengs and Rönkä, 1994); stimulate or impede product innovation (Haffner *et al.*, 1997); and, or promote trust in contractual arrangements (Ando *et al.*, 1994; Buckely, 1994). Alternatively, institutions may be very exposed to housing issues such as down turns in housing prices, housing shortages and quality.

Directly, housing investors may rely on a financial return via the developments in rental revenue, improved land value or the sale of related mortgages. Alternatively, non-economic, societal objectives may play a role. For these reasons, the observable behaviour and interests of the investor must also be understood when attempting to explain difference and change in various systems of housing provision.

According to Ball, the type of institutional arrangements that exist for channelling savings towards home purchase and rental investment are crucial to the development of housing provision (Ball, 1983: 25). Figure 5.4 illustrates the various routes for channelling savings into the mortgage sector.

Savings may be channelled directly via personal or business relations (a), contractually via special purpose savings banks (b), via commercial banks from retail deposits (c) or mortgage banks funded by funded bond issues purchased by institutional investors (d) (Boléat, 1985).

Mortgages not only flow via different institutions to housing purchasers who in turn make repayments. They are also subject to very different types of contracts for these repayments. In the Netherlands, for example, the development of new mortgage products has been rapid; each imposes different obligations on both borrower and lender and offers different types of subjective and objective risks for both parties. They require the same long-term schedule of payments spread over the loan term for the borrower, but the use of borrowed funds and instalments differs considerably. Traditionally, annuity mortgages were repaid on a defined schedule of declining instalments of principal and interest over the term of the loan.[6] Today, a wide range of mortgages exist offering fixed or variable interest rates. Some mortgages are actually repaid via the promised returns from purchased investment products. Other mortgages involve interest-only payments that are tax deductible with separate arrangements for saving towards the principal which may even double as life insurance policies (Lawson, 2005).

Governments may influence the housing finance system for a range of reasons: to increase access to housing for low-income households, reduce housing costs and thereby relieve pressure on wage levels or enhance economic growth by facilitating housing construction and related consumption. In particular, the state may play an important role by influencing the security and profitability of investment in certain forms of housing provision, specifying standards for lending such as loan to value ratios, subsidising market interest rates, providing certain tax provisions and prudential norms, thereby encouraging or discouraging flows of investment via specific channels into different parts of the housing market. Via financial policy, national banking institutions and publicly owned banks, the state may regulate the volume of credit entering the mortgage market, specify 'safe' loan to income and value ratios, cap interest rates and set a low threshold for savings interest. In an effort to promote affordability, the state can establish special purpose vehicles to allocate loans or provide a mortgage guarantee to eligible borrowers and specify allocation criteria for mortgage applicants. To encourage particular forms of housing, it may intervene in the realm of production, in the form of grants to reduce the capital and maintenance costs, tax breaks on certain materials, schemes to mechanise and save time in construction processes. The list is endless. In each nation, and at the local level, the state intervenes in the financing of housing in a myriad of intentional and unintentional ways. It is a myth to believe that the private mortgage market is without public intervention.

Nevertheless, many aspects of housing provision such as finance, construction, management, exchange and consumption are beyond the total control or influence of the state and rest in the hands of various private bodies. Indeed, mortgages, being the long-term financing method for both tenures, are not only subject to the regulatory structures and actions of the state but also other contingent circumstances, which can arise affecting the financial relations between the lender and borrower. These include rising interest rates, inflation and the fluctuating capacity to pay for housing services.

In sum, financial relations are causally significant in tandem with both property relations and the capacity of households to save and purchase housing services. Financial instruments are unavoidable under capitalist housing conditions, due to the high cost of housing relative to household income, and payments must be spread over time. Lending conditions (term, interest rate) vary according to the mode of consumption or tenure, and are subject to the institutional and market constraints affecting the entire finance system.

5.2.4 *Labour, welfare and housing consumption*

What role do *households* play in directly promoting forms of housing provision? This section provides an outline of their emergent role, as influenced by welfare and labour conditions. Welfare and labour conditions are important because they influence the manner in which housing is consumed and the relationship within households and the workplace. Yet well-developed conceptual models of this complex realm, and its influence on forms of housing provision, have yet to be developed. An outline of differing perspectives is provided later, followed by a more definitive statement.

Allen and Hamnett examine the *spatial aspects* of labour and housing markets with particular reference to commuting patterns and urban form; spatial differentiation of labour and housing opportunities; and the relative fixity of housing, relative to the mobility of employment opportunities (1991: 3–15). They contend that the relations between housing and labour markets, home and work are varied and complex, rather than static or universal, and therefore must be *understood historically and geographically*.

Randolf (1991: 16–51) stresses the *contingent nature* of the link between housing and labour markets, often operating within different spatial scales. He emphasises the following types of *contingencies*:

- determination of the number of jobs by employers;
- the relative importance of bargaining between labour and capital;
- discrimination and entrapment in labour sub-markets, particularly by gender and racial characteristics;
- spatial unevenness and mismatch in job opportunities;
- dynamic power balance of particular segments of labour markets;
- uneven flexibility of labour markets to cope with change;
- fragmentation and fluidity between segments of the labour force and
- social, historical and spatial contingency of labour markets.

Also important is the structure and function of the household and the role intergenerational wealth transfers and capital gains play in determining ability to pay for housing services. Randolf goes on to stress, as for labour markets, the social, historical and spatial contingencies of housing market processes. Together these *labour market and housing market contingencies, including the role of domestic labour, affect the relative bargaining power of workers in competing for housing services.*

By understanding housing demand *in terms of the position of workers* in the labour market a more sensitive analysis can result. Further, Watson (1991: 136–154) stresses the importance of the changing nature of home and work and the nature of work undertaken in the domestic sphere. She argues for a feminist approach to labour and work relations that is sufficiently sensitised to explain the complex interplay of culture, gender and class.

Of course, capacity to pay for housing costs is important to the rental sector as well. Landlords require regular instalments of cash to pay for operational and capital costs. Yet the payment is for housing services alone and not to the benefits of ownership (right to own and exploit the asset).

Capacity to pay for home purchase is inevitably linked to one's capacity to save. As discussed earlier, the network of housing provision, particularly the sub-sector of mortgage finance, is especially sensitive to the capacity and willingness of households to save. Incentives to save include an attractive level of real interest rates for deposits, reliability of banks, security of bank deposits from government intervention and their liability to taxes on savings and available subsidies, if any, influencing purchase (Baharoglu and Lindfield, 2000).

Capacity to pay affects not only the volume of housing investment, but the mortgage contract conditions which evolve over time, forming the dynamic institutional structures of housing investment. Mortgage arrangements are implicitly coupled with the savings capacity of households, which in turn relate to their work and welfare arrangements.[7]

For the home purchaser, the 'bottom line' remains that the 'mortgagor does not invest his capital in the house as such but in the capacity of the mortgagee to repay' (Berry, 1983b: 99). Indeed, proven capacity to make regular, adequate payments is of crucial significance to home ownership, and in addition to property rights and financial relations, forms the third dimension of the emergent relations underlying forms of housing provision.

On the consumption side, the capacity to pay for housing services may be influenced by state action in the realm of labour market policy and wage regulation, progressive taxation schedules, and targeted housing allowances (Lundqvist, 1992, see Appendix 2).

Finally, labour and welfare conditions not only concern capacity to pay on the demand side, they directly contribute to the cost of construction affecting the supply of housing. Wages in the construction sector (alongside the cost of land, development finance and building materials) must not reach a level that increases building costs to such an extent that the cost price becomes too high to extract a surplus from sale or rent of the dwelling. In such cases, production may slow down and even cease for a period.

In sum, labour and welfare relations, as with property and investment, play a key emergent role generating savings and influencing not only the capacity to pay for housing but the very supply of housing services. Once again important contingencies define these relations, not the least the position of households in the paid labour force and the role of the state in regulating wages, making transfer payments and influencing rent levels and conditions.

5.3   Emergent properties of necessary relations

Moving from this concrete discussion of housing provision earlier, section 5.3 returns to more abstract issues concerning the emergent properties of the property, savings and investment, and labour and welfare relations outlined earlier.

Drawing upon the taxonomic work of Lundqvist (1992) and Ambrose (1991), it is feasible to view the relations of housing provision outlined earlier, as generating different distributive outcomes, along commodified–individualised, de-commodified–collectivised continuums, as depicted in Table 5.1.

Yet this approach remains static, fragmented and taxonomic rather than *explanatory*. It obscures the connections between the different relations (Sayer, 2000: 6) and does not suggest how or why certain social relations hold *causal, emergent powers*. Nor does it highlight the role of *contingency* in the actual definition of social relations, which of course changes over time.

Table 5.1 Commodification and decommodification of social relations underlying housing provision

Social relation	Commodified–individualised	Decommodified–collectivised
Property rights	Private right to exploit	Public right to exploit
System of investment/savings	Savings and investments channelled to maximise private capital accumulation	Savings and investments channelled to maximise public benefit
Labour/welfare	Individualised-subsidiarity	Co-operative-universality

Table 5.2 Emergent properties of social relations underlying housing provision

Key relation	Emergent properties expressed via forms of housing provision
Property relations	Influence the nature of use, exchange, exploitation of land and subsequently, patterns of investment in land development over space and time.
Savings–investment relations	Influence the distribution of credit, entitlement and other resources amongst different societal groups over their lifetime. Ultimately, the definition of this relation influences investment in housing over space and time.
Welfare–labour relations	Influence the cost of housing construction, the capacity to consume housing resources, the labour conditions required to maintain housing costs and domestic services to reproduce 'productive' labour.

Section 5.2 contended that the 'internal' relations of property, savings–investment, and welfare–labour have *emergent* properties. Table 5.2 summarises these properties.

Emergent properties are not essential or static, but change when combined with other relations and under different contingent conditions. To use a metaphor from natural science, just as hydrogen and oxygen can combine to form water, particular social relations can combine to generate specific forms of housing provision. The power of oxygen to form water, for example, is dependant upon its relationship with hydrogen.

And so it is with certain combinations of social relations, which may tend to generate specific forms of housing provision (Castles, 1997). For example, free-hold tenure, individualised savings, regulated wages and low levels of welfare provision tend to generate and sustain more privatised forms of housing provision than those generated by a combination of communal land rights, contributory and extensive welfare arrangements.

The institutional architecture, which supports investment in housing provision, is of fundamental importance in distinguishing between dominant housing 'solutions'. Yet this basic architecture of housing provision, the property rights, circuit of savings and investment, and labour and welfare relations that influence housing consumption, is dynamic and contingently defined. There are no law-like combinations of social relations that consistently determine forms of provision. This is because contingent conditions are always present and often causally important. I now turn to the important role *contingent conditions* play in the definition of these relations and the generation of divergent forms of provision.

5.4   Contingency in housing provision

Just as hydrogen and oxygen, under certain contingent conditions, can also form ice and steam, different *contingent conditions* have a significant influence on forms of housing provision.

Contingency is a very important notion in housing provision. With its multi-dimensional relationships, the production, exchange and consumption of housing is highly vulnerable to changes in specific contingent conditions. Many different, often unanticipated actions, events and relations may influence internal dynamics of provision, and indeed have a cumulative effect on the entire housing network. For example, the level of housing production is sensitive to the availability of mortgage credit, which at any given time may be diverted to more lucrative forms of investment. It is also sensitive to increased labour and material costs, and of course changes in planning rules and development standards.

So far the emergent relations of housing provision and their contingent definition have been depicted as separate and isolated realms for ease of explanation. In reality this separation is clearly not the case. Necessary relations only ever exist in the context of contingent conditions. The following series of illustrative figures attempt to bring the concept of necessity, contingency, practice and outcomes closer to everyday reality. Figures 5.5 to 5.7 outline the type of contingencies, which influence the definition of key emergent relation in housing provision.

To begin, Figure 5.5 illustrates how property relations can be defined, under the influence of contingent conditions and the relevant risk-reducing practices.

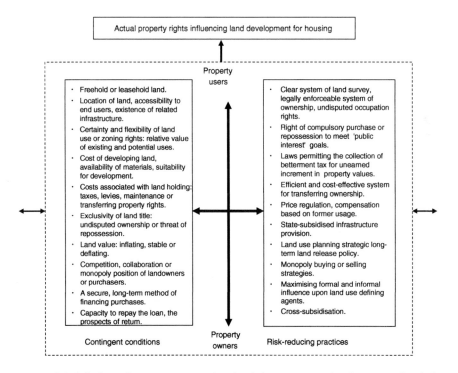

Figure 5.5 Relations between agents involved in property development, in their contingent, risk-reducing context.

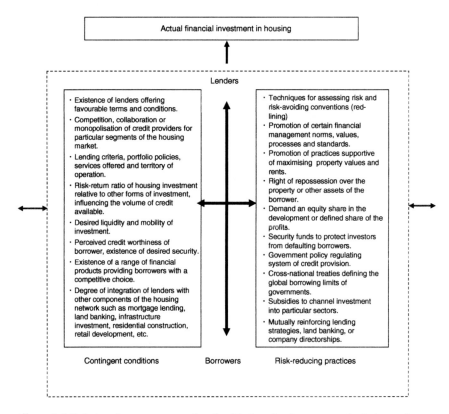

Figure 5.6 Relations between agents involved in housing investment, in their contingent, risk-reducing context.

Many different contingent conditions and risk-reducing institutions influence the definition of savings–investment relations of housing provision over time and space. Once again, concrete case study research is required to define the relations integral to forms of housing provision. Figure 5.6 abstracts the relations between agents involved in housing investment, in their contingent and institutionalised context.

Finally, Figure 5.7 illustrates the interaction between housing consumers and providers in their contingent contexts.

Further, some emergent relations have more influence upon certain phases of housing provision than others and can be perceived as primary emergent relations, linked to other more secondary emergent relations. Specifically, it is argued that property relations hold primary emergent powers over the process of land development and redevelopment, and secondarily over phases of residential investment and dwelling construction. Further, financial relations hold primary emergent powers over patterns of investment in housing production, and a secondary role in allocation and consumption. Finally, it is contended that welfare

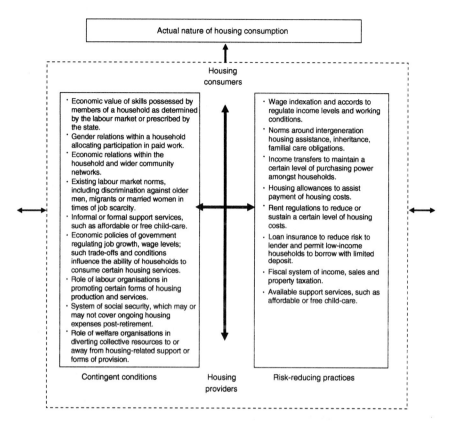

Figure 5.7 Relations between agents involved in housing consumption, in their contingent, risk-reducing context.

and labour relations hold primary emergent powers over the process of allocation and consumption and second, influence savings and investment.

Figure 5.8 should be viewed as a synthesis of Figures 5.5–5.7 and illustrates how these primary and secondary emergent powers of necessary relations, defined by contingency and agency, influence particular stages in the housing provision process.

Of course, using these ideas and concepts as prompts, historical case study research is required in order to abstract explanatory causal mechanisms at work.

But can everything be put down to the contingent context? Sayer asks 'how far, or at what depth, are social structures and processes context-dependent?' (2000: 133) and argues for a respectful exchange between narrative and analysis, cautioning against strong social constructionism, non-causal description and structural reductionism. The following section brings actors into the causal explanation, reflecting the weak social constructionist position outlined in Chapter 4.

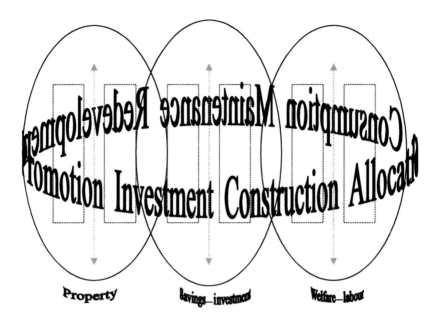

Figure 5.8 Emergent relations and stages in housing provision – promotion, investment, construction, allocation, consumption, maintenance and redevelopment.

5.5 Agency and the concept of risk

Of course, it is the actions of agents that operationalise emergent and contingent relations. Thus agency is something we need to understand by developing appropriate ideas and concepts. To appreciate the rationale for the action of particular agents operating in the network of housing provision, the concept of risk can be helpful. Risk is the indirect, experiential outcome of social relations that may influence relationships between agents in the housing network. It can be differentially perceived between different interests, professions, groups, classes and cultures – there is no fixed or concrete definition of risk. Decisions to save, build, buy, rent or invest are all made (or not made) in a context of dynamic incentive structures, which are both *materially and socially constructed*.

Yet, agents operating in housing networks are only *partly* guided by risk avoiding behaviour. In this regard the work of Nooteboom (1995), which concerns the dynamics of social relations, which shift over time under different contingent conditions, is relevant and interesting:

> we are interested in the dynamics of relations. Such dynamics include at least the following two types of phenomena:
>
> – Shifts of perception, knowledge and understanding (including mutual understanding between transaction partners), competence, goals, motives, trust and opportunism, as a relation develops.

- Events and changing conditions outside the relations: technological development shifts in supply and demand due to entry and exit of firms, etc.

Transactions are to be seen as embedded in relations that develop in time under changing conditions.

(Nooteboom, 1995: 3–4)

Nooteboom (1995) is critical of rational choice theory, where knowledge and competence are merely perceived as objective and given, rather than *learnt and path dependent*. He argues that transactions between firms are *embedded in relations that are developed over time*.

It is argued that the perspective and actions of agents are indeed selective and uneven (Sayer, 2000: 43). Importantly, agency is also *influenced by a system of ideas or ideology* that defines what is 'common sense' and guides everyday decision making. According to Gramsci (1971), major institutions in society, such as the financial institutions, the media, religious organisations and government agencies can drive ideological hegemony reinforcing certain forms of housing provision. Such ideologies may concern the role of women in domestic labour, the importance of regular work and freedom of markets, responsibilities of government, individual duties and collective welfare. Kemeny (1983, 1986, 1995) has examined the role of ideology in reinforcing home ownership in Australia and rental systems in Europe. He remarks,

Each system is informed by a specific ideology and view of how markets operate and is the product of different kinds of power structures.

(Kemeny, 1995: 5)

Accordingly, it is important to appreciate the shifting ideologies influencing housing agents over time that influences actor perceptions of risk (for a concrete case study, see Allen and Sprigings, 1999).

Risk is also a concept that can be applied to institutions affecting a cross section of society. There is often talk of the *distribution of risk*, over time, between vulnerable and less vulnerable groups in society. The state may choose to prevent poverty amongst non-working (elderly, disabled) households by *enforcing a system of savings or redistributing collective taxation to a system of benefits*. With regard to housing provision, the state may support the saving for deposits for home purchase, regulate home finance or rent levels, or intervene in the development of land and construction of housing. One rationale for such actions is to influence individual housing expenditure and thereby minimise risks to other elements of economy or society (high wage demands, long job commutes, eviction, overcrowding and substandard housing).

Yet the reasons how and why such actions are undertaken are far more complex than mere risk perception. Individual agency in the housing system is embedded in a socially and materially constructed reality. This reality encompasses different ideologies affecting the provision and consumption of housing that may emerge over time, more durable social relations affecting property rights, savings and investment mechanisms, and labour and welfare provision which may underpin a housing system, dynamic material contingencies and finally, the institutionalised everyday 'common sense' practices of actors in the housing network.

5.6   Trust and embeddedness

Embeddness is a much-abused term in sociology and urban studies. What does it actually mean and how does it relate to causality in divergent forms of housing provision? One straightforward approach is to consider embeddedness as simply 'the way things are done in a particular time and place'. But we *need to go beyond the observable* to understand social conventions. When anticipated patterns of behaviour are followed they build more certainty in future social exchange. Indeed, there is reassurance in repeated actions. Successful, predictable exchange builds trust, which generates more lasting interactions (Nooteboom, 1995: 5). In recent times, trust has been applied beyond individual exchanges and organisational culture to explain different levels of regional economic performance (Fukuyama, 1995):

> Virtually all economic activity in the contemporary world is carried out not by individuals but by organizations that require a high degree of social co-operation. Property rights, contracts, and commercial law are all indispensable institutions for creating market-orientated economic systems, but it is possible to economise substantially on transaction costs if such institutions are supplemented by social capital and trust. Trust, in turn is the product of pre-existing communities of shared moral codes or values. These communities, at least as they are lived and experienced by their most recent members, are not the product of rational choice....
>
> (Fukuyama, 1995: 95)

But is it enough to say that trust and the institutions of social exchange are historically embedded, without a *critical explanation of how or why*? Sayer argues that social exchange theory, and the lubricant of trust, idealise market interactions and

> underestimates the material aspects of economic life and [presents] an overly benign view which underestimates the instrumentality of economic relations.
>
> (Sayer, draft, 2000)

In reference to McDowell (1997), he goes on to suggest that codes of trust and embedded institutions may indeed be orientated towards hierarchical domination and 'the bottom line': oppressive, inequitable and far from 'mutually beneficial' as the term trust suggests. Indeed, systems of housing provision often incorporate uneven power resources, monopolistic coalitions, and opportunistic and exploitative players.[8] Building upon this critical understanding of the institutionalisation of trust and embeddedness, the following section concerns the relevant concepts of structural coherence, path dependency and institutional fix.

5.7 The role of the state, structural coherence, path dependency and institutional 'fix'

As stated throughout this chapter, there are no universal definitions for emergent relations underlying housing provision because they are contingently defined in an *open network* of housing provision. Further, there is *no master blue print or single agent*, such as government, which has the power to map out such a network. Certainly, forms of provision may be promoted to guide economic and social outcomes and likewise, certain social and economic outcomes may guide forms of provision. Organs of the state, such as central and local government, major welfare providers, religious movements and labour unions, may consider some forms of provision as being instrumental in reaching certain social (adequate shelter for all) or economic goals (wage moderation). They may support or discourage investment in the residential environment as a priority or direct investment into other productive sectors (agriculture, industry).

Explanations for housing provision are often strongly state-centred, focusing on policy histories and programme structures, with little reference to broader, influential, structures of housing provision influencing the promotion, investment, construction, allocation and consumption of housing. In agreement with Ball *et al.* (1988), the state itself is considered to play only a partial role in defining emergent relations and networks of housing provision. Accordingly,

> There is particularly a need to downgrade the autonomy and power of the state, which is assumed to exist in the housing sphere.
>
> (Ball *et al.*, 1988: 32)

From this perspective, the state is considered to play a *mediating, sometimes conflicting role in establishing structurally coherent networks of housing provision*. Beyond the state, one may imagine a temporary coherence or flow between different phases and stratum of housing provision.

Following Ambrose (1991) and Ball (1998), housing systems are perceived as being both a chain and a structure of provision, comprising numerous *economic interdependencies* and organisational interactions. These relationships may be enforced or undermined via the shifting ideological hegemony (Kemeny, 1995, 1983) and *uneven power relations* of various agents both internal and external to housing provision (Lundqvist, 1992). Further, various contingent conditions, external to the chain of provision, may lead to a *crisis of accumulation and social regulation undermining the neat functional–institutional fit* of the status quo.

In regulation theory, Jessop uses the term *structural coherence* to describe the interaction between modes of capital accumulation and social regulation, which form relatively stable regimes. Structural coherence is defined as

> historically contingent ensembles of complementary economic and extra-economic mechanisms and practices which enable relatively stable accumulation to occur over relatively long periods.
>
> (Jessop, 1997: 503 in Goodwin, 2001)

Such a term is also useful when explaining the long-term development of divergent forms of housing provision. One may imagine a temporary coherence in the emergent relations of housing provision: the property relations (rights, market structure and value), the system for channelling savings into housing investment and labour–welfare relations influencing capacity to pay for housing services. When these emergent relations mutually reinforce one another, a coherent structure of provision may prevail. This 'coherent cluster of emergent relations generates and is generated by numerous economic interdependencies, long term obligations, and reinforced by organisational practices and ideological hegemony' (Kemeny, 1995, 1983). Yet coherence is neither given nor static. Rather, it is subject to a wide variety of contingent circumstances and the uneven power relations of various agents both internal and external to housing provision (Lundqvist, 1992). Nevertheless, during periods of coherence it can be said that a neat structural, institutional and agency fit maintains the status quo.

Building on this perspective, coherence based upon the interdependencies of emergent relations, day-to-day practices and dominant ideologies ensures that housing solutions are neither random nor 'natural'. They result from cumulatively causal and multiple layers (structure, institutions and agency) of structured open reality. Given the relative durability of housing and urban forms, today's housing choices are 'sticky'. That is, they are heavily path dependent and *embedded in the solution, structures, institutions and practices of the past.*

Is there a law that defines structural coherence? Jessop has more recently argued that coherence is something that is inherently spatio-temporal. For this reason, concrete research is required to

> examine how specific structures and structural configurations selectively reinforce specific forms of action and discourage others. Combining these concerns leads one to examine the continuing interaction between the reflexive reorganization of strategic selectivities and the recursive selection and retention (or evolutionary stabilization) of specific strategies and tactics oriented to those selectivities. In some circumstances this interaction can result in a relatively durable degree of 'structured coherence' (or stability) in a given institutional complex.
>
> (Jessop, draft, 2000)

5.8   Defining crisis

What is it that 'undoes' structural coherence, which may have sustained a particular form of housing provision in the past, and lays the foundations for the establishment of new forms (Terhorst and Van de Ven, 1997: 80)? First, it is important to recognise that the *process of capital accumulation is an open one*, contingently defined and dynamic. Rather than being merely a closed market exchange between supply and demand, markets are inherently *imperfect*, subject to monopolies, misinformation, opportunism, resource constraints, *unpredictable contingencies*, ideological shifts and the inevitable rise and fall of profits. Markets are not only vulnerable to local conditions, but increasingly to those beyond the periphery of regions in the global arena. Capitalism easily catches a cold from many different sources and there is no reliable or permanent cure. Housing provision is part of such a world, and often comprises highly commodified relationships, subject to imperfect market relations and the chaotic, conflicting struggle for capital accumulation. Even 'public' housing is not immune: built by private contractors, financed by loan capital, with (subsidised) rent levels to cover these costs (Ball, 1983).

Given the *conflict-ridden and crises-prone nature of capitalism*, it is easy to imagine that a neat functional fit, between a particular form of housing provision and the broader political economy, may only exist for short periods of time. In an effort to moderate the 'worst excesses', institutions may constantly evolve new policies, practices and ideas. Government policies and programmes also have unforeseen and sometimes, hidden consequences. As modes of capital accumulation and social regulation are inherently spatio-temporal, the process of coherence, crises and adaptation must be concretely researched and defined (Jessop, draft, 2000).

So what is a crisis and what role does it play in providing a causal explanation for housing solutions? The following examples aim to clarify two points. First, as discussed in section 5.4, the emergent relations of housing provision are contingently defined.

Contingent relations influence the definition of necessary relations underlying housing networks. They are circumstantial relations that intersect with necessary relations to divert their 'necessary outcome'. Contingent relations may impede, mute, stifle and even extinguish the necessary relationships of a network. They are always present in open, interactive systems.

Second, emergent relations are abstractions from complex multi-dimensional forms of provision. They are not atoms but mutually dependent; thus any shift in the definition of say property relations may affect financial relations under certain contingent conditions. As explained earlier, given that housing systems are always open, their emergent relations are always contingently defined. It is therefore possible that one or more components of the emergent cluster evolve in such a way as to destabilise other mutually reinforcing economic interdependencies, long-term obligations, organisational practices and ideological hegemony.

A simple example concerns housing investment during periods of war. Housing investment does not tend to take place in disputed areas, along borders or in regions of conflict. This is because land prices and their potential to rise are too uncertain and thus provide *inadequate security to enable mortgage lenders to invest*. During such times, building materials may also be scarce and expensive. For these reasons, unstable areas often suffer from declining investments and dilapidation – compounding their economic, political and social problems.

Take the more complex example of co-operative housing, which is dependent upon communal forms of property rights, cost-rent finance and rent pooling. This coherence could be undermined by any number of contingencies including the sale of older houses which had previously enabled cross-subsidisation, deregulation of interest rates making financial costs higher than affordable rent revenue and or long-term unemployment amongst tenants leading to high levels of rent arrears eroding provisions for expansion and improvement of the co-operative. Further, coherence in the co-operative sector can also be *undermined by countervailing ideology*: by promoting more individual, private housing solutions such as home ownership, enticing wealthy co-operative tenants seeking higher quality homes from the tenure.

The earlier examples illustrate the importance of *strategic contingencies* that may erode or stifle mutually supportive emergent relations. It is worth noting that in both scenarios, coherence was disrupted by crises, creating a different risk profile for agents in the housing sector.

In periods of crises, the perception of risk, however real or imperfect, influences the actions of actors who may establish new norms, practices and institutions, leading to the development of new or adapted solutions for housing provision. Depending on the contingent conditions, risk perception and uneven power resources of key agents, a whole range of social practices and institutions may cumulatively arise to moderate (or exacerbate) the excesses of crises-prone housing provision. These may include improving the transfer of market knowledge, asserting codes of banking practice, ensuring the steady release of land for development, and regulating wages and rental conditions. Amongst many other possibilities is the regulation of housing costs, protecting vulnerable constituents and maintaining social harmony, whilst minimising the threat of wage demands to pay excessive housing costs. These actions also have their cumulative, unintended and ongoing affects.

5.9   Defining periods for analysis

This section concerns the creation of appropriate cut-off points for investigating and contrasting periods of coherence and crisis in housing history. It is contended that contrasting periods of coherence and crisis defined at the level of emergent relations can help to reveal the causal mechanisms at work in the two divergent case studies of Australia and the Netherlands.

In this way, the basis for defining periods for contrast goes beyond mere indicators of aggregated housing outcomes. Thus, the division of periods or phases will not be based upon the rise and fall of certain tenure forms. Such indicators will not reveal the causes of change and divergence. Arguments against a direct cause-effect view of causation, as distinct from a contingent one, have already been put forward in Chapter 4. Rather, division should be made at a deeper ontological level of adaptation, coherence and crisis amongst key emergent relations in their contingent context underpinning housing provision. Such a definition may mean that the boundaries appear fuzzy, as they cannot be statistically 'proven'. They are of course a researcher's construction and thus contestable. Nevertheless, precise 'switches' in forms of housing provision do not exist in real life. Modes of provision are sticky and do not change over night; rather they are subject to multiple causal mechanisms, which must be revealed by a process of abstraction and plausible notion of causality.

By contrasting appropriately defined periods of adaptation, coherence and crisis, based on contingently defined clusters of emergent relations abstracted from empirical case study research, the causal mechanisms driving divergence and change are more likely to be revealed. Such an approach is based on a clear ontological argument, a theory of emergent relations and a contingent view of causality.

5.10 Concluding statement

Housing is neither an isolated nor a static object, but surrounded and sustained by an environment of path-dependent and dynamic institutions. The manner in which housing is consumed is subject to a strategic package of emergent relations. For this reason, to understand and explain different forms of housing consumption, research must focus on the changing definition of interdependent emergent relations in their contingent context.

It is contended that systems of housing provision can be understood as the mutually reinforcing outcome of a dynamic package of coherent emergent relations of housing provision. These relations form clusters that partially generate the institutions, processes and dominant ideas of housing production, allocation and consumption. In turn, existing patterns of housing consumption also influence the development of future housing options. The system of property rights, organisation of finance and mode of housing consumption not only generates but also is mediated by the existing process of housing provision. These key or necessary relations can be contingently defined and packaged in a variety of coherent ways, over time and space.

This chapter has postulated that changes in forms of housing provision are generated when the architecture of housing provision, the emergent relations, are fundamentally redefined and the socially and materially contingent conditions permit new forms of action or inaction. Fundamental change may include the alteration of property relations shifting opportunities and risk in favour of public or private land developers, deregulation and privatisation of state-based housing loans and a shift from market allocation to queuing for housing distribution. Yet, strategic events in housing history, such as a new property law or financial instrument, may not directly lead to change. Only under the right contingent conditions will emergent powers become operational. For this reason, strategic events when linked to the definition of emergent relations and contingent conditions are of explanatory importance.

For each case study in Chapters 6 and 7, an attempt will be made to pin point and illustrate contrasting periods of adaptation, coherence and crisis. This will be done by critically rereading and reinterpreting housing history in the search for the strategic events and contingent conditions that have *reinforced or undermined mutual interdependencies*, practices and ideologies.

Part II

Diverging housing solutions: the case study evidence

6 Explaining divergent tenure patterns and urban form

The Australian case of low-density home ownership

6.1 Introduction

The Netherlands and Australia are often respectively categorised as 'Old' and 'New' World advanced capitalist countries, with different modes of welfare provision underpinning their social and economic development (Castles, 1998). The Netherlands, with its relatively strong welfare state and social rental housing, is contrasted with liberal and laissez faire home owning countries such as Australia. Contrastive comparisons are easy to make. Figures comparing state expenditure, tenure forms and housing subsidies have become more widely available with the establishment of multi-national, regional and global organisations such as the OECD, United Nations, World Bank and European Commission. However, broad-brush, empirically driven and often normatively based comparisons tend to polarise and categorise, rather than provide a considered explanation of difference.

The proposed comparison of difference and change in the housing solutions of the Netherlands and Australia seeks to highlight and explain, rather than merely emphasise the observable, obvious distinctions. It is contended that the roots of explanation can be found in the unique configuration of necessary and contingent relations present in each country: the underlying package of causal relations generating distinctive housing solutions.

The purpose of comparing the Netherlands with Australia is to demonstrate the value of comparisons that recognise the structural coherence *and embeddedness of two distinct housing solutions*. It will be argued in subsequent chapters that a unique cluster of property, investment and savings, and labour and welfare relations has been mediated by each state in radically different ways in the Netherlands and Australia.

The Dutch solution of social rental housing and urban containment has emerged over a very long period of time. It stems from the granted role of municipalities in land allocation, the role of the state in channelling housing investment, the frag-mentation of labour relations and pillarisation by religious affiliation, and the strong perceived link between housing costs, wages and international economic competitiveness. In contrast, the Australian solution has centred on land specula-tion fuelled by the prospect of urban expansion, underpinned by state-financed infrastructure provision and, until recently, a protected circuit of capital supporting affordable, individual home ownership for working households.

Considerable differences can be found in several key social relations, which intersect with and underpin the housing systems in both countries, notably the relations affecting property rights, investment and savings, and labour and welfare. For example, the institutions, market conditions and dominant ideas surrounding property rights affecting land use, development and urban form are fundamentally different in the Netherlands and Australia. Also the flow of investment into low- and moderate-income housing has taken radically different routes supporting the production of very different housing tenures. Further, the interaction of labour relations affecting wages with tenure, welfare and broader economic relations also differs in significant ways. Closer analysis of the development and interaction of these relationships is considered a fruitful pathway towards explanation of difference.

The study proposes a comparison between *the shifting housing solutions of the Netherlands and Australia during the 20th century*. The approach, outlined later, aims to make a critical contribution to conventional explanations by contrasting the packaging of necessary relations that exist in both countries and undertaking detailed research to establish their validity (Harloe, 1991: 129–130).

The Dutch and Australian housing systems have experienced a number of internal and external influences throughout their development. These influences have been internalised within the housing solution in different ways. Their responses are tied to the causal relations and sustained by path-dependent behaviour. Thus, whilst major changes may take place, traditional ideas and processes may continue to persist (in the short or long term). Analysing this process of change and contrasting various periods over time will highlight the relative 'stickiness' of particular generative causal mechanisms in each country and suggest prospects for the future.

To highlight the significance and robustness of causal clusters underlying the different 'solutions' a long trajectory of development will be examined, which extends from the mid-nineteenth to the end of the twentieth century. This trajectory encompasses various phases of adaptation, coherence and crisis, leading to the emergence, establishment, acceleration and decline of specific housing solutions emergent from the repackaging of relations underpinning distinctive forms of housing tenure and urban form in each country.

Figure 6.1 outlines the comparative strategy as follows. It is postulated (p) that the necessary social relations of labour and welfare (L), investment and savings (I) and property (P) have been differently 'packaged' and mediated by the state (S) in the Netherlands (N) and Australia (A). The research process analysing the necessary and contingent relations underpinning each period helps to revise and refine (r) the initial postulated cluster. Comparison of refined clusters provides the basis for explanation of difference between the two case studies.

Having postulated the causal boundaries influencing the development of housing systems in the Netherlands and Australia, it will be possible to put forward an empirically grounded, theoretically informed explanation of how these causal clusters have influenced the processes of housing promotion, production and allocation within each housing solution. In particular, the *different low- to*

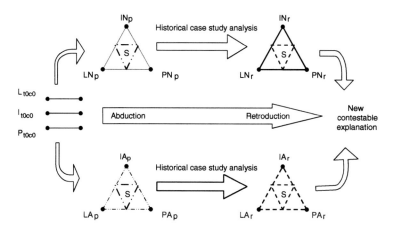

Figure 6.1 The comparative approach – refining postulated causal clusters through historical research and comparing refined causal clusters as a basis for explaining difference.

moderate-income housing solutions of compact social rental housing and low-density home ownership can be contrasted and understood towards an explanation for divergence.

In Australia, the social relations mediating housing provision have promoted and reinforced the production and consumption of highly privatised, low-density, residential environments dominated by the tenure of home ownership. Whilst a wide consensus exists about this description of outcomes, *explanations* for the Australian housing solution vary markedly, reflecting the distinctive ontological, theoretical and normative positions held by different researchers.

As argued in Chapter 5, it is considered that the most fruitful path to explanation lies in the historical analysis of a specific cluster of social relations in the property, saving and investment, and labour and welfare relations integral to any housing system in their contingent economic, political and social contexts. Different phases in housing history may be explained by the different packaging of relations in their dynamic, contingent context. When interdependencies between emergent relations break down (due to materially and socially constructed contingent conditions), a crisis of provision may occur, only to be resolved by adaptation leading to new forms of coherence, which may generate continuing housing outcomes. This chapter provides an illustration of these dynamic shifts under different conditions. It identifies phases of emergence, acceleration, deceleration and decline of the Australian 'solution' (Berry, 1998). Each phase incorporates periods of adaptation, coherence and crisis in the revision of emergent relations in a dynamic contingent context. For each phase an attempt is made to explain the housing and urban development outcomes as mediated by the synthesis of emergent housing relations and the contingent conditions that sustain or undermine them.

6.2   Observable outcomes of the Australian housing solution

This section provides a brief overview of the main features of the Australian housing solution and recent trends. Most Australians reside in large coastal cities, with the perverse exception of the nation's capital.[1] Detached dwellings with a front and back yard predominate low-density, land-use segregated, socially differentiated and car-dependent residential communities. In the scattered hinterland towns and coastal communities, home ownership is even more dominant. By the middle of the twentieth century, home ownership was established as the leading tenure in all capital cities (Table 6.1). It was the most popular housing option during the 1920s and the long economic boom that immediately followed the Second World War. The rate of owning or purchasing a private-occupied dwelling appears to have reached its peak of 70 per cent in the mid-1980s and has now stabilised around this figure. Rates of ownership vary considerably across Australia, with capital cities and south eastern regions recording higher rates than remote rural and outback areas. Typically, inner city areas have a higher proportion of rental housing than owned (ABS, 2001).

However, some researchers argue that whilst *outright* ownership appears to have reached its peak, the rate of home *purchase* may be slowing down (Table 6.2) (Beer, 1999, 1993; Berry *et al.*, 1999; Winter and Stone, 1998; Yates, 1997). Postulated causes include the changing nature of work, declining real incomes amongst working-class households, increased diversity in family types, volatility in housing prices and the cost of mortgage finance, and the desire for more flexible forms of investment.

The private rental market plays an important, yet overlooked, role in housing provision, accommodating just over 1 in every 5 Australian households. Landlords are primarily small investors, owning and renting out a single dwelling,

Table 6.1 Home ownership/purchase in capital cities, as a percentage of all households, 1911–2000

Census	Sydney	Melbourne	Brisbane	Adelaide	Perth	Hobart
1911	31	37	46	42	41	33
1921	40	45	59	52	55	43
1933	41	49	60	54	56	44
1947	40	46	60	55	56	49
1954	56	63	71	66	68	63
1966	70	74	74	74	73	71
1976	67	71	71	71	69	70
1986	67	73	72	71	71	71
1996	67	73	64	71	69	68
1999	68	76	67	71	74	74

Sources: Williams, 1984: 181–186, Troy, 1991: 2, Frost and Dingle, 1995: 31, ABS 1996, 1999, Housing Occupancy Costs, Cat. 4130.

Table 6.2 Tenure status of occupied private dwellings/households, Australia, 1911–2001 (%)

Tenure	1911	1947	1954	1966	1971	1976	1981	1986	1991	1996	2001
Owner	45.0	44.7	47.9	—	—	32.3	34.2	38.9	41.1	42.8	39.7
Purchaser	4.4	7.9	15.1	—	—	35.6	34.0	31.5	27.7	26.2	25.8
O/P undefined	—	—	—	—	—	0.4	1.9	—	—	—	—
Government tenant	—	—	4.2	5.1	5.5	4.9	4.9	—	—	5.9	4.5
Other tenant	45.2	43.4	29.9	21.4	21.8	20.3	20.3	—	—	20.0	21.5
Rent to buy scheme[a]	—	—	—	—	—	—	—	—	—	—	0.7
Other occupancy	5.4	2.6	2.4	1.9	3.3	5.6	4.1	—	—	—	—
Not stated	—	1.4	0.6	0.8	2.2	2.5	2.9	—	—	—	—

Sources: 1911–1954, Burke, Hancock, Newton (1984) using Censuses and Statistical Year Books, 1976–1996, Yates (1997) and 2001 Population and Housing Census, Australian Bureau of Statistics.

Notes
1911–1954 and 2001 data refers to dwellings, 1976–1996 refers to households.
a New category added in 2001: purchasing on a rent to buy scheme.

often via a real estate agent. The private rental sector has been described as a small-scale 'cottage' industry (Berry *et al.*, 1997), which lacks institutional investment and large-scale housing managers. Demand for rental housing has increased in recent years amongst 25–44 year olds (Elton and Assoc., 1991; Wulff and Maher, 1998; Yates and Wulff, 1999c).

Since 1945, the Commonwealth and state governments have provided housing assistance. A considerable proportion of housing funds go towards the rental sector. Indeed, in 2002, 1,209,000 tenants were receiving some kind of rental assistance. Rent allowance typically supplements the social security benefits of very low-income households (ABS, 2002). The Commonwealth State housing agreement also funds the provision of social rental housing, known as public housing, which is managed at the regional level by State Housing Authorities (SHA). Six large public landlords own and manage various forms of rental accommodation, housing approximately 1 in every 20 households. These households are primarily low-income recipients of government pensions and newly arrived migrants. Demand for public housing is high, dwellings are allocated according to a weighted list and waiting times for families in suburban areas are lengthy.

It is often remarked that the Australian state has not adequately promoted the development of alternative tenure options (Berry, 1988; Kemeny, 1983; Yates, 1997). As indicated earlier, state-supplied public housing is minimal and targeted. In 2001 there were only 40,000 people housed in public rental housing, yet there were a further 220,000 applicants waiting for the next available unit (ABS, 2002). Community-managed alternatives, such as rental co-operatives and shared equity schemes, are innovative yet negligible. Private landlords tend to be more closely attuned to capital gains via price inflation than the long-term exploitation of rental stock. Market rents and conditions are weakly regulated. Only in recent years has the Commonwealth provided low-level assistance for renters reliant upon government pensions to improve affordability. Given the limited options, available housing choices mould the aspirations of new households. These choices are becoming increasingly constrained.

The ability to pay for home purchase has been a salient factor in wage negotiations since 1907. From this period until the recent mid-1980s, broadly accessible home purchase has been an explicit public policy goal. Regulated interest rates, state-sponsored infrastructure, rising house prices, centralised wage fixation and rising wage levels facilitated the wide-spread purchase of homes during periods of Post War prosperity. However, since the 1970s, economic restructuring, labour market deregulation and declining real wages have narrowed this access (Gregory and Sheehan, 1998; Winter and Stone, 1998; Yates and Wulff, 1999a). House prices and later interest rates escalated towards the end of the 1980s. During the 1980s, the purchasing power of households was greatly affected by the sudden rise than stagnation of house prices and the volatility of mortgage interest rates. Since 1989, home loan interest rates have declined from 16 per cent to 6.6 in 2002. Whilst interest rates have dropped significantly and stabilised at lower levels, actual house prices have risen exponentially as borrowing money became cheaper. In 2002, the affordability of home purchase was at a 13-year low according to the Australian Bureau of Statistics (ABS, 2002).

Home ownership plays an important role for older households. Indeed, the Australian system of social security is reliant upon outright home ownership at retirement age (Castles, 1997). Ideally, under traditional mortgage arrangements, reduced housing costs on the payout of the mortgage are expected to improve the purchasing power of retirees and, importantly, permit the payment of lower pension rates. The renting alternative provides a stark contrast. Almost 50 per cent of elderly single renters live in poverty.

However, in recent years two incomes have become increasingly necessary to achieve home ownership (NHS, 1991: 34). Thus, single-income earners, including those with dependent children, are being locked out of home ownership (Yates, 1997) and ultimately, old age income security. Incomes are not the only factor: accessibility also varies according to the timing of purchase and the cost of mortgage finance. Households who purchased homes during the late 1980s were dramatically affected by higher mortgage interest rates, stagnating wages and the stalled rate of house price inflation (Bourassa *et al.*, 1995). Conversely, those who purchased earlier have benefited from lower interest rates and higher, longer-term levels of house price inflation.

Nevertheless, affordability problems are now concentrated amongst single-income households who rent their housing. According to the National Housing Strategy, 60 per cent of income units experiencing housing stress were private renters, especially female sole parents, people on fixed incomes, those living alone and especially those aged over 65 years (NHS, 1991: 34–35).

6.3   Beyond outcomes – explaining the core of the Australian solution

The core of the Australian housing solution, aspired to and achieved by most households, is dominated by individual home ownership. For those who can afford to purchase, both private and public renting has little to offer in terms of security, quality, saving and investment potential and social status. The purchase and exchange of detached low-rise dwellings for ownership has been facilitated by a coherent package of key social relations comprising freehold property rights, financed by long-term mortgage loans and sustained by continuous, adequate household income. For many, outright home ownership ensures a more comfortable and secure existence post-retirement with a modest pension. The contingent conditions, both material and social, which have shaped the actual definition of the key relations and promoted home purchase include state-sponsored urban expansion, a protected circuit of capital for home loans, skilled immigration and centrally regulated wage growth. Under optimal conditions, the Australian solution has generated very high rates of home purchase, especially during the 1920s, 1950s and 1960s. The later period can be considered the apex of the Australian solution. Since then the Australian model of home ownership has undergone many adaptations and revisions, leading to major reforms in the 1980s and more polarised outcomes by the turn of the century. Home ownership is no longer a feasible solution for the masses and a substantial minority of Australian households, comprising single- and low-income households, have little choice but to remain in less secure, poorer quality and lower social status housing with an uncertain post-retirement future.

6.3.1 Existing explanations for the Australian housing solution

Over the past 30 years there have been numerous attempts to explain the Australian 'solution' of low-density home ownership. This section reviews the ontological approach of this work, the explanations generated and the data presented. The ontological approach concerns the perception of how a housing system works; influencing the focus of the research, the level of analysis and type of conclusions made.

The ontological approaches of more than 20 different explanations for the Australian solution have been summarised in several tables, attached as Appendix 4. From this literature six major explanatory themes have been distilled:

• urban development and housing tenure is primarily an outcome of shifts in the mode of production;
• housing provision as a dynamic outcome of social relations in a contingent context;
• specific relations underpinning the Australian housing solution;
• arguments about the role of the state in housing promotion;
• policy analysis and normative critique and finally,
• description reveals the process.

Urban development and housing tenure is primarily an outcome of shifts in the mode of production

There are a number of urban political economists including Berry, Daly and Mullins, researchers who have applied a Marxist-informed framework to their explanations of Australian urban development. Berry (1983) examines the movement of capital and labour over time and space and postulates four stages of expansion and decline in Australian capital accumulation: colonial (1788–1847), commercial (1848–1893), industrial (1894–1939) and corporate (1930–present), each influencing patterns of urbanisation, conditioned by constraints posed by international economic integration. Each phase in urban development has been subject to crises and contradictions, which in turn have thrown up new ideas, practices and structural solutions to overcome them and continue the process of capital accumulation via urban development. He examines the spatial consequences of each stage of capitalist development in Australian cities, taking into account the complex role of numerous social relations including: state relations, international economic conditions and trading relations, industrial developments, flows of investment and labour, differentiation of economic activity, stratification of social classes, division of labour, relations of dependence and dominance of certain industries, as well as technological developments. Berry (1998) revisits his earlier historical work emphasising that urban development and housing forms are an outcome of shifts in the organisational base and technological form of industrial development. He incorporates concepts from French regulation theory and Harvey's (1989) work on the structured coherence of urban spatial forms under different conditions of production, reproduction and consumption. According to Berry, the Australian solution of home ownership has exhibited a number of phases: stabilisation at the turn of the nineteenth century, intensification until the 1970s and uncertainty in the 1990s. These phases are related to the mode of industrial and technological development, mediated by the role of the state, culturally embedded aspirations and demographic changes. The most recent transition, to a post-Keynesian city, has emerged with the deregulation of the financial and industrial relations system and a retreat of the welfare state. This has lead to increasing economic inequality, employment insecurity and privatised forms of social welfare which have polarised access to ownership. To illustrate his arguments, Berry strategically describes the process of industrial development, demonstrating the limited availability of housing options over time, and the status differentials reinforcing ownership. He points to the decentralisation of industry and retail developments which reinforced urban expansion. Other aspects such as land price gradients, the structure of the building industry and the system of credit provision are also considered influential in patterning production and consumption. Berry reviews recent trends indicating the demise of home ownership as a broad-based housing solution.

Mullins (1981) sets up a more explicit theory testing research, analysing the influence of different modes of capitalist production (mercantile/monopoly modes) upon forms of residential life. According to Mullins, residential life was, until the 1940s, influenced by the mode of mercantile capitalist development. Australian workers were reproduced under relations of urban peasantry (self-help), whilst monopoly capitalist cities centred on suburban consumerism. He compares mercantile and corporate capitalist cities forms and material services and examines urban development between 1880 and 1940, with particular emphasis upon the material provision of urban sewerage infrastructure.

In a similar vein, Daly (1988) perceives Australian urban development as an uneven unpredictable outcome of irregular capitalist development and resultant social problems. He extends and applies Berry's earlier work (1983) stressing the importance of early struggles over property ownership of housing and land. Home ownership consumption later became an important tool of Keynesian economic policy where favourable wages, working conditions and rising property values materially underpinned and bolstered this pattern of consumption. This pattern was drastically undermined by changes in the world economy.

All three scholars, Berry, Daly and Mullins employ strategic, long-term analysis of the key relations underpinning patterns of housing consumption and urban development: property rights, financial investment and labour conditions.

Housing provision as a dynamic outcome of social relations in a contingent context

Another division of approaches relates to that discussed earlier but focuses upon different sets of social relations underpinning the housing system. For example, Hayward (1992) applies Ball's (1988) analysis of the *social relations of housing production, distribution and consumption*. His approach provides a strategic compilation and analysis of land ownership, building construction, financing agents and sources from the 1880s to late 1980s. He identifies agents involved, the relations between them and their particular historical–institutional form and tries to reveal how the system of housing provision, once dominated by builder/landlords and wealthy home owners, moved towards speculative building and then to a more competitive mass-market system for providing mass home ownership.

For Williams (1984) home ownership is not a function of capitalist relations, but a contradictory outcome of *struggles over domestic property rights*. The Australian state has played a continuous role in the operations of the housing market, with home ownership receiving early cross-political support during boom, bust and crises. Alternatives to home ownership, such as public housing and private rental have been underdeveloped due to the complex architecture of the state and lack of political constituency. He also uses strategic historical analyses, focusing on the housing-related discourse of election campaigns and political parties.

Bourassa, Greig and Troy (1995) examine the influences affecting the rate of home ownership, beyond the government to *wider social and economic changes*. Home ownership rates have not increased above 70 per cent despite government policies to promote this tenure and underdevelopment of alternatives. Significant economic factors such as high interest rates, changes in housing prices and stagnating wages have made ownership less accessible for first homebuyers. Other factors such as immigration, an aging population, postponed marriages and increased divorce rates have also influenced the rate of home ownership.

Burnley (1980) emphasises *interdependence and openness of urban systems* and importance of historical factors in urban growth and social structures. His conceptual model emphasises shifting modes of production and technological change as the independent variables, linked to demographic change, social stratification and organisation, existing built forms and social pathologies. Burnley considers the distinctive pattern of Australian cities as a consequence of Western capitalist growth, accentuating metropolitan primacy, rapid urbanisation and social stratification of housing stock. In this regard, governments have been most active providing infrastructure, promoting immigration and land settlement.

Significant relations underpinning the Australian housing solution

Yet another perspective can be distilled from Australian urban research, which focuses upon a range of specific dimensions of the Australian housing solution. King (1986) emphasises the importance of switches in finance capital between investments, including forms of property development and the role of state, particularly urban planners, in maximising monopoly rent by differentiating housing markets. During the 1950s and 1960s housing-related monetary and fiscal policy ensured the extraction of absolute or ground rent from housing investments. King zeroes in on the rise of home ownership investment and links this to suburban expansion. Further, he examines the role of public policy in reinforcing differentiated housing markets, specifically via urban planning measures.

Technological development is the focus of Frost and Dingle's (1995) work which examines the growth of Australian cities bolstered by public and private investment in house construction and infrastructure provision. They emphasise the technological innovations in the nineteenth century and how they influenced the growth of cities. According to them, urban development was facilitated by the role of the state in providing infrastructure where private investment was considered too risky and unprofitable. These investments, in power, transport, irrigation, sewerage and water supply, underpinned capital accumulation in the rural, construction and manufacturing sectors.

Conversely, Castles (1997, 1997a) examines the role home ownership plays in providing horizontal, life cycle social security and influencing national systems of welfare and levels of expenditure on pensions. Drawing upon international comparisons of welfare systems and tenure, Castles argues the high rates of home ownership are incompatible with high levels of contributory funding for social security.

Arguments about the role of the state in housing promotion

Other researchers have focused upon the role of the state in housing provision, such as Dalton (1999) who provides an historical, state-centred analysis of the housing policy process. The state is considered to be a complex institutional structure of agencies, selectively contingent on the social and economic relations of the forms of capitalism within which it is located. Dalton examines four policy regimes: regional state regime mid-1800 to 1930, the central state regime of the 1930s to the 1970s, the regional state regime as the central state withdraws from the mid-1980 to the 1990s and finally, the complete abrogation of the state regime since 1994, as the state withdraws from housing policy at both the regional and central levels.

Kemeny (1983) (see also Hayward, 1992 and Troy, 1990) emphasises the ideological and political underpinning of home ownership. His critical analysis examines the role of the state in promotion of certain tenure forms and considers that the ideological and actual dominance of home ownership in Australia is a consequence of targeted state support and promotion. This has led to highly privatised urban structures, a home-centred life style and underdevelopment of more collective forms of welfare and housing tenure. According to Kemeny, home ownership has stifled more collective forms of social welfare and home ownership rates would have declined 'naturally' without government support.

Policy analysis, political power and normative critique

There has been a long history of research examining housing policy processes and these have also attempted to explain Australian housing outcomes, often providing critique on the grounds of social equity. For example, Yates (1997a) examines the shifting role of the state towards different tenures and social groups, and the distribution of risk from society to individual households. She highlights the introduction of rental assistance, considered to be a u-turn in government policy, which comes at the expense of support for public housing. Yates argues that the risks of unemployment, higher interest rates and stagnant price inflation are concentrated amongst those at the margin of home purchase. In summarising housing policies, she categorises those as having explicit or implicit support for home ownership and those concerning public and private rental tenures. Yates examines the *equality of treatment of across tenure forms* over three different periods: pre-1978, post-1978 and post-1986.

Stretton's (1970, 1978, 1986) descriptive chronology of events in city development and administration of planning also provides a normative critique which laments the decline of home ownership. Rather than develop or test any theory, Stretton introduces a number of socio-psychological explanations for the role of the state in facilitating urban development, such as extreme emphasis by the middle classes on private life, private homes and gardens, and inviolable property rights; secure social segregation and a restrained public culture; limited expectations of public life; lack of will and skills in state and local administration; and, comprehensive distrust of government, political power of public sector workers. He is concerned that the success of housing policy is dependent upon dynamic economic and financial conditions and that broad *access to home ownership* is threatened by external economic conditions. Further, Stretton regards state policy as being constrained by electoral politics, institutional capacity and divided support amongst political parties in different States. For these reasons, according to Stretton, housing policy is failing low- and middle-income households.

Further, turbulent housing policy in the state of New South Wales is perceived as a product of *political pragmatism* by Troy (1990) who provides a thematic historical account of housing policy process in this state between1901 and 1941. He argues that Australian property ownership reinforced notions of citizenship were the preferred routes to working-class emancipation.

Other policy researchers have had a different take on the purpose of policy. Whilst Jones (1972) also provides a descriptive, normative critique of the role of government, his focus has been on assistance in housing lower-income households across the nation. Like Stretton and Troy, his explanation emphasises electoral and fiscal rationale behind political actions. Governments chose policy options with limited risk to their power base and financial resources. Jones presents evidence of the dominant ideas and ideologies of different political parties through parliamentary speech notes and government reports and information on the outcomes of government policy.

Sandercock's(1975) very early work, quite different from her recent themes, provides a structured, normative critique of urban planning and development in Australia. In this work, she conceives the city as a mechanism for distributing resources. Explanations for urban outcomes can be found in the formal and informal power of agents in the urban development process who are able to influence property relations. Throughout most of Australia's European history, this has rested with landowners, and more recently, with urban planners. Dominant, pro-growth ideologies have at times unified industry with state interests. Sandercock provides illustrative examples of the policy-making process, using evidence of formal and informal decision-making processes.

Description reveals the process

According to Pugh (1976) housing provision is complex and occurs in an open, contingent-laden environment. Whilst he does not articulate key or contingent relations influencing housing provision, housing policy is perceived as a response to vexatious housing conditions and problems affecting the community. Pugh provides a chronology of housing events, providing examples of reactive policy making. Other descriptive researchers have focused upon urban development patterns rather than policies. Bunker's (1988) study covers demographic trends, population mobility and policies promoting certain forms of urban development. Urban sprawl is considered to be an aggregate of short outward moves, from the dominant central city, regulated by plans producing monotonous, jobless cities, dependent on private transport. Bunker describes various demographic trends, movements and related policies. Neutze's (1981) descriptive, empirical study of urban development in Australia contends that urban development is a consequence of market, administrative and political influences, of which the state plays an integral role. He emphasises the importance of transport technology and state infrastructure provision in urban development and makes extensive use of quantitative data, including various demographic trends.

6.3.2   A critical evaluation of explanatory progress

As can be seen from the summaries earlier, and Appendix 4, Australian housing and urban researchers have employed different ontological positions, some more complimentary than others, generating discernable fault lines in academic debate. The 'solution' of low-density home ownership has been analysed as a set of facts or events, as a story, or dominant set of political ideas, institutional arrangements or social relations. It has also been examined as an outcome of process, a mode of production or perceived as a wealth accumulating and distributing mechanism. To summarise, the key concepts that have been employed include:

- social regulation, capital accumulation and structured coherence (Berry);
- phase of capitalist development influencing mode of housing tenure (Mullins);
- urban systems as interdependent, open and path dependent (Burnley);
- housing outcomes contingently related to economic change (Bourassa *et al.*);
- tenure as an outcome of class struggle over property rights (Williams);
- key causal influences of change: shifts in financial investment (King) and technological development (Frost and Dingle);
- dynamic, historically embedded outcome of shifting social relations (production orientated – Hayward, investment orientated – Dalton);
- dominant ideology, with the state defining the form of housing consumed (Kemeny);
- housing policy as a reaction to external crises (Pugh);
- the state as a distributor of risk amongst society (Yates);
- the city as a distributor of resources which are unevenly dispersed (Sandercock);
- housing tenure as an expression of pluralist interests (Troy);
- urban development can be explained by a set of patterns, facts or events (Neutze).

Stemming from these diverse ideas and concepts are different research strategies: testing, revising and developing theories of explanation. Further, these strategies have influenced the object of analysis: economic and technological change, organisational relations and their contexts, key events, demographic change, dominant ideas, power resources of various actors, popular preferences, government policies or administrative networks. Correspondingly, the data gathered by these studies has been assembled in different ways, structured by phases of development, highlighting shifting meaning in discourse, presented as a chronology of important events, a list of policy twists and turns or a scattergun of empirical data.

A number of important themes and approaches can be abstracted from these divergent explanatory approaches. Complimentary explanations give prominence to shifting modes of capitalist accumulation, place emphasis upon the social relations and institutions involved in the production, consumption and allocation of housing, and critically examine the role of the state in these different realms. Empiricist description, rather than explanation, is more likely to be found amongst relatively unstructured, non-theorised policy and outcomes-focused research.

Over time, the research community, comprising academic researchers, policy consultants and public servants, has emphasised certain issues, theories and methodologies to the neglect of others. Explanations have been subject to the influence of dominant housing 'issues'. A normative, critical but un-theorised approach pervaded housing studies from the 1970s, highlighting the inequity of housing access and the role of the government in dispersing costs and benefits. During the 1980s, the political economists dominated the scene, restructuring historical description to highlight important economic transitions. More complex and sophisticated analyses stemming from a variety of ontological and theoretical bases have since been employed in the 1990s (Berry, 1998; Dalton, 1999; Grieg, 1999; Hayward, 1992, Johnston, 1994).

There remain, however, significant gaps in the body of research. Exploration of the relationships between housing tenure, labour relations and the social security (Castles, 1997; Winter and Stone, 1998) is emerging as a new theme, yet only a limited connection has been made between home ownership and the property relations underpinning urban expansion and the land-use planning system (Badcock, 1984, 1995; Hayward, 1992).

6.4   Postulated model of causal mechanisms

The proposed, postulated model draws selectively upon the spectrum of Australian urban and housing research outlined earlier and in Appendix 4. It is contended that more convincing explanations account for changes in home ownership in terms of the broader economic and social developments, recognise the unique institutions of the Australian state and define the social relations of housing through concrete research. These studies not only describe changes that have taken place in Australian housing history, but also explain why tenure patterns and urban forms have developed in such a unique manner.

Exemplary, recent work includes that of Dalton (1999) on home ownership policy, Berry (1998, 1994, 1983a) on the development of the Australian city and Hayward (1992) on the house building and land development industry. This work is briefly summarised in Appendix 4. Dalton provides the strongest, most detailed analysis of the role of the state as complex and differentiated, analysing the home ownership policy-making process during the twentieth century. Berry (1998,1994) examines the spatial implications of shifting modes of capital accumulation, organisation of work and class formation. Hayward (1992) provides a detailed historical analysis of the interactive social relations between housing producers and consumers, adapting Ball's structure of housing provision approach to land development and house building in Australia.

Whilst there are important differences between the explanations of these researchers, together they offer a complementary suite of methodological and theoretical concepts. These include the notion of dynamic social relations of housing provision (Hayward, 1992, drawing upon Ball, 1988, 1986, 1983), a sensitive conception of the state as complex and differentiated (Dalton, 1999 drawing upon Berry, 1983a and Jessop, 1990, 1982) and the crises-prone, contradictory process

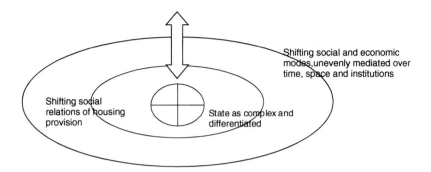

Figure 6.2 Useful theoretical concepts drawn from selected explanations.

of capitalist accumulation (Berry, 1994, 1998, drawing upon Walker, 1978 and more recently Harvey, 1989 and the French Regulation school). In addition to the ontological basis of critical realism (outlined earlier and in preceding chapters), these theoretical concepts will be utilised in the analysis of the Australian housing solution and are depicted in Figure 6.2.

The critical, social, political and economic analyses of Hayward (1992), Dalton (1999) and Berry (1998) respectively, point to a number of important phases in Australia's housing history. Whilst there are differences in their definition and labelling of phases[2], all three authors agree that the foundations of the Australian housing solution were in place by the turn of the nineteenth century. Low-density home ownership was prevalent, aspired to by a wide cross section of Australian society and supported by conservative and Labour political parties. A subsequent period of consolidation, when key institutions supporting home ownership were established, generated rising rates of home ownership until the Great Depression in 1929. Home ownership rates rose once again, to an all time high by the mid-1960s. Public rental housing was also provided and managed by state landlords for low-income earners, whilst during the same period the private rental sector diminished. Yet, by the early 1970s, it is clear that the Australian housing solution for the 'masses' has entered a period of decline. Home ownership is becoming less accessible to a growing minority of low-income households and the private and public rental sector hosts an increasingly marginalised population. Most recently the Australian solution of mass home ownership, following a radical period of deregulation, appears to be entering a new phase of uncertainty.

6.4.1 Defining phases for analysis

In contrast to Hayward (1992), Berry (1998, 1994) and Dalton (1999), *this study contends that shifting contingently defined emergent relations of property, savings and investment, and labour and welfare relations define different phases in the development of the Australian housing solution.* Based on this definition, phases of emergence (1840s–1906), acceleration (1907–1971), an intermediate period of deceleration and differentiation (1972–1985) and most recently, deregulation and reconfiguration (1983–2000) can be found. Each phase comprises a period of coherence in key relations supported by favourable contingent conditions, their contradiction leading to a crisis of provision, and adaptation facilitating a new phase of coherence. Figure 6.3 provides an abstract illustration of the periods, key relations and the concepts of coherence, crises and adaptation.

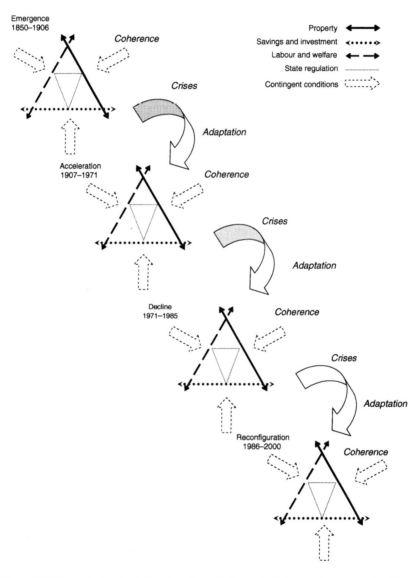

Figure 6.3 Phases in the Australian housing solution: adaptation, coherence and crisis.

First phase: emergence, 1840s–1906

The first phase in the Australia home ownership trajectory begins with the establishment of private property rights via the sale of crown land and its distribution amongst numerous freeholders. The savings and loans mechanism to fund the purchase and construction of individual, owner-occupied dwellings was borrowed and adapted from the British model of building societies. Capacity to pay for such loans was bolstered by the privileged position of skilled labour in a rapidly growing mercantile economy. The ideal of home ownership was reinforced by the experience brought by migrants from the 'motherland' and the rhetoric of political, business and labour leaders. Important contingencies undermined the successful coherence of these social relations and led to the collapse of the property market, bankruptcy of the savings and loans mechanism, and unemployment. These were related to broader contingencies, including the severe down turn of commodity prices upon which mercantile colonial cities depended, an end to the Gold Rush, collapse of the property market and poor management of building society funds.

Second phase: establishment and acceleration, 1907–1971

Continuing crisis was only averted by the intervention of the commonwealth government in the sphere of banking, finance, wages and welfare. Specifically, intervention occurred in the regulation of wages, establishment of state-owned savings banks and the refinement of rules and regulations for the allocation of mortgages, and later central regulation of State Banks. This intervention did not occur in a vacuum, but was influenced by an important selection of contingent conditions. These included: the fiscal capacity of the state to sponsor infrastructure provision and promote urban expansion, at times low interest and modest inflation rates promoting buoyant economic conditions for the protected industrial and manufacturing sector and mass migration, with employment guaranteed under internal protectionism. During the latter half of this period, the zenith of the Australian housing solution was reached with ownership rates peaking at 71 per cent. Nevertheless, the neat functional fit between key relations of provision and their contingent conditions was inevitably disrupted by the tumultuous monetary conditions of the early 1970s, which saw interest rates and unemployment sore, leading to a fiscal crisis of the state and the demise of state-sponsored, cheaply financed and consumer-driven urban expansion.

*Third phase: an intermediate period of deceleration and
decline, 1971–1985*

With the collapse of the monetary system and rise in the price of oil damaging the protected Australian manufacturing sector (Forster, 1999) and exacerbating government debt, the long boom of the 1950s and 1960s was over. The state-sponsored process of expansionary urban development temporarily stalled. Interest rates and unemployment rose sharply, dampening consumer confidence and curtailing purchaser rates. Demographic factors also played a role suppressing demand; the baby boom was over, fertility rates had dropped and European migration slowed to a trickle. During this period, home ownership became less accessible to a growing minority of low-income households, whilst the underdeveloped private and minimal public rental sector hosted an increasingly marginalised low-income population. It became clear that the Australian housing solution was entering an intermediate period of deceleration and differentiation: throughout which indecision, coping and muddling through plagued housing policy preceded more fundamental changes in the following phase.

Fourth phase: towards dismantling and reconfiguration,
1986–2000

The fourth phase, but by no means the last, gets under way in the mid-1980s. With the deregulation of the entire Australian financial system, the protected circuit of capital for home loans threatens the survival of local banks facing foreign competition. In the context of escalating interest rates, the protected circuit is completely dismantled with little protest. Non-bank lenders enter the home loan market, creating fierce competition for traditional savings banks, eliciting a credit boom. Under more favourable economic conditions in the mid- to late 1990s, consumer confidence returned and home purchase rates increased substantially amongst dual-income households, pushing up housing prices in the major cities. Modest intervention to secure broader access to ownership was discredited and curtailed and there was little commitment to the development of affordable housing alternatives. Yet behind the euphoria lay a hidden crisis, as single-income households were priced out of the Australian dream and young couples continued to delay their purchase plans.

6.4.2   Theorising the role of the state in the Australian housing solution

Throughout each phase, the state has established the rules for land markets and credit provision, channelled funds into home ownership finance, and more recently dismantled the protected circuit of mortgage capital. Changes in patterns of investment have been vulnerable to shifts in the global economy including the decline of commodity prices during the mercantile years of the 1880s, the Great Depression, changing interest rates, monetary collapse, oil prise shocks and deregulation of the protected financial sector. Residential investment has also shifted across different processes and tenures in housing provision, moving away from the development of private rental terrace housing in the 1880s to largely detached home ownership since the 1920s. The strategic intervention of various social classes, their organisation and absence, has also influenced the system of housing provision over time in different ways. Early migrants were well resourced, skilled and well paid; able to afford what similar workers in the home country could only dream of. Skilled workers organised themselves under protective unions and were represented politically by the Australian Labour Party. Their negative experience of landlordism led to the perception of home ownership as a route to working-class emancipation. They neither acknowledged the distributive risks of commodified property relations nor appreciated the benefits of public landlordism. There was no space or demand for political parties to develop alternative tenures and no mass movement for demanding alternative modes of allocation. Absence, therefore, has a power of its own.

The treatment of the state and contingent relations, discussed earlier, is insufficient and requires further expansion. Building upon the notion of housing tenure as the mediated outcome of contingently defined necessary relations, the role of state is one of mediation and regulation of property rights, capital investment and welfare provisions. Following Jessop (1990) this form of regulation and mediation must be concretely researched to establish the unique form and role of the state.

Towards a more concrete treatment of the Australian case, Dalton (1999: 60) extends the work of Berry (1983b: 110–111) to provide a typology of state interventions in the Australian system of housing provision. His framework of market supporting, supplementing and displacing forms of state intervention has been applied to the four proposed phases of emergence, acceleration, deceleration and decline, in Table 6.3.

There are limitations of such a state-centred approach. Dalton (1999) does not abstract the contingent relations that may influence state roles, in his state-centred analysis of policy making and home ownership. Beyond the role of the state, it is also very important to examine the key (state-regulated) social relations underlying provision and their concrete definition. The state may provide an important regulatory and sometimes economic context for housing provision, yet the actual production, allocation and consumption relies upon much broader property, investment and household relations mediated by those with the state and capital.

6.5   Analysis and contrast of different phases in the Australian housing solution

To summarise, the main features of the proposed explanatory model are strategic historical analysis, which contrasts different phases in the development of the housing solution, and examines periods of adaptation, coherence and conflict between underlying property, financial and welfare relations in their contingent context, towards an explanation of housing outcomes.

Moving forward with this proposed explanatory model, the following section begins to apply the approach by addressing the following set of questions for each phase of the Australian housing solution:

- How were the *property relations* contingently defined during each phase of development in the Australian mode of housing provision? How did this definition influence the *development of land* for housing?
- How were the *savings and investment relations* contingently defined during each phase of development in the Australian mode of housing provision? How did this definition influence *investment and production* of dwellings?
- How were the *labour and welfare relations* contingently defined during each phase of development in the Australian mode of housing provision? How did this definition influence the *consumption* of housing?

Table 6.3 Forms of state intervention in the Australian housing system over time (building upon Dalton, 1999: 60)

State form	Emergence	Acceleration	Decline	Reconfiguration
Market supporting	• Establish private property rights and allocate land to individuals • Support system of building societies as a means to save and invest in housing	• Subsidise cost of infrastructure provision • No tax on capital gains or imputed rent	• Cost of infrastructure provision transferred to land developers • Improve urban amenity • Promote innovation in urban development	• Deregulate centralised wage fixation processes • Privatise social security provision • User pays principles in infrastructure provision • Promote consolidation and permit denser housing forms • Removal of interest rate controls • Privatisation of land commissions • Privatisation of loan insurance corporation
Supplementing	• Subsidise suburban expansion • Expand role of State Banks in home finance	• Plan and co-ordinate urban expansion • Develop housing estates to attract large industrial complexes	• Target public housing to those who cannot afford home ownership • Provide mortgage assistance and permit tax deduction of mortgage interest	• Limit expansion of public housing • Fiscal incentives for investment in private rental accommodation of mortgage

• Regulate investment and establishment of credit foncier mortages • Ration finance for certain households and forms of housing consumption • Target finance to those able to pay	• Establish home loans insurance corporation to protect banks and broaden loan access • Interest rate controls and restrictions channelling finance • Mortgage assistance	• Expand system of income transfers to cope with economic restructuring and declining purchasing power	• Decline of targeted home ownership schemes • Provide minimal rent assistance, target and support • Force wage earners to save for their own social security • Give cash grants to first home buyers
Replacing	• Regulate rents and prices • Provide public housing for those who want it	• Attempt to establish land commissions	
• Regulation of wages and conditions • Establish universal, needs-based pension system collectively funded			

- How did property, savings and investment, and labour and welfare relations *interact* with each other and endogenous factors in each phase to influence the *mode of provision?*

What follows is an empirical illustration of four phases in the development of the Australian housing solution.

6.5.1   Emergence and establishment, 1840–1906

Outline of key events and housing outcomes

The most significant period in Australian housing history is the earliest period of European colonial settlement when important foundations of home ownership, private property rights, individual mortgage finance and subsidised infrastructure provision were established. These basic structures provided the framework upon which all future adaptations have been hung.

Home ownership came to dominate the Australian system of housing provision at an early stage. A staggering 41 per cent of the 473,000 Melbourne households owned their home by 1890 (Frost and Dingle, 1995b). Nationally, ownership was widespread amongst diverse occupational classes, with 44 per cent of unskilled workers and 53 per cent of professional and managerial elites owning or purchasing their homes by 1888–1889 (Davison, 1981; Hayward, 1992). Both inside and out, homes were more spacious and better serviced than those of equivalent households residing in 'Old World' cities (Frost, 1991: 126). Renting was also widespread, but increasingly unpopular.

The aspirations of settlers and mass evictions during the 1880s left a marked impression on the growing and influential labour movement. Following Federation in 1901, nationalism fuelled the desire to own a stake in one's new country and secure freedom from the parasitic landlord. The following table provides a brief overview of key events in early housing history.

Violent dispossession of indigenous aboriginal population by European colonialists	1788–
Establishment of a system of private property rights by the colonial administration	1800
Land sales by the Crown to free settlers	1840s
State-promoted land settlement and migration of skilled, resourced free settlers.	1840s–
Establishment of building societies to channel savings into home ownership	1847–
Gold Rush, excess capital channelled into property and construction	1850–1880
State system established for taxing land owners and registering land exchange	1858–
State-sponsored infrastructure provision	1890s
Collapse of the property market and bust of private banks and building societies	1890s
Mass evictions and repossessions of property	1890s
Organisation of labour movement, formation of Labour party	1890s
Federation and nationalism, male adult franchise	1901

The description of housing outcomes, outlined earlier, requires further explanation, as Hayward makes clear:

> home ownership rates in themselves mean very little...to understand the costs of benefits and constraints that are attached to home ownership it is necessary to understand the relations between the variety of agents associated with the provision of housing for home ownership.
>
> (Hayward, 1992: 203)

So why did Australians go down the *ownership* path when renting was the norm in the 'Old World', and when countries such as the Netherlands took a markedly different approach to housing their working class?

Examples of coherent relations, contingently defined during the period of emergence

Following the process of abduction outlined in Chapter 3 (section 3.3) the following paragraphs use the ideas and concepts outlined in Chapter 5 and section 6.4 to produce a new description for analysis. This section illustrates how property, finance and welfare relations were contingently defined during this early phase of emergence, to form a unique and coherent system of housing provision, which was disrupted by strategic contingent conditions.

CONTINGENTLY DEFINED PROPERTY RELATIONS

Australian cities were initially founded during a wave of European industrialisation and colonisation. The administering colonial armies possessed considerable experience in establishing new towns. Their land surveyors were trained to value and implement principles of social order, civility and facilitate the administration of trade, using symmetry, balance and regularity in street patterns and lot sizes. All Australian cities are based on a colonial grid, and located to maximise their economic potential (Proudfoot, 2000: 12–13).

Settlement became highly concentrated in cities and towns. Indeed, by the turn of century Australia was considered to be one of the most urbanised countries in the world.[3] This concentration was reinforced by the role of cities as ports and administrative centres for the export of wool and wheat and import of goods and materials to facilitate the establishment of the colony. By 1891, 42 per cent of Victoria's population resided in Melbourne, higher than Sydney with 34 per cent of New South Wales' population.[4]

Having assumed imperial ownership by the Crown, the colonial governors quickly established a system of *property relations*: claiming lands in the name of the Crown, legalising squatters claims, establishing a system of land title and permitting their legal exchange and undertaking massive and rapid land auctions. These events promoted individual land ownership, increased certainty for financiers, removed barriers to small-scale private rental investment and reduced the cost of land transactions (Dalton, 1999: 95).[5]

Critically, only a narrow elite benefited from the sale of land surrounding trading ports during the 1840s, just prior to the discovery of gold and mass immigration of prospectors. Large tracts of developable land passed into the hands of very few. In his study of early land purchasers, Hayward provides a vivid description of the land market during this period.

> The original purchasers of the land, being wealthy merchants, professionals or recent immigrants, had no interest in encouraging or engaging in residential construction activity themselves... but could afford to use their land holdings either as long term investments, or, if the situation so arose, as a means of making short-term speculative or developmental gains through sub-division and sale.
>
> (Hayward, 1992: 180)

With the establishment of municipal governments in the 1840s[6] and the introduction of a local land tax, such owners were discouraged from holding land. Subsequently, many released land onto the market the size of existing suburbs. Parcels were sold to other speculators, who further subdivided land into streets of residential lots for purchase by owner builders.

Whilst the core of many cities was indeed orderly and planned, beyond the central streets grew a jumble of 'crowded, tightly built, badly serviced terrace precincts' (Proudfoot, 2000: 18). These areas were developed when the organs for delivering basic infrastructure were yet to be established. By the time dedicated state agencies were launched, the image of these 'unhealthy' inner precincts persuaded those with additional resources to seek more spacious allotments in the outer areas, serviced by new lines of trams and trains.

Suburban development and land price speculation was further driven by the enormous flow of capital from the 1850s' Gold Rush and the role of the state in providing physical infrastructure. A bold programme of rail development during the 1860s and 1880s connected ports and lightly populated areas to cities, which under conditions of excess capital (winnings from the gold fields, mass migration and growing commodity trade) facilitated an extraordinary building boom. Roads, rail, water, sewerage and later electricity and communication services were financed by government borrowings and taxation revenue. This strategic public investment secured and subsidised the development of expanding suburbs. Thus began the process of publicly sponsored suburban sprawl of major cities. The demand for urban expansion heightened with the arrival of migrants from England, many seeking wealth in the nearby gold fields, and the employment in local industries (some protected by government tariffs).

The pattern of land ownership influenced the form of housing production, quality and price in different areas. Owner builders, contract builders, speculative jerry-builders or master builders dominated different suburbs. By the 1880s, low-density speculative commuter suburbs were created around railway stations at some distance from the central city (Frost and Dingle, 1995b: 25). During this founding period the transition from controlled convict settlements, based on order and control, to the laissez-faire sprawl of a booming mercantile metropolis was complete.

Yet, falling international commodity prices and the inevitable end of the Gold Rush thrust colonial Australia into deep economic depression leading to the collapse of the property market and the financial ruin of a wide range of investors, including private banks and Building Societies. As investors tried to recoup their assets, rent hikes, evictions and overcrowding became the norm for half the population. A long period of unemployment, industrial unrest and under-investment continued until well after Federation in 1901, leading to poor housing conditions and shortages.

CONTINGENTLY DEFINED SAVINGS AND INVESTMENT RELATIONS

In addition to the property relations supporting home ownership defined earlier, the relations between savers and investors were also defined in such a way as to support individual home purchase. The *financial relations* of housing provision in the new colony were subject to investment constraints and opportunities offered by the imperial governors' administration, growing local markets and trading partners in the 'Old World'. Adapted from the British model, privately owned financial intermediaries known as Building Societies provided an early vehicle for the recycling of local savings into home loans for members. These institutions were regulated by the Colonial administration (operating from Sydney) in 1847 to channel investment into residential development.

Likely members would have included new settlers, with skills in high demand, which brought reasonable levels of capital to the colony. The high cost of passage discouraged migration of the poor; thus more affluent, skilled migrants were the norm (Frost and Dingle, 1995b). The restrictive lending practices of Building Societies required that borrowers first owned the land they purchased and subsequently occupied the dwelling produced, institutionalising the link between individual land ownership and access to capital. The high deposit threshold greatly restricted access to less wealthy borrowers and minimised risks for the Building Society. Drawing upon the work of Butlin (1964), Hayward quotes,

> Money would only be lent for house construction on the condition that the borrower could prove not only the ownership of land, but also the erection of house walls. In addition the full interest costs of the loan had to be repaid irrespective of whether the loan was repaid earlier than was required. These conditions clearly favoured owner builders, and represented an important obstacle to the formation of speculative building firms.
>
> (Butlin, 1964 in Hayward, 1992: 189)

To repay the loan within the necessary 5 to 7 years, owner builders often became accidental landlords, purchasing a larger parcel of land for the development of terrace housing. They constructed a row of houses, one for themselves and the others for rent, with the profits derived from renting channelled into mortgage repayments. Today, this form of housing provides a distinctive character to the inner cities of Melbourne, Sydney and Adelaide.

With the relaxation of financial requirements in 1882, individual households were encouraged to borrow for housing purchase. Again, much of the capital required for purchase was provided by Building Societies and also private banks, which provided up to two-thirds of the cash required. This was directed towards workers with sufficient assets, able to pay regular mortgage payments over 7 to 12 years, at a cost of about one-quarter of average skilled wages (Frost, 1991: 119–120). For the first time, builders did not have to own the land they built on. Builders and purchasers could form contractual arrangements for the staged payments of construction. Thus another linkage in the system of mass home ownership was set in place (albeit not firmly at this point).

Some builders tried to reap rewards by building in advance of purchase (speculative building), or by jerry building, cutting standards and adopting more efficient building techniques. Technological advances in the building process and materials, such as balloon frames and galvanised iron roofing reduced a builder's dependence on costly skilled labour (Hayward, 1992: 186). Such dwellings were often intended for the growing working class employed in one of the protected manufacturing industries. Nevertheless, labour shortages and craft associations generally sustained high labour costs and quality. Well-organised unions restricted the entry of less-skilled workers and influenced standards of construction and specialisation (Dingle and Merret, 1972).

Small building companies were dependent upon landowners for work, contracting a handful of specialised skilled craftsmen to complete commissions. As mentioned earlier, builders were initially reliant on short-term credit under conditions of regulated labour, thus standard designs and quick production techniques were keenly adopted. Conversely, larger master builders built custom-designed mansions for wealthy elite, and employed a hierarchy of skilled tradesmen.

Unlike their British counterparts, Building Societies were permitted to buy and sell mortgaged freehold and leasehold land with member reserves. During the land boom of the 1880s Building Society funds were increasingly channelled into speculative land and housing development. Farms on the fringes of the cities were purchased at inflated prices and converted into building allotments or estate companies that flooded the market and remained vacant for years to come. These actions were generated by the Building Societies' blind commitment to a home for all, a false belief in the security of land as an investment and, most importantly, their corrupt administration (Cannon, 1995: 18–20).

An externally and internally driven property crash inevitably led to the collapse of many Building Societies. Some were dependent upon larger financial institutions and when they raised their interest rates and called in overdrafts the situation rapidly deteriorated for the Society sector. Public mistrust was fuelled by bank closures, and led to a run on all banking institutions in the early 1890s. Repossessions of homes from defaulting purchasers forced many into the rental sector or onto the street.

CONTINGENTLY DEFINED LABOUR AND WELFARE RELATIONS

The *capacity to pay for home ownership* and lack of alternative options played a key role in defining the relationship between households and the consumption of housing services during the period of emergence of the Australian housing solution. As mentioned, for many new settlers a house and garden was a dream in the 'Old World' that became an economically feasible reality in Australia. Further, the high cost of emigration discouraged low-income groups from taking passage. The nature of work and low labour intensity of farming attracted a strong city-based, mercantile class with a high disposable income. Workers were more likely to be engaged in commercial services for the export and manufacturing sectors than the lower-paid labour-intensive industrial sector (Frost 1991: 114–115; Frost and Dingle, 1995b: 23).

There was a shortage of unskilled labour to construct new homes, and building workers in Australia could earn twice as much per week as in Britain. Comparatively, the incomes of new settlers were high, rising and relatively evenly distributed. They sustained high housing expectations and boosted demand for new, quality housing (Frost, 1991: 114–115, 123; Frost and Dingle, 1995b: 23).[7]

Lower housing purchase costs, due to labour saving construction methods, promoted affordable access and enabled escape from overcrowded poor quality housing in the city centre. Declining cost of materials and innovation in construction, balloon frame, light weight galvanised iron roofs, mechanised brick-building processes, prefabricated plaster and joinery work, limited the range to straight forward 'pattern book' designs. Innovations in materials, despite high wages, kept the cost of building new houses within the reach of working-class households (Frost, 1991). By the mid- to late nineteenth century, home ownership was prevalent across the spectrum of Melbourne society, and noticeably amongst the working classes, as illustrated in Table 6.4.[8]

However, with the economic depression of the 1890s followed by the First World War, housing shortages and high rents forced almost 40 per cent of new migrants to live in canvas tents and temporary sheds (Coghlan, 1969: 2124 in Williams, 1984). Others were evicted from rental accommodation or lost their homes through defaulting mortgages.

Table 6.4 Home ownership rates by occupations, Melbourne, 1888–1889

Occupation	Home ownership rate
Professional and managerial	53
Shopkeepers and independent trade	54
Clerks and shop assistants	46
Artisans	48
Service and unskilled	44
Not in workforce	54
Miscellaneous and unknown	50

Source: Davison, 1981: 184 in Hayward, 1992: 207.

Synthesising key relations in their contingent context

The housing outcomes generated during this emergent phase (1850 and 1906) in the development of the Australian housing solution were notable for the inclusion of widespread home ownership and absence of large-scale investors in the private rental sector. The key relations of property, investment and savings, and labour and welfare relations worked together to generate this outcome under favourable contingent conditions – for a time. These included the promotion of individual land ownership underpinned by the existence of *freehold property rights* promoting speculative land market exchanging *small parcels of land* subdivided, with substantial capital gains, from larger pastoral and raw tracts. The new colonial state and entreprenuerial transport companies played an increasingly important role in the *provision of infrastructure*, sponsoring and supporting suburban expansion. This infrastructure incidentally *subsidised the cost of urban development*, reducing the real cost of land. The emergent Australian solution was financed via *deposit secured mortgages*, with collatoral provided by land title, from Building Societies and Banks. These institutions were reliant on the savings of members and returns on investments, which were primarily in real estate. Australian Building Societies were an adaptation of the British model, and provided credit for owner builders and later purchasers of housing. Further, the *capacity of households to save* in a booming mercantile economy and favourable labour market was strong. The actual circuits of investment and consumption, building on the conceptual discussion in Chapter 5 (section 5.2.3) and empirical evidence presented in this section, are depicted in abstract terms in Figure 6.4.

However, first it should be noted that this figure, as with those in the remainder of this chapter, depicts an abstraction from complex, multi-dimensional reality. Abstraction enables key relationships in the mode of provision to be more clearly seen. More extensive connections between the mortgage banks and the capital market and tenants to the labour market are not shown, *but are assumed and discussed in the surrounding text.*

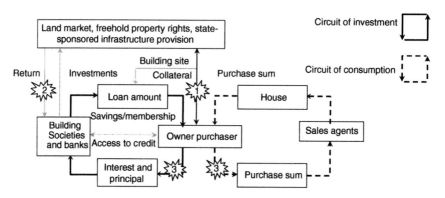

Figure 6.4 Abstraction of the flow of capital during emergent phase of the Australian housing solution (1850–1906).

As depicted in the figure by the star-shaped explosions, this coherent form of provision was undermined by a *cumulative series of crises* in the land, finance, labour and inevitably housing markets. These crises emanated from a much wider economic depression during the 1890s caused by the collapse of international commodity trade and the end of the Gold Rush. A crisis of *investment* followed, leading to the collapse of the *over-heated property market* (1), which seriously affected the *financial position of building societies*, who had speculated heavily in this market with members' reserves and were largely responsible for directing their savings into mortgages for home ownership. As banks and building societies collapsed (2), many subscribers lost their entire savings during this period. *Unemployment and loss of income* prevented the continuous payment of mortgage premiums (3) and the homes of many borrowers were repossessed in a *deflating market*. As house prices plummeted, investment flowed into the less risky rental sector. Indeed, for a short period renting was more affordable than ownership. Yet as rents rose amid scarcity there were many evictions and considerable social unrest. From its earlier established base in the union movement, the Labour Party was formed and took office in government (an international first). The dream of home ownership became intertwined with the ideology of nationalism, egalitarianism and emancipation of the working class from suppressive landlord relations. This was the beginning of a new phase of adaptation in the Australian housing solution.

6.5.2 Establishment and acceleration, 1907–1970

Outline of key events and housing outcomes

To ameliorate the housing crisis, governments laid out the directions of future urban expansion, greatly assisted by the State Banks. These banks not only financed home purchase but specified desirable construction costs, preferred house plans and promoted and developed model suburbs. Government authorities provided important infrastructure such as roads, electricity, communications, sewerage and water connections. By 1933, despite the Great Depression, home owner-purchase rates reached 49 per cent in Melbourne, with even higher rates recorded in the rural areas and the major capital cities of Brisbane (59 per cent), Adelaide (52 per cent) and Perth (55 per cent) (Frost and Dingle 1995b: 31; Troy, 1991: 2; Williams, 1984: 181–186). However, the states activities were severely curtailed by the Great Depression. During this period, many home purchasers were forced to leave their homes following mortgage default. A housing crisis continued throughout the Second World War, and only recovered under favourable political and economic conditions. To overcome housing shortages caused by a dearth of investment during the Depression and the Second World War, the Commonwealth (in partnership with regional state governments) embarked on a major programme of public housing production in 1945. Such housing, initially built for renting, was sold at heavily discounted prices from 1953. The 1950s was a period when the vested interests in home ownership narrowed politically feasible options and undermined the sustained development of alternative housing tenures.

The following key events emerged during the adaptation of property, finance and welfare relations during the period of accelerated home ownership:

System for regulating wage labour introduced	1907
State Banks take over home finance role and introduce credit foncier mortgage	1910
Subsidised finance for veterans of the First World War	1918
State Banks finance, design and produce model suburbs for working households	1920s
Severe economic depression, again mass evictions and repossessions	1929–1933
Pent-up demand following Great Depression and the Second World War	1945–
Commonwealth government implements Keynesian economic programme	1945
Central bank regulates housing interest rate and reserve deposit ratios	1945
Commonwealth State Housing Agreement (CSHA) funds public rental housing	1945
Mass immigration of working-class migrants	1950s
Stable secure employment growth, rising wages	1950s
Relocation of industry to the suburbs	1950s–1960s
New CSHA emphasises home ownership and sells public housing at discounted prices	1953
State-subsidised expansion of suburbs	1950s
CSHA funds diverted to co-operative credit societies	mid-1950
Establishment of Home Loans Insurance Corporation	1965
Deposit assistance via Home Savings Grant programme	1965

The rising entry of new purchasers to the home ownership sector is clearly visible in Table 6.5. From 1947 to 1966, rising prosperity and cheap finance facilitated strong growth in the rate of ownership. Many new owners moved across from the private rental sector. Public renters were also encouraged to become owners via heavily discounted prices of public rental stock.

Examples of coherent relations, contingently defined during the period of acceleration

The following paragraphs illustrate how property, finance and welfare relations were contingently adapted and repackaged following a long economic crisis, to promote accelerated rates of home purchase.

Table 6.5 Australian housing tenure, 1947–1976 (%)

Housing tenure	1947	1954	1961	1966
Owner without a mortgage	44.7	47.9	47.5	—
Owner with a mortgage	7.9	15.1	22.4	—
Total owner	52.6	63.0	69.9	71.4
Public renter	—	4.2	4.2	5.2
Private renter	—	29.9	23.2	21.5
Total renter	43.4	34.1	27.4	26.7
Other	4.0	2.9	2.6	1.9

Source: ABS Population and Housing census, various years in Neutze, 1981: 153.

CONTINGENTLY DEFINED PROPERTY RELATIONS

The laissez-faire *property relations* established in the 1840s were modified by actions of the Savings Banks in the 1920s and following the Second World War, the implementation of Keynesian economic policy and state-led urban planning in the context of rapid industrialisation.

Following Federation (1901) and the return of the First World War soldiers, the Labour party had spoken passionately about the individual ownership of land as a basic foundation of civil society. Thus private property rights remained untouched, despite the problems of speculation and a campaign against exploitation by slum landlords.[9] Labour came to power in 1910, forming the first trade union-based government in the world. They created a new and important role for the State Saving Banks, which were able to define the type of dwellings to be financed and even prepare and develop model suburbs such as Garden City in Melbourne. By tightly controlling both allocation of loans and the type of investment, State Savings Banks could minimise their own risks.

Following the Second World War, governments planned the expansion of metropolitan areas, developed extensive cottage estates on the suburban fringe and redeveloped inner-city slums. The Commonwealth government enforced the development of metropolitan plans at the state level for the private development of land.[10] Government priorities for inner areas during this period included the improvement and redevelopment of rental housing (McLoughlin, 1993: 40, MMBW (1954) Melbourne Plan). In 1961, the Victorian government actively sought sites for the development of public housing, surveying inner city areas, designating slums, repossessing property and redeveloping whole neighbourhoods with high-rise public housing estates.

Despite these initiatives (model estates, urban plans), property relations remained highly commodified and ownership largely rested in the hands of non-state agencies and interests. In some areas a single speculative builder developed an entire suburb producing monotonous, standardised housing estates. In other suburbs, contract builders who were commissioned by individual land purchasers produced a more varied urban landscape. The primary efforts of the state focused upon the use of the finance system as a vehicle for intervention in the housing market and supported both these modes of construction.

CONTINGENTLY DEFINED SAVINGS AND INVESTMENT RELATIONS

During this phase, we can also see signs of adaptation towards coherence in the realm of *savings and investment*. The crisis of the 1890s forced many purchasers out of their homes and into the rental market. For a brief period, for the first time in decades, capital investment flowed into this tenure. However, this investment was curtailed by the high cost and shortage of materials with the onset of the First World War, leading to widespread housing shortages, overcrowding and generally poor housing conditions. By 1900, investment in repairs and new housing was at its lowest in 40 years, leading to a drastic housing shortage in 1910–1911 (Williams, 1984: 173).

So how were the financial relations adapted and repackaged to ameliorate the housing crisis? The state responded by improving the *security and stability of the financial system*: regulating Savings Banks to take over Building Societies' role in home lending, and introducing assistance programmes to facilitate ownership amongst working households.

In 1910, the Victorian parliament passed amendments to the Savings Bank Act, which enabled public banking institutions to provide finance for home purchase. Public housing, on the other hand, was to be provided by local government, but legislation to this effect failed between 1914 to 1920. From 1915 to 1923 the national Labour government, with the narrow support of the conservative opposition, established a tax on imputed rent: 'on the grounds of equity between tenants and owners within the income tax system' (Williams, 1984: 173). Speaking against the proposed tax, conservative parliamentarian E Johnson stressed the ideal of home ownership over renting:

> Every inducement should be given to encourage men, especially working men, to get rid of the exactions of the landlords, and acquire their own homes. This sub-clause has a penalising tendency upon every person who endeavours to get a roof over his head far from the obnoxious visits of a landlord every Monday morning.
>
> (Parliamentary Hansard, 1915, Vol. 78: 6590 in
> Williams, 1984: 192)

Clearly home ownership was the tenure of preference. One of the most important pieces of legislation in the history of housing assistance is the Commonwealth War Service Homes Act, passed in 1918 (under Conservative leadership). This Act made provision for cheap loans to enable the rent-purchase of homes for returning soldiers and their dependents. The newly established state-owned government Savings Banks became the primary vehicle for such loans.[11]

However, measures such as the War Service Homes and state-provided public housing built in the 1920s were insufficient to compete with the private sector and keep rents down (Williams, 1984: 175). Housing shortages ensured pent-up demand and escalating rents. During this period an Interstate Commission on the Basic Wage estimated considerable housing shortages across the major cities, including a 9,000 dwelling backlog in Melbourne. Yet state initiatives in rent control, public housing and home finance were patchy and limited. The Savings Banks continued to ration their loans for new homes at a specified cost and amortisation period to households within a narrow income range. The Commission argued for a national remedy involving the government at all levels.

During the late 1920s political pressure remained for a more expansive programme to promote home ownership, particularly emanating from the conservative Nationalist Party[12], who saw home owners as a new source of conservative votes (Williams, 1984: 179). In opposition, Labour remained vocally supportive of home ownership. Parliamentarian Makin spoke of Labour's desire to increase home ownership in order to release workers from 'the grasping greed of the landlords', promote a better home life and improve citizenship standards.[13] This stance was said to represent the expressed interests of the unions and workers' self-help movements.

However, the Great Depression arrived in 1928 and lasted for five gruelling years, stalling any united housing effort. Many workers, including those from the middle classes, lost paid employment, were evicted and/or had their homes repossessed. Those evicted included the returned soldiers assisted by the War Services Homes Act.[14] As ownership levels fell, families shared their homes to cope with the burden of housing costs. Others organised and established the Unemployed Workers Movement to fight evictions by encircling homes to fend off the landlords' thugs.

As a sign of *financial shifts* to come, a Royal Commission, held in 1936–1937, examined for the first time Australia's monetary and banking system. In a dissenting opinion, future war time Prime Minister J B Chiffley gave an indication of his Keynesian economic policies in his dissenting opinion to the Commission.

> Banking differs from any other form of business, because any action – good or bad – by a banking system affects almost every phase of national life. A banking policy should have one aim – service to the general good of the community. The making of profit is not necessary to such a policy. In my opinion the best service to the community can be given only by a banking system from which the profit motive is absent, and, this, in practice only by a system entirely under national control.[15]

The Commission recommended policies to curb the autonomy of banks and direct investment to improve economic management (Crough, 1980: 9). However, all initiatives were set aside as international conflict in Europe and Asia dominated the attention of the Commonwealth government.

Nevertheless, Keynesian economic policy gathered momentum during and immediately after the Second World War. Chifley took over Labour leadership in 1941 and committed the government to a massive programme reforming the banking sector and establishing a major programme of public works. These included the production of public housing to address the considerable post Depression and Second World War backlog, financed under a Commonwealth State Housing Agreement (CSHA). The 1945 CSHA contributed 27 per cent of new housing in the immediate post-war period; primarily low-density dwellings in new suburbs close to growing industrial estates and higher-density inner-city apartments replacing designated slums.

A broad-based, union-initiated campaign to secure the right to housing (ACTU and AU, 1944) was transformed into a campaign for cheap housing finance dominated by the house building industry (Dalton, 1999; Hayward, 1992). Under Labour, home finance was regulated by the Reserve Bank, interest rates were fixed at 1 per cent below the bond rate and minimum reserve deposit ratios were set. Savings banks were compelled to lend at favourable rates but, in return, were permitted to pay out lower rates of interest on savings accounts. Later, in 1964, mortgage insurance enabled banks to lend to a wider range of borrowers at a deeper loan to value ratio (90 per cent) (Berry *et al.*, 1999: 8).

These actions created what became known as a 'protected circuit of capital', promoting and securing high levels of investment in home purchase. Following Labour's Chiffley and Evert governments, conservative coalition governments dominated federal politics for almost two decades. In a polarised political climate, they distanced themselves from Labour's socialist housing programme and diverted funds from public rental housing to establish co-operative housing societies. These co-operatives were linked to professional organisations and unions, which in turn nurtured a growing middle class of home purchasers.

CONTINGENTLY DEFINED LABOUR AND WELFARE RELATIONS

The role of *wage levels in the capacity of households to purchase* their homes was a subject of debate in the early period of adaptation of this second phase. Workers campaigning for better living standards had become far more organised, unionised and struck in key industries: shipping, mining and farming.

Pacification came in the form of assistance for war veterans and later working households to purchase homes, as mentioned earlier. Importantly, a centralised system of wage arbitration was established during the late 1800s and the establishment of a universal, collectively financed and needs-based system of social security from 1909. A contributing wage case, known as the Harvest Judgement (1907), developed principles that *acknowledged the cost of home purchase in setting male wage levels*. This centralised system became an important institution for determining the level of the male wage, affecting the ability of working households to afford home ownership.[16] Yet without work, as during the Great Depression, neither rents nor mortgages could be paid and once again, many lost their homes.

During the 1950s the capacity of households to purchase housing services on a single male income increased. It was a time of strong economic growth, rapid industrialisation and once again immigration from the 'Old World'. The Commonwealth government's protectionist economic policies required imports to be replaced by locally produced products. International companies settled 'behind the tariff walls' in the middle and outer suburbs of large Australian cities. This decentralisation of job opportunities reinforced continuing suburban expansion.

Immigration, near full employment and rising wages also boosted demand for new homes. Farms on the edge of the city were converted into new suburbs by state housing agencies, speculative developers and home purchasers. These suburbs, laid out by regional planning authorities,[17] were accessible by car, closer to new work opportunities and serviced by state and locally provided infrastructure. Secure jobs and rising incomes spurred demand for new housing production and accelerated domestic consumption. New households filled their homes with consumer items produced locally in the protected manufacturing industries. By the end of the boom, a significant and politically powerful 70–73 per cent of households in capital cities were purchasing, rather than renting, their own homes (Troy, 1991: 2). During this period, no political party could afford to ignore the wishes of the homeowner.

Synthesising key relations in their contingent context

Once again, drawing upon the empirical evidence mentioned earlier and concepts outlined in Chapter 5, Figure 6.5 attempts to abstract and synthesise the key property, investment and savings, and labour and welfare relations underpinning the consolidation and acceleration of the Australian solution of home ownership (1907–1971).

During this period the Commonwealth government intervened to address the shortage of housing investment and established a key presence and role in housing finance via national and state agencies (1). *State Banks under Commonwealth direction replaced the home lending role once played by Building Societies.* They issued targeted, capped and conditional loans for approved housing plans and engaged in land development of entire suburbs, thereby minimising their own risks and managing housing market outcomes. Following pent-up demand, home purchase rates increased rapidly during the 1920s and subsequently many suburbs were developed on land dormant since the 1890 property crash via speculative building activity, until the Great Depression. After the Second World War, the *volume and cost of home finance became regulated by the Reserve Bank.* Interest rates were fixed at 1 per cent below the bond rate and minimum reserve deposit ratios were set. Savings banks were compelled to lend at favourable rates but in return were permitted to pay out lower rates of interest on savings accounts. This agreement became known as the *protected circuit of capital* in the housing market. Further, The *Home Loans Insurance Corporation* was established to improve and widen access amongst low- to middle-income households to housing credit (3).

For a brief period, a new sector of publicly commissioned and managed rental housing was sponsored by Commonwealth and state governments, to renew dilapidated areas and provide cheap workers housing. Yet, with economic stability and growth restored after the Depression and the Second World War, home ownership quickly resumed its dominance in the 1950s.

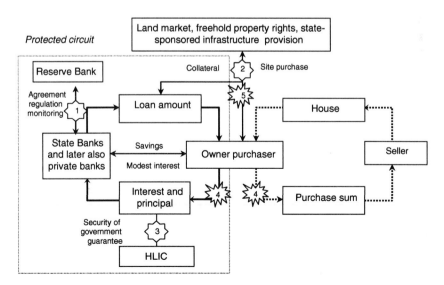

Figure 6.5 Abstraction of the flow of capital during acceleration of the Australian housing solution (1907–1971).

In 1956 private banks entered the home loans market and supported a long boom generated by *industrial protectionism, migration and growth in household wealth*. State and municipal governments continued to provide physical and social *infrastructure to support urban expansion*. Regional planning agencies took over the strategic planning role from individual municipalities and metropolitan *planning provided guidelines for developers* active on the urban fringe, further promoting expansion and speculation in the land market. During the long boom, coupled with the protected circuit and state-sponsored infrastructure, *strong stable employment and conditions* supported rising purchase rates and sprawling expansion of cities until the early 1970s.

Yet coherence was not sustained under conditions of *rising unemployment and the increasing cost of building*, which undermined capacity to pay and delayed new purchases (4). Further monetary conditions and welfare demands affecting state finances *diminished the capacity of the state and local government to continue sponsoring urban expansion* via the provision of infrastructure (5).

6.5.3   An intermediate period of deceleration and differentiation, 1971–1985

Outline of key events and housing outcomes

This phase illustrates the significance of 'counterproductive' contingent relations in the actualisation of the Australian housing solution. Whilst the cornerstones of the Australian housing solution remained in place during this period, important contingencies such as high unemployment and stagnating wages eroded disposable incomes. High interest and increasing demands on the welfare state also undermined public investment in urban areas.

Key, defining events include:

End of the long boom, economic decline and restructuring	1970s–
Fiscal crisis of the regional and local state, inability to service urban expansion	1970s
Increasing interest rates for home loans, declining affordability of purchase	1970s
Government attempts to capture land betterment impeded establishment of land commissions	1974–
Rising levels of unemployment 4–11 per cent, especially amongst blue collar workers and young job seekers	1972–1983
Expansion of income support	1972–
Reserve Bank advises removal of controls on home lending	1975
Intermittent mortgage assistance and tax deductibility programmes	1972–1983
Uneven rise in house prices, favouring inner urban areas	Late 1970s, 1980s
Campbell inquiry recommends deregulation of financial system	1981
Union campaign for superannuation	early 1980s
Shortage of capital in protect circuit	early 1980s
Economic recession and unemployment	1982–1983

Table 6.6 Housing tenure – 1971–1981 (%)

Housing tenure	1971	1976	1981[a]
Owner without a mortgage		31.5	33.2
Owner with a mortgage		35.1	33.0
Total owner	68.6	67.6	63.2
Public renter	5.8	5.0	4.9
Private renter	22.1	25.9	20.3
Total renter	27.9	30.9	25.2
Other	3.4	2.5	2.9

Source: ABS Population and Housing census, various years in Neutze, 1981: 153.

Note
a Burke, Hancock and Newton, 1984.

A snapshot of housing outcomes, in terms of tenure distribution, can be derived from Table 6.6. One can see that the rate of new purchasers is beginning to fall, a trend that later continued in the 1980s. Public rental continues to provide only a small, now declining contribution to overall housing options.

Examples of coherent relations, contingently defined during the period of deceleration and differentiation

The following paragraphs illustrate how property, finance and welfare relations were contingently adapted and repackaged during the period of decelerating rates of home purchase and marginalisation of alternative tenures.

CONTINGENTLY DEFINED PROPERTY RELATIONS

Important changes occurred in the role of the state in supporting *private property* development. To counter the expansionary and road-dominated urban planning of the 1960s, urban consolidation emerged as a new theme in the 1970s. Various interests including Commonwealth and state planning agencies managing urban policy promoted consolidation above the dreaded image of a sprawling and hollow city. Denser cities, better utilising public infrastructure, especially transport, appealed to very different interests – environmental movements campaigning against the intrusion of freeways and urban sprawl into the green hinterland, cash strapped governments with high interest debts and companies with investments in the central city, such as the large insurance giant Australian Mutual Provident (AMP). Nevertheless, the new policy, first promoted by the Commonwealth's Department of Urban and Regional Development, was met by institutional hostility amongst diverse instrumentalities at the State and local government level (Housing Commission, Road Construction Authority and various local councils) and corrupted by speculative property interests. The costs associated with government intervention and subsequent scandals undermined further interventionist planning efforts.

With insufficient resources, high rates of interest on borrowed debts, local and state governments were unable to keep pace with the provision of roads and drainage for subdivided land. This so-called crisis in collective consumption (Jakubowicz, 1984: 150) pushed former public responsibilities into the lap of developers. Not only did this have the effect of increasing the price of land but shifted costs to landowners, buyers of sites and ultimately home purchasers. To make matters worse, many land developers left the market, further restricting supply and inflating house and land prices. The Commonwealth government attempted to establish public land commissions and development corporations to process raw land and moderate the price of new housing lots. It was frustrated in this task by existing landowners on the urban fringe with strong links to state politicians, upon which the Commonwealth was dependent to implement the new land policy. Further, corruption in the ranks of the executive played a role in discrediting state government activity in the land market. Appendix 5 provides a more detailed illustration of the relations sustaining the Australian system of property rights and the power of institutions opposing change.

In evaluating the effectiveness of the land commissions, Neutze (1978: 83) argues that their limited funds to purchase in an already inflated land market had a limited impact on prices. The land commissions were unable to dominate the market and failed to even recover the cost of providing infrastructure.[18]

CONTINGENTLY DEFINED SAVINGS AND INVESTMENT RELATIONS

Contributing factors influencing the affordability of home purchase not only include purchase price and household income but also employment and mortgage conditions. Interest rates can stimulate or stifle affordability and home purchase rates. Job security promotes consumer confidence and purchasing propensity.

For most of the post war period, interest rates had been relatively low, around 4 per cent, with stable low rates of inflation and almost full employment fuelling consumer confidence. Yet the long boom of the 1950s and 1960s was soon over with the collapse of the international monetary system in the early 1970s causing the end of low interest government loans and the rationing of capped home loans by stage savings banks. Soon after followed the first rise in the price of oil, seriously damaging the protected Australian manufacturing sector (Forster, 1999) leading to massive job cuts and subsequent social security demands, further exacerbating escalating government debt.

By the mid- to late 1970s and well into the 1980s home loan interest rates and unemployment had risen dramatically. During the 1970s there were also attempts to change *the financial relations* of home ownership. Resistance was not in the form of popular movements or political parties, but emerged from major financial institutions. As early as 1975, the Reserve Bank was recommending an end to the regulation of home finance. The government took no action, avoiding possible electoral backlash. However, by 1978, senior government economists came to view the protected circuit as the cause, rather than the prevention, of declining home purchase affordability. Banks were constraining the volume of home mortgage finance released in the protected circuit. The Commonwealth intervened, lending 150 million dollars of its own funds to Savings Banks. Bank deposit ratios were also altered to free more finance. On the demand side, mortgage assistance and tax deductibility of interest was offered to first homebuyers until the early 1980s.

Stalled investment in the Australian economy and the actions of the banking sector prompted the establishment of the industry-dominated Campbell Inquiry (1981). The Inquiry argued the need for the wholesale deregulation of the financial system and more competition between financial institutions. Specifically, it recommended the removal of mortgage restrictions on Savings Banks. In the context of rising interest rates, Savings Banks began to shrink their home mortgage portfolio, tightly rationing the allocation of home loans during the early 1980s. Unemployment (13 per cent) and high home loan interest rates (12.5 per cent) peaked in 1983 and both were a major election issue.

CONTINGENTLY DEFINED LABOUR AND WELFARE RELATIONS

The *relations of housing consumption* were also changing during the 1970s. Throughout the period, there remained a strong preference for home ownership across occupational and income groupings. However, economic restructuring in the labour market created a considerable rise in unemployment amongst blue-collar workers.

Changes in household dynamics and expectations also influenced the capacity of households to consume services. The feminist movement facilitated the acceptance of female participation in the paid workforce. Birth control gave women the choice of smaller families and delayed marriage. Whilst housing prices rose faster than average earnings, two-incomes kept ownership within reach. On the other hand, the rise in two-income households priced single-income households out of the market (Wulff, 1992 and Yates, 1997 in Winter and Stone, 1998: 8). Thus, during the 1970s, lower- and single-income earners had declining access to purchase. Conversely, those households who purchased in the 1950s and 1960s stood to gain from rising property values, especially in desirable areas. High interest rates were every homeowner's enemy, and they blamed governments – not the banks – for their sustained rise.

In the social rental sector constrained public housing budgets and continuing sales of the most desirable stock led to the targeting and marginalisation of public housing. Far from being homes for returning war heroes, public housing came to represent homes for the 'idle ne'er-do-well, no-hopers or the dregs of an achieving society' (McLoughlin, 1993: 97).

Synthesising key relations in their contingent context

Once again, we can abstract and synthesise these contingently defined key relations of property, investment and savings, and labour and welfare during this phase of deceleration in the Australian housing solution. Home ownership ceases

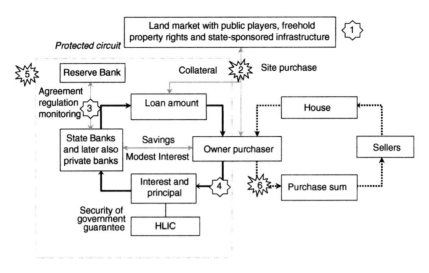

Figure 6.6 Abstraction of the flow of capital during reconfiguration of the Australian housing solution (1986–2000).

to grow and we see sporadic rates of production, we also see a number of initial adaptations and looming threats. These adaptations address particular crises affecting the Australian solution and are depicted in abstract terms in Figure 6.6. First, the Commonwealth government *attempts to intervene in the highly commodified, freehold property market* to moderate land price speculation by establishing public land corporations, but is stymied by entrenched property interests and corruption (1). *Land developers, in concert with subsidiary construction companies, continue to control supply* of land and pace of new housing construction, greatly influencing both house prices and outcomes. After a long period of deflation, a *crisis in collective consumption and stifled developments*, land developers are forced to pay for the cost of infrastructure. However, this is largely passed on to new purchasers on the urban fringe via increased housing prices, generating affordability problems (2). The *government attempts to boost production and improve affordability* by further interventions in the protected circuit affecting home loans. To address the shortage of *housing investment*, the Commonwealth lends AU$150 million to State Banks to issue home loans (3). These efforts are complimented by a *brief period of mortgage interest deductibility* (4).

Yet the protected circuit, the *financial corner stone of Australian home ownership is weakening*. The regulation of mortgage interest comes under increasing scrutiny by advisors in the Reserve Bank and Treasury Department. An industry-dominated inquiry recommends abolition (5). Only electoral politics stalls removal of the protected circuit. Further *wage growth stagnates* and only the entrance of women onto the job market sustains home purchasing power. However, the housing choice of single-income households begins to narrow (6).

6.5.4 Dismantling and reconfiguration, 1986–2000

Outline of key events and housing outcomes

This phase illustrates the significance of shifting the founding relations of housing provision. During this phase the neat functional fit, that promoted broadly accessible home ownership during times of evenly distributed economic prosperity, was dismantled. During this most recent phase, a number of fundamental changes have occurred in the relations that have mediated the Australian housing solution for almost 50 years. The interest rate on mortgages fluctuated considerably, creating affordability problems for many new purchasers during this phase. The protected circuit of capital in home finance has been dismantled and the institutions protecting wages and conditions marginalised. Further, the role of some public land agencies continues to be under threat.

The Australian solution of low-density home ownership was changing and new patterns and forms of housing consumption tentatively emerged. The housing outcomes of this most recent period in housing history have proven to be disturbingly uneven. Ownership is no longer a widespread option, available to working-class households.[19] As can be seen from Table 6.7, whilst the number of outright owners has reached a peak, a falling proportion of households are entering the market. The proportion of mortgage defaults has increased significantly (Berry *et al.*, 1999) and delayed purchase has led to a rise in long-term renting.

In their analysis of housing careers, Winter and Stone suggest that during this period, the social connotations associated with home ownership have also altered. Ownership has become less strongly linked to major life events such as family formation or childbirth, yet the authors are unable to detect a new, emerging social meaning (1998: 51–52). Affordability problems continue to concentrate in the private rental sector and public housing is increasingly targeted to those in greatest need (and high support needs), who are unable to be housed in the private sector.

The prospect of remedial state action was further limited as the goal of widespread home ownership no longer represented a political priority for the Commonwealth government. The electorate no longer supported public intervention in the regulation of home loans. The Government's gaze shifted towards

Table 6.7 Household trends in tenure type, 1980–1994

Tenure type %	1980	1990	1994
Outright owner	38.3	42.4	41.8
Purchaser	33.6	29.2	28.3
Public renter	4.8	5.8	6.2
Other renter	20.2	19.8	21.4
Other	3.1	2.8	2.2
Total	100.0	100.0	100.0

Source: Survey of Housing Occupancy and Costs (8724.0);
Survey of Income & Housing Costs and Amenities (unpublished
data); Australian Housing Survey: Selected Findings (4181.0).

levels of investment, the balance of trade, inflation and interest rates. Domestic housing policy was merely a secondary issue holding a low profile and position in the Commonwealths executive hierarchy.[20] The following table summarises key events during this phase.

Deregulation of the Australian financial system	mid-1980s–1990s
Opening the Australian economy by reducing tariff barriers	1980s–1990s
Introduction of nine-year Wage accord during recession	1983
Removal of interest rate ceiling	1986
Introduction and demise of Commonwealth then state-initiated – mortgage assistance	early 1980s–1997
Introduction and massive rise of rent assistance	1985–
Focus on inner city revitalisation and international competition	1980–1990s
Promotion of flexible, performance-based planning regulation	mid-1980s
Stock market crash, shift to property investment	1987
Commercial property boom and bust	1980s–1989
Demise of State Bank, privatisations	late 1992
Promotion of alternative forms of personal investment	1990s
Compulsory superannuation and privatisation of public super funds	1990s
Concept of super for housing dropped	1995
Workplace Relations Act marginalised unions during period of high unemployment	1996
Corporatisation of Victoria public land agencies in preparation for full privatisation	1998
Increasing targeting of welfare payments (Work for the Dole and Active Welfare policies)	1998–

Examples of coherent relations, contingently defined during the period of dismantling and reconfiguration

The following paragraphs illustrate how property, finance and welfare relations were adapted and contingently redefined during this period of dismantling and reconfiguration.

CONTINGENTLY DEFINED PROPERTY RELATIONS

The *property relations* of housing provision became increasingly commodified over the last two decades of the twentieth century. The process of largely private land development on the urban fringe, where most new houses were being built, continued at a slower pace during the 1980s. Public land commissions, which were promoted by the short-lived Commonwealth Labour government during 1972–1975, remained in place but altered in ambition and purpose. Public land developers, such as the Victorian Urban Land Corporation[21], exhibited diminished social charter by the end of the 1990s and were forced to compete, like any other commercial entity, delivering shareholder dividends alongside other large national development companies such as Delfin, Australand, Mirvac and Lendlease and larger house and land developers such as Jennings, Wimpy and Pioneer.[22]

After many years on the back burner, urban consolidation returned in the mid-1980s and early 1990s as a theme for residential development at the Commonwealth level. Yet whilst big on vision, little was sustained except an array of demonstration projects promoting joint ventures between the impoverished public rental sector and private investors. The basic mechanism influencing urban form remained untouched: highly commodified property relations, individual home purchase, development boosterism and the continuing dominance of the private vehicle over mass public transport.

By the mid-1980s, consolidation also took on a new meaning, shaped by the lessons of the 1970s and hardened by the economic liberalism of Canberra's political elite. Denser, more affordable, appropriate and equitable development was the aim, which could utilise public infrastructure more efficiently. Actual initiatives involved infill development, redevelopment of public housing estates and the conversion of non-residential buildings for housing, permitting the doubling of houses on traditional allotments and subdividing smaller blocks in new areas. Publicly sponsored private development was also a tool of urban consolidation, redeveloping under utilised public lands in the city centre. In the late 1990s, private freeways, universities and casinos were opening, sponsored by entrepreneurial State planning agencies and development corporations, via generous land deals, profit (and loss) sharing arrangements and planning compromises. Fringe development could also occur under the new consolidation, just on smaller blocks with more dwellings per hectare. Yet higher-density housing and inner-city apartment living certainly didn't prove to be more affordable, equitable or desirable amongst new purchasers, and was criticised by numerous commentators and researchers (Bunker, 1986; Forster, 1999; McLoughlin, 1991; Troy, 1999).

Metropolitan planning agencies placed far greater emphasis on urban consolidation (rather than continuing investment in expansion),[23] inner-city rejuvenation and the development of major (inner city) projects, in order to compete with other Pacific Rim cities and attract international investment. Central city governments were transformed into market agencies for 'Living Cities'. Second order central city office buildings, left vacant since the 1987 office boom and bust, were converted (primarily by their liquidators) into new lifestyle apartments. The inner-city municipality of Melbourne experienced a profound increase in multi-unit dwellings, contributing 28 per cent to the city's dwelling stock since 1992 (Watling, 1999).

During this period of intense inter-city competition,[24] local planning processes were subordinated, third-party rights curtailed and a special task force established to speed up projects in the state's best interest – despite local opposition (Lewis, 1999; Ogilvy, 1998). In one state, all elected local Councils were abolished for a period of two years, amalgamated and temporarily managed by appointed commissioners who oversaw an extensive programme of pro-growth development facilitation and privatisation of public enterprises (Mowbray, 1996; Shaw, 1998).

Planning research agencies, such as the Metropolitan Services Co-ordination System, simply forecasted housing demand and monitored land supply, rather than lead or control urban expansion, providing regular maps of underdeveloped and suitably zoned land. At the local government level, municipalities were no longer the initiator or regulator of land development. Rather, they became more passive facilitators of infrastructure partnerships. Land development companies such as Delfin continued to have an important role mediating between different agents in housing provision system. This prominent development company assembles large parcels of land, obtains planning permission, subdivides and markets building lots in conjunction with preferred building companies. Past performance in joint venture projects enabled Delfin to establish a positive and fruitful rapport with key government partners. See Appendix 6 for an example of Delfin's new urban development practices.

CONTINGENTLY DEFINED SAVINGS AND INVESTMENT RELATIONS

Internationally orientated economic policy not only affected the property relations of housing development but reshaped their financial relations. By the end of the 1980s, commentators remarked on the 'sweeping changes' that had transformed the Australian financial system[25] to prepare for a more open, export-orientated economy.[26] Perkins attributes the speed of deregulation to the acceptance of the industry to change. Freedom from government regulation would enable them to better compete with not only local credit unions, unit trusts, cash management trusts and building societies, but also the international financial institutions which were now entering the country and operating on the foreign exchange market (Perkins, 1989: 1–7).

These more global changes to the Australian financial system were to have a profound effect on the *financial relations* of housing provision, unleashing a volume of credit for home purchase. From 1986, banks and building societies were no longer bound to the Reserve Bank constraints that had created the 'protected circuit'. Instead, they could invest with more freedom and diversity (Perkins, 1989: 44–45). Larger banks did well out of the new arrangements via mergers and takeovers.[27] Yet they too faced strong competition from innovative new players such as Aussie Home Loans.

Analysis undertaken in 1989[28] found that following deregulation, the interest rate immediately rose by 2 per cent and remained above the 1986 level for three years. Latent demand[29] for finance led to a dramatic increase in lending, greatly inflating house prices. In the context of rapidly inflating purchase prices and later very high interest rates, only two-income households were able to borrow sufficient mortgage credit. Interest rates have since subsided, but remain high in relation to real interest rates. Thus, the benefits of an inflated market were distributed unevenly, not only by income but also by region, concentrating the wealth amongst owners of (inner city) houses in areas of rapid price rises (Fincher, 1991: 130).

Interviews undertaken for this research in 2000 with staff from the Commonwealth Bank[30], reveal the organisational impact of deregulation, privatisation, declining interest rates, see Table 6.8, and increased competition upon mortgage lenders. Under pressure to compete, the Commonwealth instituted radical moves to

Table 6.8 Home loan interest rates, 1991–2001

Home loan interest rates	1991	1992	1993	1994	1995	1996	1997	1998	1999	2000	2001
%	15.1	11.9	9.9	8.9	10.0	10.3	8.3	6.7	6.6	7.0	7.6

Source: Australian Bureau of Statistics, Cat. No. 4102, Australian Social Trends Companion Data.

curb costly branch services (closing branches, introducing supermarket banking and increasing over the counter fees) and increase the quality of their customer base (taking over more 'elite' banks such as Colonial, targeting more lucrative customers via internet). During deregulation, lenders became more selective and risk averse – targeting 'quality' customers and rejecting less lucrative traditional clientele.

Given the increasing diversity of loan products on the market, lucrative customers were more difficult for the large, increasingly unpopular Commonwealth Bank to retain or capture. New products were introduced and more customer-oriented practices established in what was considered to be a 'cut throat' market. Despite these efforts, other commercial banks and mortgage retailers were quickly outmoding the Commonwealth's efforts. A new sector of mortgage brokers emerged to 'assist' borrowers with complex choices. Unable to secure a commission, mortgage brokers did not include Commonwealth Bank's products amongst their panel of preferred mortgages. Mortgage originators, such as Aussie Home Loans, with limited branches and thus minimal overheads, captured the lion's share of new borrowers during 1999–2000.

In addition to the deregulation of financial markets affecting the home loans sector, guarantee arrangements have also been privatised. The insurance of mortgages has moved from being a public monopoly to a private one. The Home Loans Insurance Corporation, established in 1964 to broaden access to home ownership, was privatised in 1997 and purchased by the financial giant GE Capital. Recent research on the sector found a 50 per cent increase in mortgage arrears and defaults during the early 1990s (Berry *et al.*, 1999: 14–15). State initiatives in mortgage security schemes for low-income purchasers (FANMAC and NMC) have been phased out following high interest rates, defaults and major losses in 1997.

By the end of the 1990s the apparent benefits of home loan deregulation and competition finally appeared, with the new Conservative coalition government basking in popularity under declining interest rates (both home loan and official) and strong economic growth. During this time, home loan rates dropped to 6.7 per cent in 1998–1999.[31] In an apparent policy reversal in July 2000, the Commonwealth government announced the introduction of a non-means tested, $7,000 and later $14,000 grant to assist first home purchasers. This was the first form of direct, universal home ownership assistance in 15 years. Whilst the new grant could be seen as a reversal in housing policy trends, its primary goal was to avoid the potential, post Goods and Services Tax (GST) downturn, predicted to strike the housing construction sector.

An 'artificial' housing boom followed. The home ownership rate in 1997–1998 amongst working couples with dependent children reached 78.8 per cent. Yet, strong demand resulted in massive price inflation, around 20 per cent in Sydney and Melbourne, leaving-single-income earners and new purchasers in these areas increasingly out of the market. Access declined partly due to uneven changes affecting the *welfare relations* of different households, which in turn, have influenced their position in the housing market.

CONTINGENTLY DEFINED LABOUR AND WELFARE RELATIONS

As mentioned earlier, the ability to purchase housing services, both ownership and rental, diminished during the late 1980s with rapidly rising interest rates and stagnant wage growth. House price inflation, which rose considerably between 1986 and 1988, was the most important factor reducing access of low-income first homebuyers to finance, especially in Melbourne[32] and Sydney. Further, real incomes, constrained by a national wage accord that lasted nine years (Stilwell, 1986), were further eroded by the imposition of compulsory super annuation payments. Formerly, most workers relied upon the receipt of the government's old age pension. First, the government's pension became means tested and then private pension arrangement became compulsory (to avoid post-retirement poverty despite owning a home outright). Yet wage rises did not compensate for this new imposition nor exceed house price inflation, stifling the ability of new buyers to save for a home deposit.[33] Fearing a downturn in purchase rates, the real estate lobby unsuccessfully campaigned for the release of accumulated pension contributions for home deposits.

Pertinent is the research by Yates (1994)[34], which reveals a widening group of middle-income and young households delaying their decision to purchase or simply remaining in private rental accommodation. In her review of the evidence on income distribution, employment and purchase[35], Yates (1994) explains that

Table 6.9 Households spending >30 per cent of their gross weekly incomes on housing, 1994

Tenure type	Lowest quintile %	2nd quintile %	3rd quintile %	4th quintile %	Highest quintile %	Total %
Owner	14.3	3.7	1.0	0.2	0.3	4.9
Purchaser	66.3	56.1	38.9	17.5	7.5	26.1
Renter	50.7	42.5	11.0	4.3	0.9	26.2
Total	**30.2**	**25.2**	**16.0**	**8.3**	**3.7**	**16.7**
Recent first home buyer	57.7	53.2	42.6	18.8	7.6	29.2
Recent changeover buyer	27.1	26.5	31.5	19.0	11.4	21.3

Source: Australian Housing Survey (unpublished data).

increasing inequality between incomes is reducing the expected proportion of new home purchasers entering the market (see evidence in Table 6.9). McClelland (1993) echoes this claim, raising the possibility of increased social division and reduced cohesion, exacerbated by poor growth and individualised welfare obligations.

In a combined analysis of Australian Bureau of Statistics Household Expenditure and Income Surveys, Yates (1997) continues to provide further evidence that home ownership has reached its peak and indeed, may have begun to decline. She stresses the significance of a *range of uncertainties* facing new purchasers, in addition to socio-demographic and lifestyle changes:

> increasing inequality in earned incomes have also contributed to increasing uncertainty and insecurity in relation to labour market income. The liberalisation of the financial sector, which brought with it the deregulation of interest rates, has contributed increasing uncertainty about the future of interest rates. The increased availability of mortgage finance has contributed to increased uncertainty about the stability of dwelling prices. The changing demographic structure of the population and the increased uncertainty about future immigration policies have led to increased uncertainty about future trends in dwelling prices.
>
> (Yates, 1997: 42)

Recent relief, in the form of rising rates of employment and lower interest rates, has tempered housing stress for the time being and for some households. Nevertheless, there remains widespread concern amongst housing analysts, for low- and single-income households.

Synthesising key relations in their contingent context

In sum, the housing outcomes during this period were tumultuous and there are some signs of decline in the rate of home purchase. The three corner stones of the Australian solution of mass home ownership have been fundamentally altered. In their hey day, these were state-sponsored infrastructure provision, protected circuit of capital and steady wage growth. The crises in collective consumption, which arose in the 1970s and impeded public sponsorship of infrastructure has been ameliorated by urban consolidation, lower standards of land development on the urban fringe and greater influence of private land development companies in planning estates and economies in development and construction: higher density (smaller plots) and construction quality (standardised plans favouring larger builders).

Major changes have taken place in the home finance sector, depicted in Figure 6.7: the *protected circuit has been abolished* (1), new financial institutions have entered the market to compete with traditional savings banks (2) and the public HLIC has been privatised (3). In the 1980s interest rates were very high, but dropped in the late 1990s amidst intense competition and product innovation between new and traditional mortgage lenders. Access to home ownership

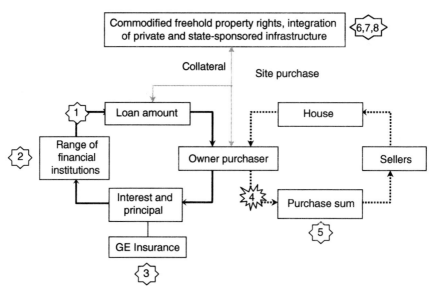

Figure 6.7 Abstraction of the flow of capital during reconfiguration of the Australian housing solution (1986–2000).

amongst single-income and low-income households has been substantially narrowed by rapid but uneven house price inflation and rising interest rates during the late 1980s and once again a *dramatic increase in (inner) urban house prices* during the late 1990s (4). Increasing house price inflation has been facilitated by strong white-collar employment growth and low interest rates relative to house price inflation. To assist first homeowners in an inflated market, government provides *one-off grants to assist purchase* (5). Changes continue to occur in the land market, with public land agencies being privatised and forced to deliver substantial dividends, as with other commercial developers amidst intense land trading on the urban fringe (6). There have been some developments in the relationship between state government agencies, land developers and building firms with regards to infrastructure provision, with *land developers assuming a key role in planning and standard setting*, government agencies as more passive partners (7) and building firms as 'pattern book' contractors (8). Finally, the promotion of existing supplementary tenures such as social housing has also been weak.

6.6 Abstracting the causal mechanisms

The emergent relations of property, investment and savings, and labour and welfare were differently defined and packaged during each phase of the Australian housing solution. During each phase, the state played a dynamic role under different political circumstances and shifting economic modes of production.

In sum, the emergence of the Australian housing solution of low-density home ownership took place during the years of colonisation and federation. During this period, the cornerstones of the Australian housing system were set in place: a system of private property rights, state-sponsored infrastructure provision, channelled mortgage finance and moderate, regulated wage growth. Successive phases in Australia's housing history have cummulatively built upon and modified these key features. In the most recent phase, introduced in 1986, two key relations, channelled mortgage finance and regulated wage labour, were removed and a third, state-sponsored infrastructure provision substantially altered. Since 2000 a grant for first homeowners has been introduced.

Today home ownership is no longer an option for the 'masses'. Rather, housing outcomes are increasingly polarised by household type and income level and the location and timing of purchase. Declining access to home ownership for a growing minority of households may lead to the development of alternative housing solutions for Australian households. Yet this will take time, and is not likely to occur whilst governments are committed to ameliorative one-off non-structural actions such as the first homeowners' grant that merely supports further house price inflation. Perhaps a crisis of 'strategic significance' (Harloe, 1995: 50) will generate a new housing solution. This is most likely to emanate from the inherent conflict between deregulated contract work, long-term variable mortgage contracts and post-retirement security for men and women, singles and larger households.

6.6.1   *Abstraction using relevant concepts and ideas*

A number of abstractions have been made from the analysis provided. These abstractions can be found in Table 6.10 and are further developed in section 6.6.2 and the comparative conclusions presented in Chapter 8.

However, Table 6.10 does not communicate the dynamic interaction and cumulative causation between contingent conditions and key relations generating the process of coherence, crises and adaptation across the Australian home ownership trajectory. However, it does provide a neat abstraction of relevant contingencies. The challenge of providing a new and dynamic interpretation, using the abstractions mentioned earlier, is undertaken in the following section.

6.6.2   *Retroductive analysis of the Australian housing solution*

In this section a number of poignant contrastive and counterfactual questions focus the retroductive analysis, employing the ideas and concepts developed in earlier chapters and summarised in Figure 6.3, and illustrated by the empirical evidence and Figures 6.4–6.7 presented in section 6.5.

Why begin a new colony with ownership?

A formative causal mechanism, from which home ownership later emerged, was the establishment of exchangeable freehold title via the rapid sale of land claimed

Table 6.10 Social relations over time, contingent relations and housing outcomes

Relations/phase	Emergence 1840–1906	Establishment and acceleration 1907–1970	Deceleration and decline 1971–1985	Dismantling and reconfiguration 1986–2000
Property	Private property rights allocated to individuals, investment supported by state infrastructure investment	Private property rights protected by land-use segregation, urban plans lay out future suburbs, governments lead urban expansion, developing estates and redeveloping slums	Public infrastructure fails to keep pace with expansion, land commissions make little impact on market and housing costs, land owners retain raw land rather than develop	Land commissions privatised, continuing constraints limit government infrastructure provision. Partnerships dominant mode of development, with developer leading planning processes
Financial	Building societies established yet crash during property collapse, State Banks permitted to provide home finance, development of new loan instruments, measures to reduce risk instituted	State Banks regulated by Reserve Bank to channel funds into home finance, public mortgage insurance corporation protects banks and broadens borrower access	Protected circuit of capital constrains financial institutions; State Banks ration loans, shortage of mortgage credit	Deregulation of financial system, removal of mortgage regulation, decline of State Banks and introduction of new players

Welfare	High and relatively evenly distributed incomes, well-organised labour movement, wage earners' welfare state established	Centrally fixed wages, labour shortages moderated by immigration, high rising wages, low unemployment	Economic restructuring, high unemployment amongst low-skill occupations, increasing dependence on income transfers	From corporate agreement to relative deregulation of wages, push for self-reliance through private superannuation
Contingencies	• Flow of investment from Britain, Gold Rush, property boom, lack of regulation • Collapse of commodity prices in Europe, end of Gold Rush, collapse of property market • Recovery then global economic Depression	• Shortage of materials and high cost of labour • Protected economic growth in manufacturing and minerals extraction	Oil crisis and global economic downturn leads to a decline in manufacturing industry, transfer of infrastructure responsibilities to land developers	Opening of the Australian economy, economic restructuring, globalisation of investment, competitive positioning of Australian cities
Housing outcomes	Few tenure alternatives. Relatively broad access to home ownership, yet poor housing conditions, evictions and repossessions during economic crises	Strong shift from rental to home ownership, rapid rise in home ownership, some provision of public rental housing	Home ownership rates remain stable, but less affordable for new entrants, other tenures show signs of social marginalisation	Signs of decline in rate of home ownership, marginal assistance to renters, weak promotion of tenure alternatives

by the Crown (despite resistance from indigenous people) to raise cash for the new colony. New private landowners, holding vast tracts extending from the city grid, had no intention of developing their holdings for residential use. Speculation was the goal, which at times stymied urban expansion. The initial land auctions greatly undermined the position of the state in land ownership and urban planning in all areas beyond the essential ports. Further, electoral franchise was rooted in property ownership, and the landed gentry were placed in a powerful position to diminish any legislative threats. Nevertheless, the needs of an expanding state prevailed and sitting land speculators were eventually forced, by the threat of taxation, to develop or sell their holdings. Indeed, taxation was necessary to establish instrumentalities that could implement state-sponsored urban expansion. Speculators released their holdings onto the market in smaller, albeit suburban size packages to land developers. Yet once again, the prospect of capital accumulation via speculative investment dominated progress.

The extraction of profit occurred primarily at the early stages of raw land conversion and subdivision and not in the development and construction phase. During this period, areas were made accessible by an expanding network of road, rail and trams, greatly assisted by the new state instrumentalities. Smaller lots were subdivided along narrow streets and lanes maximising potential yields and were sold to owner builders. Construction involved small-scale, often father-and-son firms. Finance for home purchase required eventual owner-occupation, allocated to members of savings clubs or Building Societies.

The land speculators boom and the supply of home ownership were bolstered on the demand side by a growing local economy (import replacing industry, rising commodity prices and flow of capital from the Gold Rush). Consumer aspirations were indeed path dependent, shaped by the culturally and materially constructed preference for home ownership amongst new migrants from Ireland, England and Scotland who were both skilled and well resourced. There was no significant industrial sector employing a large and lowly paid workforce that would be satisfied with cheap and basic housing. Rather, it was port and commodity related trade and commerce that were the main sources of employment, leading to the establishment of a well-paid mercantile class able to accumulate savings and secure loans for the purchase of new homes.

But why not begin with renting?

It is unlikely that the new colony could have begun with rental housing. First of all, investment capital was not attracted to the long-term and unknown benefits of landlordism in a rapidly growing mercantile economy. There was no reliable and experienced vehicle for the secure management of such housing assets or their tenants. Far less risky investments could be made elsewhere, and in the formative years of rapid urban expansion, it was thought (mistakenly) that no safer investment existed than real estate.

The structure of the building industry also played a causal role impeding the establishment of a rental sector. The industry was and still remains dominated by small owner builder firms constructing dwellings using simple and standardised designs, with limited capacity or experience to build multi-unit dwellings. Master builders, with their hierarchy of skilled labourers, were sufficiently occupied, building mansions for the growing social elite (largely comprising sheep and cattle farmers wealthy from favourable land deals).

Further, there was no demand for mass rental housing amongst both employees and employers. The cities were expanding as bases for mercantile activities rather than industry and work was relatively well paid, generating enviable wages and potential household savings. These were captured by banks and Building Societies, which provided conditional loans for owner purchase.

Finally, as mentioned earlier, the social status of new migrants and their emerging national identity placed much value on home ownership. This was bolstered by memories of the homeland and the rhetoric of all political parties and importantly, the strong and growing labour movement. Conversely, there existed a socially and materially constructed opposition to landlordism.

For these reasons, rental housing did not emerge to displace home ownership at the core of the Australian solution. This was due to a multiple and cumulative series of causal mechanisms: the nature of the property market, the underdevelopment of the landlord sector, the absence of a large and low-paid workforce and the aspirations of new, relatively wealthy migrants and the mechanism for channelling savings in individual home loans. Thus, there was and remains a poorly organised, unprofessional private rental sector, comprising petty and accidental landlords.

Whilst the Australian solution dominated by home ownership maintained a period of coherence for several decades after the 1850s, its open housing system inevitably fell prey to negative contingencies and crises. These included a massive fall in commodity prices upon which mercantile cities were dependent, the end of the Gold Rush which had brought so many migrants and fuelled consumption, collapse of the inflated and overheated land market and finally, the subsequent crash and closure of many building societies and banks.

Why not radical change in strategy after the crises? Why a
financing solution rather than a property one?

The most visible face of the crisis mentioned earlier was represented by the repossession actions of banks and their eventual closure. Popular politics directed blame towards the banks and building societies, even though often-legal speculative investment in the highly commodified land market played a large role in their downfall. So began the Australian tradition of 'bank bashing' and loyal preference for government-owned State Savings Banks.

Whilst speculation was an important cause of the housing crisis it could have been curtailed or outlawed, but was not. Despite public scandals and disgrace amongst certain key banking, property and political elite, the power of speculative land interests remained in the upper echelons of governing chambers of parliament at the state level. No legislation could be passed which threatened their interests.

Further, ideological concepts associating ownership with patriotism were promoted and protected the sanctity of private property from public intrusion. Indeed, such problems persist. In the 1950s, Sydney's precious Green Belt policy was scrapped and its main proponent, the Cumberland City Council abolished by vested property development interests in state parliament. In the Victorian parliament 20 years later, the establishment of public land agencies and more recently tenancy reforms were severely frustrated by corruption and vested property interests.

Yet, in the early years of the nineteenth century, land ownership was strongly associated with emancipation of the workingman. Despite the continuous threat of repossession of homes by the banks, the labour movement perceived private rental landlords as mere parasites of workers' wages. Indeed, the wage debates of 1907 highlighted the futility of wage rises in the context of market rents. But rent regulation was not the favoured solution. Rather, a mechanism to facilitate ownership, such as State Bank loans for modest homes, was supported by both capital and labour.

A public housing programme was established after the war,
why did this not develop as an important solution?

Public housing was established to address serious and immediate housing shortages amongst returning soldiers and redevelop areas dominated by slum dwellings. This Commonwealth government initiative followed a long period of decline in housing investment and production that began with the Great Depression and mass unemployment. This had all but extinguished expressed demand and curtailed the role of the state in housing finance and urban expansion. Beyond this, public housing was an important mechanism to stimulate economic development in a climate of industrial restructuring. Many housing-related industries were assisted as a direct result of the public housing programmes. Further, substantial contracts specified the use of particular materials, labour saving devices and skills, ensuring efficient use of scarce post-war resources. The concrete industry was particularly favoured.

Allocation via waiting list ensured the 'appropriate' distribution of low-rise public rental houses and flats to skilled workers, close to areas of mass employment in the newly industrialising cities. A different strategy was employed in the inner suburbs, where dilapidated terrace houses were completely demolished and their inhabitants selectively rehoused in these areas. Plans for modern high-rise buildings were borrowed from Britain and their concrete towers broke the low-rise skyline of the inner city terraces.

However, the public housing programme did not flourish, and the most desirable dwellings were sold at discounted prices to their inhabitants. There was no organised constituency to support the expansion of public housing. The labour movement still considered home ownership a source of worker emancipation. Conservative politicians utilised nationalist cold-war rhetoric to promote the dream of ownership and dismantle the 'anti-Australian' socialist housing programmes. Later, inner-city environmental groups, appalled by the destruction of both buildings and communities and the high-rise buildings that replaced them, joined the anti-Commission campaign. The budget of the Housing Commissions was and remains subject to a politically vulnerable and complex fund sharing agreement, providing ample room for disruption and curtailment.

Further, much was to be gained from developing housing privately in the rapidly expanding post-war suburbs. State-sponsored urban expansion, coupled with the mobility of the private car, promoted an ever-outwards migration from the city centres fuelled by new household formation and immigration programmes. Many land developers had combined forces with building companies, and wanted a slice of the action. With low interest rates and household wealth secure and stable in the 1950s and 1960s, private home ownership in new suburban locations came within reach of a wide array of single-income households.

If the Australian solution centres on state-sponsored infrastructure, cheap finance and adequate wages, why were these conditions altered in the 1980s?

For many decades, urban expansion was sponsored by state-provided infrastructure provision. There was no betterment or capital gains tax to claw back these subsidies from landholders and home purchasers. The reduced cost price of serviced building sites was partly transferred to purchasers of new homes but largely flowed into the hands of land developers. The cost to the state was spread over generations of city dwellers via collective taxation. This neat functional fit was eroded by economic crises (unemployment, high interest rates) generating heavy demands on state spending and constraining funds for necessary infrastructure. New financing mechanisms for infrastructure provision have been developed, which emphasise user pays principles and private sector partnerships. The cost of developing land has risen, standards have dropped and densities risen on the urban fringe.

Housing remains dependent upon cheap finance. Yet the home loans sector forms only one small, albeit nationally important part of a much larger and increasingly global capital market. Time and time again, we see how negative monetary conditions can erode favourable housing credit and labour conditions and how the rate of new purchase subsequently drops. By the mid-1970s additional and very powerful non-housing actors came into play, emanating from the private banking sector, as did public servants from the Reserve Bank and Treasury Departments of the Commonwealth. Their message was consistent: open up the protected Australian economy, deregulate the relatively closed Australian financial system and introduce new players to increase competition and the flow of investment. The monetarist doctrine of Reganism and Thatcherism promoted the deregulation of financial markets across the globe, as a monetarist tool to fight inflation. In Australia, this was portrayed as the only course of action for a national economy starved of foreign investment in the 1980s. Further, a national wage accord which lasted for most of the 1980s ensured that wage growth was minimal to improve the international position of Australian industry. Simply put, the investment demands of industry were considered more important than the immediate housing aspirations of new purchasers, and perhaps the proposed solution would serve both in the long run.

Further, the private and State Banking sector, the Reserve Bank and those within Treasury (including the future Labour prime minister) advanced arguments undermining the logic behind interest rate regulation in the home loans sector. The protected circuit came to be seen and promoted as part of the problem in a time of home loan scarcity (rationing by Savings Banks) and rapidly escalating interest rates (capped versus non-capped interest rates). Both were an anathema to those calling for open competition. Following deregulation, home loan interest rates actually rose by 2 percentage points and remained high for three years. Those contemplating home ownership delayed their purchase. Those with variable loans either weathered the storm by compensating with additional work, or lost their homes through mortgage default and repossession.

Indeed, home ownership as a 'mass solution' remains in the last instance dependent upon adequate household income, and the ability to pay for housing is strongly related to one's position on the labour market. Inflating house prices surpassed declining real wages, stifled by Labour Accords in the 1980s and deregulation in the 1990s. The growth in part-time work compensated for the suppression of wage levels. Centralised wage fixation processes were increasingly replaced by work place agreements favouring those with the most effective union, with scarce skills in demand or in a growing and profitable new sector. Thus, two decades of economic restructuring and deregulation have affected employees at opposite ends of the spectrum quite differentially. Today, lower-skilled workers in the blue-collar industries, even households with two such incomes, are far less likely to purchase a home. The housing crisis has arrived for these households and for others it is merely delayed. The growing minority of longer-term renters, with no housing asset to compensate for modest post-retirement pensions, faces a very bleak future indeed.

7 Explaining divergent tenure patterns and urban form

The Dutch case of compact social housing provision

7.1 Introduction

This chapter provides a further contribution towards explaining shifts in the Dutch trajectory of housing provision. It is the second of two cases for contrast and comparison of the generative mechanisms promoting divergence in national housing solutions. Evidence is presented for the unique definition of key social relations and their synthesis in order to provide a plausible explanation for the development of compact cities that, unlike Australian cities, became dominated by *social housing* in the Netherlands from the 1950s to the mid-1980s. Thus, it is *not* intended to provide a detailed, descriptive chronological biography or policy history. Rather, this chapter focuses upon possible causal relations that may have generated the Dutch 'solution' using the ideas and concepts put forward in earlier chapters.

The structure of this chapter is similar to the Australian case. It begins with the observable outcomes of various phases in the continuing evolution of the Dutch housing 'solution' and tries to define its core features. This is followed by a critical review of existing explanations from a range of research offering very different modes of explanation in the Netherlands. A postulated explanation is put forward that selectively draws upon previous empirical and theoretical work, as well as new perspectives and concepts outlined in previous chapters.

This postulate is tested and revised by analysis of the various phases in Dutch housing provision: the end of laissez-faire liberalism; foundations addressing the housing crisis; acceleration under favourable contingent conditions; and most recently redefinition and reregulation of key relationships. For each metamorphosis of the housing 'solution', the key events and housing outcomes are briefly summarised. Step by step, the contingently defined relations of property, savings and investment, labour and welfare and their synthesis will be examined. At the conclusion of the chapter, an abstraction of the causal mechanisms from this description will be put forward. This will form the basis for contrast and comparison with the Australian case in Chapter 8.

7.2 Observable outcomes of the Dutch housing solution

By the year 2001, 100 years after the first housing law formally established the Dutch system of social housing provision, the Netherlands had evolved to become both a nation of social renters and increasingly, home purchasers. It continues to have one of the largest social housing sectors in Europe, with 36 per cent of total stock provided by approved housing associations, municipal housing companies and non-profit institutions for low- and middle-income households. Just over half of these dwellings are considered low rental (56 per cent between 300 and 427 Euro per month). There were 643 social housing landlords in 2001, providing just over 2.3 million of the nation's 6.5 million dwellings (Aedes, 2001; VROM, 2001). Many of these landlords are of considerable size providing more than 4,000 dwellings and 59 providing more than 10,000. The number and composition of these landlords have changed significantly in recent years, with mergers and transformations leading to the rapid decline of the municipal housing sector, as indicated in Table 7.1.

Social housing, known as *volkshuisvesting*, is unevenly distributed across the country. As can be seen in Table 7.2, a large proportion of housing in the four largest Dutch cities, particularly Amsterdam and Rotterdam, comprise rental dwellings, which are predominantly provided by social landlords.

Rental housing is also provided by the commercial sector, comprising small private landlords and larger institutional investors being primarily pension funds. Significant numbers of tenants receive relatively generous rental assistance, which is provided on the basis of rent paid and household income. This is paid directly to tenants, via the municipality, or directly to the association in return for reduced rent (Kemp, 1997).

Table 7.1 Social housing landlords, 1990–2001

Social landlords	1990	1992	1994	1995	1996	2001
Housing corporations	824	805	793	774	763	619[a]
Municipal housing companies	213	188	125	81	63	24[a]
Total social housing stock ('000s)	1.854	1.950	2.167	2.265	2.295	2.347

Source: VROM/DGVH, Key data for social renters, 1996, CBS, Financial Monthly Figures.

Note
a AEDES cijfers.

Table 7.2 Tenure distribution, the Netherlands and major cities in 2000

Area by tenure	Social rental (%)	Private rental (%)	Purchase (%)	Total dwellings (100%)
The Netherlands	36	12	52	6,520,500
Amsterdam	56	27	17	369,300
Rotterdam	59	15	26	283,800
Den Haag	39	27	34	212,500
Utrecht	45	14	42	101,100

Source: Cijfers over Wonen, VROM, 2001.

Over the past five decades, home ownership has increased in the Netherlands from 28 per cent in 1947 to 52 per cent in 2000 (VROM, 2001). In recent years the average price of dwellings, particularly in and around the Randstad, has increased dramatically. Individual home purchase has been financed via individual mortgage finance, the most common being savings and annuity, and promoted by more permissive lending criteria based on two incomes, various government schemes and significant tax incentives.

In addition to these unique tenure characteristics, a defining feature of Dutch housing provision concerns urban form. The compactness of numerous towns and larger cities, regularity of dwellings and sharp distinction between town and country are distinguishing attributes (Terhorst and Van de Ven, 1997: 14). A constellation of moderately sized, compact cities in the west of the Netherlands known as the Randstad loosely encircles an open area of agricultural and recreational space known as the Groene Hart. For the past three decades housing densities have been declining. Between 1991 and 1998, lower-density neighbourhoods comprising free standing, maisonette and row housing have dominated new production, particularly in the newly announced VINEX locations of the Randstad (DGVH/RPD, 2001; Woonmilieu Database, Ottens, 1989). In contrast to urban expansions of earlier years, dwellings in these new, more spacious urban areas are intended for purchase, with construction undertaken by development companies.

7.3 Beyond outcomes – Explaining the core of the Dutch housing solution

The Dutch solution of compact cities with their large proportion of social rental dwellings alongside subsidised and unsubsidised dwellings for rental and purchase was formerly, but tenuously established in the early years of the twentieth century. The Dutch housing solution is notable for its prominent inclusion of private nonprofit housing associations managing social housing, which contrasts starkly with the marginal and residual role of state-provided 'public' housing in Australia. Behind this observable phenomenon can be found a set of social relations characterised by the strong role for larger municipalities in land development, planning and housing development, favourable government loans and object subsidies for the construction of dwellings by a variety of providers for different forms of consumption, and the regulation of rents sustained by modest household incomes and supplemented by rental allowance.

The output of social housing has been enabled and curtailed by a variety of state actions operating under various contingent conditions, which have influenced the definition of core emergent relations underpinning provision. The explicit motivation for government intervention has shifted from a concern for public health and slum clearance, to welfare, the housing shortage, producing low cost employment and keeping rents low, and more recently, to urban renewal and housing those who cannot afford market alternatives. A variety of contingent factors has shaped and been shaped by government efforts. Amongst many others, these include the market position of municipalities in negotiating development outcomes, the availability of investment for constructing dwellings, the level of interest rates and inflation, the cost and supply of labour and materials, and the incomes of households. How these important contingencies affected the development of the Dutch housing solution will be examined in section 7.5.

7.3.1   Existing explanations for the Dutch housing solution

Why has social rental housing dominated Dutch cities since the 1950s, and why has the Netherlands strayed from this long-established route in recent decades?

This section and sections 7.3.2 and 7.3.3 consider the contribution of three decades of *Dutch housing studies*[1], which have emerged amongst and sometimes isolated from the different currents in social science and explanatory housing research that were previously outlined in Chapters 3 and 4.

This section examines the dominant 'project' of housing research in the Netherlands and the traditions and institutional relations that underpin different explanatory pathways emanating from various research schools. Indeed, there is not one, but many different approaches to explaining the Dutch case, yet only a few hold the academic and policy spotlight. Housing production has been perceived as an outcome of government policy in the context of need, effective demand and demographic change, or as a string of random events to which policy has correctively responded. Alternatively, social housing provision has been considered as a civilising and pacifying process, connected to shifting modes of economic production and the entire process of industrialisation and urbanisation. The entire 'system' has been viewed as one devised by central governments, currently influenced by the move towards European Monetary Union and increasing integration of finance and property markets. Some researchers emphasise the importance of the individual city entrepreneurs, architects and professional movements, whilst others stress the intertwined central–local state relations embedded in shifting modes of accumulation. All these modes of explanation have something to offer, yet some are more contestable than others from a realist ontological vantage point.

The following paragraphs categorise Dutch housing explanations by their central 'project':

- empirical studies and policy commentary,
- explanation, via demographic and economic modelling, for forecasting purposes,
- explanation via ideas and institutions to promote better understanding,
- explanation via international contrast, contrasting differences and similarities,
- critical explanations exploring the civilising process and gender relations,
- explanation via state theories of pillarisation and the passive welfare state,
- explanation with attention to local contingencies in a broader political economy.

Table 3 in Appendix 1 summarises these streams in Dutch housing studies.

Of these diverse explanatory schools, the first two, policy commentary and prognoses, are more widely practised and typical of Dutch housing studies. A critical evaluation of progress takes place in section 7.3.2. Possible reasons for the path taken in Dutch housing studies follow this review, in section 7.3.3.

Explanation via normative critique

It is widely recognised that there has been a strong tradition of *empiricism and muted positivism* in Dutch housing studies. Empirical research places great emphasis upon careful, objective observation of housing events. The selection of these events is not explicitly guided by concepts or theories drawn from social science, but from the observable shifts and manoeuvres in politics and policy-making. Two authors have dominated this tradition, providing a valuable and detailed record of central government initiatives, particularly those pertaining to the social rental sector.

Van Beusekom (1955), housing policy activist and professor of Architecture (Delft), provides a classic notebook biography of Dutch social housing from the mid-nineteenth to the mid-twentieth century. He recalls the administrative and political events contributing towards the history of housing-related legislation and its implementation. His notes of vignettes deliver a personal account of key public debates and their resolution, providing a dialogue of policy development in a tumultuous socio-economic context. He pays particular attention to the role of central government in subsidising provision and the various institutions, professional bodies, civil servants and other key players involved in 100 years of Dutch housing policy.

For more than 25 years, a major correspondent of such events continues to be Hugo Priemus, who established the OTB Research Institute for Policy Sciences and Technology in Delft. His extensive publications, many in English, concern the various twists and turns in contemporary Dutch housing policy. Priemus follows a long tradition of pragmatic–normative research, charting the policy contours of housing history (in many of which he has played an influential role) with commentary and policy recommendations. Nevertheless, no observation is without certain assumptions and normative standpoints; indeed, certain theories of explanation do permeate his analysis and policy prescriptions. For example, Priemus (1990, 1992, 1996) gives analytical prominence to government intervention in market interactions and promotes state intervention to mediate external forces or abuses to achieve desired market outcomes as well as economic and political equilibrium (1995). In this manner, Priemus provides influential normative critique, and maintains an active hand in policy debate.

Explanation via demographic and economic modelling

Another important tradition in Dutch housing research has been market analysis and prognosis. Towards this end, the Dutch variants of demography and welfare economics have played an important role, defining key concepts in the subsidy of housing production and consumption, and predicting and forecasting housing trends and policy options. This mode of research is fully institutionalised in the policy process. Forecasts play an integral role in a housing system where the government wishes to maintain stable levels of housing production through various subsidy schemes, thus minimising market risks and housing shortages.

Dieleman *et al.* (1985) offer a strong demographic and rational economic perspective, predicting future demand for social housing. Their work considers demographic developments to be the décor against which developments in social housing respond. Their 1985 report considers how household growth, income developments and financial prospects will influence the levels of social housing required and outlines some policy options. More recent work by Dieleman maintains a predictive perspective, focusing on the impact of rising income, tenure preferences and housing prices upon affordability and residential segregation (1996b).

The extensive work of Van Fulpen, undertaken for the Social Cultural Planning Bureau, is also illustrative of this prominent and well-developed approach. He defines, models and predicts the consumption costs for tenants, testing alternative models of social housing finance, and different subsidy options (1985, 1984, 1983a,b, 1982). His 1985 work, *Volkshuisvesting in Demografisch en Economisch Perspectief (Social Housing in Demographic and Economic Perspective)*, provides a good example of predictive modelling approach applied to the Dutch housing market. He uses quantitative multi-variant analysis to examine the effects of demographic and economic factors upon the quality and quantity of housing demanded. Van Fulpen applies his model to the housing market in order to simulate possible outcomes. The explanatory power of his work depends on the model's implicit assumptions, including ideal types, aggregated consumer preference and rational behaviour, and the extent to which they resemble reality. Key to Van Fulpen's analysis is the realm of consumption, which is perceived as dependent upon quantifiable demographic, macro- and micro-economic factors.

Neo-classical models of equilibrium, competition and free markets permeate much housing research in the policy field. The conceptual model developed by Conijn, concerning the financial and economic basis of social housing provision, assumes a market in perfect competition where demand and supply are in balance and the role of government is left out 'as the study focuses on the operation of housing' (1995: 173). Econometric models of this nature, tend to utilise empirical data or expressed, available recorded outcomes, building a closed model of different dimensions of the housing market, as devised by the researcher and influenced by his or her ontological perspective. Such models are not inclined to emphasis the less overt and often unpredictable, causal influences affecting housing, such as the socially and materially embedded modes of housing production, exchange and consumption of housing services and important non-housing influences. Indeed, highly aggregated econometric models are not insightful when trying to explain spatial variations, the seemingly irrational institutionalised practices and ideas about housing, and the housing systems continuing vulnerability to unpredictable external shocks.

A recent example of econometric modelling for predictive purposes was undertaken by the Cultural Planning Bureau (Rele and Van Steen, 2001) concerning the system of subsidising housing in the Netherlands with an emphasis on the distributional effects of various measures, including a low tax on home equity (relative to other assets) in the ownership sector and housing allowances and low rent levels in the rental sector. As with many econometric studies the researchers develop a variety of equations representing various subsidy forms and calculate their aggregate effects on public finances. Whilst these equations imply statistical accuracy they do employ many assumptions including 'best guesses' of pure cases of subsidisation, their weighting and average effects and also remove certain possibilities, in an attempt to avoid 'distorting fluctuations' from their analysis. For this reason, the findings are not abstracted from complex and uneven empirical reality but derived from a conceptual model developed by the researchers, enabling relatively straightforward recommendations. Employing their model, Rele and Van Steen conclude that the benefits of subsidisation are greater for low-income renters and for mortgaged rather than equity-financed purchases. Recent conditions in the housing and labour market, such as the growth in white collar employment and escalating house prices, have increased the indebtedness of new owners, skewed subsidies towards them (via substantial tax deductions) and also promoted further price inflation. From their analysis, the authors suggest that a reduction or abolition of tax subsidy would reduce prices and increase access for first homebuyers, providing an apparently objective contribution to the highly charged politics surrounding this aspect of housing policy.

Explanation via ideas, professions and institutions

Econometric models, however inclusive, fundamentally differ in terms of ontology, epistemology and purpose from geo-historical studies. Van der Schaar, using a loosely defined institutional approach to understanding and explaining housing history, provides a leading example. He has updated and refined his comprehensive body of historical work for analysis of housing institutions. His seminal work, *Groei en Bloei van het Nederlandse Volkshuisvestingbeleid* (1987), remains one of the more thorough accounts of outcomes in the policy process to the mid-1980s and remains a key reference for scholars of housing history. This text places emphasis upon the instruments of policy in the context of other forces: market developments, formal political decision-making processes, and the lobbying and advice of government officers and representative organs. More recent work provides a concise historical account (1998) of the shift in policy emphasis from public health to environmental quality. Whilst events, rather than causes, are the focus, a number of explanatory themes are implicit. These include the importance of property relations in defining development players and their conditions, the small government ideology and preference for private (capitalist) rather than public entrepreneurship, and the quest to maintain production, with the state playing a corrective role to address 'abnormal' market conditions.

In more recent work, Van der Schaar (1999) gives his analysis a more distinct institutional emphasis. Policy phases are considered to be influenced by social demands and needs, the dominant ideas of political coalitions (minimal state provision, goal of normal market relations), and professional interests, punctuated by reactions to exogenous economic crises and other circumstances. Most recently (2001), he reiterates that social housing is first and foremost a matter of policy, whilst certain economic relationships are of crucial importance, namely the inter-play between costs of building, incomes, market conditions and government subsidies and the constant struggle for a return to 'normal' market relations.

The following historical explanations focus upon the ideas of key professional organisations upon the delivery and development of the Dutch housing solution. Unlike those above, the following explanations have had far less influence in policy and professional circles.

Grinburg (1977, 1982) provides a historical study of Dutch housing form, with an emphasis on the various concepts, traditions and ideologies shaping architectural practice, in relation to shifts in administrative and economic power between 1900 and 1940. Grinburg's descriptive study emphasises the significance of the ideas and motivations of housing promoters upon different forms of housing provision, such as: paternal philanthropy and economic self-interest of industrial landlords; economic liberalism of speculative jerry builders; the paternalistic–speculative character of early associations; the workers' co-operative movement for self-owned dwellings and the principles of liberal-paternalism underpinning the Housing Act. He mentions specific influences in the establishment of the Housing Act: the fear of fire and disease amongst the better housed; the power of speculators over government; and the role of social welfare groups, health commissions, building committees and city architects. Steiber (1998) offers a similar perspective, with an emphasis upon the Amsterdam school of architecture and urban design, stressing the importance of various supervisory committees which officially regulated the built environment during the early twentieth century.

The role of professions and their struggle for societal status is considered to have played an important role in defining social housing policy. Hajer and Reijndorp (2001) examined different periods of provision and the influence of medical practitioners, engineers, architects, urban planners and community workers upon the promotion of 'ideal' housing outcomes through the development of various housing institutions, programmes and projects. According to his analysis of the current period, professions have played a prominent role in the institutionalisation of supply and individualisation of demand.

Organisational histories also provide a relevant body of empirical research. A good example is the work of De Ruijter (1987), on the Dutch Institute for Planning and Housing (NIROV), which gives much attention to developments in housing and planning between 1850 and 1940. He focuses on the role and ideas of professions: architects, housing reformers, pressure groups, planners and professional bodies such as NIROV. His lengthy study of the Dutch Housing Act examines the concepts and arguments of different pressure groups, individual reformers, political parties and social movements active in the field of housing reform. These include: the movement for private–public health and professional pressure for social hygiene; movements to improve the living environments of workers; the idea that better housing could achieve social reform; the sanctity of private property; the role of the labour movement in organising for better housing conditions; the autonomy of municipalities and the role of government to restore equilibrium in dysfunctional markets. De Ruijter makes use of a wide variety of qualitative historical materials such as letters, journals, speeches, plans, photos, songs and posters. Other official administrative histories typically review regionally aggregated housing indicators, national programme initiatives and government legislation, whilst emphasising the role of individual civil servants and politicians (for examples, CDWV, 1952; see Kooiman, 1943; Van der Schaar *et al.*, 1996).

Historical accounts of policy have commonly focused on the succession of rules and regulations developed by central government that have 'defined' various housing programmes of the day. In recent years, Dutch policy science has applied more elaborate techniques towards an explanatory strategy grounded in rational action neo-interactionism (Kickert, 1991; Klijn, 1996; Klijn and Teisman, 1992; Koppenjan *et al.*, 1993). Klijn applies this explanatory approach to post-war housing policy. He examines how individual action is channelled and contends that actors are connected to each other in a policy network by mutual interdependency and engaged in an ecology of games (1996: 335). His empirical research compares the housing policy networks and games employed by relevant actors in three cities: Den Haag, Rotterdam and Groningen.

Explanation via international contrast

The comparative approach in Dutch housing studies has become more prominent in recent years, fostered by the establishment of various international agencies and research networks (European Commission, European Network for Housing Research (ENHR), European Social Housing Observatory (CECODHAS). Nevertheless, theoretically structured comparative studies (Barlow and Duncan, 1994; Harloe, 1995; Kemeny, 1995; Lundqvist, 1989) have had little influence upon formal policy research. A lack of analytical and empirical depth often undermines broad comparative explanations. More descriptive, explorative studies focusing on various policy mechanisms and trends, such as Oxley and Smith (1996), Kemp (1997) and Macrone and Stephens (1995), have emerged with stronger institutional support and contributed to the policy debate.

Some authors have described Dutch housing as 'corresponding in many ways to that in Britain and France, but lags behind by a number of years' (Prak and Priemus, 1992). Implicit is the notion of a mono-linear pattern of development, with forerunners and laggards passing various milestones. This approach is also found in the work of Boelhouwer and Heijden (1992) who contrast the progress of seven European nations along certain phases of development.

Often quoted, but of little formal influence in Dutch studies, is the work of Harloe (1987, 1994, 1994a, 1995) who has long been interested in explaining the relationship between different periods of capital accumulation, via an analysis of housing history. Harloe examines the historically inherited legal status and institutional format of systems of housing provision in Europe. In particular he considers the constitutional, governmental and political systems and macro-economic policies surrounding social housing. In a number of studies he has compared the political, social, ideological status of the social sector with the private market. Drawing upon the work of Block (1987) and Gourevitch (1986), Harloe (1995) has tended to divide developments according to a number of urban development and economic phases. For each phase he contrasts the emergence, growth and decline in social housing developments in different countries in Europe (including the Netherlands) and the United States of America. He discusses a wide range of concrete political and economic factors leading to rise and decline of different forms of social housing in each country, and the recent rise of owner occupation, including: religion, social class, ideology, politics of tenure, the necessity for coalition building, major destructive events (the Second World War), labour markets and wage levels, the extent of urbanisation and the level and form of economic development.

Harloe contends, 'institutional differences derive from the particular nexus of economic, political and ideological factors which surrounded the emergence of social housing in each country' (1987: 128–129). The form of intervention, mass or residual, depends on the degree to which housing need threatens existing social and political systems. At certain times, social housing can maintain political stability, ameliorate class conflict, stimulate the economy, dampen wage demands and generate employment. In recent work, Harloe considers that interest in mass social housing has dissipated, and will only return when housing needs hold '*strategic* significance for the functioning of societies' (1995: 50).

The work of Van Weesep (1986) on condominium conversion in the Netherlands, Britain and the United States of America is a rare example of theoretically informed comparative explanatory research. Drawing upon the realist philosophy of Keat and Urry (1975) and Sayer (1982, 1984) he argues that despite similarities in the conversion process, differences in tenant protest and the legislative response in these countries have been generated by important variations in the structure and powers of government, the nature of real property law and landlord–tenant statutory relations (Van Weesep, 1986: 43). In tandem with Pickvance, Van Weesep stresses the importance of understanding the historical, cultural and political variations in comparative research (1986: 57).

Through the past decade, Boelhouwer and Heijden (1992) have developed a comparative framework to contrast developmental phases in the Dutch housing policy and test the validity of convergence theory (Donnison, 1967) with six other West European countries. Their explorative work describes the housing outcomes of different demographic, market and institutional interactions in each country. Their VROM-sponsored study partly intended to generate theories of explanation and contribute towards the convergence–divergence debate in European housing studies (see Doling, 1997: 89–91; Klienman, 1996: 169–170). Whilst the outcomes of each housing system are concisely described, their generative processes are not fully explained (cf. Boelhouwer and Heijden, 1992: 55). Nevertheless, whilst the theoretical ambitions of the project were not achieved in 1992, work still continues in an explanatory direction (Heijden, 2000).

Explanation via the civilising process (Elias, 1939)

Moving from descriptive, explorative and contrastive historical studies of entire systems of housing provision, we now move towards those investigating particular explanatory themes in Dutch housing provision: first, studies focusing upon the consumption dimensions of housing provision.

Deben's historical study (1988) of housing consumption of the period 1850 to 1969 follows the influential German sociologist Elias, to focus on the control aspects of Dutch housing provision, particularly to *civilise, discipline and supervise the working class* according to the standards of housing reformers, landlords and management professionals. Deben's explorative and descriptive study focuses upon the groups involved in civilising working-class residents, the design standards for dwellings, the house rules, the interest of landlords in managing tenants, and the wider circle of interests in housing provision and research. Three periods are investigated, divided according to the focus of behavioural change: behaviour of the family, correct use of the dwelling and dwelling environment and desirable interior decoration. Deben uses a wide range of historical, qualitative material indicating desirable living standards and rules, emanating from guides, congress reports, housing association rules, exhibitions, tenancy rules and journals. More recent work (Deben, 1993) examines the rules governing tenancy between 1850 and 1980: again focusing on the civilising intent of housing managers upon working-class residents.

There are a variety of Dutch housing studies that examine *gender relations* in housing history, with a primary focus upon consumption. Van Meijel, Renou, Van Schendelen, Veneijer and Verloo brought together a collection of perspectives on women, residential life and the built environment in 1982. Their book partly examines the economic relations of Dutch women in the home, the standardisation of dwellings and living environments, and an analysis of family and neighbourhood relations.

Other historical contributions include De Regt (1984). She examines the system of early working-class housing provision, with specific attention to its role in reinforcing certain gender relations and roles. Further, Van Moorsel (1992) provides a detailed analysis of the role of women, as promoted by the Stichting Goed Wonen between 1946 and 1968. She covers themes such as the separation of women in the home from men at work; provides a historical background to the system of housing provision (from 1850); and analyses the role of rational and phenomenological design concepts. In her book *Power and Gender in Social Movements* (1992), Verloo analyses the power relations and mechanisms influencing women's role in resident movements (action, reform and resistance) in Rotterdam and Nijmegen between 1965 and 1985 and makes critical comments on the usefulness of the 'civilizing' theory of Elias.

Explanation via pillarisation and the passive welfare state

A substantial body of research, from political science, historical sociology and political economy, has tried to explain the unique form and relations of the Dutch welfare state, which is considered to be 'much more a task of empirical research and associated theorising than a quest for statistical correlations' (Kersbergen and Becker, 1988: 497). A number of explanatory concepts have been developed in the process: the theory of pillarisation; the passivity of the Christian democratic welfare with its principles of subsidiary welfare; the corporatist model of decision making and negotiated adjustment to change.

There is only room here to mention a few key proponents, in order to provide a taste of this rich conceptual work. A special section dealing with Dutch state theory and housing is provided in section 7.4.2. Lijphart developed a theory of Dutch pilliarisation (first in English) in 1968, prompting lively debate and analysis on the peculiar nature of the Dutch state (Daalder, 1989; Schuyt and Van der Veen, 1986; Stuurman, 1983) via the

> pillarisation of its society and as a consequence of this extraordinary political influence of the church and religion. This in turn favoured the predominance of paternalist Christian – in particular catholic – social doctrine of social policy. 'Caring' for 'the weak', for the victims of unemployment or sickness, therefore has been a central political and ideological issue.
>
> (Kersbergen and Becker, 1988: 495)

Daalder (1989) emphasises the importance of political and institutional coalitions, which channelled collective savings via non-state organisations for the delivery of social goods and services.

> A pattern first seen in the equal financing of public and religious schools after 1917, was thus extended to many social sectors, including social insurance, health care and many other forms of culture and recreation. Such a process has been reinforced by the Dutch bureaucracy itself... their joint activities implied a strong upward pressure for government expenditures and services.
>
> (Daalder, 1989: 15–16)

From this vantage point, contemporary corporatisation and passivity in the Dutch welfare state have been explored (Daalder, 1989; Kersbergen, 1991; Kersbergen and Becker, 1988; Kersbergen and Verbeek, 1997; Therborn, 1989). It is considered that de-pillarisation and declining economic prospects are the causal mechanisms eroding paternalism and reshaping welfare politics today (Kersbergen and Becker, 1988: 496). In their empirical study of different sectors of the Dutch welfare state, Visser and Hemerijck (1997) examined dynamic forms of corporatism defining wage policy (regained), social security (unrestrained) and labour market policies (truncated) over the past 15 years. They argue that corporatist transformation within different sectors of policy can be explained in terms of their differing levels of societal support and institutional integration (Visser and Hemerijck, 1997: 183). Whilst this conceptualisation is interesting it remains largely disconnected from empirical research on the housing sector.

Salet (1999, 1994, 1987) is one of a few urban sociologists to examine recent shifts in housing policy, with explicit reference to the peculiar Dutch state and unique structure of housing provision. In brief, he characterises the Dutch welfare state as comprising interdependent government and non-government organisations, which have emerged from religious and ideological social pillars of Dutch society in the early twentieth century. Salet (1999) applies *an institutional approach to examine regime shifts in Dutch housing policy* since the 1980s. He highlights the private nature of Dutch social housing providers, which nevertheless function in a highly regulated environment. This relationship has sheltered housing providers from both the demands of consumers and competition from alternative providers. Of specific interest is Salet's interpretation of recent changes in the various institutions, norms and rules governing housing policy, resulting in a move away from direct intervention towards a new balance in public–private relations that places more emphasis on self-regulation and entrepreneurship. With these changes, Dutch social housing has emerged as a more resilient sector when compared with other European countries. However, social policies promoting affordability and social integration may become more difficult to sustain.

Political economy has not dominated explanations in Dutch housing history, as is the case in Australia. However, there are a number of studies and the work by Nycolaas (1974) provides an early example. He places the history of housing and related policy within the dynamic process of capital formation, labour relations, rent politics and economic crises from the mid-nineteenth century to the 1970s. Nycolaas argues that governments have successively failed to withdraw support from the financial relations of production and consumption, preventing so called normal market relations from ever taking place. Further, the involvement of the central government in housing production was significant, via various incentives, grants and contributions, to ensure a flow of investment in the housing sector. During periods of economic recovery, government support for the housing sector diminished, as part of the drive to achieve 'normal' market relations.

Difference and change at the local and regional level

Moving from broad theories explaining the Dutch nation state, a number of enlightening studies focus on uneven development, examining the underlying *social structures that have generated difference and change at the local and regional level*. The following research demonstrates that such 'small-scale' research can provide theoretically rigorous and spatially sensitive explanations for different housing and urban forms.

Jurriens (1981) examines the role housing organisations played in producing a system of social control amongst mine workers in the Southern province of Limburg. Local Catholic patricians played a moderating role, establishing housing associations which reinforced solidarity between the church and industry that were able to exert effective control over the social lives and habits of mine workers. The associations united Christian principles with the achievement of adequate housing, reinforced by the authoritarian and hierarchical position of the priest and industrial power of mine management. Their housing policies and programmes prevented concentrations of workers in cities from forming a large organised proletariat, by isolating them into small colonies and retaining the familiar village form.

Whilst not exclusively focusing on housing per se, Terhorst and Van de Ven (1997) postulate and provide evidence for the causal mechanisms generating divergence and change in the urban 'trajectories' of Amsterdam and Brussels. Their theory rests on the different definitions and interaction of specific rules of the state: territorial, fiscal and franchise over time and space, with particular emphasis on the property rights governing the collective or private character of urban development. The authors examine consecutive regimes, from the eighteenth to the twentieth century, comparing, amongst other themes, the structure of housing provision in each city. Commodified and privatised housing in sprawling and fragmented Brussels is contrasted with collectively organised social housing in consolidated Amsterdam. Abstracting from extensive concrete research, Terhorst and Van de Ven argue that divergence is plausibly explained by the cumulative effect of the different packaging of rules governing property rights that regulate public access to social and material goods.

7.3.2   A critical evaluation of explanatory progress

The earlier review highlights the very different pathways to various explanations of Dutch housing history. It has been argued earlier that empiricism and muted positivism currently dominate Dutch housing studies. Further, there is little dialogue or debate between the different disciplines examining housing provision. Historical explanations have been conceptually and thematically fragmented, applying very different units of analysis, from ideological categories to social pillars, social class to demographic cohorts. Consequently, postulated explanations are diverse and include: a response of housing shortages; need to generate employment; lack of private capital; threat of social unrest; inadequacy of private philanthropy; dominance of certain professions; ideology of government coalitions; rational preference of households; demands of political constituencies; weakness of the socialist movement; performance of associations and proactive local government involvement.

Amongst these diverse factors are several overarching explanations that permeate historical housing studies. Most common is the idea of state-led trigger response to the prolonged shortage of housing, especially after the Second World War (Boelhouwer *et al.*, 1990) and, second, the constant struggle for 'normal' market relations (Nycolaas, 1974; Schaar, 1998) in 'abnormal' market conditions. Third, the form of provision, via non-profit housing associations, is often attributed to the strongly pillarised nature of Dutch society (Murie and Priemus, 1994; Terhorst and Van de Ven, 1997), the erosion of which is undermining the traditional power blocks engaged in welfare provision (Salet, 1999). A number of policy watersheds are regularly identified: the Great Depression, the Second World War, the monetary crisis and oil price shocks followed by the fiscally austere climate of the 1980s. Whilst these events may indeed be important, they are common to many western countries. Indeed, more explicit attention may pin down their actual role in defining the unique Dutch housing solution.

Yet, by far the most prominent mode of explanation in Dutch housing studies is not explanation at all, but normative description, grounded in the traditions of empiricism and pragmatism. Research that models and predicts the operation of regulatory instruments, rather than provide a critical explanation of them, sits comfortably in the main stream. Yet, a number of assumptions remain unchallenged in this 'objective' empirical work, particularly the equilibrium thesis that casts the central state in a normative and corrective economic role and the emphasis upon national aggregates that hide regional and local variations in housing provision.

With few exceptions international sociological debates concerning urban and housing phenomena have only been given marginal attention (cf. convergence, state theory, structure/agency, locality studies, regulation theory and postmodernist critique) and the causal mechanisms underlying housing transformation are buried beneath policy debate or obscured by empiricism.

7.3.3   A possible explanation for progress in Dutch housing studies

As outlined earlier, the dominant field of housing studies in the Netherlands differs markedly from its Anglo-European counterpart. The empirical, contrastive and predictive modes of explanation have dominated Dutch housing studies for the past 25 years. Why is this so? The following points provide a partial explanation.

First, housing is widely perceived as a 'technical' rather than a 'scientific' field of study. From its earliest beginnings, the motivation for the Dutch housing solution of social housing provision was driven by a number of professions in the civic arena, namely medicine, engineering, architecture and social work. Within academia, alongside engineering and architecture, housing emerged as a self-contained field (such as health, education and transportation), to professionalise the large housing association sector. Second, via key research institutions, set apart from the social sciences, Dutch housing research has taken a more pragmatic course, responding to the housing shortage and later, the demands of urban renewal and housing choice. Independent from European intellectual movements, such housing studies have given prominence to the functional concerns of the state and become firmly embedded in policy studies. Thus, analysis tends to focus upon various government subsidies and other forms of intervention, which maintain stable rates of supply and minimise risks for the private housing market. Even international research maintains a strong policy outcome focus, perhaps neglecting the driving forces that have shaped distinctly different forms of housing provision across Europe. The generative mechanism may be the power-sharing model of corporatist governance that exists between academia, housing providers and the central state facilitating a more constructive, consensual dialogue in the policy-making process. Senior researchers double as policy advisors and the roles are often interchanged.

On the other hand the Dutch social sciences (economics, sociology, political science and geography) have, to some degree, ignored housing as a field of study for a range of reasons. They have viewed housing as an object of study that *belongs* to the realm of policy research. From this perspective, the Dutch system of social housing was merely considered as an aberration of market forces, a product of government policy and electoral politics. Only a few researchers perceived the Dutch housing solution to be embedded in and contributing towards the emergent social relations and power structures of Dutch society.

Thus, explanation for this unique form of provision, established for more than 100 years, has not benefited from lively theoretical debate and a critical approach to housing studies has barely emerged.

7.4 Postulating a model of causality in Dutch housing provision

From a realist ontological vantage point, it is considered that more attention is required to *tease the generative processes from their actual outcomes and events*, thus abstracting the causal mechanisms from the substantial, existing body of descriptive, historical work.

Causal mechanisms are postulated to exist in the packaging of key relations of housing provision, which operate under dynamic contingent conditions. These relations concern the geo-historical definition of the property relations influencing housing development, investment and savings mechanisms, and welfare and labour relations influencing capacity to pay for housing services, as contended in Chapter 5. How these relations are contingently defined and packaged (accidentally or intentionally) is considered to be of generative significance in promoting specific housing solutions.

Yet housing provision is a long-term, cumulative and path-dependent process, which is embedded in the structures of society (including state and market structures) and subject to unpredictable contingent conditions. Change is rarely attributable to single causes and the relationship between cause and effect rarely straightforward, immediate or observable. Changes take time to mediate the system of provision, which comprises many different related components subject to influences outside the housing system itself.

Thus any explanatory study must look far back into history, to examine the various phases in housing development and abstract both the necessary and contingent relations. For this reason this study examines aspects of housing provision prior to the development of the Dutch housing solution (from the mid-nineteenth century) to the present day. A number of phases within this long trajectory have been defined to enable contrastive analysis between different 'packages' of key relations in their contingent context. These phases are outlined in section 7.4.1 and briefly illustrated by Figure 7.1. Further, specific attention is given to the unique and dynamic nature of the Dutch state with its roots in pillarisation, corporatism and a Christian Democratic subsidiary welfare state, and a discussion of these concepts consequently takes place in section 7.4.2.

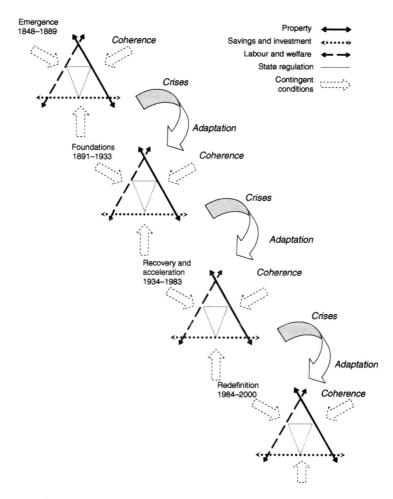

Figure 7.1 Phases in the Dutch housing solution: adaptation, coherence and crisis.

7.4.1 Defining periods for analysis

Specific to the case, it is contended that a number of phases can be derived from the shifting of contingently defined relations of housing provision. *Each phase comprises several periods: adaptation, coherence and crises.* Coherence can be said to occur when key property, investment and savings, and labour and welfare relations sustain, alongside contingent conditions, a succinct and relatively stable form of provision. Given the conflict-ridden and crises-prone nature of capitalism, it is easy to imagine that a neat functional fit, between a particular form of housing provision and the broader political economy, may only exist for short periods. Thus periods of coherence are followed by periods of crisis, which may in turn lead to a period of adaptation. Adaptation enables production to reestablish and is evident via the initiation of new practices, ideas and institutions. Adaptation may precede another, albeit temporary period of coherence. Based on this definition, the following division of Dutch housing history is proposed.

First phase: laissez-faire liberalism in crisis, 1848–1889

We cannot begin to understand the Dutch housing solution by merely examining founding legislation or periods of high production. Given the path dependency of any housing history, we must look to the social relations and conditions from which the solution has emerged. For this reason, an appreciation of the nineteenth-century conditions of constrained development under laissez-faire capitalism in an industrialising economy is essential alongside an understanding of the pre-industrial nature of Dutch urban political economy.

Thus, the first phase for examination begins in the mid-nineteenth century. This is characterised by highly commodified capitalist relations of housing provision in urban areas, involving the exploitation of land, construction and letting of dwellings in a time of economic restructuring (from agrarian and mercantile to industrial economy). The efficacy of economic liberalism is questioned under conditions of severe land and housing market scarcity, generated by constraints on city expansion, private ownership of land and dwellings and mass urban migration, which resulted in speculation, low building standards, overcrowding and exorbitant rents.

The laws of laissez-faire liberalism and sanctity of private property rights, once upheld by religious ethics and guarded by the landed gentry, were gradually undermined by various initiatives in the civic and industrial sectors. Expanded electoral franchise and unionisation of industrial workers provided vehicles and voices for reform. New players challenged the existing monopoly capitalists, who had controlled municipal chambers, and fed a growing movement to ameliorate the worst excesses of the housing crises.

Second phase: foundations for change in a turbulent context, 1891–1933

The foundations of the Dutch housing solution emerged following a period of housing crises, civic protest and a broad-based movement for reform in cities but did not produce significant numbers of social houses nor contribute greatly to production.

Nevertheless, an important building block was the redefinition of public property rights, enabling the municipalities to intervene (expropriate, designate land use and dispose) amongst dispersed private land owners operating in a highly commodified land market and dispose of suitably developed land to private entrepreneurs for the expansion and renewal of their cities. Such extensive property rights were legitimate in a climate of urban dilapidation, crisis in capital accumulation and threatening health and social conditions. Municipal land development removed the most risky phase of development from the hands of the private sector and increased the certainty of development outcomes. The establishment of municipal land companies absorbed the risks associated with land development and avoided the delays, uncertainty and non-cooperation of speculative private development.

The dearth of private investment was to be addressed by the provision of central government loans and various subsidies to approved non-profit associations and municipal housing companies. Government loans were set at market rates for a 50-year term. Such long loan terms were preferred by the private sector: being secured by the government delivered a lower interest rate and the term was 20 years longer. With the standardisation and enforcement of building standards, jerry building was outlawed and thus a further risk to long-term housing investment was minimised. Building standards ensured that dwellings constructed would generate rents throughout the 50-year term of the mortgage.

Approved housing associations were perceived as legitimate beneficiaries of favourable land and capital provisions, as they were willing to develop and firmly manage affordable housing for low-income workers and their families to reproduce a healthy, harmonious, wage competitive labour force. These organisations pioneered the pillarised empires of welfare provision and social control, emerging from a divided but tolerant multi-faith constituency. Calvinist opposition to subsidising private enterprise was whittled away by establishing social tasks for approved recipients (private housing associations), and channelling surpluses to a 'deserving' cause.

Only in extreme economic conditions did these measures prove insufficient to continue high levels of housing production. These conditions persisted until a global economic crisis drastically curtailed the flow of private investment into many sectors of the Dutch economy, including housing construction. With interest rates rising and governments demanding the repayment of earlier subsidies, social housing associations were fast approaching financial ruin and various measures were being called for to adapt to the new economic conditions.

Third phase: recovery and acceleration of the Dutch solution 1934–1983

This phase begins with a period of adaptation and modification. To prevent insolvency of associations, the Dutch government ensured the financial continuity of associations by providing advances to pay interest on government loans. Private investment in the housing sector continued to fall away and was only later secured by central government subsidy.

Wartime and German occupation introduced an entirely new set of political, economic and housing conditions. The construction sector is resuscitated by the reemergence of social housing production: this time with governments commissioning the development of large social housing estates via municipal housing corporations and associations. In 1947, the central government regulates to force associations to manage their own finances more closely and establish emergency reserves to be managed by municipalities, giving the latter substantial control over new investments.

Cities such as Amsterdam and Rotterdam, with powerful municipal housing companies and a growing constituency of social renters, lobbied to increase their share of rental production. During this period, the public property rights and development capacities of municipalities[2] were fully exploited, leading to the redevelopment of large inner city areas and creation of new suburbs. New production techniques were employed to minimise labour costs, maximise output and address overt demand. From these subsidised and increasingly regulated producer relations emerged a sizeable and moderately well-off constituency that came to enjoy affordable and secure tenancy. During this period, the Dutch social housing solution has reached its zenith.

Inevitably, inflation increased building costs, which demanded higher rents, exploitation or subject subsidies. Whilst attempts to tax wealthy tenants in low rental dwellings failed, new financing mechanisms were introduced, such as the Dynamic Cost priced method to curtail government outlays and spread them out over a longer period. Yet the costs of this 'ideal' system radically escalated during unanticipated periods of rapidly declining inflation.

By the end of this phase, government budgets and continuing subsidy mechanisms came under increasing scrutiny. Fraudulent activities by some associations reduced political support for the associations. Dynamic methods of subsidy and various other schemes are presented as costly and open ended in an austere financial climate favouring deregulation. This time the reformers were not calling for a traditional solution to the growing housing crises, but rather radical adaptation to save it.

*Fourth phase: securing 'independent' relations for land
development, finance and individualisation, 1984–2000*

In the fourth, most recent phase radical changes have been introduced, shifting the political and financial risks away from governments towards social housing providers, banks and tenants. Government lending for social housing has all but ceased. Object subsidies have sharply declined. Housing associations must finance their production directly via the capital market. Further, they must generate profits and consume reserves 'internally' to be able to build non-profit social housing.

To attract private investment into housing production, the central government announced new building locations, inviting and providing more certainty to non-government for profit players in the land market. This inadvertently led to speculation and escalating land prices, weakening municipal control in co-operative development negotiations. Further, increasing rents, favourable tax incentives and generous access to credit enticed large numbers of moderate-income households away from the 'protective' fold of social rental, into home ownership for the first time in Dutch housing history.

Today the housing-related welfare of many Dutch households is in the hands of contribution-based social insurance, individual rent subsidies and more liberalised labour, mortgage, land and housing markets. This new period of coherence is far from the protective, sometimes exploitative, constraints of producer and tenancy politics. In this context, new relations of housing provision have emerged, with the housing, employment and mortgage markets playing an increasing and inter-dependent role in the individualisation of risk and wealth in Dutch society. Whilst need is strong, housing production has slowed considerably in both the ownership and social housing sectors. In an economy approaching recession, some housing commentators suggest we are resting on the cusp of yet another crises, this time affecting indebted homeowners dependent on two incomes.

7.4.2 Theorising the role of the state in the Dutch housing solution

Scarce research has been undertaken in Dutch housing studies that specifically theorises the role of the state in housing provision (with the exception of those authors mentioned in section 7.3.1, Jurriens, 1981; Nycolaas, 1974; Salet, 1999, 1994; Terhorst and Van de Ven, 1997, who go far beyond policy research). For this reason, it is worth returning to explanations of the Dutch state in general, which have emphasised the importance of pillarisation in the development of welfare services in this country. As with many other aspects of social life, including education, health and the media, the effect of pillarisation on the architecture of housing provision from the early twentieth century has been profound.

Stuurman (1983) critically applies and revises Lijphart's (1968) *theory of pillarisation* and it's influence on the development of the Dutch welfare state from 1750–1920. He outlines the developments in historical materialist terms, from an oligarchic–mercantile–protestant and aristocratic Republic to the modern Dutch welfare state. This shift is explained as a process of transformation across existing social, economic and political structures through changing modes of capital accumulation, forced by modern industrial capitalism. Class and sexual struggle are just two of many factors influencing the development of the modern Dutch state and social structure.

Importantly, twentieth-century conflicts were filtered through the pillars of Dutch society: Protestant, Catholic, Socialist and Liberal. Between 1900 and 1965, these pillars provided a mechanism of social control, identity and pacification and this division stymied the incursion of a unified socialist doctrine. Nevertheless, it was also an unseen and unintended consequence of different socio-political conflicts between liberals and conservatives, workers and capital, men and women, which after 1920 gave the Netherlands political and social stability and a liberal–confessional state.

Swedish policy scientist Göran Therborn (1989) is one of few international researchers to recognise the specific form of *welfare provision under the pillarised Dutch state*. He charts the relationship between the state, labour movement and church from 1830, and the origins of welfare pillarisation through various struggles including the financing of denominational schools, divisions in the trade union movement and development of confessional parties. According to Therborn, this institutional groundwork led to the emergence of the subsidiary welfare state and the passive role of both the labour movement and the state in direct welfare provision (1989: 106).

Whilst Lijpardt, Stuurman and Therborn have little to say about housing policy, their analysis can contribute much to our understanding of the pillarised origins of housing associations and why Catholic, Protestant and later socialist housing associations came into being with privileged access to government loans for the construction of rental housing.

Yet the grip of pillarisation has weakened since the mid-1960s and thus, we need other theories based on more recent shifts in history to progress our understanding of relations between the state and the Dutch housing solution. Recently, both empirical and theoretical research on this topic have flourished in the field of political science. With Uwe Becker (1988), Esping Anderson (1992) and Verbeek (1997), political scientist Kees Van Kersbergen has developed an approach from a substantial body of concrete research and abstraction. He argues that Christian democracy has led to the development of a *passive welfare state*, lacking the explicit commitment to collective services and full employment that tends to characterise more social democratic welfare states (1992: 193). Christian democracy depends on market forces to create employment and distribute income. The state merely redistributes the benefits, reinforcing traditional notions of family, social harmony and the principle of subsidiarity in welfare participation.

Recently (1997: 258), Kersbergen, with Hemerijk, has attempted to explain recent reforms in the Dutch welfare state from the perspective of *contingent conditions and institutional legacies* that have enabled policy makers to alter the 'rules of the game' during the 1980s and 1990s. They argue that researchers must be sensitive to change, rather than hold on persistently to notions of path dependency, lock-in and electoral hazard (263). Accordingly, the complex dialectic between corporatist-negotiated adjustment and welfare reform can best be understood

> by studying the interaction between the rules of the game of social policy-making (institutions); the characteristics of particular social programmes (policies); and the political systems (politics).
>
> (1997: 259)

Of course, many theories are coloured by the stable from which they come. The theories mentioned earlier emanate from the discipline of political science. Towards a more inter-disciplinary perspective, the work of economic and political geographers Terhorst and Van de Ven (1997, 1995) is of special interest and relevance. The authors emphasise the distinctiveness of the Dutch state, which exists in a very open economy dominated by trade, transport and agriculture, where the central state is highly dependent on *national* institutions to promote growth and distribution (pension funds, housing associations). For this reason, the fiscal relationship between central and local governments is extremely centralised, through which particular forms of housing and urban form can be promoted via various laws, policies, programmes and schemes.

In 1997, Terhorst and Van de Ven proposed a more complex and integrated notion of a dynamic state structure to explain divergence and change in urban and housing outcomes between the eighteenth and twentieth century. In abstract terms, the state consists of territorial, tax and electoral rules that vary over space and time to influence urban development outcomes. To test their claim, they examined a number of phases in Amsterdam's history since 1830, during which the state took on a contrasting character, defined by the interrelations of the contingently defined state structures. The researchers presented an immensely detailed case study of various regimes and the crises that divided them, to illustrate the influence of the changing structure of the state upon Amsterdam's development. A much-reduced version of their findings is provided in Table 7.3. The table, although concise, betrays the dynamism of periods of coherence and crises it depicts.

To conclude, a number of ideas and concepts developed in state theory – outside housing studies – provide fruitful insights towards an understanding of the state's role in housing in the Netherlands. These include theories of pillarisation, the passive corporatist welfare state and the nature of relations between the national economy and the local and central state. These theories provide clues for the different role the Dutch state plays in housing, with regards to land development, the channelling of individual and collective savings and the relationship between wages and housing costs. Further, the important role of the larger Dutch municipalities such as Amsterdam and Rotterdam in tandem with the central state in promoting the land lease system and municipal social housing is of particular relevance.

Both Terhorst and Van de Ven (1997) and Australian housing researcher Dalton (1999) are concerned with the dynamic reconfiguration of the state when defining different phases in housing history, yet differ markedly in terms of their definition of the state and its causal role in housing provision (see Dalton, 1999: 86 and Chapter 6, Table 6.3). This is not only due to the different nature of the state relations in the Netherlands and Australia, but also to differing notions of causal relations underpinning state action. A sharp 'local' contrast can be made between Terhorst and Van de Ven's rules of the state and the state-centred work of planning theorists Faludi and Van der Valk (1994). The latter emphasise the role and position of planning professionals in chains of decision making affecting policy formation, within a dominant self-preserving doctrine. In contrast, Terhorst and Van de Ven perceive the state as being embedded in the power structure of the social relations of society, and reflected in its electoral, fiscal and territorial rules. From this perspective, they place more emphasis on relevant influences shaping the very nature of the state in order to understand its role in urban and housing development.

7.5 Analysis and contrast of different phases in the Dutch housing solution

Rather than a housing policy centred basis for periodisation, this analysis divides housing history according to shifts in the *core features of the housing solution* as

Table 7.3 Actual rules of the local state influencing Amsterdam's urban development, 1830–1997 (distilled from Terhorst and Van de Ven, 1997)

Regime	Territorial structure	Tax rules	Electoral rights	Urban outcomes
Until 1865	Uncertain division of private and public rights, no basic road plan and limited potential for expansion	Regressive, benefiting landed gentry, uncertain benefits from costly new development	Landed gentry and commercial interests	Development piecemeal, concentrated within defence walls, overcrowding
1866–1914	Territorial expansion by mergers and annexation, municipal sale of cheap peripheral land promotes conditional expansion, development of land lease system	Introduction of an income tax, special central government grants, private financing of infrastructure, establishment of housing associations	Limited franchise extended to middle-class men	Growing immigrant working class, speculative building, inadequate infrastructure and municipal-planned housing development
1918–1978	Initial expansion then consolidated Amsterdam, urban development on municipal-owned land	Progressive income tax, special grants to finance local services channeled via social pillars	Universal suffrage for men and women over certain age	Construction of subsidised dwellings at below market price for the working class, pillarised social services
1978 – pause or prelude?	Boundaries almost static, subdivided in districts	Fiscal crisis, private investment sought, districts have no tax raising powers	Universal suffrage, territory subdivided into districts with own representatives	Deconcentration of population, attack on social housing role, stimulation of owner-occupation

identified in sections 7.3 and 7.4. This division *follows the dynamics of change, from adaptation and coherence to crisis* and broadens the focus to include non-policy influences affecting production, exchange and consumption. For this reason, there will always be debate over the precise division of the chosen periods. When did adaptation actually begin? When did crisis lead to an end of coherence? I welcome this debate, but stress that the basis for definition is *changes in key relationships* influencing housing provision, and these are not directly reflected in the ebb and flow of housing outcomes or specific events. Thus the Depression, post-war recovery and the golden age of Dutch housing provision have not been designated as distinct or complete phases.

The goal is to reach an empirically plausible explanation for the Dutch 'solution' of compact, social rented housing as a prominent but receding feature of housing provision in the twentieth century. To summarise, the main features of the proposed explanatory model are strategic historical analyses, contrasting different phases in the development of the housing solution and examining the process of adaptation, coherence and crisis, with attention to the contingent definition of property, savings and investment, and labour and welfare relations. Moving forward with this proposed approach, the following questions help to focus on analysis in each phase as proposed in section 7.4.1:

- How were the *property relations* contingently defined during each phase of development in Dutch housing provision? How did this definition influence the *development of land* for housing?
- How were the *savings and investment relations* contingently defined during each phase of development in Dutch housing provision? How did this definition influence *investment and production* of dwellings?
- How were the *labour and welfare relations* contingently defined during each phase of development in Dutch housing provision? How did this definition influence the *consumption* of housing?
- How did property, savings and investment, and labour and welfare relations *interact* with each other and endogenous factors in each phase to influence the *mode of housing provision*?

The following sub-sections analyse four cumulative phases in Dutch housing history, illustrating the given postulates, which have cumulatively contributed towards the development of the Dutch housing solution.

7.5.1　Housing relations under conditions of economic liberalism, 1848–1889

Outline of key events and housing outcomes

The last half of the nineteenth century provided an important pretext for the development of the Dutch housing solution. Industrialisation and economic growth offered the prospect of work to many in the depressed agricultural sector.

This new mode of accumulation required a different set of urban conditions including the expansion of industrial and residential areas and the development of related infrastructure such as roads and canals.

There were a variety of housing outcomes produced during this period, namely, petty landlordism (renting of single rooms in a larger dwelling), speculative market rental housing, philanthropic rental housing, non-profit ownership and rental dwellings provided by workers associations, and a small number of paternalistic housing initiatives undertaken by industrialists.

Towards the end of a period of urban-based economic growth, a growing professional and industrial elite and an increasingly organised working class were in conflict with the established landed gentry and merchants who controlled municipal chambers. Uncoordinated private land ownership and speculative investment were incapable of providing adequate housing at a reasonable cost, threatening not only people's health and reproductive labour conditions but also city growth, curtailing efforts to harness the new industrial economy.

Economic liberalism and entrenched land and development interests could not ameliorate the threatening health and housing conditions of the new urban working class. In the last quarter of the nineteenth century the agricultural depression pushed many labourers to the cities in search of paid work and housing conditions reached a crisis point.

The following table provides a selection of key events during this period.

Late industrialisation attracts rural workers to cities	1850s
Slow city migration, insufficient housing, overcrowding and poor health and living conditions amongst productive workforce	1850s–
Few industrialists build housing for their workforce	1850–
First mortgage banks promote investment in housing, time of speculation and jerry building	1860s
Fiscal reforms reducing reliance on local tax base	1865, 1897
Debate over the development of agricultural land and the role of municipalities in infrastructure	1873
Law permitting development of land beyond city walls	1874
Agricultural depression, massive inflow of labourers to cities	1878–1895
Free unions possible for the first time	1886

Examples of coherent relations, contingently defined during the period of emergence

CONTINGENTLY DEFINED PROPERTY RELATIONS

With the threat of city invaders long gone and their function as tax barriers[3] diluted by central government fiscal reforms, the walls and moats that surrounded newly industrialising cities became a tight girdle constraining development during the new era of industrialisation. The residents of walled cities were literally becoming hemmed in, forced to reside in cellars, back to back and other infill dwellings, and single rooms subdivided from once larger dwellings (Nycolaas, 1974: 16). It became widely accepted that claustrophobic and damp living conditions exacerbated the relatively high infant mortality and short life expectancy of city dwellers in Holland, Zeeland and Utrecht (Beusekom, 1955: 23).

In cities such as Amsterdam, the influx of job seekers only exacerbated overcrowding, worsening the threat to health and indeed property values. Infill development consumed productive gardens and other available spaces. After 1865 development jumped the defence walls and moat surrounding the city. Whilst the elite hankered for more exclusive and luxurious living quarters, the prospect of higher-density housing development was more lucrative for developers and landlords.[4] Speculators turned to even higher-density developments for their profits, yet their cost-cutting and jerry building techniques undermined the quality of dwellings.

In 1874 the central government enacted a law permitting the destruction of city walls.[5] Municipal mergers and annexations were also permitted, allowing the expansion of formerly constrained and overcrowded cities. Yet local authorities were at first reluctant to engage in an active land policy and in particular, to encroach upon existing private property. Many were still controlled by the established landed gentry; electoral reforms were yet to come. Thus, by the 1890s many of the problems of poor development standards and dilapidation remained. Only a small number of larger cities asserted (albeit weakly) their authority, stipulating required street plans and building envelopes. Amsterdam chose to pursue an active land banking policy, purchasing strips of agricultural land on the periphery of the city and using its own land holdings to negotiate standards and conditions with building developers. However, the implementation of planning aspirations relied upon the fickle construction industry.

The cost of infrastructure provision, diffuse land ownership and the structure of the municipal tax base was a major impediment to the development of land around cities. A national campaign to permit the forced reclamation of private land and development of infrastructure by municipalities, and ensure more spacious streets, plains and parks, was fought in 1882 (Van Beusekom, 1955: 28–29). The local tax burden was significantly reduced by fiscal centralisation, which allocated revenue on a per capita basis, rather than property values.

CONTINGENTLY DEFINED SAVINGS AND INVESTMENT RELATIONS

By the mid-nineteenth century, Dutch savings and institutional investments favoured land, mortgage and foreign bond investments. These were channelled by financial practices arising from years of Napoleonic rule in the previous century. As capital shifted from the depressed agricultural sector during the mid-nineteenth century, it flowed into mortgages to support the speculative housing market in various cities.

Catering to these investors, a number of mortgage banks were established in the 1860s and readily issued 30-year mortgages at market interest rates, promoting lucrative speculation and attracting investors from a range of non-housing backgrounds. As credit flowed into a tight land and housing market, urban land prices soared and exorbitant rents were demanded from tenants in the poorest quality dwellings (Searing, 1971). In the major cities, investors maximised profits from expensive land by commissioning the construction of high-density, low-quality buildings known as *revolutiebouw* (Nycolaas, 1974: 23–24). These buildings were substantial, filling entire parcels of land and up to six storeys high. Apartments were let at exorbitant market rents in a tight housing market (Grinburg, 1982: 21–22).

As an alternative to these exploitative relations of private tenancy, some workers established building co-operatives during the 1860s and 1870s, to generate savings and channel them into loans for home purchase. Yet as the cost of ownership relative to savings became prohibitive, the goal was switched to the development of rental co-operatives for members (Nycolaas, 1974: 23).

After 1870, investment in housing declined as more secure and profitable investments could be made elsewhere. This led to a serious shortage of capital in the rental housing sector, which further exacerbated overcrowding and dilapidation. Escalating housing demand, with the influx of former agricultural workers, was almost totally unanswered, leading to extreme overcrowding and poor housing conditions.

Whilst economic liberalism was under question, a socialist alternative did not emerge. Typical initiatives to address the housing issue embraced capitalist relations of ownership, production and consumption. Following the example of English housing activist and social reformer Octavia Hill, a small number of wealthy citizens invested capital for a modest return, to finance rental housing for workers. Such projects must be economically viable, with tenants paying sufficient rent to permit a modest return on investment. Such relations of consumption were considered to be in the best interests of the tenants, who would learn the discipline of work and respect the value of good housing. Consequently, the very poor and job seekers could not benefit from such schemes. Indeed, workers were to be civilised, improved and managed and the unemployed were perceived as damaging elements (Deben, 1993; Nycolaas, 1974: 20–24).

The results of philanthropy were limited and on a small scale. Further, a small number of industrialists experimented with ideal workers communities. Again this investment was totally inadequate to meet the broad demand for workers housing.

CONTINGENTLY DEFINED LABOUR AND WELFARE RELATIONS

Prior to mass industrialisation during the 1850s, for many the home was a place of work – for the whole family. Without modern industrial techniques, hundreds of families worked for a distant overseer at the kitchen table or on home looms. With their small incomes, they bought their daily provisions from the overseer's supplies. In addition to childcare and labour-intensive domestic duties, it was also common for women to undertake additional paid work in the home: processing prawns, peas, beans, coffee, cigars and needle work. Women were in demand as their wages were lower than for men (Meijel *et al.*, 1982). These precarious and exploitative labour and tenure conditions left little or no capacity for saving, nor any means to improve material conditions.

The quality of the workplace, often still the home, and its effect on productivity was an issue of primarily economic and health concern. Medical practitioners expressed this concern, as well as architects and engineers who called for improved urban design. In 1851 municipalities gained the right to make laws in the interest of public health and order (Gemeentewet). In 1853 the Royal Institute for Engineers (of which King Willem III was amongst the board members) promoted the adoption of standards for dwellings, specifying certain densities, street widths, physical infrastructure, standards for construction techniques, which could promote better light and air circulation. Yet without defining the means of implementation, these standards were of no immediate significance. Further, design standards of new dwellings were of little relevance to those in existing hovels unable to afford better housing.

Late industrialisation brought not only economic restructuring, but enabled the growth of the workers movement, which subsequently fuelled efforts to improve housing and tenure conditions. As mentioned earlier, during the 1870s a small number of industrialists constructed paternalistic communities, based on the ideal that a healthy and peaceful living environment would promote a more productive, managed workforce (Meijel *et al.*, 1982).

Many families rented single rooms, let from owners of larger dwellings and land-lords in the rapidly constructed, low-quality, speculative sector. Extreme scarcity of housing and agricultural decline ensured a supply of desperate tenants, with little choice but to pay a large proportion of their new wages in rent or double up in small apartments, rooms and cellars. Constrained urban expansion compounded exploita-tive tenure relations and played a significant role in the appalling housing conditions of the new urban worker. During this period, housing the poor, sick and unemployed lay precariously in the hands of small petty landlords reliant on rents for their own household income and old age security[6], and larger landlords dependent on mortgage capital. Beyond housing, there were a small number of paternalistic philanthropic institutions providing very basic shelter and care for the sick.

Finally, overcrowding in compact cities fostered diseases transmitted via air and water, to which no social class was immune. It became common knowledge that health conditions in the Netherlands were worse than elsewhere in Europe (Van Beusekom, 1955: 23). The threat of sickness was real and widespread. Elites demanded public intervention for protection. Lobbying for change were numerous public interest and professional associations such as medical practitioners, engineers and architects, arguing for a greater role of governments in securing better living conditions.[7] This message was strengthened by strikes and social unrest during the years 1889–1890.

Synthesising key relations in their contingent context

Towards abstraction of the key causal mechanisms underlying change in forms of housing provision, Figure 7.2 outlines the mode of capital accumulation under conditions of economic liberalism, pinpointing areas of crises.[8] This mode of provision produced high-density, low-quality market rental housing generating

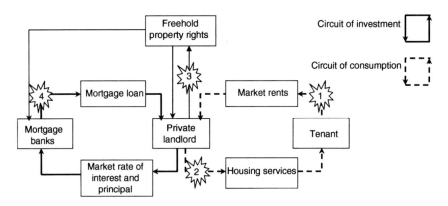

Figure 7.2 Abstraction of the flow of capital during economic liberalism (1848–1889) and
relations subject to crises.

profits for land developers, building constructors and rental income for petty and
larger landlords. It synthesises particular, contingently defined social relations
concerning property rights, investment and savings, and labour and welfare.
Contingent conditions sustaining this mode of capital accumulation included
freehold property rights providing collateral for *mortgage loans*, availability of
30-year fixed rate loans, scarcity of housing supply and a *strong demand from
immigrant families*. Under conditions of market scarcity, rents escalated. Tenants
must either pay or face eviction, and with strong migration from agricultural areas
an evicted tenant was easily replaced.

A number of crises affecting key social relations sustaining this circuit of
investment and consumption undermined the coherence of this mode of accumulation. First, the labour *relations* affecting the consumption of housing (1) were
disrupted by the *limited capacity of tenants to pay high rents*. Low-skilled, low-
paid workers in over supply were not in a labour market position to demand
higher wages and thus pay higher rents. Second, the extraction of profits under a
low-rent regime was only possible via the delivery of low-quality housing
services. Yet quality was so low that *poor housing conditions* contributed towards
major health problems, *affecting a range of social classes* (2). Third, constraints
upon urban expansion led to a *scarcity of available land* under commodified
conditions, and thus very high prices. This influenced the nature of housing
developed: high-yield, high-density rental housing. As prices rose and sites
diminished, profits from the exploitation of rental housing became far less
certain (3). Finally, there was *no steady flow of capital* under these changing
economic conditions; *investment shifts away* from mortgage investment in rental
property, towards other more lucrative and less risky ventures (4).

During this phase, *the local state*, dominated by an oligarchy of landed gentry,
merchants and industrial elite, was unable to address the new *demands of
industrialisation* for urban expansion and cheap workers' housing. Whilst some

speculators made enormous profits from the exploitation of land and buildings, immigration and declining housing investment led to a much *broader housing crisis*, and its consequences touched a range of social classes living 'cheek by jowl'.

7.5.2   The first unsteady foundations of the Dutch solution: 1890–1933

Outline of events and housing outcomes

In this subsequent phase, 1890–1933, professional bodies and private developers increasingly looked towards the central state for support to promote investment in housing production, which had been greatly eroded by adverse economic circumstances by the end of the nineteenth century. These conditions were exacerbated by the economic crisis of 1907, which further undermined investor confidence in the building sector. Following a brief recovery, the First World War diminished Dutch trade and transport, isolating the country and increasing the cost of scarce building materials (Beusekom, 1955: 67). The subsequent but short-lived economic boom of the 1920s generated a rise in living conditions (wages and social welfare) and a range of housing outcomes including non-profit social rental dwellings depicted in Table 7.4. From the early years of the century, housing associations *dominated social housing* production, with municipal housing companies playing a complementary role. Social housing provided more than half of all dwellings built between 1916 and 1920. After 1920, their role in production

Table 7.4 Total number of dwellings built, 1906–1933

Year	Total number of built dwellings	Built by housing associations and municipalities			
		Number	Association	Municipalities	% of total built
1906	25,000	23	9	91	0.1
1908	20,000	467	84	16	2.3
1910	20,000	977	94	6	4.9
1912	25,000	1,370	90	10	5.5
1914	17,000	2,413	94	6	14.5
1916	10,000	4,955	96	4	49.5
1918	10,000	7,478	80	20	75.0
1920	25,000	21,659	62	38	87.0
1922	45,496	20,430	67	33	45.0
1924	46,712	12,310	71	29	26.4
1926	48,833	7,665	62	38	15.7
1928	47,335	6,733	82	18	14.2
1930	51,501	7,379	68	32	14.4
1932	41,341	5,165	72	28	12.5
1933	44,425	1,664	59	41	3.8

Source: Department of Reconstruction and Housing (1950) *Housing Associations in The Netherlands*, Government Information Office, The Hague.

diminished[9] as private house construction increased dramatically until the onset of the Great Depression.

The following table provides a selection of key events of the period.

Dutch welfare state emerges: compulsory education, health care and limited workers insurance, union organised contributory unemployment insurance	1900–
Government legislates to support private organisations with 50-year loans (Woningwet), New Building Code and beginning of planned extension of cities	1901
Advances distributed to housing associations and municipal housing companies for slum abolition and rehousing low-income residents	1910–1915
First World War	1914–1918
Government assists borrower to pay interest on housing loans	1915
Government assists builder to pay for high cost materials	1916
Universal suffrage and proportional representation for men and women 25 years and over	1917–1919
Massive increase in government loans lifting social housing output	1918–1920
Government subsidises private construction and sale of social dwellings	1920
Government loans used to ensure private housing production	1923
Private construction becomes dominant norm and social housing lending forbidden	1925–
Price limit on land for social housing development	1926
Housing associations burdened by cost rents and affordability problems amongst tenants	1927
Depression limits financial outlays of government for housing development	1929

Examples of key housing relations, contingently defined during this period of foundation

CONTINGENTLY DEFINED PROPERTY RELATIONS

It was not until 1892, with soaring land prices and the undersupply of developable land, that the National Commission of Inquiry for the Workingman argued for municipalities to provide land to housing societies for the provision of housing. Further, it recommended that infrastructure should ensure that such land was ripe for building, and be provided by the municipality for a modest charge.

Initially stymied by the dominance of liberalism in the national government during the 1890s, socialist politicians continued to lobby for legislative interventions in private property rights via the right to inspect and condemn uninhabitable dwellings and stipulate planning conditions for new developments. With broadening eligibility to vote, the Radical Liberals and socialists increased their numbers in the municipal chambers, and with a new step toward fiscal centralisation, they demanded that more funds be directed to address local welfare.

In 1896, a major change in municipal land policy was passed by the influential city of Amsterdam. Municipal land would be leased, rather than sold.[10] The Amsterdam councillors responsible for this and other Radical Liberal initiatives would later enter national parliament and influence the content of the first Dutch housing legislation. Indeed, their influence can be found in the Housing Act of 1901, which stipulates that *municipalities*, rather than organised private interests, should be made responsible for the *supply of developable land* around cities. As noted earlier, speculative activities and multiple private interests had stymied co-ordinated land development. Land development was a risky business often requiring the expensive, labour intensive construction and co-ordination of many different owners, in order to proceed (Badcock, 1994: 427; Groetelaars, 2000: 3). The law permitted the expropriation of property from slum landlords in the public interest, to be compensated at *market value* (Terhorst and Van de Ven, 1997: 258).

Yet, the implementation of the law was slow and difficult. According to Nycolaas (1974), the housing law did not fit neatly into the demands of industrial capitalism and there was vocal opposition from parliamentarians,[11] building and landowners concerned about any intrusion upon their private property rights.

The Housing Act, known in Dutch as the *Woningwet*, required local government to plan and provide for *growth*. Again this was met by resistance at the local level.[12] Later, such planning was made compulsory in 1921, with local governments defining land uses and laying down streets to open up land for *urban expansion and prevent undesirable housing conditions*. The exploitation potential of land became partly defined by permissible land uses and developable plot sizes. By providing public areas, parks, streets and underground services, municipalities assumed responsibility for less profitable tasks, minimising the risk for the developers, whilst defining how an area should be developed. Land companies were a powerful force leading to the revision of the act in 1921, when detailed and long-term land-use plans became compulsory, and in 1931, required co-ordination between municipalities on planning matters (see Nycolaas, 1974: 35; Kooiman, 1943: 120–121 and Terhorst and Van de Ven, 1997: 218 for details). Private land holdings could still be expropriated, but must be purchased at market value and the dispossessed had to be carefully protected.

As mentioned earlier, a number of cities, such as Amsterdam and Rotterdam, played an influential role in defining national housing (and land) policy. Rotterdam established a municipal land company to process land for housing development. Many municipalities attempted to maximise local revenue and thus minimise the burden of servicing expanding suburbs by selling landholdings to the highest bidder, yet this often priced out the development of affordable workers' housing. In 1926 a law was passed limiting the price of land (Grondprijslimiet) to be developed for social rental housing.

Amsterdam chose a particular land policy to promote the development of well-planned affordable housing: long-term leasing, with land rents initially based on cost rent rather than market prices, only sufficient to cover the costs of acquisition, preparation and loss of idle capital. Cost pooling was also practised, cross-subsidising expensive sites for social housing via less expensive ones. The financial practices of the Amsterdam land department were internally integrated and thus, less subject to scrutiny than more self-contained land corporations that were administratively and financially at arms length (Terhorst and Van de Ven, 1997: 287–291). This municipality became a monopoly purchaser and farmers simply waited for their land to be purchased at the highest market price.

Importantly, the Housing Act legitimised the provision of interest bearing loans and contributions to approved private housing associations. The government's financial role was formally legislated following a series of inadequate philanthropic efforts towards the end of century. The *Woningwet* permitted government advances of credit to private housing associations for the provision of social rental housing of a reasonable quality to improve hygiene and services for workers.

Financial resources for Housing Act loans were gathered from the capital market under the government's umbrella, achieving lower-market interest rates with the government's security, for the new housing sector. Loan payments for social housing could be spread over 50 years (Schaar, 1987: 80), rather than 30. Spreading payments over a longer period could enable cost rents to be low enough for low-income workers, in a low-inflation environment. Such housing was built in new and redeveloped areas processed by municipal land companies. Further, the quality of housing was greatly enhanced by the new building code and its enforcement.

Yet conditions in the building and capital market were unfavourable. Materials were scarce and prices exorbitant, interest rates were also climbing. Combined, these factors limited investment in private housing production. To stimulate construction in 1914, under 'abnormal' market conditions of the First World War, the Government provided assistance to associations to pay interest on housing loans. Assistance was also extended to the builder in 1916 to subsidise the increasing cost of materials (Feddes, 1995: 346). Between 1918–1920 government loans were greatly increased, lifting social housing output and keeping 'idle hands' busy.

Thus it took almost two decades for Housing Act loans to be widely distributed to housing associations and municipal housing companies for slum abolition and rehousing low-income residents. Periods of sustained production of social housing were limited to the few years between 1916 and 1922, and were stimulated by the crises contributions.

As exorbitant building costs gradually returned to 1915 levels and interest rates declined, interest in private housing construction returned (Feddes, 1995, figure 8.1 and p. 346). With the financial markets briefly restored in the mid-1920s the central government curtailed its own lending programme. To make matters even worse for housing associations during the Depression, the central government insisted that all former subsidies received since 1901 be repaid (Schaar *et al.*, 1996: 127).

Subsequently, a different set of conditions in the capital market undermined the newly established Dutch housing solution of social housing. In comparison with the more recent developments employing cheaper materials and finance during the 1920s, social housing already built earlier was far more expensive and reliant upon secured annuity loans established during a time of higher interest rates. The comparison for renters was stark, with cost rents far higher than those for newer dwellings, set at market rates. For those with adequate and secure incomes, it became favourable to purchase homes (Feddes, 1995: 347).[13] Social housing rents were set to repay a (much higher) cost price of building and financing dwellings, and especially at this time of looming unemployment and stagnating wages they were much higher than the market rents of the private sector. By 1929 the Great Depression limited financial outlays of government for housing development and the entire rental-housing sector was in crisis. With mass unemployment, indebted housing associations struggled to meet their obligations on government secured loans.

CONTINGENTLY DEFINED LABOUR AND WELFARE RELATIONS

I now turn to the welfare and labour relations underpinning the wobbly foundations of the Dutch housing solution.

Nycolaas (1974) refers to the 1890s as a period of enlightenment and public openness. The broadening political elite, freedom to form unions, the existence of multiple political parties and a free press challenged the old power base, which had used co-option and protection to remain powerful. Concern amongst the populace was fuelled by a series of reports by health committees and medical practitioners, detailing the poor living conditions in many towns and villages across the Netherlands (Beusekom, 1955). Armed with new evidence, public interest groups called for local action to clean up slum dwellings.

Following on from the health concerns of the elite, the Health Act was closely linked to the Housing Act and passed in the same year. A hierarchy of health committees and health inspectors was of growing influence, highlighting poor housing conditions and steering developments in housing policy. Rather than resisting the influx of poor, as a burden on the municipal tax base, centralisation and redistribution of tax revenue gave municipalities more financial freedom to address welfare issues.

By the turn of the century, unrest amongst workers threatened social and economic order and culminated in demands for improved labour conditions and social welfare. Revolutions in Russia, Central Europe and Germany fuelled the organisation of Dutch workers into (now permitted) labour unions and motivated their struggles. Concessions were made, such as voting rights for women, better public services, unemployment benefits and pensions for older workers, and the government's active interest in working-class housing (Nycolaas, 1974: 34–46).

It became increasingly legitimate to establish some basis for modest welfare provisions for the poor worker. From an extremely narrow base, suffrage was expanding to middle-class Protestants, Catholics and Socialists who formed numerous political parties comprising conservative, liberal and progressive factions. Each had its own answers for dealing with the 'social question'. For Catholics a clear message was delivered by Pope Leo XIII, who argued that rapidly changing times required closer co-operation between different social classes. He appealed for the better distribution of property and argued for social policies supporting the development of social welfare. With the new flow of centrally dispersed general funds and special grants, and an army of health inspectors, municipalities were well-informed and better resourced to take action and provide some poor relief, and improve housing conditions in the interest of public health and safety.

Yet the solution was not municipal socialism, as in the United Kingdom. Whilst social goods would become increasingly financed by the central and local state, their delivery would be privately managed and administered. Philanthropic and religious institutions mobilised to keep the socialists from controlling new welfare services. Beginning with the provision of housing and later education, they formed what would later become the organisational architecture of the Dutch welfare state and greatly influence social policy development.

Partly due to the weakness of the socialist movement, welfare relations under-pinning the Dutch housing solution were strongly defined by the entrepreneurial role of religious organisations. Representation was divided along class *and* religious lines according to variants of Calvinist nationalism, Catholic isolationism, liberalism and socialism. During the closing years of the nineteenth century and the early twentieth century, religious groups joined other civic and professional groups arguing for a housing solution and the dispersal of collective resources via their local networks of provision.[14]

For some in government and industry, social housing policy was a tool for moderating wage demands and managing the working class. Rental, rather than co-operative or individual ownership was their preferred tenure for reproducing a flexible, contained labour force. Social landlords considered that workers should be managed and their domestic behaviour 'improved' via the rental of quality dwellings from housing associations.[15] Further, such households did not have the means to finance home purchase nor maintain their dwellings, which housing reformers feared would inevitably fall into the hands of exploitative landlords. Further, it was argued that workers would become too attached to their own homes and this would reduce their flexibility in seeking employment.

Yet in times of high unemployment and continuing fixed loan repayments, social housing associations were forced to seek assistance from the central government. Many evicted non-paying tenants, whilst others faced financial ruin.

Synthesising key relations in their contingent context

Figure 7.3 below abstracts the 'ideal' relations of provision as promoted by the conditions of the 1901 Housing Act. This new mode of provision is radically dif-ferent from the previous one, but *shaped by and emergent from specific crises* in the land, finance and housing markets. This consequent mode of provision introduced a number of *new players to finance and provide housing*, under very different land and housing market conditions. This new system was based on the financing of rental housing via a 'closed' system of government-secured loans and cost rents.

First, to address the lack of private investment and accelerate renewal of slum areas, the central government replaces and adapts the role played by mortgage

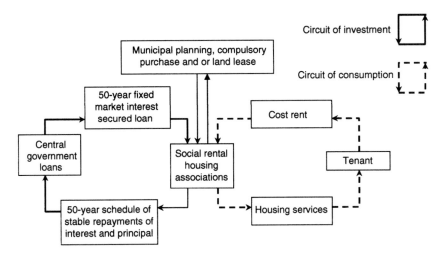

Figure 7.3 Abstraction of the flow of capital via the housing market, as envisaged by the 1901 Housing Act.

banks in the provision of credit. Favourable market interest rates are achieved by the *presence of a government guarantee securing the repayment of interest-bearing, fixed market rate, 50-year loans.* Second, *housing associations* have replaced private landlords as legitimate managers of rental housing. Importantly, they are committed to the *cost rental of their dwellings*, that is, rents are fixed on the basis of the cost of the loan, maintaining and managing rental dwellings. This marks a radical change from the rental regime of the previous model, where market rents were the norm and subject to fluctuations in the tenancy market. Finally, the private monopoly conditions stifling urban expansion, housing quality and renewal have been overcome by the *powerful role of municipalities in the expropriation of land, enforcement of building standards and targeted release (or lease)* of ready sites onto the construction market.

However, given the open, contingently defined nature of the housing system, particularly vulnerable to change in the land, finance, rental and labour markets, *ideal cost rent conditions were never sustained* (see Figure 7.4). First, the cost of producing housing escalated as imported *building materials became increasingly costly* during and soon after the First World War. Trade relations were hampered (indeed the port was blocked) causing major shortages and price rises in building materials that could not be made locally. This required additional financing, which impacted upon the level of the cost rent (1). Second, during a brief boom period in the 1920s *land prices soared*, further contributing to high object costs and influencing the level of cost rents (2). Third, social housing *cost rents* based on higher costs during 1916–1922, were *noticeably higher than those in the market* rental sector during the 1930s (3). Finally, as wages stagnated and mass unemployment threatened tenants were simply *unable to pay relatively high rents*

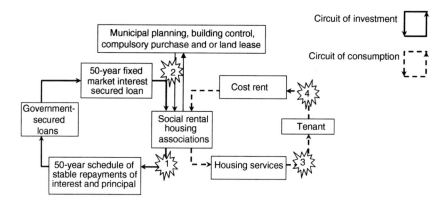

Figure 7.4 The 1901 Housing Act model subject to contingencies and crises.

in the social housing sector leading to many evictions and the financial ruin of the social housing sector (4)

A further abstraction (Figure 7.5) illustrates the adaptation of the 'ideal' solution under periods of crisis, which path dependently builds upon the Housing Act model outlined in Figure 7.3. Reference has been made to a number of adaptations that concern the production of cost-rent social housing by private housing associations.

The *first* adaptation delivered *contributions* for slum clearance and *housing for the socially disadvantaged* in 1904, where the rental income that could be derived was too low to meet cost-rent payments (1). Much later, following almost stagnation of the housing sector *interest rate contributions* were introduced in 1915 to compensate borrowers and enable them to keep rents low. This subsidy was split between central and municipal governments (2). Soon after in 1916, *contributions* were made towards the inflated *cost of materials* and again split between central and local government (3). Yet following a period of rent freezes and regulated increases in the market sector from 1916 to 1921, cost rents in the social housing sector were relatively high, making it far more vulnerable to capacity to pay issues. In 1919 crisis contributions were paid to housing associations where the *state paid 75 per cent of the difference between cost rent and market rent* (4). To reduce the cost of social housing, and thereby the level of the cost rent, a *maximum price limit for land* intended for social housing development was established in 1926 (5). The last adaptation in this phase was a 'hidden subsidy' from 1934, which subsidised the cost of *market interest on government-secured loans* in order to once again reduce cost rents.

One *serious crisis remained* which eventually undermined the mode of provision outlined earlier. It concerns the consumption of housing under conditions of mass unemployment (6). No housing system reliant upon rental income is immune to labour and welfare developments affecting its tenants. Thus during the

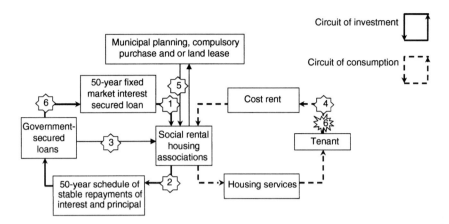

Figure 7.5 Abstraction of the flow of capital via the social housing sector, with various adaptations of the core housing solution (1916–1934).

Great Depression many households had no paid work and thus no income to spare on any level of housing costs. Mass evictions and the collapse of many housing associations was the result. This issue is addressed by the following adaptation of the housing solution examined in the following subsection.

7.5.3 Recovery and acceleration of the Dutch solution, 1934–1983

Outline of key events and housing outcomes

The long economic crisis, beginning with the Great Depression and continuing well after the Second World War, eroded confidence in 'normal market relations' and 'viable' housing production and consumption without sustained government support. The housing sector had completely collapsed during wartime (see Table 7.5), and a new mode of accumulation had to be reestablished. In the previous phase a number of initiatives were introduced as mere crisis measures: sporadic lending for social housing, advances for paying high market interest on government loans, subsidies for inflated material costs and short-term rent freezes. Importantly, many of these crisis measures became institutionalised in the Dutch housing solution. Further, the Second World War inflicted much damage and destruction to the larger cities such as Rotterdam and The Hague and a substantial number of dwellings were lost, compounding the problems associated with a long period of declining investment in housing production and maintenance.

For a decade after the Second World War, housing policy was heavily influenced by macro-economic policy, which pursued a low wage strategy to increase the international competitiveness of exports. The overarching principle

Table 7.5 Total number of dwellings built, 1934–1949

Year	Total number of built dwellings	Built by housing associations and municipalities			
		Number	Association	Municipalities	% of total built
1934	52,591	4,875	85	15	9.2
1936	30,285	2,579	89	11	8.5
1938	38,375	2,862	73	27	7.5
1940	17,661	2,638	74	26	15.0
1942	8,355	2,570	75	25	31.3
1944	675	179	50	40	30.0
1946	1,593	369	44	56	27.3
1948	36,391	29,423	41	59	80.8

Source: Department of Reconstruction and Housing *(1950) Housing Associations in The Netherlands*, Government Information Office, The Hague.

of full employment was tightly coupled to a policy of wage containment. This strategy was to be achieved by reducing living costs and specifically, keeping housing rents as low as possible. Long after the Second World War, rents were frozen at 1934 levels. During this period planning and redevelopment policy became highly centralised. The national government was chiefly concerned with redeveloping areas destroyed by the war and addressing the housing shortage.

The period from the 1950s to the mid-1960s can be considered as one of temporary coherence in the Dutch solution, with key relations operating under favourable conditions of regulated land supply, loans at below-market rates of interest (2 per cent relative to 4 per cent in the 1960s), sustained by institutional integration between the state and social partners and facilitated by electoral concerns. Correspondingly, production of social housing reached a high point during this period and with rising welfare, home ownership rates gradually began to rise.

Yet this neat institutional fit soon began to show signs of fracture. In the mid-1960s, the stranglehold on wages and rents, the economic backbone of the central government's strategy, was weakened. By this stage, housing associations had become dependent on generous and costly object subsidies. Increasing tenant incomes and growth of home ownership undermined the legitimacy of this costly system. A new financial system, Dynamic Cost Price (DKP) was introduced based on steady rent and wage increases. Yet the prognoses upon which this system was based were false. The international monetary collapse and oil crises of the 1970s ended a regime of high employment, wage growth and low inflation, altering the financial dimensions upon which increasing repayments could be based. When the new (amended) system was finally introduced in 1975, it later proved exorbitantly expensive and loans ballooned exponentially by the end of the decade. Yet a broader crisis threatened despite these looming budgetary constraints. With the near collapse of the home ownership sector by the end of the 1970s to the early 1980s, despite looming budget deficits the government

Table 7.6 Housing production in the subsidised rental and owner-occupied sector, 1979–1982

Year	Subsidised rental	Owner occupied, subsidised	Owner occupied, unsubsidised	Total
1979	31,700	27,800	30,000	89,500
1980	50,000	36,000	27,700	113,700
1981	70,800	30,100	16,800	117,700
1982	89,200	26,000	8,100	123,300

Source: CBS, Monthly figures building industry, in Terhorst, P and Van de Ven, J (1995) Table 1: 348.

once again steered investment into the social housing sector, as demonstrated by Table 7.6.

The following table summarises many of the important events that took place during this phase in Dutch housing history.

Government reduces interest on advances 'hidden subsidy'	1934
War time – no exploitation of housing, increased property tax	1940–1945
Strict rent control based on May 1940 levels	1940–1958
Legal basis for private housing companies to be subsidised	1950
Exploitation shortage subsidy introduced	1950
Expansion of subsidised housing programme	1952–1965
Various initiatives to promote home ownership	1957
Rent control eased	1958
Below market interest loans replaced by object subsidy	1960s
Housing associations gain priority for developing housing over municipalities	1965
Drive to equalise subsidies across tenures	1966
Preference for privately subsidised rental housing	1966
Land costs for social housing set to cover costs of developing infrastructure	1968
Associations preferred over municipal companies in municipal land allocation	1969
Interest on social housing loans increased to market level	1969
Increased allocation of subsidies during politics of need, production, rents and profits	1969
Government experiments with individual rent assistance system	1970
Introduction of dynamic cost-rent system	1972–1973
Subsidy policy maintained but adapted to relate to incomes rather than cost price	1974
Rent controls to keep rents down	1975–1978
Subsidies for new build housing introduced, yet not taken up by private builders	1975
Increased subsidies for production in rent and ownership sector	1978
Social housing loans partly turned over in guarantees and partly privatised	1978
Government sustains investment levels in the ownership and rent sectors	1978
Budget austerity, central government contemplates major reforms	1981
Policy emphasises home ownership via sale of social housing	1983

Examples of key housing relations, contingently defined during this period of acceleration

CONTINGENTLY DEFINED PROPERTY RELATIONS

A major change in property relations occurred during the Second World War, when occupying German forces dictated a strongly centralised land use, construction and housing policy. These actions had important implications, which consequently influenced the level and type of private housing investment. Repossession laws were extended and land-use planning became more centralised. Diverse local planning rulebooks were homogenised and powers usurped by the new national planning service. All new development and extensions required not only local permission, but central approval as well. Later during the occupation, all new building works were forbidden, and materials and labour resources were redirected for defensive works along the Dutch coast (Schaar, 1987: 93).

Under these highly regulated conditions, it was also forbidden to profit from the exploitation of tenancy and a tax on the value of property was introduced. Rents were fixed at 1934 levels since 1940 and remained in place until 1951, then adapted by nation-wide rounds of increases. These measures, amongst others, gave a persistently negative signal to potential investors, stymieing their role in housing provision. Later in the 1960s, a number of national plans defined the terrain within which local development could occur. These plans affected property rights by designating acceptable areas for growth, specific land uses and the development of supporting infrastructure, such as major roads and public transport services. Each plan held a different spatial emphasis and influenced the creation of quite different urban environments.

Yet despite these national plans, actual land preparation, involving the drainage of land, plot division, supplying infrastructure and ensuring space for defined forms of urban development, continued to be carried out by the municipalities.[16] Building ripe land was then disposed to building developers for the construction of approved dwellings. This process ensured that development took place in accordance with local plans and housing objectives, within national parameters, with sale proceeds, central government subsidies and/or other higher value sales, cross-subsidising the costs of site preparation. In some cases, municipalities acted commercially, sometimes making enormous capital gains.[17]

Until the mid-1960s municipal housing companies, closely associated with municipal land companies, shared information and technical expertise, thereby minimising project management costs. Together they dominated the important social housing sector of major cities. Yet, Christian politicians[18] considered that such companies held an unfair advantage over private housing associations, which in some areas were becoming marginalised and professionally under-developed. The role of associations was strengthened and their realm of development activity broadened beyond the low-income renter (Schaar *et al.*, 1996: 126–136). In 1965, municipal housing companies were only allowed to implement development plans when the local housing association was unwilling or unable to do so. The diminution of municipal control was intended to separate land development priorities from the construction of viable social housing projects and thereby reduce the risk of 'non-commercial practices' favouring municipal housing companies. Further, the central government issued directives in the so-called Brown Booklet that fixed land costs for social rental dwellings in zoned areas. Land price covering subsidies were only provided for urban areas of importance to national housing policy (RIGO, 1991: 3–4).

A brief mention should also be made concerning property rights pertaining to individual tenants, which were substantially strengthened during this phase. Protection for tenants against eviction was strengthened. Further, to prevent excessive rents and the development of a black market, allocation was formalised and waiting lists established. In 1978, the level of rent was regulated according to a point system based on the quality and quantity of the living space.

CONTINGENTLY DEFINED SAVINGS AND INVESTMENT RELATIONS

In 1934, to prevent the collapse of the housing association sector and widespread default on government secured loans, the government reduced interest demanded on its loans to housing associations, on the condition that rents would be kept low (Schaar, 1987: 92–93). This 'hidden subsidy' remained in place until the early 1960s, and was then replaced by more visible object subsidies.

The occupying forces and post-war governments radically extended many of the crises measures applied or discussed before the war. As mentioned earlier, rents were frozen for a considerable period and it was forbidden to profit from the exploitation of dwellings. Government legislation forbade increases in mortgage interest. Without this flexibility, and in the face of numerous other disincentives, private investors simply turned away from the housing sector (Schaar, 2001: 4). Without investment, the private rental sector completely stagnated and very few new homes were built.[19]

It became increasingly necessary for governments to invest in order to address the massive housing shortage and build at high density and tempo. In path-dependent fashion, the non-profit institutions and financial mechanisms, which had addressed the housing crises of the early twentieth century, were called back into action. And once again, during the 1950s to 1960s, social housing production returned to centre stage. The production of new dwellings was regulated by the Reconstruction Law, which outlined approval processes, desired building standards and financial provisions for housing construction. The subsidy programme underpinning high housing output was greatly expanded. To reduce labour costs, time-saving technologies were developed such as modular production, producing standardised often-monotonous residential areas. Long-term contracts were offered to companies who applied these building techniques and could realise large-scale projects.

Yet frozen rents inevitably sank far below the cost price of building and managing rental housing. Consequently, rental income was totally insufficient without rent rises or a substantial exploitation subsidy. Landlords and their representative associations lobbied central government leaders for a quick and considerable increase in rents (25 per cent). Unions argued that incomes must also rise to compensate. Yet low rents were important for low wages intended to promote a more competitive export economy. To overcome this conflict, a pact between unions, landlords and the central government established a scenario of low rents and wage moderation in return for sustained social welfare provisions. Terhorst and Van de Ven explain,

> [l]abour unions were only willing to participate in a tripartite reconstruction pact as long as prices of basic consumer goods remained under control and the embryonic welfare-state system was extended in order to protect families with dependent children that mostly relied on one wage-earner only, from the risks of old age, unemployment, sickness and accidents at work.... Within this framework, rent control played a crucial role in the post–war reconstruction period.
>
> (1997: 293)

Nevertheless, there was much debate over rent policy between the central government, landlords, unions, the Socio Economic Research Council and other housing organisations, during the 1950s and 1960s. The quality of new dwellings was heavily constrained by the freezing of rents. Various ideas and proposals were exchanged including rent increases for subsidised and unsubsidised dwellings, tying rent increases to financing conditions, and taxing rents to finance new dwellings, in order to attain the ideal of cost price rent whilst preventing excessive wage demands. The stalemate was broken in 1955, but rents were merely increased by 10 per cent above the level of 1940 and no rent tax was introduced (Schaar, 1987: 101–109).

During the early 1960s, landlords once again demanded considerable rent increases and this time the government was more receptive. Wages began to increase alongside employee contributions to welfare (Terhorst and Van de Ven, 1997: 294–309). It was economically feasible that tenants could pay more.

Turning briefly to developments in alternative sectors, by the 1950s individual home purchase was narrowly distributed amongst the middle and upper classes in urban areas, whilst being more widespread in the countryside. The substantial down payment required (30 per cent) to secure a home loan was simply too high for modest-income earners. Efforts were made to improve access amongst low- and middle-class city dwellers by way of mortgage guarantee (established in 1957), mortgage interest deduction and object and subject subsidies (Mersmann, 2002). The conditions for obtaining a guarantee were devised by individual municipalities, leading to a variety of schemes. Payments of interest and premiums, in the case of default, were secured by the central government. These efforts reduced the risk of lending, enlarged the volume of available credit and lowered the interest rates, thereby assisting a number of households to enter home purchase.

After a long period of mass social housing construction, the new centre-right government attempted to accelerate the promotion of home ownership in order to 'balance the market', and importantly reduce the costs of government object subsidies to the social housing sector. Renters were disorganised and unable to mobilise effective opposition. After more than a decade of high production, subsidies for social housing came under increasing scrutiny in the mid-1960s. Secular inflation set in from 1965. A new discussion emerged, arguing for the targeted allocation of social housing to low-income households and the taxing of wealthy renters in subsidised accommodation. Under these residualising conditions, home ownership was clearly promoted as the tenure of preference.

Yet the problem of escalating central government object subsidies continued to plague both government and housing associations.[20] The push for improved dwelling standards and urban renewal increased the cost of dwelling construction and thus costs rents, demanding further object subsidies. A new method of financing social housing known as DKP was developed, which built upon the principle of cost rent and promised to ease the burden of this growing subsidy for both landlords and governments – providing wages and rents continued to grow; it was implemented in 1975.

Yet the prognoses upon which the DKP method was based were not fulfilled. The oil crises disturbed stable patterns of international economic growth, wages stagnated and unemployment rose, leading to a growing dependence on social security. Broad access to individual rent subsidy compensated financially disadvantaged tenants. Capital shifted towards more secure investments, contributing to a major decline in residential construction.

Despite the central government's promotion of home ownership in the late seventies, the second oil shock and subsequent economic recession eventually led to the collapse of the housing market in 1979. During this period inflation was hovering around 13 per cent. In this context, the government decided to expand the social housing programme and once again, the share of social housing rose considerably (Boelhouwer *et al.*, 1990: 95).[21]

CONTINGENTLY DEFINED LABOUR AND WELFARE RELATIONS

Momentarily, before the 1937 election, the socialist movement attempted to break the stagnation of depression by promoting the establishment of a federation of building firms, employers, employees, the government and relevant professions, to divide up the housing quota and tackle unemployment. Without the necessary support of larger political parties, the plan was barely discussed before its rejection. The housing shortage and the lack of investment remained a major issue and the Second World War only worsened the housing crisis.

Unemployment and wage levels remained the key to unlocking the crisis in the housing sector after 1945. After a long and difficult crises, compounding poor living conditions, the government promoted a policy of full employment, contributory social security and public health, as well as broadly accessible social housing (Vlek, 1998: 9). As mentioned earlier, labour unions accepted low wage growth in exchange for work and welfare safeguards.

In the 1950s, wages were generally linked to cost of living (Van Zanden, 1997: 80), kept low by the freezing of prices, regulation of rents and strict dwelling allocation. Wage levels were of great social, economic and political significance. It was a time of the single breadwinner, where women remained at home attending to unpaid domestic duties, and men worked to provide sufficient income to cover all household expenses.[22]

Under this domestic regime, income security could not easily be bolstered by a second income. Thus social security became an important safeguard against income loss and enabled the maintenance of household order. The Dutch welfare state rapidly expanded under a highly corporatist regime of employers, unions and government, based on a system of employee benefits. The dominant principles of the day, orthodox confessionalism and anti-communalism, worked against more collective, taxation funded arrangements. The social partners (unions and employers) played a key developmental and administrative role, alongside state representatives – facilitating corporate-managed schemes and preventing the development of purely state alternatives.

An acceptable path was found via the development of self-governing insurance associations based on principles of subsidiarity and corporatism. Schemes were non-profit but cost-led, with the Minister for Social Security having the final word on premium levels to cover yearly expenditures (Therborn, 1989: 212–213). These institutions provided the so-called exit strategies for the unemployed. They came to play an increasingly powerful role, not only in labour market policy and negotiations, but also as a large, long-term investor in the private rental market.

Beyond exit strategies, other measures were required to protect modest household income. As rents were progressively increased above the rate of inflation and wage rises, they consumed an increasing proportion of the household budget. Rents, from a very low base, were rising faster than housing costs in other tenures.

Indeed, during the mid-1960s rents for new dwellings in urban renewal areas were no longer affordable for low-income households. Yet there were other renters who paid a very small proportion of household income on rent. In 1966, centre-right politicians called for a tax on wealthy renters in subsidised dwellings. They argued that social housing should only be allocated to lower-income households. This added further fuel to the hot debate over rent levels, dwelling quality and object subsidies.

During the 1970s, housing and planning policy focused upon perceived social, physical and economic problems in older inner-city neighbourhoods. Renewal converted affordable lower-quality dwellings to more expensive higher-quality ones. The gap between new cost rents and old cost rents was beyond the capacity of tenants to absorb. Some projects even remained vacant, unable to attract paying tenants.

Eventually, the 1974 Rent and Subsidy Policy promoted a system of object subsidies for quality and urban renewal to ensure that new social rental dwellings were accessible for those on a low-income and project-targeted demand subsidies. Later the 1975 Individual Rent Subsidy (IRS) was introduced which was not tied to costly new housing projects but available to any tenant of any type of dwelling paying under 5,000 guilders rent per year and meeting declining income to rent ratios (Boelhouwer and Heijden, 1992: 63).[23] With the IRS there was no longer a direct link between cost rent, allowances and object subsidies.

Synthesising key relations in their contingent context

An important *adaptation* during this phase was the comprehensive *tackling of the relationship between wages, rents levels and the cost of housing production.* Object subsidies played an important role in managing the level of cost rents in the social housing sector. As part of national economic strategy, which aimed to improve the Netherlands' international export position, wages were kept deliberately low. As housing costs often consume the largest proportion of the household budget, control over rents paid and many other aspects of domestic expenditure were closely regulated. For this reason the *low wage policy* appears prominently in Figure 7.6. Privately provided social housing, via approved associations and municipal housing companies, was considered the best vehicle to *keep rents low and control wage demands.* For this reason, *social housing was central to post-war recovery, low labour costs economic strategy and addressing the housing shortage.* From this basis, subsequent generations of baby boomers facing *continuing and severe housing shortages,* merely 'stepped into the shoes' of a well-established post-war housing and employment solution, sustaining the system of social housing provision well beyond its initial short-term purpose.

The figure incorporates a number of measures, which emerged since the Great Depression to the mid-1970s. First, from 1934 the government provides a 'hidden subsidy' in the form of *subsidising the interest rate on government-secured loans* until the early 1960s. This subsidy is replaced by explicit object subsidies. Also since 1934, *building quality and techniques were rationalised to reduce the costs of construction,* later producing modest mass-produced high-density dwellings (1). To secure greater certainty in development outcomes, *municipalities became active in land development and in large cities housing development,* under strong

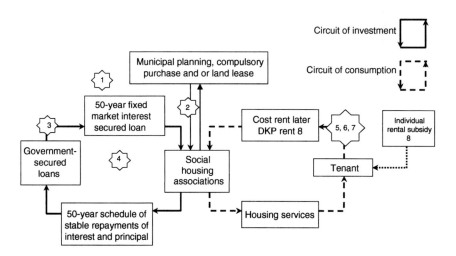

Figure 7.6 Abstraction of the flow of capital via social housing sector, with further adaptations of the amended housing solution (1934–1978).

central planning from 1945 (2). *Loan programmes* for social housing production via housing associations and municipal housing companies were *greatly expanded* from 1950 (3). In the context of frozen rents and suppressed wage growth during the1950s, *object subsidies were extended to housing associations to cover exploitation shortages*, aided by stringent cost calculation (4).

One of the major debates by the mid-1950s concerned the balance between object and subject subsidies, rent levels and the capacity of tenants to pay. Rises in interest rates during the 1950s, inflation in the cost of construction and increased housing quality demanded either reduced new construction (despite persistent shortages), higher object subsidies or substantial rent increases. All three alternatives were politically unpalatable to the government and social partners. As economic prosperity improved in the late 1950s, the *strangle hold on wages and rent increases was broken*. Increased rents only marginally helped to recover the rising standards and cost of housing improvement in 1959 (5). During the late 1960s and 1970s the Dutch welfare state expanded considerably, extending into unemployment insurance, income support and importantly *rental allowance* (6). This *loosened the link between cost-rent social housing and low-wage labour relations* and tightened the link between labour relations and developments in welfare provisions. In the 1970s, the cost of meeting construction costs shifted to a greater degree from object subsidies to housing associations to tenants, who were more secure under new welfare provisions (7). The cost of Individual Rent Subsidy was generously funded by royalties from a resources boom,[24] which helped to reduce the impact of a number of economic shocks (monetary collapse, oil crises, wage stagnation and unemployment) during the 1970s until the early 1980s.

Further attempts to claw back the object subsidies were made via the introduction of the Dynamic Cost Price rent system in 1975 to capture association gains that were possible towards the end of the mortgage term. Yet further developments in rent policy moved central government subsidy policy further away from the notion of object costs and subsidising the payment of cost rents. No longer were *subject subsidies* only directed towards tenants in costly individual projects, but were *broadly available* and set according to income levels and a point system for housing quality (8). In this sense they are more a *policy of welfare* than one of covering exploitation deficiencies.

7.5.4   Securing 'independent' relations for land development, finance and individualisation, 1984–2000

Outline of key events and housing outcomes

In the context of a stagnating economy, inflation, unemployment and rising public sector debt, fiscal austerity concerns dominated the development of the Dutch housing solution in the early 1980s. This was the era of monetarist economic policy: inflation was enemy number one. A prominent feature of this phase were the attempts by the central government to diminish its role in social housing provision, shifting financial responsibilities towards housing associations, banks and tenants and the opening up of the land market. The inner areas of major cities continued to have very large social housing sectors of smaller rental dwellings accommodating an increasingly marginalised population. In contrast the composition of outer suburbs and new locations were quite different: single family dwellings for middle-class households, more often for purchase than social rental. Notable is the growth in home purchase and house price inflation during the 1990s amidst a favourable fiscal, monetary and labour market climate.

Liberalisation occurred in both the financing of social housing construction and setting of rents by associations. The sector has been encouraged to become more financially self-sufficient, accessing finance directly from the capital market, merging with other associations, undertaking more commercially orientated projects and selling housing stock. Rents have been able to increase above the rate of inflation. Assistance has been targeted to lower-income households via the Individual Rental Subsidy, whilst home purchasers have been lured by inflating house prices, low interest rates on mortgages and advantageous fiscal benefits (tax deductibility of mortgage interest, low imputed rent tax).

In the second half of the 1990s, the economy began to recover. Strong employment growth enticed more women into the job market. Lenders responded to these trends by offering credit calculated on the basis of two incomes. In tandem with generous tax advantages and market scarcity, house prices boomed in sought after locations.

The following table provides a selection of key events of the period.

WSW institution established to secure capital market loans for housing improvement	1983
Several large municipal housing companies in financial difficulty	1986
Parliamentary inquiry into building subsidies	1986
Strengthening transparency of government's financial management role	1987
Parliamentary commission pushes for equity in financial treatment between social and private housing.	1988
Central government forces cities to build for the market (VINEX)	1988
Central Fund for Social Housing (CFV) established to improve financial position of housing associations	1988
Housing in the 1990s promotes financial self-sufficiency amongst social landlords, sales of social housing	1989
WSW expanded to cover loans for newly built social housing	1989
Additional government funds allocated to WSW in order to strengthen security	1993
Brutering agreement cancels outstanding government loans repayments in exchange for future subsidies	1994

Examples of key housing relations, contingently defined during this period of restructuring

CONTINGENTLY DEFINED PROPERTY RELATIONS

For most of the twentieth century, municipalities have played a relatively safe and predictable monopoly role in the planning, purchase, development and targeted release of land for new housing development.[25] However, an important shift in the municipality's role in the land development process occurred in the mid-1980s, opening up the bidding process and specifically promoting development around major cities in the Randstad region.

In the context of economic stagnation, unstable land prices and unemployment, the land development companies of smaller towns suffered major losses (Needham, 1988: 73). The Fourth Report for Spatial Planning ended the growth and new town policies that had created cities such as Almere and Zoetermeer. The new policy concentrated development in and around a select number of major cities and promoted the construction of housing for purchase. Of course, such a policy influenced the land market and investments in these and less-favoured areas.

Importantly, an addition was made to the Fourth Report in 1994, known as VINEX. This supplementary policy argued that environmental problems justified the need to minimise car transport. This could be achieved via the expansion of existing urban areas with transport infrastructure. Numerous locations were openly specified, each sufficient for approximately 5,000 dwellings – before municipalities had the chance to secure land ownership. To enable these municipalities to realise their housing plans, the central government negotiated targeted packages with regions and provinces, to subsidise land costs and contribute to the development of public transport and green spaces. According to Terhorst and Van de Ven, environmentalists, the agricultural sector, pension funds and the planning profession were a powerful coalition behind this policy (1997: 319).[26]

In a more open land market, the land companies of Randstad municipalities were no longer sole players able to pay market prices for the purchase and processing of former agricultural land for housing development. By publicly announcing its intentions early on, the central government awakened dormant players to enter the land market, promoting land speculation and increasing land prices – sometimes above municipal capacity to purchase.[27, 28]

There are not only more players in the market, but they possess different resources and thus different powers of negotiation.[29] According to research by Korthals Altes and Groetelaers (2000), municipalities remain important players in the land market, but their task has become more complex and risky with less say over the content of future housing developments. Municipalities, once accused of profiting from their monopoly position, must now operate more transparently and encourage more opportunities for privately constructed dwellings for home purchase, in order to promote choice (Remkes, 2001). Yet the choice is not for everyone. The proportion of social housing in new areas has declined, leading some to argue that new urban areas will only be accessible to a narrow range of household incomes (Terhorst and Van de Ven, 1997: 327) and the poor will continue to remain in less wealthy city centres.[30]

In addition, the State Secretary (Remkes) demanded the sale of social dwellings, especially in larger cities, in the interests of 'consumer choice' despite resistance from 'independent' housing associations.[31] Yet entrepreneurial housing associations implementing this policy have also come under scrutiny. The State Secretary has ordered the closure of sales offices run by associations, which mediated between tenants and associations, and demanded that existing real estate agents, operating in the private-for-profit sphere, exclusively handle the sales of social houses.

A new law, giving preference to expanding municipalities, aims to partially restore their diminished market position in new residential developments. These municipalities can use this law to fulfil provincial or central government plans in and around their cities, such as the establishment of parks, new houses, industrial areas and infrastructure. They can also demand conditions for the right to exploit land, without having to expropriate it. Only when planning conditions are not met, can the municipality compulsorily purchase in the public interest. However, municipalities must not use the law as a means to become a project developer, which continues to be discouraged by central government.

To further restore the weakened position of municipalities, a new national land policy was launched in 2000 and later passed by parliament in 2001. It requires land exploitation permits to be obtained by landowners and a contribution made to a fund for public infrastructure. When infrastructure is unable to be provided by the developer in a timely manner, municipalities can choose to expropriate required land in order to implement plans, paying inflated market rates and cash compensation.

By September 2001, the level of housing produced was half that anticipated by the State Secretary for Housing and crisis meetings were being held with industry representatives. These groups blamed local and provincial government urban planning requirements and processes for the slow down (*de Volkskrant* Newspaper, 8 September 2001). Other experts blame the developments of the 1980s, which weakened the position of the state in land release:

> the most important cause of the stagnation is the market parties, including housing associations and sometimes municipal land companies. They and not the government now define the rhythm of building production, and have much interest in scarcity.
>
> (Muñoz Gielen, 2002)

CONTINGENTLY DEFINED SAVINGS AND INVESTMENT RELATIONS

Not only has the monopoly position of the municipality been challenged, but also the role of the central government. Its former role in channelling finance into the housing sector has been curtailed and privatised. By the mid-1980s, in a climate of financial austerity, the role of the central government in financing housing associations came under question.[32] In 1986, allegations of fraudulent activity by investors manipulating subsidy systems in the building sector began to emerge.[33] It was argued that subsidies should shift from the dwelling to the tenant, rents should rise and a proportion of social rental dwellings be sold (Murie and Priemus, 1994: 113).

Until 1988, government-secured loans had financed housing associations and municipal housing companies, set at market rates.[34] Institutional investors as well as social housing providers received object subsidies to ensure high levels of building activity, rents increases were moderate[35] and controlled to ensure affordability and wage restraint. Further, generous demand side subsidies, rental-housing allowances, were also provided to eligible tenants.

By the end of the 1980s under pressure from the Ministry of Finance, the central government proposed to withdraw completely from arranging finance for social housing production. Much emphasis was placed upon the private and transparent nature of social housing provision, separate and independent from government. In this context housing associations were forced to become more financially independent and autonomous.

In 1993 the government initiated the process of cancelling all outstanding government-secured loans to housing associations and municipalities, in advance of forthcoming subsidies for renovation and construction. The so-called *Brutering* or grossing up process made it feasible for associations with good reserves to obtain funds independently from the capital market (for further details see Appendix 2) during a favourable interest rate climate. The central government temporarily secured the rent revenue stream, by permitting increases above the rate of inflation for several years.[36] Whilst rents continue to increase, the incline has been moderated.

Associations had to support improvements and stock expansion through their own reserves (enhanced via favourable market conditions, the Brutering process and rent increases above inflation), private loans, financial restructuring and economically driven development strategies. Initially, the capital market was unfamiliar with the character and quality of social housing as an investment. Further, the financial health of associations varied considerably, making the market cautious and interest rates potentially crippling. Towards this aim, the

Table 7.7 Rent price developments, 1990–2000

Year	Inflation (%)	Rent increase[a] (%)	Real rent increase (%)
1990	2.5	3.3	0
1991	3.1	5.9	2.8
1992	3.2	5.6	2.4
1993	2.6	5.4	2.8
1994	2.7	5.2	2.5
1995	2	4.7	2.7
1996	2	4.1	2.1
1997	2.2	3.7	1.5
1998	2	3.4	1.4
1999	2	3	1
2000	2.2[b]	2.5[c]	0.3

Source: CBS/VROM, 2000 table 6.2.

Notes
a exclusive rent harmonisation.
b prognosis CPB.
c Huur Brief 2000.

National Housing Council (Nationale Woningraad) and Ministry of Housing, Physical Planning and the Environment (VROM) proposed the establishment of the guarantee structure for reducing the risk and thereby the cost of capital loans. Two financial institutions have since been established to secure loans at more favourable interest rates for all associations (WSW) and improve the financial structure of poorer ones (CFV). For more details on these institutions see Appendix 3.

Housing associations are now operating in a dynamic financial environment where minor changes in the rate of inflation, interest or rent can have major implications for financial reserves, solvency and ultimately rents charged.

The primary investor in social housing in the Netherlands is the publicly owned Bank of Dutch Municipalities (Bank Nederlandse Gemeenten, BNG)[37], with commercial banks and pension funds playing a lesser role. Its dominant position in social housing finance has concerned AEDES, the combined umbrella group for association sector. They have initiated the establishment of another specialist mortgage provider, with stronger ties to one of the larger commercial banks (ABN/AMRO).[38]

The Dutch government now plays a diminished but essential role in financing social housing yet faces little direct risk. The current role of the government in housing is one of guiding the operation of 'independent' associations, determining rent policy and permissible increases, providing housing allowances to tenants, collecting imputed rent tax and permitting substantial tax relief for home purchasers.

During this phase in the history of the Dutch housing solution, home ownership has assumed far wider ideological prominence than any other. The proportion of social rented dwellings has declined with the promotion of owner occupation through central government taxation incentives, flow of funds into home mortgages and a flow of investment into free sector land and housing development. The proportion of home purchasers and outright owners increased from 42 per cent in 1981 to 52 per cent in 2001 (VROM, 2001). On average, Dutch households became much wealthier in the second half of the 1990s, not only via their income but also via the appreciation of housing assets amongst homeowners (DNB, 2000: 32). Indeed, wealth appreciation was largely derived from dramatic rises in house prices, especially between 1995 and 1999 and is considered by industry groups to have played a large but unacknowledged role in national economic growth (NVM in RICS, 2002).

During the 1990s, capital flowed from less profitable sectors of the stock exchange and bonds market into the property sector. Financial institutions, such as ING and various pension funds, invested heavily in the residential property market. Construction firms such as Hollandsche Beton Group (HBG), Volker Steven and the BAM Group were major recipients.[39]

Investment in mortgages at the lower end of the market was promoted by the relaunch of the mortgage guarantee.[40] A fund based on borrowers' premiums enabled the creation of the National Mortgage Guarantee in 1995. This triple A rated guarantee facilitated a lower interest rate for modest borrowers. In case of default, payment of interest and mortgage premiums was secured by the Foundation Guarantee Fund, which was backed by government guarantee in the context of an inflating housing market. With standardised, nationwide conditions and promotion via mortgage retailers, 80 per cent of mortgages received a guarantee in 1995. However, with house prices in major employment centres rising rapidly, fewer purchasers could borrow within the loan to income ratios required and the NHG's share of the market has plummeted to 50 per cent (Mersmann, 2002).

The market for mortgages grew exponentially in the second half of the 1990s. As competition amongst lenders intensified new institutions such as the secondary mortgage market, new mortgage products and marketing devices were developed, which fully exploited the government's policy enabling the deduction of mortgage interest.[41] The development of the secondary mortgage market is just one cause behind the large volume of credit that has flowed into the home loans sector. Coupled with developments in the supply of mortgages are those at the consumer interface. Rising rents (due to the removal of object subsidies and new financial relations in the social housing sector) pushed higher income tenants into the home ownership market. Yet this was a market based on two and not one income. Dual income households were encouraged to borrow under a much more permissive lending regime, a growing job market and generous tax incentives.

Purchase prices in sought after housing markets skyrocketed, partly based on 'double income' capacity to pay and a flush of available credit. Far from the ideals of emancipation movement promoting greater participation of women in the paid workforce, today many households have become locked into mortgages requiring high monthly premiums and thus, two full time incomes in a more precarious labour market. According to a European survey by the Royal Institute of Chartered Surveyors, Dutch households have taken on more debt than any other in Europe.

> Undoubtedly, the biggest problem facing the housing market is that the boom was sustained by a huge increase in mortgage lending that has made the country's home owners some of the most indebted in Europe.
>
> (RICS, 2001)

The European and National reserve banks are concerned about the implications of over indebtedness for national financial security. The Dutch National Bank has cautioned lenders that their borrowers are vulnerable to the inevitable decline in house prices, when the boom finally busts or taxation policy changes[42] and indeed marginal changes occur in interest rates.[43]

CONTINGENTLY DEFINED LABOUR AND WELFARE RELATIONS

In the previous phases, the Dutch welfare state had emerged from the negotiated consensus between the social partners rooted in dominant Christian ideology, rather than the division between labour and capital (Reijden, 1989) and supported by resource royalties in the 1970s. Yet over the past decade, the general directions of government policies in the socio-economic field have been strongly influenced by monetary and fiscal policies in an intra-governmental European context. Thus national corporate interdependency has taken place within an internationally orientated economy, which has given little room for manoeuvre and government ambition (Geelhoed, 1989).

For the first time since 1945, economic growth during the early to mid-1980s did not bring additional employment. Labour intensive industries were moving their plants to low-wage countries in Asia, Eastern Europe and Africa. A second-generation birth wave brought a massive influx of young school leavers into the job market, whilst technological change meant that the skills of their parents were increasingly obsolete (Vlek, 1998). New migrants were also competing for low-skilled work, and as job opportunities for the low skilled diminished, long-term unemployment amongst older members of the labour market became entrenched. By the beginning of the 1980s, a gap emerged between the skills offered and those demanded in the labour market. Structural unemployment was and remains concentrated in the major cities such as Rotterdam and Amsterdam.

Since the 1980s there has been ongoing discussion between unions, employers and the central government about lowering labour costs to a minimum wage level to increase labour demand. During these negotiations the concept of the single male breadwinner, bringing home sufficient pay to cater for all the family's needs has diminished. At this time, an increasing proportion of women were joining the paid, predominantly part-time workforce in the service sector, complimenting the declining real wages of traditional male breadwinners.

The Wassenaar Labour Agreement of 1982 specified moderate wage demands in exchange for reduction in working hours and preservation of the system of social welfare (Terhorst and Van de Ven, 1997: 313). Collective work agreements contained wage demands, particularly amongst labour intensive industries, and have been internationally praised as the mechanism for subsequent job growth in the late 1980s and mid- to late 1990s. Further, major transport infrastructure projects have been fostered to promote private investment and generate employment in the distribution and service economy.

Yet during the 1980s and 1990s, Dutch welfare provisions came into regular and increasing conflict with monetarist fiscal policy driven by the entry requirements for the European Monetary Union (Vlek, 1998). Under this paradigm, governments are considered best if they are small, their public services privatised and driven by market principles. In this context the social security buffer has come under scrutiny, driving the call for more targeted, reduced benefits and to discipline beneficiaries to look for work.

As mentioned earlier, the social welfare system is largely a contributory one, paid for by the policy premiums and taxes of low- to middle-income earners. Between 1976 and 1998 cuts in social spending raised 40 million guiders annually in savings on all social benefits, workers' insurances, social provisions and pensions (Vlek, 1998: 7). In recent years individual social contributions by employees have been criticised by employers. According to some employers, wages diverted to pensions present a break in consumer spending, harm international competitiveness and fuel wage demands. Yet premiums are desperately needed to feed a system obliged to an aging membership, yet relying on declining number of policyholders and investment dividends. The sector has lobbied hard for an increase in premium, which is regulated by the central government.[44]

Individual Rental Subsidy falls outside the individual insurance circuit. It is funded from general taxation revenue and is universally available to all tenants within certain rent and income limits. As mentioned in the previous phase, it is no longer a direct, project-specific demand subsidy relating to the cost-rent system, but more a general welfare policy available to eligible tenants. Expenditure on rental allowances rose considerably during the 1980s despite efforts to contain it.[45] After years of circling debate and increasing cost to the state, the State Secretary (Heerma) recommended a number of measures to secure budget savings and reduce the financial burden: limiting subsidies to young people, sharpening the quality discount and limiting the rent that could be subsidised to 700 guilders. These provisions were to deliver 45 million guilders savings every year beginning in 1988. Yet the cost to the central government has continued to grow.[46]

Today rental subsidy is the central government's only vehicle for influencing housing-related welfare. It can adjust the eligibility criteria (income, rent levels, etc.) and the level of payment provided. Whilst some commentators have argued that rent subsidies have been too broad and deep, other aspects of rent policy have clearly not favoured tenants in recent years. During the mid- to late 1990s, the government permitted rent increases above the rate of inflation (see Table 7.7), kept the eligible upper rent limit for subsidies low, encouraged more targeted allocation of housing and promoted the sale of social housing to financially able tenants.[47,48] These actions were motivated by the central government's strategy to protect the primary revenue source of the social landlords and secure their financial continuity, and thereby stabilise the association sector in the new financial context (outlined in this subsection earlier).

This financial and political context has played an implicit role defining the implementation of the social task of housing associations (to target low-income households and those in housing need). In practice, associations have undertaken entrepreneurial activities, built for profit, sold stock, liberalised and raised rents and merged with other associations. The market orientated activities of some associations, in the context of greater freedom to set rents, have reduced affordability for some low-income families. Increasing homelessness has also been noted (Priemus, 1996). According to Van Kempen *et al.*,

> the operating risks of the housing associations were redefined to closely resemble those of large-scale private land lords. It is likely that this will entice them to adapt their operating rules and management strategies, resulting in severe erosion of the position of low-income households in the housing market.

> (2000: 512)

Home ownership, once the preserve of wealthier Dutch households, is now being heavily promoted as a mainstream option by central government.[49] The government's explicit goal is to encourage the housing consumer's self-sufficiency (Vermaat, 1996). To this end, social landlords have been encouraged to sell existing stock to suitable sitting tenants. VINEX housing is primarily built by private firms for sale and not social rental. Further, households are enticed by generous (but regressive) taxation concessions, which enable the deduction of the cost of home finance. By 1995 almost one in every two households owned or was purchasing a home (NRW, 1997: 13).

Synthesising key relations in their contingent context

Figure 7.7 depicts the *fundamental changes* that have occurred during the 1980s and 1990s, redefining the very core of the Dutch solution. *First* and foremost, we see that the *central government is no longer in control of the volume of the loan programme for social rental housing.* Housing associations must now access the capital market directly. They have improved their access to this market by obtaining a guarantee (WSW), which in the last resort is secured by the central and local government and financial reorganisation (CFV). Second, the monopoly position held by municipalities in the land market has been diminished. New players include project developers capable of implementing development Plans.

The government is *no longer in a position to use the social sector as a counter-cyclical tool* during times of low production and high housing need. It has *lost considerable control of the nature and level of housing outcomes* produced. Production levels are alarmingly low, and scarcity is keeping prices high. Further, a number of current and potential crises could lead to the demise of the social housing sector itself. Problems include speculative activity in the *land market, rising prices* above those feasible for social rental exploitation, the slow *'eating*

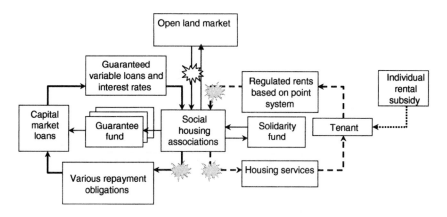

Figure 7.7 Abstraction of the flow of capital via social housing sector, following the withdrawal of the state from issuing loans (1979–2000).

away' of housing association reserves during less favourable interest rates, increasing *residualisation of the tenant base* as more wealthy tenants are both pushed and pulled out of the sector and finally, almost *total reliance on subject subsidies* to achieve housing welfare, whilst other costs are unchecked. Further, increasing *entrepreneurial activities may erode the legitimacy* of the sector undermining any future government assistance. Finally, there are already emerging signs that *young dual-income couples cannot afford to enter the home ownership market.*

7.6   Abstracting the causal mechanisms

Section 7.5 has redescribed and abstracted key relations underlying various shifts in housing provision in the Netherlands, with particular emphasis upon how contingencies have influenced the definition of core property, finance and welfare and labour relations during periods of coherence, crises and adaptation.

As outlined in section 7.3, the Dutch solution of compact cities with its large proportion of social rental dwellings alongside subsidised and unsubsidised dwellings for purchase was formally, but tenuously established in the early years of the twentieth century. It is notable for its prominent inclusion of private associations managing social housing, which contrasts starkly with the marginal and residual role of state-provided 'public' housing in Australia. Behind this observable phenomenon can be found a set of social relations characterised by the strong role for larger municipalities in land development, planning and housing development, favourable government-secured loans and object subsidies for the construction of dwellings by a variety of providers for different forms of consumption, and the regulation of rents sustained by modest household incomes and supplemented by rental subsidy. Contingent conditions have played an integral role in the development and dynamics of these core relations of provision, influencing the level and type of dwellings produced and their spatial patterning.

For the purposes of analysis, relevant contingencies can be considered to be those that influence the key relations of provision: property, saving and investment and labour and welfare relations. Take for example the initial period of economic liberalism between 1848 and 1889, which generated a serious housing crisis. During this time the property market was operating under conditions of scarcity, monopolised by private speculative interests and constrained by municipal government, politically and fiscally out of step with the demands of the new industrialising economy. Development was constrained not only by obsolete defence walls but also by the strength of private property rights, which precluded government co-ordination and fiscal constraints of municipalities, which undermined their capacity to pay for costly infrastructure works. Of course, these contingencies affecting property rights must also be synthesised with those affecting institutions of investment in the built environment at the time and the labour and welfare conditions of city residents and new migrants. To facilitate this process, section 7.6.1 abstracts the contingent conditions of relevance to key relations underpinning changes in the Dutch housing solution.

7.6.1 Abstraction using relevant concepts and ideas

To enable a more straightforward contrast between each phase, Table 7.8 abstracts from section 7.5, shifting definitions of key relations, under periods of coherence and crisis, in the development of the Dutch housing solution. It also abstracts the contingent conditions of influence and the relevant housing outcomes.

7.6.2 Retroductive analysis of the Dutch housing solution

Beyond the simple contrast provided by Table 7.8, retroductive reasoning is required to progress explanatory analysis. Whilst the table is useful for highlighting contrasts, it merely categorises relations and does not tell us much about the integrated dynamics between them and how they generated particular housing outcomes – and indeed, non-outcomes. Rather, this process of abduction must be complimented by contrastive and counterfactual questioning to expose the causal mechanisms operating to influence the development of the Dutch housing solution. The following series of questions and possible answers, drawing upon the evidence provided in section 7.5 and abstractions in Figures 7.2–7.6, are dedicated to this goal.

Why was home ownership for workers not an alternative in the formation of the Dutch housing solution?

The Dutch housing 'solution' has emerged from very different roots than those established during a similar time period in Australia. First and foremost it emerged from existing pre-industrial cities, with a medieval mercantile past. The contours of these earlier cities can be seen in the circling defence walls, tight inner cities and narrow irregular street patterns. These contours and the power structures that maintained them constrained and influenced the development of industrial cities and their housing solutions. Yet, beyond this brief preliminary explanation can be found a specific coherence of property, investment and labour relations, which underpinned a specific type of housing provision during the late nineteenth century.

From the outset, conditions present in the Dutch property market of pre-industrial medieval cities bore no resemblance to those in colonial Australia. Renting housing was the norm and circuits for individual housing credit for ownership were quite undeveloped. The land market was monopolised by a landed gentry, merchants and industrial elite who constrained supply and gained their wealth from speculation. Small exchangeable and affordable parcels of land, suitable for modest housing developments, were completely absent form the market. Larger parcels were scarce and thus land prices high. Such conditions necessitated high yield developments and multiple tenancy apartment buildings were the norm.

Another causal mechanism can be found in the definition of labour relations and market position of urban workers. Labour conditions in new industries and the home were often poor but workers fleeing the economically depressed countryside were isolated and unorganised. Unlike their Australian counterparts,

Table 7.8 Phases in the definition of Dutch housing provision, 1848–2000

Phase	Liberalism and crisis 1848–1889	Turbulent foundations 1890–1933	Recovery and acceleration 1934–1983	Redefinition 1984–2000
Land rights development	Dominance of private speculation, costly land development requires voluntary co-operation of private parties, electoral franchise limited to landed gentry, fiscal base reliant on rising property values	Increasing role of municipality in land banking, leasing, development control and repossession, broadening electoral franchise, revenue base expands with fiscal decentralisation	Municipalities monopolise land markets surrounding cities, social housing given primacy, strong central government role in planning urban renewal and new urban expansion	Municipal role challenged and numerous commercial players enter the land market surrounding cities, central government designates areas for expansion, speculation returns to the market and impedes productivity
Savings investment	Non-housing investment flows into city, mortgage banks support speculative development of high-density rental housing, industrial expansion stifled by limited sites and lack of workers housing	Central government plays a pivotal role allocating housing finance to specific providers, subsidises increasing interest payments, rising material costs, yet later caps social housing rents and demands subsidy repayments	Central government expands its role, with particular emphasis upon social housing development, rent levels fixed, exploitation subsidies provided, efforts to guarantee home loans, legitimacy of role questioned and new financing model introduced, proves costly	Central government withdraws from direct financing role in social housing, replaced by government-backed guarantee and solidarity fund, growth and innovation in home mortgage and secondary mortgage market maximising advantageous fiscal conditions
Welfare/labour	Poor labour and working conditions, piece work,	Strikes and social unrest, strengthening role of the	Wages suppressed but rents regulated and later rental	Structural unemployment amongst low skilled, accord

	expensive housing, no capacity to generate savings, excess labour supply, extremely limited and paternalistic welfare provisions	labour movement yet without formal political representation, pacification of the labour force and pillarisation of publicly sponsored private welfare state	allowances greatly expanded, unions and government focus on jobs rather than wage growth, later wage growth slowed by economic decline and unemployment	for wage moderation, growth in high-skilled employment and related wages, Welfare cut backs, asset wealth amongst owner occupiers substantial
Contingencies	Local state constrained by fiscal and electoral base, tight land market promotes speculation and high yield development, industrialisation, agricultural depression, mass migration, over supply of labour	Fiscal constraints of the local state overcome, but in a turbulent economic climate, costly materials and scarce private investment, strong role of religious organisations garnering public resources for welfare provision	Lack of interest in housing market by capital market, later market conditions stabilise but eroded by monetary collapse, oil price rises, unemployment and low wage growth, investors campaign to protect investment in central cities	Substantial interest by mortgage market, capitalising on increasing value of existing homes, double incomes and rising incomes amongst certain workers, city gentrification but areas of social disadvantage receive attention
Housing outcomes	High density, rental apartment dwellings, over crowding, serious and widespread health epidemics. Some attempts at housing alternatives: co-operatives, philanthropic rental housing	Cost-rent social housing provided by municipal housing companies, assisted private rental construction, limited dwellings for ownership, crisis follows mass unemployment	Substantial expansion of below-market rent mass social housing provided by social landlords, decline in private rental housing, gradual increase in home ownership, collapse of housing market, last spasm of social housing production	Rapid increase in home ownership, mores spacious new dwellings outside city centres, over production rates decline, sale of social housing strongly promoted, rising household indebtedness and industrial colonies

Dutch skilled and semi-skilled workers were 'disposable', easily replaced by the thousands of work seekers leaving the depressed agricultural sector. Working conditions were extremely poor and wages minimal. In some cases, workers merely received tokens, which could only be exchanged for provisions from the employer's store.

These contingently defined labour conditions and housing costs suppressed the capacity of households to save, not only for hard times, but also for better housing. Additional resources may have improved their capacity to change their housing situation and attempts were made in the formation of home ownership co-operatives. However, the price of ownership outstripped savings capacity and the co-operatives' goal of home ownership was switched to renting.

For every system of savings is a corresponding one of investment. As mentioned, for many workers the capacity to save was minimal. The required down payment for a mortgage loan was prohibitive. Further, mortgage banks had far safer investments to make than small-scale 30-year mortgages for low and insecurely paid home purchasers. Conversely, capital did flow into the private rental sector, where more certain profits could be made from building at high density and low quality. Rental investment was a safe investment, providing the building survived the 30-year mortgage! Thus, via the circuit of mortgage credit and housing development, the rental sector flourished for a time. Landlords were in a strong market position to exploit the abundant supply of tenants. Rents were set at market rates and eviction for non-payment was the norm. This exploitative mode of provision pervaded until unsafe buildings and poor living and health conditions threatened a range of social classes and stifled orderly expansion of the newly industrialising cities. The local state was fiscally and politically incapable of resolving the crisis. Constrained by limited revenue and controlled by a propertied elite, few reforms were possible until electoral and fiscal conditions were adapted. Indeed, this period was of 'strategic significance' in the formation of the Dutch housing solution (Harloe, 1995: 50).

Emerging from a period of social unrest, expanding electoral franchise and calls for reform, the Housing Act of 1901 outlined the central government's intention to provide *50-year annuity loans* with fixed payments, rather than the norm of 30, for registered associations of renters for the construction of social rental housing and contributions towards operational costs to keep rents as low as possible. The terms of the loan required *rental associations* to commit to regular fixed repayments over a very long period, rather than purchase for individual home ownership. Life expectancy then, and now, certainly did not permit individual mortgages of a 50-year maturity. Yet such terms were possible with rental associations; they were conceived as relatively permanent institutions. Further, the *new building code ensured that buildings produced remained standing and exploitable* beyond the maturity of mortgage finance, matching the financial commitment made by central governments. These important, linked provisions shifted the risk of investment towards the state, which in turn managed the land development process via municipalities, setting building standards and non-profit management standards for approved *registered* associations. Registration enabled the government to ensure that loans were being issued to *responsible landlords*, who would manage their stock efficiently, yet *not profit excessively from their advantageous position*. Eventual surpluses (after loan maturity of 50 years) had to be spent on furthering housing provision. In turn these associations selected tenants most able to sustain rental payments and enforced strict standards of tenant behaviour.

Indeed, the Housing Act emerged from a period of strategic crisis and provided the basic framework for the Dutch housing solution. The framework comprised municipal land development; 50-year government-secured loans at the lowest market rate possible and cost rents. Yet exposed to the contingencies of an open economic system, this framework was not enough. When the cost of building materials and urban renewal rose, object subsidies were provided; when interest rates rose, the government paid the difference between market and below-market rates to keep cost rents low, when frozen or stagnating wages were insufficient to cover cost rents, further object subsidies were provided which later shifted to subject subsidies. Despite the ebb and flow of contingent conditions, and the sporadic outputs of social housing, the basic structure of the Dutch housing solution remained in place until the mid-1980s.

Why were social landlords private and not public?

A peculiar aspect of the Dutch housing solution is the reliance upon private rather than public landlordism for the management of social housing funded by government loans. Such private landlords are not of commercial origin, but rather a non-profit private vehicle to resolve the question of accommodating working households, including those on a moderate income. An explanation for this phenomenon can be found in the historical and spatial coherence of key social relations affecting the development of housing policy following a period of urban crisis. This crisis was partly generated by economic liberalism and dysfunctional housing market dominated by speculative interests, and was responded to in the context of an emerging Christian corporatist welfare state.

Unlike municipal landlords in the United Kingdom or State Housing Commissions in Australia, Dutch housing associations emerged as the most legitimate vehicle at a time when the crisis of economic liberalism undermined faith and trust in commercial landlordism, yet public ownership and control was tainted with revolutionary communist idealism. Social unrest had erupted in numerous towns and cities, often over housing conditions, but no strong advocate existed for the de-commodification of housing relations. In contrast to the labour movement, the network of Christian-based interest groups was deeply rooted in the daily lives of Dutch households. Almost everyone belonged to a church, social group or society of religious origin, which in turn influenced social networks, work ethics and domestic life. Most labour unions belonged to one or another camp, being protestant or catholic and later non-aligned.

The capitalist ethic was intertwined with religious doctrine. Even profits had to be generated from philanthropic housing initiatives and market rents charged; more collective or subsidised alternatives would simply dilute the hard working ethic of deserving tenants. Private non-commercial organisations, and not the state, were considered the most suitable mode of social regulation in a time of social upheaval across Europe. They were in a central position to reform anti-social behaviour amongst tenants and protect them from the dangers of socialism. Further, housing associations were a natural forerunner of the pillarised welfare state. Typically collective facilities such as schools, recreation clubs and health funds later became rooted in the pillars of the Christian corporatist welfare state.

Why social rather than private rental housing in the 1950s?

Social housing formed an integral part of the central government's low-wage strategy following a long economic crisis and the material destruction brought by the Second World War. It was the only institutional response that could be steered by the government to repair war damage, address the housing shortage and charge low rents. Social landlords were committed to a long-term social task via cost-rent housing, rather than market rents for private profit. They were established in this task before the War and were called upon once again, to address the new housing crisis. Yet housing associations and their tenants became a force of their own and were subject to competitive electoral politics between the Catholic and Labour parties. The housing shortage continued in the 1950s and the baby boom generation and new colonial migrants needed to be housed. Expansion of the existing framework of housing provision, via housing associations was a path-dependent and politically acceptable strategy.

From its dominance in the late nineteenth century to near extinction in the 1950s, the private-for-profit rental sector has been subject to numerous contingent conditions eroding investor confidence and reducing the number of active players in the market to large institutional investors. Throughout the War, it was forbidden to profit from the exploitation of dwellings. Rents were frozen at 1934 levels. The low wages of tenants and shortages of materials also curtailed profitable exploitation. Later various additional housing policy measures promoted declining investment. These included strong tenancy legislation, centrally regulated rents and indeed competition from both the regulated affordable social housing sector and the subsidised and fiscally attractive home ownership sector.

Together, these measures undermined the flexibility and security of rental investment and broke basic conditions for commodified tenancy relations (security of tenure, rent regulation) of interest to small-scale investors and petty landlords. Today, the largest investors in the small private rental market remain Dutch pension funds. These investors seek low-risk, long-term investments in order to pay their obligations to long-term policyholders, and use rental property as a hedge against inflation. A number of pension funds are now capitalising on their debt free, inflated assets and selling rental stock, sometimes to sitting tenants.

Why discontinue the system of government-guaranteed loans and curtail municipal-led land development in the 1990s?

Despite continuing housing shortages, the seeds of stagnation were planted in the Dutch housing 'solution' by the late 1960s. Following protracted struggle between housing associations, central government, unions and the Social Economic Research Council, the strangle hold on wages and rents was broken in the 1960s. The central government's hidden interest subsidy, which had created below market-interest rates for housing associations, was exposed by explicit object subsidies. To reduce the burden, a new system of Dynamic Cost Rent (DKP) was introduced in 1975 to claw back object subsidies in the latter years of the mortgage. By the mid-1970s, the finance of social housing associations became tied to calculations of the DKP system and low-income tenants became eligible for rent subsidy. Yet, as always the new financial system was subject to unfavourable contingent conditions. In the context of stagnant wage growth, unemployment and deflation, rents did not increase sufficiently in a deflated market, and the DKP system proved exorbitantly expensive for the central government by the late 1970s.

Yet alongside these troubles in the social sector, the private housing market was in crisis and the building industry in deep recession. Despite looming budgetary constraints, economic malaise and the near collapse of the home ownership sector, the government steered investment into the social housing sector once again, using the trusted neo-Keynesian strategies of the past. Yet such a strategy ran counter to the growing ideological hegemony of small government, financial deregulation and privatisation promoted by the conditions for Economic Monetary Union. This ideology was bolstered by the yearly reminder of the housing debt presented in the government budget, demonstrating the ballooning nature of housing loans committed under the DKP system and allegations of building fraud eroding confidence in housing associations and municipalities.

A number of important changes were legitimised in this climate of fiscal austerity and greatly influenced the dependent relations between central government, housing associations and municipalities. With these changes, municipalities would no longer hold a monopoly position in the land markets surrounding their town centres and thus would be less able to direct the pace and composition of housing construction. To some degree this initiative was unintentional and stemmed from the announcement of potential development areas by central government, which of course attracted speculative purchasers. Municipalities were not permitted by law to expropriate land from owners with a capacity to implement development projects (unlike farmers). Later, municipalities were strongly discouraged from becoming too active in the land market. Instead the central government gave preference to private companies in building homes for purchase rather than associations providing social housing. In this context, the task of municipalities in fulfilling planning objectives became more complex, involving multiple players, and housing outcomes became less certain.

Importantly, the financial relations of social housing provision were also altered with the shift away from directly secured loans (which were ballooning exponentially) towards those accessed directly by associations from the capital market. The balance sheets of housing associations were greatly enhanced by the Brutering calculation, which cancelled existing loans in exchange for future object subsidies. Dutch housing associations now obtain a financial guarantee (WSW) and contribute to a mutual fund (CFV) to strengthen their market position and obtain all loans on the capital market. To date access to this market has been relatively easy given the strong asset position, improved rental income and management experience of social landlords. The sector has been encouraged to become more financially self-sufficient, merging with other associations, undertaking more commercially orientated projects and selling housing stock. Sandwiched between the openness of the capital market and margins of rent policy, associations have also had to become more attuned to their economic potential, pursuing more 'active' rent policy (which in turn pushed out those who could afford home purchase) and development strategies, which include the construction of dwellings for sale and profit.

In tandem with these developments in the social sector, home purchase has been encouraged by the discounted sale of social housing stock, the relaunch and promotion of the National Mortgage Guarantee, and generous tax advantages. Purchase prices in employment centres have escalated. Within the finance sector, a number of developments have fostered the growth of home purchase: a more permissive lending regime based on two incomes, establishment of a secondary mortgage market and the establishment of the brokering sector generating markets for new mortgage products.

Also related are developments in the Dutch labour market. Following recession, wage constraint and labour market restructuring, there has been substantial employment growth in the mid- to late 1990s, particularly amongst the financial services, technology and construction sectors. In this context, the social task of the housing associations appeared to be less pressing (apart from the demands of structurally unemployed and 'silent' asylum seekers) in the face of apparent labour market prosperity. Further, following the welfare 'excesses' of the 1970s and 1980s, the central government has promoted a libertarian ideology of self-reliance, by targeting welfare benefits and individual rent subsidies more closely. Home ownership, once the preserve of wealthy and non-city dwellers, is now promoted as the mainstream housing 'solution' for all 'able' Dutch households. In contrast, the social housing sector is considered by some in the central government to be a receptacle for households unable to compete in the private-for-profit sector.

Indeed, the coherence of the long-established social housing solution has been broken and a new one is emerging, dominated by those with an interest in home ownership. Some of these interests are contrary to national polices of choice, affordability and quality, as the politicians demand the sale of social housing and market parties accidentally or implicitly promote production scarcity, further inflating house prices.

To sum up, this chapter has outlined observable characteristics of the Dutch mode of housing provision, identified its core features and provided an overview of explanatory approaches in Dutch housing studies. It has also provided a rationale for a new approach and applied this to different phases in housing history. These have been contrasted and analysed for their underlying causal mechanisms via contrastive and counterfactual questioning.

Chapter 8 will now contrast and compare the underlying causal mechanisms of the two divergent case studies, Australia and the Netherlands, and discuss a number of theoretical and substantive issues.

Part III
Summary and conclusions

8 Explaining and comparing housing 'solutions'

8.1 Introduction

We have come a very long way in our journey of understanding and explanation, since the first lay impressions of housing and urban conditions in Australia and the Netherlands posted at the very beginning of this book. It is now time to contribute towards a more theorised explanation for divergence between the two countries.

As proposed in the problem statement in Chapter 1, the research has focused upon the contingent definition of specific social relations, which were postulated to hold emergent properties with regards to forms of housing provision. It was argued that the contingent, geo-historical definition and packaging of specific social relations, primarily concerning property rights, saving and investment and finally, labour and welfare, would play an integral role explaining divergence in forms of housing provision. In order to test the plausibility of these arguments two illustrative case studies in Australia and the Netherlands examined various shifts in their long-term housing trajectories, contrasting specific periods of adaptation, coherence and crisis. For every phase, close attention was given not only to the contingent definition of these relations but to how they were synthesised in a coherent albeit crisis-prone manner to promote a specific mode of provision. Contrastive questioning and counterfactual thinking at the conclusion of each case sharpened the definition of causal mechanisms generating specific housing outcomes and inhibiting others.

This chapter provides an opportunity to reflect upon the theoretical and analytical progress made so far and contributes towards an explanation for divergence in the two very different housing 'solutions'. We are only able to move in this direction now, because we have reached the stage where we can compare at the level of generative causal mechanisms, as argued in Chapter 3. However, this is not the end of the story. Fulfilling the promise of the retroductive approach, it is also timely to revisit and sharpen our earlier postulate towards a stronger explanation for further testing and revision.

Towards this goal, a number of relevant theoretical conclusions are put forward in this chapter that respond to the initial postulated explanation outlined in Chapters 3 and 5 and subsequent findings in Chapters 6 and 7. First, the case study findings highlight how core relations can promote fairly stable institutions, such as the protected circuit of capital and municipal land development companies that may delimit future developments and sustain others in path-dependant fashion. Second, these institutions may be subject to various adaptations to cope with dynamic contingent circumstances. In this sense change can be considered not only to be path dependent but also cumulatively causal. Thus, a revised postulate should stress the power of path dependency, institutional fix and cumulative causation in sustaining particular modes of provision. Third, as critical explanation also asks why sustained housing institutions are later subject to challenge, I also take a closer look at the notion of contingency and risk. Fourth, these conclusions concern the way we conceptualise different forms of housing provision and its importance in reaching an understanding of the core relations, both emergent and contingent, and their interdependencies underpinning specific modes of provision.

Furthering the 'critical' role of realist research this chapter postulates the consequences of recent developments in both the Australian and Dutch housing solution, contemplating future housing scenarios, with specific attention to the shifting distribution of risk between households and space for potential state/ market manoeuvre.

8.2 Explaining divergence: comparing causal mechanisms

This section integrates and contrasts empirical case study research to examine how key relations have been defined and packaged differently to generate divergent forms of provision in Australia and the Netherlands. From the formative decades of the two housing solutions, different sets of risk perception were found to exist in the field of land development, finance, construction, exchange and the consumption of housing services. These differences guided the actions of agents in the network of housing provision, which produced and were reproduced by dynamic structures of provision. Further, periods of coherence were punctuated by periods of crisis, leading to the reformulation of new routes of accumulation in the housing sector.

It is helpful to focus upon specific contrasts between the different phases in the trajectories of the two cases in order to highlight the existence of differently defined emergent relations of provision, the interdependencies between them and their synthesis in the form of flows of investment and consumption, supported by various institutions and undermined by contingent conditions. To this end, drawing upon analysis from the case study research, an explanation is developed in response to a number of contrastive questions. This process contributes towards a dynamic, multi-causal explanation for divergence and concerns the following:

- the period of crisis in the late nineteenth century, preceding the evolution of adaptive modes of provision,

- the channelling of investment and supportive institutions established in the early twentieth century,
- the sustained development of these solutions during the 1950s and 1960s, and
- their reconfiguration in the late 1980s and 1990s.

8.2.1 Why did social housing not emerge as the solution in the late colonial period and why did home ownership not emerge as the solution in the urbanisation of Dutch cities?

First of all, the institutional structure and market conditions of the land market during the formative years of new colony were very different. In Australia, following the Crown land sales of the 1840s, urban land was largely in private hands. An efficient system of property rights and subdivision facilitated transactions between agricultural owners, land developers and homeowner builders. The preparation of land for development was a much simpler albeit labour intensive process, requiring tree clearing to enable simple wooden houses to be erected. Second, the urban workforce was largely better off, especially compared to their European counterparts, and largely engaged in mercantile or construction activities rather than hard labour of mass or cottage industries. In particular, the labour market position and wages of skilled workers in a mercantile economy was much stronger, wages were relatively high enabling them to save. Third, savings institutions modelled on British Building Societies required the vesting of land title as security for construction finance. Small parcels of land for this purpose were rapidly released onto the land market in the 1860s and 1870s when the colony was awash with migrants and successful gold seekers. Loans from Building Societies were only provided for the construction of owner-occupied dwellings. In this way, thrifty (or fortunate), skilled workers were able to realise housing aspirations that were a distant dream in their overcrowded impoverished country of origin. Figure 8.1 depicts the circuit of investment and consumption during the hey day of home ownership in the 1870s.

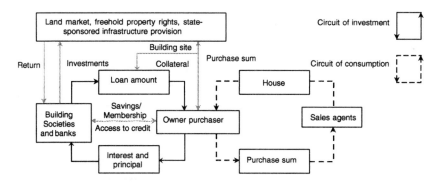

Figure 8.1 The Australian solution in the formative years.

Unlike their British counterparts, the reserves of Building Societies were able to be invested in the land market. When this over-heated market collapsed, many Building Societies lost their reserves and thus the circuit of members savings that could be recycled into rationed home loans. An inevitable housing crisis followed, with repossessions and widespread homelessness. The response to this crisis is discussed in section 8.2.2.

In contrast the property relations and land market conditions were radically different in Dutch cities during the last half of the nineteenth century. Land ownership was fragmented and it was difficult to co-ordinate necessary reclamation, site preparation was costly and municipal revenues for basic infrastructure provision were insufficient. The landed gentry that dominated municipal chambers under conditions of limited electoral franchise blocked any intrusion into their property rights. An outmoded and static urban form and a regressive fiscal and political structure stifled the development of adequate housing for workers in new industries, impeding industrialisation. Further, Dutch wages were low and precarious in the mid nineteenth century. A high proportion of household income was spent on rental housing costs. As a consequence, households had little over to save at the end of each month. Individual mortgages schemes, which rely on the ability to save for a down payment and make regular installments there after, simply did not get off the ground. In the sphere of production, the construction of high-density rental dwellings was the norm to maximise yield on scarce expensive land often within tightly constrained city boundaries. For a time investment capital flowed from other declining areas of the economy into the speculative land and housing markets. Figure 8.2 illustrates a simple abstraction of the flow of investment and consumption into housing around 1870.

Migration, overcrowding, poor housing conditions and severe health problems led to a much broader crisis in housing provision, touching upon a range of social classes. In the context of broadening electoral franchise and a more centralised

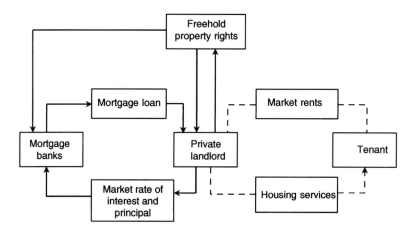

Figure 8.2 The Dutch solution in the pre-social housing years.

fiscal revenue, municipalities were increasingly in a position to respond to the constraints of speculative land relations, poor quality construction and exorbitant rents. They could not, however, address the problem of vacillating levels of investment in the housing sector. Shaped by the crises of the former mode of provision, municipalities broke the impasse in the land market with expropriation rights and market compensation, tightened control over the quality of construction, and designated slum areas for urban renewal. Central government secured finance of housing for workers, to be managed by non-profit private landlords. The reasons why this new 'solution' was able to be established are discussed in section 8.2.2.

8.2.2 Why was mortgage finance channelled via State Savings Banks and households in Australia and central government and associations in the Netherlands?

The primary financial institutions channelling capital into housing production in each of the two 'solutions' are very different, and so too are the borrowers and their risk profiles. In the second phase of the Australian solution, we see that State Savings Banks have taken over the role of financier of housing services from Building Societies. Following the spectacular rise and fall of the property market, many Societies collapsed or became ensconced in corruption scandals; in the process members lost their homes and were forced into less desirable rental housing and temporary shelters. The governments of Victoria, New South Wales and other states responded by improving the security and stability of the financial system and certainty in development processes. In this climate, state-owned banks emerged as the only legitimate and viable vehicle to channel investment into property. No longer beholden to the narrow interests and savings capacities of Society members and (corrupt) board members, State Banks could pursue broader 'public' objectives under Commonwealth legislation. With many young soldiers returning from the First World War, these banks were used as a vehicle to distribute Commonwealth housing loans. They developed systems to minimise the risks of default to the banking sector at large, and established the mechanism of credit foncier mortgages. They also became involved in the land development process directly, setting maximum standards for dwellings and rationing the allocation of home loans to 'safe' borrowers. Figure 8.3 depicts this new situation.

The Netherlands provides a useful contrast highlighting the role uneven and socially structured risk plays in constraining and enabling policy alternatives. At the turn of the century, the concept of home purchase for working households was far from the political agenda. The potential of Building Societies was not widespread or well known. Workers were not considered capable of maintaining a housing loan, given their weak labour market position. Landlordism was certainly despised by some, but the few experiments in social housing suggested that renting, by definition, did not have to be excessively exploitative. Politically, it was considered a question of balancing the goals of good housing with sound financial management and tenant discipline. Avoiding the self-interest and speculative problems of the previous phase was paramount. Given the dearth of private

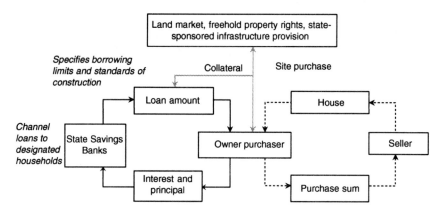

Figure 8.3 The foundations of the Australian solution *c*.1925.

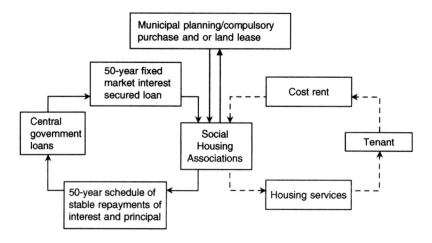

Figure 8.4 The foundations of the cost-rent social housing solution under the Housing Act 1901.

investment for quality housing, government loans were channelled via registered associations committed to these goals, as depicted in Figure 8.4.

Yet social housing never became public housing, financed, owned and managed by the state. Private associations, often originating from one of the denominational pillars of society, must register their commitment to the delivery of cost-rental housing, repaying a fixed schedule of loan principal and interest via cost rent-revenue. Philanthropic and religious organisations mobilised to keep the socialists from controlling state resources. Indeed, private non-profit housing associations were an important institutional stepping stone towards the development of the vertically structured corporatist welfare state in the Netherlands.

8.2.3 Why did Australian households express their wealth and status via home purchase in the 1950s and 1960s, whilst Dutch households did not?

The mechanisms supporting the expansion of home ownership were well developed by the 1950s. Urban planning of metropolitan areas promoted urban expansion and provided maps for speculative purchasers. State agencies continued to 'roll out the services' connecting potential urban areas with basic services, making land in these areas accessible, developable and valuable. Building upon existing financial institutions, the flow of investment into home mortgages was bolstered by the Commonwealth government, which instructed the Reserve Bank to negotiate a protected circuit of capital for home loans delivered by State Banks and established the Home Loans Insurance Corporation. The protected circuit lowered interest rates below the bond rate and the guarantee enabled a wider range of households to borrow with smaller initial deposits. The financial risks to State Banks were further minimised by a buoyant inflating housing market, urban expansion underpinned by state-sponsored infrastructure provision and strong labour market conditions. This scenario is depicted in Figure 8.5.

Australian politicians on both sides of the political spectrum supported the expansion of home ownership during the 1950s and 1960s. This was bolstered by the collective memory of mass evictions during the Great Depression. Indeed, the party with the strongest support for the ideology of home ownership remained in office for almost twenty years after the Second World War. Ideology also played an important role minimising the development of the public housing programme, established in the period immediately following the Second World War. In the subsequent cold war era of anti-communist patriotism, conservative politicians promoted homeownership as the goal of every worthy citizen, whilst demonising

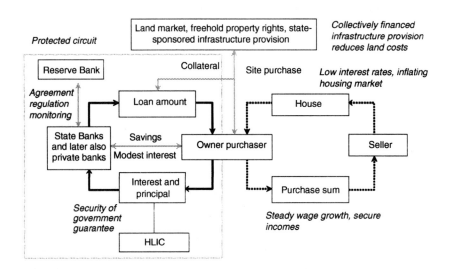

Figure 8.5 The Australian solution under a protected circuit of capital.

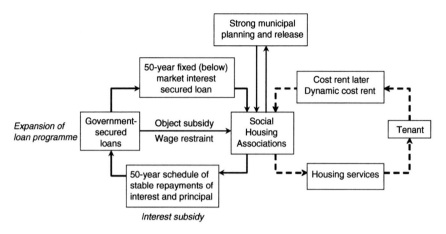

Figure 8.6a The Dutch solution under conditions of wage constraint.

public housing as dangerous socialism. This government also enjoyed an era of strong and protected economic growth and widespread post-war prosperity. During this time, the strong labour market position of skilled workers was bolstered by employment in the new industries 'jumping the tariff walls' and this meant that home purchase, in a low interest scenario, was indeed within the reach of a wide social spectrum.

If we turn to the Netherlands during this period, we see a contrasting set of perceptions, contingent conditions and emergent structures, crystallising to promote very different housing choices. First and foremost, the Netherlands was emerging from a period of post-war recovery that institutionalised a number of special measures affecting housing investment, wages and rent levels. Again labour market conditions and strategies were a decisive constraint in defining the housing solution. A centralised low-wage strategy necessitated low housing costs. In the context of post-war destruction and massive housing shortages, a market solution could not deliver efficiently or effectively. The low-wage scenario necessary to promote Dutch exports could only be sustained via the expansion of the existing social rental sector, with land development monopolised by municipalities opening sites for housing associations, rents frozen and kept below cost rent and exploitation shortfalls compensated by central government subsidies. This scenario is illustrated in Figure 8.6a.

In a tightly constrained housing market, Dutch households queued for long periods for their housing. They had little choice. In this context, home ownership remained the domain of the wealthy urbanite or country dweller until prosperity returned in the 1960s.

As depicted in Figure 8.6b, Individual Rental Subsidy was first introduced as a pre-condition of urban renewal, as cost rents for improved dwellings, constructed under more costly conditions, were substantially higher. Later rental allowance was provided to all tenants, regardless of the dwelling type.

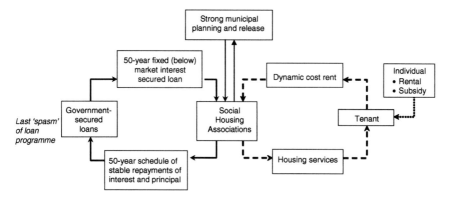

Figure 8.6b The Dutch solution under conditions of welfare.

8.2.4 Why did state support for home purchase decline in Australia and increase in the Netherlands during the 1990s?

Given the scenario outlined earlier, what could possibly have generated the reverse stance taken by the Australian and Dutch governments towards their favoured housing solutions during the 1990s? The changing definition and perception of risks can help us to understand this shift in both cases, but to explain them we need to dig deeper to appreciate the underlying shifts taking place in urban political economy. In the Australian case, intervention in home finance is challenged by the much larger finance sector, in the context of dwindling domestic investment and chronic long-term unemployment. Regional governments and fringe municipalities face a crisis in financing urban infrastructure and the burden of provision shifts to land developers who pass on these costs to new home purchasers. Housing investment becomes more risky, house prices on the urban fringe decline for a period and this materialises in the form of negative equity with acute individualised consequences. With interest rates climbing, purchasers in the 'mortgage belt' lobby for a new policy response. During this period, deregulation of the financial sector is in full swing, opening access to foreign banks. Labour leaders and the union movement support this change, as a means to gain investment and produce employment. Yet it requires the constraints of the protected circuit of home finance be lifted from Savings Banks, to enable them to compete for customers in the context of a far more open market, offering alternative saving and investment opportunities. With new mortgage retailers competing for customers and interest rates peaking at 18 per cent, voters saw deregulation as the only way out. During this time the government's national mortgage guarantee (HLIC) was privatised and with it the last vestiges of Australian home ownership policy seemed to disappear without immediate electoral consequences. Increased competition did, however, increase the volume

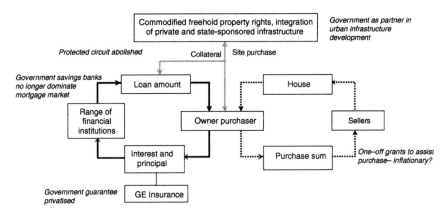

Figure 8.7 The Australian solution under deregulation.

of credit available; apparently generating lower interest rates several years later and promoting innovation in mortgage products. The abundance of credit also raised prices in the housing market beyond the affordability of traditional single-income households, formerly the intended beneficiaries of the Australian dream of home ownership. Risks are now concentrated amongst over indebted households, reliant on two incomes in a flexible casualising labour market and more 'open' interest rate scenarios. Figure 8.7 depicts the new scenario.

In the Netherlands housing policy mediated the problems of fiscal austerity, unemployment and under-investment in the domestic economy in a very different manner, yet building upon the institutions of the past. Fiscal austerity translated into a drive to reduce the very visible state contribution of object subsidies for social housing provision (climbing exponentially as ballooning loans under the failed DKP arrangement). A way out of central government obligations became apparent when the capital markets began to appreciate the strong asset and revenue position of associations, and viewed them as safe, secure forms of investment. Institutions were established to facilitate the shift from central to capital market loans, including the exchange of future subsidies for payout of government-secured loans (Brutering), expansion of an existing guarantee fund and establishment of a solidarity fund to assist weaker associations. Risks could be passed onto the tenant via rent increases and minimised and spread more evenly across the housing association sector through improved assets and reserves. Loans remain guaranteed, yet in the very last resort, by central and local governments, as depicted in Figure 8.8.

Home ownership is fast becoming the dominant form of housing consumption in a package of housing options in the Netherlands. Support for home ownership is more difficult to explain, as it is not necessarily a rational choice for many households with generous welfare provisions and future pensions and affordable and secure rental housing options. It can be said that home ownership was an extension of the government's ideological commitment to minimise dependence

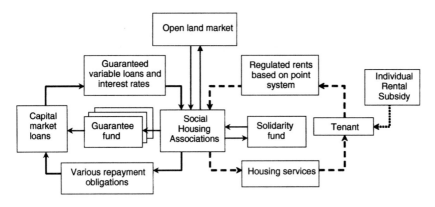

Figure 8.8 The Dutch solution under reregulation.

upon social housing subsidies and was willingly promoted by the central government. Yet in trying to reduce one form of revenue 'dependence' another far more regressive one has taken hold. Generous, untargeted tax provisions have encouraged extensive borrowing, to lend more extensively, bolstering house prices and catapulting many new purchasers into the category of Europe's 'most indebted' households. Indeed, today's house prices place many outside the eligibility requirements of the National Mortgage Guarantee and its share of market coverage is declining sharply. These issues will be discussed in the following section.

8.3 Future housing scenarios and the distribution of risks across the housing system

It is not the intention nor focus of this book to predict future housing scenarios, but some mention must be made of the issues raised by the empirical conclusions of each case study and outlined in section 8.5. These conclusions suggest that risks are concentrating amongst single-income households and their opportunities for participating in the favoured tenure of home ownership are limited. Further, in the Netherlands, whilst the position of housing associations may currently be strong, favourable conditions are unlikely to prevail. Towards the end, a brief contribution is made for the consideration of those in a position to alter the future course of housing history.

8.3.1 The Australian dream for whom?

The Australian case drew attention to a number of contemporary threats to the culturally embedded aspiration of Australian home ownership. These include the deregulation of home finance, diminution of centralised wage fixation processes, polarisation of household incomes and increasing privatisation of social security provision. It is contended that slowly and unevenly, signs of a new housing solution are emerging. These signs include an overall decline in rates of home purchase, the promotion of new forms of housing consumption and mass production, and privatised process of urban expansion in some cities.

After more than two hundred years of housing provision centred on low-density homeownership, what will this new deregulated solution offer the next three generations of Australian households? Current initiatives in housing provision suggest that uncertainty and tenure polarisation are likely to prevail. Housing policy supporting widespread home ownership is minimal, since the dismantling of mechanisms to influence the cost and distribution of home loans and influence the cost of urban land development. Further, the current simplistic allocation of grants for uncapped first home purchase only serves to inflate housing prices at the bottom end. Indeed, Beer (1999) paints a gloomy picture of housing in the year 2030:

> the pattern of home ownership and housing wealth in Australia had changed markedly: it no longer constituted the same percentage of national assets as 20 or even 30 years previously and its distribution had become much more uneven.... The lack of adequate investment in roads, schools, urban rail systems and other infrastructure helped reinforce the apparent monotony of the great swathe of further metropolitan regions. People and their houses were therefore differentiated by location but also by their own characteristics – their jobs and employment experiences, their migration patterns and demography. The decline of the nuclear family and once 'conventional' modes of life generated winners and losers – the cashed-up 'never had children', the families struggling to keep their tenuous toehold in the middle class and those whose families broke up, with many banished forever from home ownership and access to housing wealth.
>
> (Beer, 1999: 87)

Other researchers (Berry, 1998; Berry *et al.*, 1999) predict that the declining rate of new purchasers entering home ownership poses a number of implications not only for households but for the housing *industry*. These include a possible downturn in fringe and outer suburban development and increased selectivity and premiums for higher-risk home loans resulting in the social-spatial patterning (red-lining) of home finance. Berry *et al.* (1999) also raise concerns over the effectiveness of the private rental market and current levels of rent assistance to meet the needs of those 'expelled from home ownership' or of those who retire as renters, without their own homes as a form of social security.

At present, the most likely solution appears to be the expansion of minimal Commonwealth assistance to entice households into home ownership, new forms of lease ownership financing arrangements and undoubtedly, increased polarisation between single and dual-income households. Without fundamental change, a long-term scenario could leave an increasing minority of households in post-retirement poverty in unregulated and insecure rental accommodation.

8.3.2 Will the Dutch housing miracle turn sour?

We have seen by the end of the Dutch case study the withdrawal of central government from any direct role in the finance of social housing provision, whilst subsidies to the individual renter continue. Apparently this has had no effect upon the social housing sector, which has taken these changes in its stride and is enjoying the freedom. But what are the long-term consequences? What will the current solution offer households in the twenty-first century?

The government is no longer in a position to use the social sector as a counter-cyclical tool during times of low production and high housing need. It has lost considerable control of the nature and level of housing outcomes produced. Production levels are alarmingly low, and the land market appears stymied by complex negotiations, projects are delayed and with continuing scarcity housing prices are extremely high in major cities. Further, a number of current and potential crises could lead to the diminution of the social housing sector itself.

First, contingent conditions in the land market are greatly affecting the position of housing associations in new urban areas. These include new market players, with far greater resources, operating in the land markets surrounding cities and speculating on rising land prices. Housing associations are not merely passive operators in this game. Yet, more risky profit-orientated developments and inflated land prices could easily 'eat away' housing association reserves during less favourable times.

Second, in the shift from government-secured loans to more open capital market arrangements, associations may become more vulnerable to unfavourable market circumstances (interest rate rises) without the capacity to renegotiate government-secured loans or top up repayment shortfalls with additional government contributions. For the moment they remain subject to central government rent policy, protecting tenants and setting rent increases. In this sense their room for manoeuvre is limited, but the current level of rental assistance is neither guaranteed nor set in stone.

Third, to date housing associations have been favoured in the politics of rent setting and tenants have absorbed rent increases above the rate of inflation in the 1990s. Whilst rental assistance has continued to be targeted to lower-income households via the Individual Rental Subsidy, lower real thresholds have pushed higher-income tenants out, especially those lured by low interest rates on mortgages and advantageous fiscal benefits into home purchase. Associations may become heavily reliant upon a more residual tenant profile, and thus more reliant upon rental allowances to keep the revenue flowing, as in the United Kingdom, and these cannot be guaranteed in a dynamic and open economy where other sectors may capture the government's priorities (consider the changes in the Australian financial sector affecting the protected circuit).

Fourth, increasing entrepreneurial activities may erode the legitimacy of the sector undermining any future government assistance or favourable regulatory changes.

Turning to the rapidly emerging home purchase sector, ownership has been encouraged by inflating housing prices, the discounted sale of social housing stock (albeit not in the numbers demanded by central government), the relaunch and promotion of the National Mortgage Guarantee and generous tax advantages. Purchase prices in employment centres have escalated. Within the finance sector, a number of developments have fostered the growth of home purchase: a more permissive lending regime based on two incomes, establishment of a secondary mortgage market and a brokering sector generating markets for new mortgage products.

Related to these developments are those in the Dutch labour market. Following recession, wage constraint and labour market restructuring, there has been substantial employment and wage growth from the mid- to late 1990s, especially amongst the financial services, technology and construction sectors. In this much-publicised context, the social task of the housing associations has been less pressing (apart from the demands of 'silent' asylum seekers and long-term unemployed). Further, after the 'excesses' of the 1970s and 1980s, the central government promoted a culture of self-reliance, targeting welfare benefits and individual rent subsidies more closely. Home ownership, once the preserve of wealthy and non-city dwellers, is now promoted as the mainstream housing 'solution' for all 'able' Dutch households. Yet there are already emerging signs this scenario will not continue. Young dual-income couples increasingly have difficulty entering the home ownership market. If the predicted recession arrives, many recent purchasers reliant upon strong dual-income employment may be exposed to mortgage default (Lawson, 2005), as in Germany, the United Kingdom and Australia.

8.4 Conclusions – critical realism, housing studies and comparative research

8.4.1 Conceptualising different forms of provision: core relations and interdependencies

Critical realism places much emphasis upon the process of conceptualisation in explanatory research, for this can determine and influence any subsequent line of enquiry. For this reason, Chapters 3, 4 and 5 carefully examine not only alternative modes of perceiving forms of housing provision and key emergent relations of provision, but also the process and causes of change. Increasingly, throughout the case study process, the causal significance of an *integrated core of relations* became apparent. Thus not only the process of abstraction is important, which highlights contingently defined emergent relations of provision, but also the way these relations work together to form a causal mechanism sustaining coherence. Thus, in addition to the process of abstraction, much thought needs to be given to interaction and synthesis and the notions of mutual interdependency and structural coherence, first raised in Chapter 5. Towards this end I make two concluding comments.

First, synthesis can demonstrate the mutual interdependency between different aspects of the same phenomenon. We need to know how different necessary and contingent relations work together in order to generate specific outcomes. For example, how does a certain definition of property rights compliment or conflict with a certain route of savings and investment to promote certain housing outcomes? Are there some combinations that tend to work together and others against? Throughout the research a number of different *interdependencies* were revealed, which arose from specific definitions of property, investment and savings, and labour and welfare relations and sustained specific housing institutions. They include, but are not limited to, the relationship between mortgage credit, individual land ownership and savings capacity: and further, the relationship between annuity loans, object and operational costs and cost-rent revenue. Of course interdependencies are *vulnerable to change* where contingent conditions alter the nature of one or more key dimensions. Such interdependencies and their contingent conditions were carefully abstracted from each case. Towards this end a number of important diagrams, illustrating dynamic circuits of investment and consumption during periods of coherence and crisis, were discussed at the conclusion of every phase in each case study.

Second, to sustain coherence and facilitate flows of capital via these two different routes unique institutions were established in each country. Focusing on home ownership in Australia, we see the establishment of freehold land title, a protected circuit of capital in the home lending sector and state-sponsored infrastructure provision facilitating land purchase in expanding suburbs. Turning to the Netherlands, we see a system of government-guaranteed loans, municipal land development and cost-rent social housing. Section 8.5 compares the *unique contingencies that initially generated very different sets of mutual interdependencies and the contingent conditions that changed them.*

In sum, stemming from the ontological approach of critical realism, the research has focused upon the key dimensions being the necessary and contingent conditions pertinent to the housing phenomena to be explained, how they have worked together to generate certain outcomes and been sustained by the development of particular institutions. This approach differs from empiricism, historical biography, as well as inappropriate generalisation and theory determinism.

8.4.2 Path dependency and cumulative causation

More often than not the reasons for differences between social phenomena are vaguely attributed to individual actors, environmental factors, tradition and more recently, embeddedness and path dependency. Sometimes, universal laws such as market preference or 'class struggle' are called into explanatory service. Chapters 4 and 5 closely evaluated alternative conceptual approaches to change and argued that the concepts of path dependency and institutional fix offered potential but must be grounded in concrete case study research. It is now time for evaluation in light of the case study research, and the following four conclusions are made.

First, the case study analysis certainly revealed a strong thread of *path dependency* supportive of the 'history matters' camp in explanatory social science (especially institutional economics and historical sociology). Each country's solution responded to its severe housing crises at the end of the nineteenth century very differently, in adaptive, path-dependent fashion. They established modes of housing provision by the early twentieth century which responded to specific opportunities and constraints in the realm of property rights, investment and labour relations, which have not been fundamentally changed until the end of that century. Changes have certainly occurred, but they have been ameliorative and cumulative, responding to specific crises and building upon the structures of provision established by the 1920s. In the main, the problem of housing the working masses in the twentieth century has been addressed by a system of social housing provision based on costs rents in the Netherlands and individual mortgaged finance home ownership in Australia.

Second, we need to both recognise and question the structural stickiness of these different modes of housing provision. Towards this end, it is contended that they are temporarily fixed and resistant to fundamental change for one very important reason: they are both underpinned by very long-term social contracts in the form of mortgage finance. Australian home ownership is based upon the availability of deposit-secured household mortgage credit, for terms of up to 30 years. Likewise, Dutch social housing was financed by 50-year annuity loans to associations that necessitated a fixed schedule of repayment based upon cost rents. These very different social contracts form the basis upon which investments are made supporting two very different housing solutions for the 'masses'. Time exposes these contracts to adverse potential risks and unforeseen influential contingencies and for this reason, various modes of intervention arise to reduce these risks.

Third, the notion of institutional fix, in which practices and processes have a power of their own and may well be sustained beyond their initial stated purpose, was found to apply in both cases. It has clearly been demonstrated by the continued expansion of social rental housing from the mid-1960s to the early 1980s. The notion of institutional fix was highlighted in the answers to contrastive and counterfactual questioning which concluded each case.

Fourth and finally, this brings us to the importance of *cumulative causation*. The earlier description of interdependencies, path dependency and institutional fix falsely implies an overwhelming functional agenda played out by the actions of the state and capital. Nothing could be further from reality. The social contracts present in each case and mentioned earlier were time and time again subject to conflicting circumstances beyond their control: inflated building costs demanding larger loans and higher costs rents, the differential between rents in the cost-rent and market rent sectors in the Netherlands and the crises of state-sponsored urban expansion and credit rationing by banks opposing the imposition of the protected circuit of capital in home loans. Attempts to create 'closure' in circuits of investment and consumption were repeatedly undermined. Recall the initial failure of cost-rent social housing under the Housing Act, the demise of the Dynamic Cost Price Rent system in the Netherlands and the end of the protected circuit of mortgage capital in Australia. This issue brings us to address that of contingency and risk, first raised in Chapter 3.

8.4.3   *Contingency and the notion of risk*

It was originally contended that contingencies are any conditions that influence the emergent relations of housing provision, that is, the system of property rights, investment and savings, labour and welfare. Further, contingencies were not limited to the realm of state housing policy or programmes, or the decisions of policy makers – but to the wider social relations of the economic, political and civic institutions affecting state/market relations. At first glance this may seem a very *broad definition*. Far beyond mere actions of policy makers, it extends to the very power relations of society and its processes of capital accumulation. However, a number of simple examples demonstrate the feasibility and appropriateness of such a definition. Take for instance labour market conditions in Australia during the colonial era inflating wages to permit savings amongst skilled workers; and later the entrance of women into paid employment increasing the borrowing limits for home purchasers. Contingency may include any new process, event or idea, such as technological developments in mass housing construction, lowering labour costs and increasing production, and establishment of a secondary mortgage market, facilitating a new flow of credit into the home mortgage market. These are all examples of contingent conditions, which have had *some bearing on the nature of emergent social relations underpinning housing provision.*

For this reason it is never enough to merely point to events in housing history, for events cannot explain, even significant ones such as the Great Depression, the Second World War and the oil crises. For one must explain what it precisely was about these events that influenced the core property relations, investment or labour relations, and in turn how this influence subsequently affected forms of housing provision. This link is what makes them contingent relations and part of any causal mechanism explaining change. Further, it is not possible to neatly isolate contingencies from emergent relations; they are always there together in concrete, multi-dimensional reality. Thus any explanation for divergence will consist of multiple, overlapping causes, which cannot be expressed in simple statements or as equations drawn from closed conceptual models.

Embedded in this dialectic between contingency and necessity are conscious actors who perceive risks according to their socially and materially constructed vantage point in the housing system. Specifically, housing risks are perceived as being intimately entwined with key relations of property, finance and labour in a complex and open housing system.

8.5 Concluding discussion

It is finally time to step back to assess the value of conducting comparative housing research that is inspired by realist ontology and evaluate how this may progress critical explanations in the field. Towards this end a number of broader insights can be made.

In review, Critical Realism is a theory of the nature of reality. Whilst it is not a substantive theory for divergence in forms of housing provision, like any ontology it greatly influences our perception of the subject under scrutiny and the methodological strategy. For this reason, any ontological choice should be explicit and justified.

Some academics argue that regulation theory is an adequate alternative to critical realism. Indeed there are important ontological similarities: regulation theory assumes the existence of influential social relations and encourages concrete research. Its primary focus is the interaction between regimes of capital accumulation (RCA) and modes of social regulation (MSR). In doing so it encourages the use of historical case study research to examine these interactions. Critical realism demands the abstraction of generative causal mechanisms from the field of study (whatever field this may be in both the natural and social sciences). The process of postulating, testing and revising potential models of generative mechanisms is far more open than that proposed by regulation theory. For this reason, I would argue that the choice between critical regulation theory and critical realism is a false start. For CR precedes any discussion of the substantive, it can be used as an ontological spring board for whilst regulation theory argues that we must examine interactions between MSRs and RCAs.

Further, CR offers more comprehensive ontological vantage point. In the field of housing research, it forces the researcher to postulate a feasible model of the generative causal mechanisms influencing housing outcomes. In doing so, it perceives all levels of reality – not just one – as being relevant foci or dimensions for research. Therefore the experience of housing provision, the material outcomes as well as the underlying relationships are all considered to be important as together they can influence important developments and outcomes in housing provision. Combined, these different dimensions of housing reality can form causal mechanisms which always operate in the midst of contingent relations. From this perspective, the open nature of housing systems which influences and is influenced by exogenous circumstances needs to be appreciated.

Empirically, the notion of emergence and causality in Critical Realism encourages the researcher to look beyond historical events and quantified outcomes and try to imagine the kind of emergent relations and contingent conditions which generate forms of provision. Consequently, detailed case study research is required, which examines the long-term, path-dependent and cumulative development of housing provision.

The first part of this book provides a comprehensive range of concepts which can be adapted for individual housing research. It defines a number of abstract relations: affecting property rights; the circuit of savings and investment in housing; and the household income and welfare provisions which influence the capacity to consume housing services. These emergent relations are contingently defined and packaged together to influence housing outcomes.

In summary, the research emphasises the importance of identifying and abstracting these key emergent relations through concrete research, rather than focusing upon chronological events or outcomes. Second, it stresses the significance of contingent conditions (both material and social) in defining these emergent relations. The importance of packaging and mutual dependency between emergent relations in establishing coherent forms of provision, and supporting the establishment of relevant institutions and practices is a third aspect of this research. Fourth, the path dependency of these institutions and practices, even beyond their official 'use by' date, is an important aspect in the evolution of housing systems. Finally, the shifting distribution of actual risk and risk perception between financiers, providers and consumers of housing services can propagate crises in housing provision.

Whilst positivism and to a lesser extent interpretivism dominate the comparative research world, very few housing researchers have applied realist ontology in comparative studies. According to realist thought, forms of housing provision are unique to time and place. They are unique expressions of complex, dynamic, underlying necessary and contingent relations. Thus each system must be explained from this 'embedded' starting point which necessitates place specific, detailed longitudinal research. For this reason, the ontological approach (realism), epistemology (retroduction) and methods applied (longitudinal case study) have influenced the *choice and number of countries for comparison*.

The chosen research strategy assumes from the very beginning that each form of housing provision is a unique expression of social relations, which are embedded in a specific time and space. Thus comparison is not a 'like with like' experience, or a type with type model. Comparison occurs at a deeper level or explanation – a comparison of *necessary causal relations*, operating in *contingently different contexts*.

Given the explanatory aims and demands of the research, the number of cases has been limited to two. Australia and the Netherlands both offer systems of housing provision which are known and accessible to the researcher. Necessary contacts could be made easily and material readily found for analysis. In both countries the system of housing finance was undergoing immense change. However, given the pace of change, little research had been undertaken which critically attempted *to explain why this transformation came about*. The second part of this book attempts to address this gap.

From a sea of empirical detail, which has all but drowned comparative housing studies, the cases in this book try to sift out the emergent relations and causal tendencies. For this reason you will not find a chronology of housing events, important as these events may seem. For it is not a history of housing that has been attempted, but an explanation based on a justified set of ideas and concepts. For each phase in the history of housing solutions, specific dimensions were examined. Different periods of crisis, coherence and adaptation were defind and the contingent definition and packaging of property, investment and savings, and welfare and labour relations were concretely examined.

Ultimately this book has sought to explain the differences between the Netherlands and Australia in terms of their housing solutions, and conclusions are put forward in the final of three parts. This section seeks to provide what no other comparison has done before: define the causal generative mechanisms and compare them in order to explain difference. These causal mechanisms are outlined in previous sections of this chapter, aided by contrastive and counterfactual enquiry. This approach has many advantages over others: it does not attempt to correlate the outcomes of systems which may be subject to many different contingencies, it does not rely on standardised data sets but forces the researchers to be empirically rigorous and curious to explain the many unrecorded dimensions of housing provision, it encourages the constant revision of postulated models rather than simple testing of the researchers' hypothesis. What is sought is explanation, but this is always fallible and open to debate and revision.

Risk has not been central to realist-inspired studies in the past. Yet in this book, risk is taken more seriously and used in two ways. First, it is employed as a prompt to avoid functionalist/rational notions of agency, which can perceive individuals as unconscious dopes or pawns of a master planner. Second, it is also used to highlight the shift in responsibility for housing provision and finance across households, industry and the state.

Many aspects of housing provision, from land development to tenancy, involve the interaction of people. Embedded in a set of social relations, these individuals are influenced by their uneven, filtered and bounded perception of risk and trust in complex housing interactions, and in their material and socially constructed contexts. For this reason, they do not act unconsciously or in the same manner in different circumstances. However, depending on the power resources and contingent conditions influencing the actions of individual and collective agents, cumulative housing transactions may evolve to influence the norms, processes and institutions of housing provision. Repeated, path-dependent interactions may form an institutional architecture of laws, administrative processes and bureaucracies, which in turn may evolve to consolidate a particular form of provision and limit the choices and course of action undertaken by conscious, thinly rational individuals.

Last but not least, the concept of risk has been used as a prompt to normatively evaluate the impact of changing systems of housing provision upon different groups and classes in society. The research has abstracted key changes in two different forms of housing provision, both involving the withdrawal of the state from the land development process and the circuit of housing finance. In the Netherlands, high land prices and a multitude of competing developers have greatly reduced the output of social rental dwellings and promoted mortgage financed home purchase. In Australia, the volume of mortgage credit provided by the protected circuit was eagerly replaced by a host of new players, yet the flood of new credit generated high housing prices. Both these cases reveal the worrying impact of these fundamental changes upon the distribution of housing wealth and supply outcomes.

This book has provided just one example of how Critical Realism can inspire comparative housing research. It is hoped that it will be a catalyst for ongoing debate and research in the housing field.

Appendices

**Appendix 1 Ambrose's state – market – citizen relations
and the chain of provision (1991, 1994)**

Ambrose (1994) proposes a model of state – market – civil society relations, illustrated here, that underpin any chain of housing provision. In his book *Urban Process and Power* he analyses the shift in power balance between the state

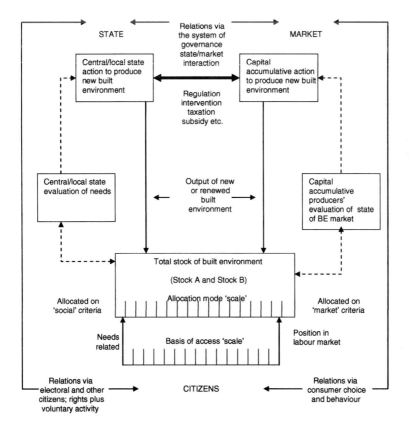

Appendix 1 (a) Ambrose's chain of provision (1991, 1994)

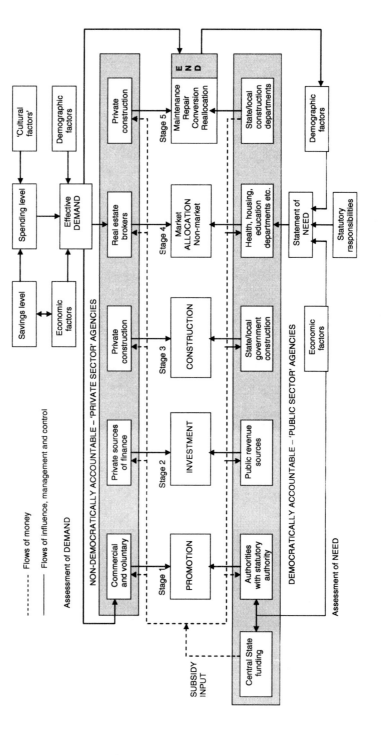

and market and the influence of these shifts upon the built environment (1994: 12–13). A polarised characterisation of the state and market is proposed: on the one hand the state is perceived as democratic, responsive to need and allocating on this basis, and on the other is the market, undemocratic, responsive to effective demand and allocating on the basis of capacity to pay. This abstraction 'floats' beneath the chain of provision, as illustrated by Appendix 1(b).

Appendix 1 (b) Doling's (1997) elaboration of Ambrose's chain of provision

Building upon Ambrose's notion of a chain of provision (1991, 1994), Doling (1997) alludes to a relationship between finance, land and labour and subsidy to four phases of provision: development, construction, allocation, repair and maintenance.

FINANCE			
DEVELOPMENT	CONSTRUCTION	ALLOCATION	REPAIR AND MAINTENANCE

LAND	LABOUR

SUBSIDIES

In particular he stresses the necessary relationship between labour, materials and the construction or production phase and land title and the allocation of consumption phase. Further, it is actors, operating in open economic context, that undertake the process of housing provision. He cautions against ontological isolationism, that ignores important contextual conditions. Specific examples of influential contexts are provided, including wage developments, interest rates, prosperity, rates of return in other sectors of the built environment, demographic developments, technology and lifestyle changes.

Appendix 2 State interventions in consumption and production of housing (Lundqvist, 1992)

Lundqvist (1992) highlights the role of the state in the definition of purchasing power and dwelling prices. His concept does come close to the notion of contingent-defined relations, but is too state focused and neglects broader socio-economic contingencies and non-state institutions and processes.

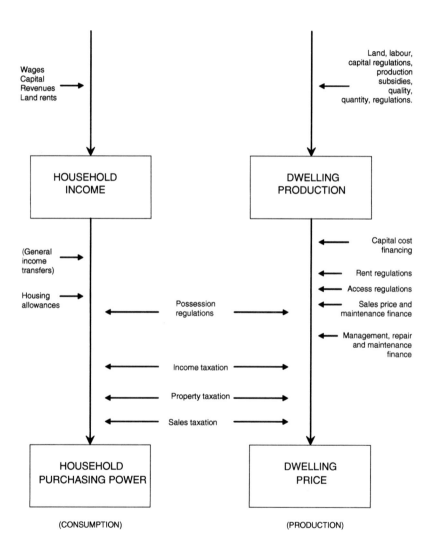

Appendix 3 Structures of housing provision
(Ball, 1998, 1992, 1983; Ball *et al.*, 1988)

The structure of housing provision thesis (SHP) was developed by Ball and via the work of Harloe and Martens (Ball, 1998, 1992, 1983; Ball *et al.*, 1988). In a recent review of various approaches (1998), he maintained that the SHP approach is still valid and useful as a prompt for empirical research in comparison with actor-centred and institutionally focused approaches. According to Ball, a structure of housing provision

> specifies the nature of the social agents involved in the provision of a particular form of housing and their inter linkages. Producers, consumers and financiers in different guises all have their place within structures of provision. Actual structures of housing provision, however, are empirical constructs and cannot be theoretically deduced, although obviously theory has to be applied in their analysis.
>
> (Ball, Harloe and Marteens, 1988: 29)

Not only are the agents and their relations important, but their contexts: government policies, economic strategies such as wages, competition in the money market and movements in interest rates (1983: 18–19).

Almost twenty years ago, Ball (1983) provided a detailed examination of the home ownership in Britain, using SHP as a prompt to ensure comprehensive coverage of the various interconnected relations and their contingent contexts, as illustrated here.

Structure of owner-occupied housing provision in Britain
(Ball, 1983: 18)

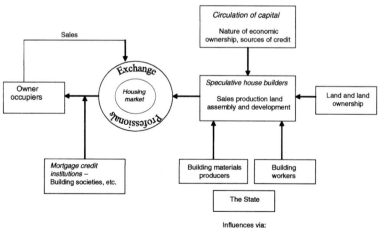

Appendix 4 Explanatory themes and ontological approaches

Urban development and housing tenure are primarily outcomes of shifts in the mode of production

Approach	Explanatory model proposed	Data presented	Key proponent(s)
Explanation via shifts in the organisational base and technological form of industrial development	The Australian solution of home ownership has exhibited a number of phases: stabilisation at the turn of the nineteenth century, intensification until the 1970s and uncertainty in the 1990s. These phases are related to the mode of industrial and technological development, mediated by the role of the state and culturally embedded aspirations and demographic changes. The most recent transition, to a post-Keynesian city, has emerged with the deregulation of the financial and industrial relations system and a retreat of the welfare state. This has led to increasing economic inequality, employment insecurity, privatised forms of social welfare which have polarised access to ownership	Berry provides a selection history of the changing nature of industrial development, also demonstrating the limited availability of housing options over time, and the status differentials reinforcing ownership. The decentralisation of industry and retail developments reinforced urban expansion. Further, the gradients of land prices, structure of the building industry and the system of credit provision have also influenced patterns of production and consumption. He reviews recent trends indicating the demise of home ownership as a broad-based housing solution	Berry (1998)
Explanation via uneven and unpredictable outcome of key contingently defined relations	Stresses the importance of early struggles over property ownership of housing and land. Home ownership consumption later became an important tool of Keynesian economic policy. Favourable wages,	Strategic, long-term analysis of the key relations underpinning patterns of housing consumption and urban development: property rights, financial investment, and wage and conditions	Daly (1988)

			Reference
		working conditions and rising property values materially underpinned and bolstered this pattern of consumption. This pattern of consumption was drastically undermined by changes in the world economy	
Explanation via the movement of capital and labour over time and space	Postulates four stages of expansion and decline in Australian capital accumulation: colonial (1788–1847), commercial (1848–1893), industrial (1894–1939) and corporate (1930–present), each influencing patterns of urbanisation, conditioned by constraints posed by international economic integration. Each phase and form has been subject to crises and contradiction tendencies and responded by reestablishing structural solutions in the form of new stages of accumulation	Examines the spatial consequences of each stage of capitalist development in Australian cities, taking into account the complex role of state relations, international economic conditions and trading relations, industrial developments, flows of investment and labour, differentiation of economic activity, stratification of social classes, division of labour, relations of dependence and dominance of certain industries, technological developments	Berry (1983)
Explanation via theory testing research, analysing the influence of different modes of capitalist production (mercantile/ monopoly modes) upon forms of residential life	Residential life was, until the 1940s, influenced by the mode of capitalist development. Australian workers under mercantile capitalism were reproduced under relations of urban peasantry (self-help), whilst monopoly capitalist cities centred on suburban consumerism	Compares mercantile and corporate capitalist city forms and material services. Examines urban development between 1880 and 1940, with particular emphasis upon the material provision of urban sewerage infrastructure	Mullins (1981)

Housing provision as a dynamic outcome of social relations in a contingent context

Approach	Explanatory model proposed	Data presented	Key proponent(s)
Explanation focusing on broader socio-economic factors influencing the rate of home ownership	Home ownership rates have not increased above 70 per cent despite government policies to promote this tenure and under development of alternatives. Significant economic factors such as high interest rates, changes in housing prices and stagnating wages have made ownership less accessible for first homebuyers. Other factors such as immigration, an aging population, postponed marriages and increased divorce rates have also influenced the rate of home ownership	Provides a history of home ownership and alternative tenure developments; examines the role of governments, the type of policies introduced and the impact on housing affordability. Introduces a number of additional factors influencing affordability, namely: immigration, household formation and unemployment	Bourassa *et al.* (1995)
Explanation examining the social relations of housing production, distribution and consumption	Reveals how the system of housing provision, once dominated by builder/landlords and wealthy home owners, moved towards speculative building and then to a more competitive mass-market system for providing mass home ownership	Strategic compilation and analysis of land ownership, building construction, financing agents and sources from the 1880s to late 1980s	Hayward (1992)
Explanation perceived as path dependent, subject to demographic changes, the policy and economic environment and the capacity of the existing	Pattern of future development will take the form of low-density development on the urban fringe, the emergence of urban wastelands (without adequate government response) with under-provided infrastructure, employment	Empirically examines all aspects of the postulated model: incomes, employment, economic growth, industrial restructuring, fiscal and monetary policy; population growth, household change and residential	Burke and Hayward (1990)

system of housing provision to respond	opportunities and community facilities. Choice for young households: accessibility to urban resources or cheap housing	differentiation; instability in the housing sector, lack of innovation; under-provision of infrastructure, constrained capital funding, land speculation, house price differentiation, polarisation of incomes and housing outcomes, rental tenancy and the policy environment	
Home ownership as a contradictory outcome of struggles over domestic property rights	The Australian state has played a continuous role in the operations of the housing market, with home ownership receiving early cross-political support during boom, bust and crises. Alternatives to home ownership such as public housing and private rental have been underdeveloped due to the complex architecture of the state and lack of political constituency	Historical analyses, focusing on the housing-related discourse of election campaigns and political parties	Williams (1984)
Explanation via shifting modes of production and technological change as the independent variables, linked to demographic change, social stratification and organisation, existing built forms and social pathologies	The distinctive pattern of Australian cities is a consequence of Western capitalist growth, accentuating metropolitan primacy, rapid urbanisation and social stratification of housing stock. Governments have been most active in this regard providing infrastructure, promoting immigration and land settlement	Examines main factors in nineteenth-century urbanisation between 1800 and 1850, 1860 and 1900 as well as demographic patterns until 1914	Burnley (1980)

Significant relations underpinning the Australian housing solution

Approach	Explanatory model proposed	Data presented	Key proponent(s)
Explanation considers the role home ownership plays in providing horizontal, life cycle social security and influencing national systems of welfare	Drawing upon international comparisons of welfare systems and tenure, Castles argues the high rates of home ownership are incompatible with high levels of contributory finding for social security. Outright home ownership provides a form of social security that necessitates lower pension payments. However, access to ownership is unevenly and inequitably distributed. Minimal, universal payments are inadequate for households in other tenures, still paying rents in old age	Reviews the history of home ownership in Australia, taking into account the relative affluence of workers at the turn of the century and limited interruption to supply during both World Wars. Examines the electoral appeal of home ownership, leading to its promotion by across the political spectrum and current threats to accessibility: high interest, unemployment and rapidly increasing house prices. Draws upon the Luxembourg Incomes Study, comparing welfare systems, payments and housing tenures	Castles (1997, 1997a)
Explanation examines the role of technological development, public and	The transmission and adoption of innovation in the nineteenth century influence the growth of cities. This was	Provides a number of examples that illustrate the relationship between technology and urban development	Frost and Dingle (1995)

private investment in house construction and infrastructure provision

facilitated by the role of the state in providing infrastructure where investment was considered too risky and unprofitable for the private sector. These investments, in power, transport, irrigation, sewerage and water supply, underpinned private sector growth in the rural, construction and manufacturing sectors

Explanation emphasises switches in finance capital, including forms of property development and the role of state in sheltering this investment and urban planning in maximising monopoly rent by differentiating housing markets

During the 1950s and 1960s housing-related monetary and fiscal policy ensured extraction of absolute or ground rent from housing investments. The breakdown of mechanism underpinning the housing boom has necessitated the role of urban planning in protecting and differentiating property values, with regressive equity effects

Focuses upon the rise in home ownership investment, linked to suburban expansion. Examines the role of public policy in reinforcing differentiated housing markets and the switching of finance capital across different sectors of the built environment

King (1986)

Arguments about the role of the state in housing promotion

Approach	Explanatory model proposed	Data presented	Key proponent(s)
Explanation via historical, state-centred analysis of the housing policy process	Examines four policy regimes: regional state regime from mid-1800 to 1930; the central state regime of the 1930s to the 1970s, the regional state regime as the central state withdraws from the mid-1980 to the 1990s and finally, the complete abrogation of the state regime since 1994, as the state withdraws from housing policy at both the regional and central levels	Analyses the history of the state's involvement in home ownership through detailed policy and administrative historical research, drawing upon a range of documentary sources and interview material revealing the formal and informal processes and influences upon decision and non-decision making concerning housing policy	Dalton (1999)
Explanation emphasises the ideological and political underpinning of home ownership	Ideological and actual dominance of home ownership in Australia are a consequence of targeted state support and promotion. This has led to highly privatised urban structures, a home-centred life style and underdevelopment of more collective forms of welfare and housing tenure	Home ownership rates would have declined 'naturally' without government support. Home ownership has stifled more collective forms of social welfare	Kemeny (1983). See also Hayward (1992) (1990) and Troy (1990)

Policy analysis and normative critique

Approach	Explanatory model proposed	Data presented	Key proponent(s)
Explanation examines shifting role of the state and the distribution of risk from society to individual households	Highlights the introduction of rental assistance, considered to be a u-turn in government policy, which comes at the expense of support for public housing. Argues that risks of unemployment, higher interest rates, stagnant price inflation are concentrated amongst those at the margin of home purchase	Summarises housing policies, categorised as explicit and implicit support for home ownership and those concerning public and private rental tenures. Examines the equality of treatment across tenure forms over three different periods: pre-1978, post-1978 and post-1986	Yates (1997)
Explanation provides a chronological account of the housing policy process	Housing policy development is irregular and a product of political pragmatism. Property ownership reinforced notions of citizenship as a route to working-class emancipation. State Banks promoted access via the credit foncier loan instrument	Reviews development of NSW housing policy between 1901 and 1941. Provides a detailed administrative history of housing initiatives and failures	Troy (1990)
Normative critique of housing policy and feasibility of alternatives	The success of housing policy is dependent upon dynamic economic and financial conditions. State policy is constrained by electoral politics, institutional capacity and image, and divided support amongst political parties in different states	Focuses upon the accessibility of home ownership under changing economic conditions and policies	Stretton (1978)
Structured, normative critique of urban planning and development in	Explanations can be found in the formal and informal power of agents in the urban development process to influence property relations. Throughout most of	Presents illustrative examples of the policy-making process, providing evidence of formal and informal decision-making processes	Sandercock (1975)

(continued)

(Continued)

Approach	Explanatory model proposed	Data presented	Key proponent(s)
Australia. Conceives the city as a mechanism for distributing resources, yet broader theory is not articulated	Australia's European history this has rested with landowners and more recently urban planners. Dominant, pro-growth ideologies have at times unified industry with state interests		
Descriptive, normative critique of the role of government assistance for housing lower-income households	Explanation emphasises electoral and fiscal rationale for political actions. Governments chose policy options with limited risk to their power base and financial resources	Presents evidences of the dominant ideas and ideologies of different policies through parliamentary speech notes and government reports. Provides a scattering of descriptive information on the outcomes of government policy	Jones (1972)
Descriptive, normative critique set in historical context of uneven city development	Provides a number of fragmented explanations for role of the state in facilitating urban development, such as extreme emphasis by the middle classes on private life, private homes and gardens, and inviolable property rights; secure social segregation and a restrained public culture; limited expectations of public life; lack of will and skills in state and local administration; and, comprehensive distrust of government, political power of public sector workers	Chronology of events in city development and administration of planning policy	Stretton (1970)

Description reveals the process

Approach	Explanatory model proposed	Data presented	Key proponent(s)
Explanation as chronology with a normative focus	Housing policy is a response to vexatious housing conditions and problems affecting the community	Chronology of housing events, providing examples of reactive policy making	Pugh (1976)
Explanation via description of urban development patterns	Urban sprawl is an aggregate of short outward moves, from the dominant central city, regulated by plans producing monotonous, jobless cities, dependent on private transport	Bunker describes various demographic trends, movements and related policies	Bunker (1988)
Descriptive, empirical study of urban development patterns and policies in Australia	Contends that urban development is a consequence of market, administrative and political influences, of which the state plays an integral role. Emphasises the importance of transport technology and state infrastructure provision in urban development	Extensive use of quantitative data, again various demographic trends, movements and related policies	Neutze (1981)

Appendix 5 Illustrative example of private property relations

In the late 1960s and early 1970s the Commonwealth government's Department of Urban Development and the Australian Institute of Urban Studies argued that a lack of serviced land was inflating land prices and threatening affordable access to home ownership (Neutze, 1978: 72). The local consideration of planning applications had also provided an opening for communities to voice their concerns about the quality of development, standard of services supplied and impact on the environment. Developers perceived delays caused by planning processes as a costly imposition, providing another reason to leave the industry (Neutze, 1978: 74). Small investors taking advantage of the lack of tax on capital gains held on to vacant land and watched it rise in value (Neutze, 1978: 82).

Housing costs were a pressing issue during the early 1970s, with media commentators predicting 25 and 40 per cent increases in the land costs.[1] The incoming Whitlam Labour government was acutely aware of the price difference between land for rural and housing purposes, and the lucrative gains for owners on the urban fringe. The new Department of Urban and Regional Development (DURD) wanted to harness this unearned increment for public purposes, whilst providing sufficient land to keep housing costs down. Land costs in growth areas were to be checked by processing land sales through development corporations, urban land councils or land commissions.[2]

DURD was dependent upon the co-operation of state governments, which was by no means uniform. Throughout the early to mid-1970s, the Victorian government frustrated and resisted the Commonwealth's programme[3]. From a pool of $103 million of Commonwealth loan funds for land acquisition and development, relatively little was spent in Melbourne in 1974–1975: $8.7 million compared with Albury-Wadonga, $42.3 million (Neutze, 1978: 80, quoting Commonwealth Budget Paper, 1975: 28). Land acquired was eventually sold for housing purposes and the loans repaid. The impact was minimal, with less than a quarter of development sites provided via the public sector at $1,000–2,000 below those in the private sector.

The Victorian government in 1975, three years after a federal request by the Prime Minister, tardily established its own Urban Land Council. Contrary to the Commonwealth objectives, Victoria channelled profits of land sales to service authorities in order to encourage the further expansion of the private sector's operations in the land market.[4] The Housing Commission acted as land purchaser rather than land developer. Thus began one of the most notorious land scandals in Victoria's history. The Minister for Housing inflated the value of specific areas on the urban fringe by referring to their development potential, regardless of current planning constraints, suggesting that the Government would soon purchase large tracts of raw land for satellite cities (Kilmartin, 1988: 166). The role of the Minister and the Commission was later scrutinised by a Board of Inquiry which drew attention to the close financial relationship between the development industry and the ruling conservative Liberal Party. The resulting Gowans report[5], released in March 1978, found that the Commission

> paid too much for it what got, so that vendors or their intermediaries achieved rewards in excess of what the community thought was fair, and failed to fulfil the hopes of early land and housing relief which optimistic forecasts had led people to expect.
>
> (Gowans report, 1978: 13)

Later a Royal Commission examined the methods of purchase and valuation, to ascertain whether any corruption took place and found the Ministry's actions inept, inefficient, ad-hoc and unplanned with the Minister unable to discharge satisfactory control over the land purchasing function.[6]

The Victorian land deals of the 1970s completely eroded public confidence in the role of government in the land markets and justified the cessation of the development of large housing estates. The renamed Urban Land Authority (ULA) was originally established in 1979 to dispose of remaining government-owned land, including land purchased by the Ministry of Housing. It dispersed the Commission's Pakenham land across a variety of uses. During the course of the 1980s, the ULA struggled to recoup the costs incurred by the Commission when it first purchased land in Sunbury and was unable to afford the cost of housing low-income families on the public housing waiting list.

Subsequent Victorian governments have pursued a modest programme of purchasing existing individual houses and the redevelopment of existing estates – increasingly with private sector partners.

Appendix 6 Illustrative example of new urban development

Caroline Springs provides a typical example of the process of urban development on the fringe of Australian cities. In 1992, planning consultants, representing farmers and land developers made a submission to rezone the land from agricultural to residential purposes for a self-supporting and diverse housing development for 30,000 people. With zoning in place, the owners approached Delfin to convert 800 raw lots into the community of 'Caroline Springs'[7]. Delfin sells its expertise in development and marketing and project management and receives a proportion of the profits of the sale of the developed land. They ensure the provision of all necessary infrastructure and negotiate with local governments to secure funding for certain style of social and transport amenity to realise their ideal of a community in which to 'live, learn, work and rest'[8].

Builders compete for display space on the estate. Only those able to deliver the most marketable product are permitted on site and included in Delfin's catalogue of house and land packages (Delfin, 2000). This high cost, risky venture leads to the participation of a small number of larger builders who can achieve economies of scale (Hayward, 1992). Small builders are simply unable to compete. One

Appendix 7 Explanatory themes and ontological approaches

Approach	Explanatory model proposed	Data presented	Key proponent(s)
Empirical studies with implicit normative critique	The selection of these events is not explicitly guided by concepts or theories drawn from social science, but from the observable shifts and manoeuvres in politics and policymaking, with commentary and policy recommendations	Empirical research places great emphasis upon careful, objective observation of housing events	Priemus, 1990, 1992, 1992a, 1995, 1996, Van der Schaar, 1987
Explanation via demographic and economic modelling	Primarily market analysis and prognosis. This mode of research is fully institutionalised in the policy process. Forecasts play an integral role in a housing system where government wishes maintain control over public spending, stable levels of housing production through various subsidy schemes, thus minimising market risks and housing shortages	Selected variables according to researchers conceptual model including manipulations of official data sets ('pure' cases, weighted indexes)	Van Fulpen, 1985, Dieleman et al., 1985, Conijn, 1995, Rele and Van Steen, 2001
Explanation via ideas and institutions	These explanations focus upon the ideas of key professional organisations on the delivery and development of Dutch housing. Histories vary from personal biographies, organisational histories and policy chronologies to more explanatory geo-histories presenting empirical arguments from selected events in housing history for particular theories	Official administrative histories typically review regionally aggregated housing indicators, national programme initiatives and government legislation, whilst emphasising the role of individual civil servants and politicians	Van der Schaar, 1987, Grinburg, 1977, Steiber, 1999, De Ruijter, 1987. For official histories, see Kooiman, 1943, CDWV, 1952, Van Beusekem, 1955, Van der Schaar et al., 1996
Explanation via networks, rules and games	Dutch policy science in employing increasingly elaborate techniques towards an explanatory strategy grounded in rational action neo-institutionalism. These studies examine how individual action is channelled and contend that actors are bound to each other in a policy network by mutual interdependency and engaged in an ecology of games (Klijn, 1996: 335)	Klijn (1996) provides quantitative analysis of local policy networks, their rules and games in three cities, Den Haag, Rotterdam and Groningen, concerning the redevelopment of post-war housing areas	Kickert, 1991 Klijn, 1996, Klijn and Teisman, 1992, Koppenjan et al., 1993, Klijn, 1966

Explanation via international contrast	The comparative approach to housing research has become more prominent in recent years, fostered by the establishment of various international agencies and research networks (European Commission, ENHR, CECODHAS). Whilst the outcomes of each housing system are concisely described, there is often little room for their generative processes to be fully examined, leaving the reader with a list of differences and similarities	The strategy for data collection varies from collation of comparable statistics, individual housing histories, consistent collection of simiar 'facts', to comparison of underlying generative mechanisms defined in a contingent context (Weesep, 1986)	Van Weesep, 1986, Boelhouwer and Van der Heijden, 1992, Papa, 1992, Boelhouwer, 2000, Van der Heijden and Haffner, 2000
Explanation exploring the civilising process and gender relations (Elias, 1939)	Studies emphasise particular explanatory themes and concepts in Dutch housing provision often testing, revising or employing concepts from Elias' civilisation thesis, with a focus upon gender relations of provision	Historical research with an emphasis upon household norms and domestic relations in a socio-cultural setting	Deben, 1988, 1993, De Regt, 1984, Van Meijel et al., 1982, Van Moorsel, 1992, Verloo, 1992
Explanation via pillarisation and the passive welfare state	A substantial body of research has tried to explain the unique form and relations of the Dutch state, yet few have linked this to housing provision. A number of explanatory concepts have been developed in the process: the theory of pillarisation; the Christian democratic subsidiary welfare; the corporatist model of decision-making and negotiated adjustment to change	Research influenced by state theory from political science and institutional economics focusing upon class formation and sources of power amongst governing elites	Lijphart, 1968, Schuyt and Van der Veen, 1986, Stuurman, 1983, Van Kersbergen and Verbeek, 1997, 1991, Therborn, 1989, Salet 1999, 1994
Explanation via local differences	Moving from broad theories explaining the Dutch nation state, a number of enlightening studies focus on uneven development, examining the underlying social structures that have generated difference and change at the local and regional level. Unlike nationally aggregated models and grand state theories, smaller-scale geo-histories attempt to provide a more comprehensive and sensitive explanation for differences in housing and urban forms	Cross disciplinary use of historical, economic and political studies illustrating unique contingent shifts in key social relations	Jurriens 1981, Terhorst and Van de Ven, 1997

small builder suggested that only the largest, Jennings, Pioneer and Wimpey, had a chance. These players could cut the cost of labour, materials and, through key alliances with financial institutions, offer attractive financing deals to new buyers (such as payment for three months rent for deposit). Subsequently, small builders play almost no role in fringe development, and rely on medium density infill, extensions and renovations for work.

Appendix 8 The Brutering Agreement

For several years, since 1987, a number of housing associations refinanced fixed rate public loans with low-interest capital-market loans. Observing this development, the government considered withdrawing completely from channelling finance, and established a self-serving fund for associations to assist each other in times of financial stress, thus transferring the umbilical chord of financial responsibility from the central government and control to a collective organisation of providers.

Housing associations were considered to be in a sound financial position in 1993 (CECODHAS, 1994: 3). They had large financial reserves, considerable assets, secure increasing rental income and were providing well-maintained good quality housing. Many associations had plans for expansion and were working with partner organisations. The government assumed that the capital market could provide loans to associations at a rate of 7 per cent, if inflation remained low (3 per cent) and rent growth continued (5 per cent pa).

In 1988, Enneus Heerma, State Secretary of Housing from the centre/right-wing Lubbers-De Korte Cabinet, introduced *Housing in the 1990s*: a policy of privatisation, decentralisation and withdrawal (Priemus, 1990). The Heerma Memorandum (1989) sought reduced government spending on housing, increased targeting and promoted the financial independence of associations and companies. Social targeting required identification of groups to be housed preferentially, specifying income groups and seeking 'optimum' (targeted) use of stock. In line with Heerma's policy, government loans and subsidies were dramatically reduced in the 1990s. *Fixed* annual subsidies were provided to associations, introduced in 1988 and were tapered off during the first half of the 1990s, ceasing in 1995. Heerma ended dynamic costing and introduced the *net cash value method of subsidy, where risk of increasing rates of interest shifted from central government to landlord*. To 'compensate' landlords were permitted more freedom to adjust rent and operating (allocations) policy. In a domino like fashion, risk was therefore passed onto sitting and waiting tenants.

The Government initiated the Brutering Agreement of 1995 to implement its policy of financial independence, reduced public subsidy and decentralisation. Originally, the government wished to provide a lump sum operating payment to housing associations and require them to sell some housing to tenants. This was unacceptable to housing associations, and to counter the proposal they evolved the concept of Brutering, or putting the counter back to zero, by cancelling forthcoming subsidies and outstanding loan repayments. For the central government the agreement was to reduce its involvement, cut operating and capital subsidies, and increase the role of municipalities in financial monitoring and allocating social housing.

Co-operative negotiations between the government and housing associations concluded in late 1993 and the Brutering Agreement was signed by the Association of Dutch Municipalities (VNG), National Housing Council (NWR) and National Christian Housing Association (NCIV). The final agreement ensured that future operating and capital subsidies from the central government were paid in advance to associations. In exchange all outstanding loans were paid to the central government in one action. The agreement was finalised by referendum amongst housing associations in March 1994. By 1995 the Dutch national parliament has passed a Brutering Act, and final settlement took place.

The payment involved an operating advance of 35,000 million guilders by the central government and advance repayment of 30,000 million guilders by the housing associations.

In return for lost subsidies the associations were granted the following measures:

- rents able to rise 0.5 percent over inflation with a minimum floor of 3.5 percent and maximum of 6.5 percent
- specific dwellings with a cost rent structure were given public subsidies to phase out this method of financing and enable rents to rise at the same rate as other dwellings
- extension of existing social housing guarantee fund to cover capital market loans for new construction in social and for profit sector
- extension of non-profit housing activity into commercial development
- system of local negotiations to ensure development meets local needs.

(CECODHAS, 1994: 3–4)

Appendix 9 Guarantee fund for social housing and central social housing fund

The Guarantee Fund for Social Housing (WSW) was established in 1984 to provide security for association loans. A second instrument, financed by contributions of member associations, is the Central Social Housing Fund (CFV) to assist weaker associations, thereby increasing confidence of financial markets. In this way associations, through the CFV and WSW, co-operate to build a stronger, financially independent sector able to access the most favourable terms of private investment.

As mentioned earlier, housing associations and municipal housing agencies must finance their activities via the capital market. Further the government will not directly guarantee funds borrowed by associations. To reduce the cost of such funds, and thereby contain rents, associations try to obtain a guarantee in order to reduce the cost of capital finance.

The WSW was revised in 1989, to apply to all loans by registered social landlords and municipal housing agencies. However, Municipal Housing

Companies and non-profit Institutions are not allowed to participate in the WSW. Alternative private sector loan arrangements, without the assistance of the WSW or local governments, may also be negotiated between associations and private lenders. Yet, loans secured by the WSW attract interest at 1 per cent below market rate with a fixed maximum rate (Vermaat, 1996).

In summary, the WSW guarantee comprises capital resources of the housing association; guarantee funds held by the WSW; and a 'catcher' role shared by central and local government. To date the guarantee fund has not been called upon. In 1997, the WSW was nominated AAA status by the credit rating agency Standard and Poor. This was obtained on the basis of current operational procedures, revenue, indemnities and the existence of government counter-guarantees. This rating confirms WSW's security to external interests, broadens the potential range of institutional investors in social housing developments and gives confidence to the sector.

The primary security for investors is the financial continuity of individual associations and the housing sector as a whole (WSW, 1997). The Central Fund for Social Housing (CFV) is an important public instrument for improving the financial health of weaker associations through reorganisation, amalgamation, asset sales and rent policy (see next subsection for details).

Loans and their corresponding guarantees are linked to a housing complex nominated by the association, which serves as collateral. The size and condition of the loan must correspond with the going concern value and economic life span of the nominated building. The WSW has the right to establish a mortgage on the nominated building. In the event of insufficient funds the two 'catchers' wish to be assured of the precise asset they are securing.

The next layer of security is provided by the guarantee capital of the WSW. This capital originates from a single lump payment by the central government of 70 million guilders, investments of the fund and the annual contributions of participating associations. Currently, 660 members pay 850 guilders per year to participate. Active members are also required to set aside 3.75 per cent of their guaranteed loans that can be called upon in case of emergency.

A final, last resort security is provided by central and local government. In the case that the WSW guarantee capital falls below the minimum required, central and local government will provide interest free loans. Agreement to secure the fund is secured by civil contract.

Guarantee certificates are issued for new construction and improvements to existing dwellings owned by an association. Housing associations must be members of WSW to apply for a certificate of guarantee and must comply with strict financial continuity and solvency criteria. This criteria is based on amount of financial reserves, provisions for repairs, rental and subsidy income plus operating costs. To enable an assessment of current financial status and solvency, participants must reregister each year providing annual accounts, auditor's opinion, financial projections and other detailed financial information.

To obtain a guarantee housing associations submit a detailed project proposal with financial concepts and projections to the WSW. Depending on the complexity of the project and the time taken to provide all required information, certificates are issued within 6 weeks and are only valid for 12 months. Certificates are issued on a strictly standard agreement, developed by the board of WSW and approved by the state.

The Central Housing Fund (CFV)

The Central Fund for Housing (Centraal Fonds voor de Volkshuisvesting, CFV) was established by the Dutch government in 1988 to improve the overall financial viability of housing associations. Through the proportionate contribution of members, funds and expertise are directed towards poorer associations in a mutual effort to improve their financial sustainability. A board comprised of national association experts manages CFV resources. Through efforts to reorganise and restructure, poorer associations are given three years to regain financial health and, through the WSW guarantee, access to private funds (Priemus, 1992: 10). If they are unable to restructure, they may be amalgamated with more viable associations.

The CFV and WSW work closely together to form a safety net for weaker housing associations. If an association is refused a WSW guarantee to expand or improve stock and still wishes to obtain funding, it can apply to the Central Housing Fund for assistance. Assistance is in the form of financial aid to associations alongside an agreed reorganisation plan (CFV, 1997). Whilst the CFV is a public body, it is funded by a levy on housing associations. Each year the Minister determines the amount required and contributions are calculated (NRW, 1997: 35). Since 1988 the CFV has provided 600 million guilders of support to weaker housing associations and has a remaining 225 guilders to allocate.

Those eligible for assistance must submit a reorganisation plan, which evaluates the reasons for their poor financial position and includes rectification measures. These may include co-operation or merger with a stronger housing association, asset sales or rent increases. The reorganisation plan must include a rent policy, long-term maintenance budget and calculation of actual business value. CFV support is made in instalments on the basis of demonstrated progress with their reorganisation plan.

Currently, municipalities assess the financial solvency of associations on an annual basis. Now and then a municipality may have ignored signs of financial problems. In such cases the CFV can demand that the municipality also assist by providing reorganisation funds.

Glossary

What follows is a quick reference and simple definition of a number of terms used in this book. Much has been written elsewhere on these concepts and what immediately follows is merely a launching pad. At the conclusion is a list of recommended reading in the Critical Realist and related fields.

Ontology   What claims can we make about the nature of reality. What should be the object of study? What does reality comprise; is it only what we can see with our own eyes or something beyond this? There are many different classical and contemporary philosophical theories, some stemming from realist, constructivist or positivist views of reality. Which one do you subscribe to?

Epistemology   What claims can we make about the way we can gain knowledge about reality? Given your chosen ontological perspective, what is your theory of knowledge? What is the logical process in your research and how does it influence your research strategy?

Methodology   What is the logic of your research strategy? You have many choices, for example: deductive, inductive, abductive and retroductive. Which one do you choose for your research and why? Is it coherent with your theory of what is real, that is, your ontology, and how you can gain knowledge about it, in other words your epistemology?

Abstraction   If reality is complex, as realists suggest it is, research phenomena can better be understood by taking away single dimensions or components to identify and conceptualise causal processes between them. What dimensions should be examined in your research phenomena? How do these dimensions necessarily relate to each other and what are the possible, but unpredictable contingent relations?

Abduction   This thinking process involves the interpretation and recontextualisation of the phenomena under research, using a plausible, justifiable set of explanatory ideas and concepts. This new interpretation is known as a postulate, or hypothetical conceptual model, which is developed in thought, in order to produce a new explanation of what is actually going on.

Retroduction   This thinking process follows that of abduction. It tests the initial postulated description or explanation, using methods such as contrastive and counterfactual questioning. Does the model adequately explain what is going on? Does it provide the most competitive explanation?

Open system   Realists consider that social and natural phenomena are typically open to influences outside their necessary relations, whose influence cannot be predicted. What are the contingent relations, beyond those integral to the object of study, which could also influence your phenomena?

Critical realism   This is an ontological theory which argues for the appreciation of experiential, actual and real levels or dimensions of reality. It emphasises the abstraction and conceptualisation of complex concrete phenomena, which encompasses all these realms, in order to facilitate the search for a feasible causal explanation. In doing so it argues that social and natural life are complex, structured and open, and we must sort out the contingent from the necessary relations influencing phenomena in order to progress causal explanation.

Experiential realm   The empirical world as observed and experienced by some, to varying degrees of consciousness.

Actual realm   The outcomes or events which occur, as a consequence of underlying generative mechanisms operating in open, complex, structure systems. These events may or may not be recorded in official histories or data sets.

Real realm   This level is all that exists but may not be experienced and observed or actualised. This realm comprises objects, systems or relationships which have emergent powers, such as the family to produce children or employers to hire and fire. These emergent powers may or may not be activated under different contingent circumstances. Nevertheless, they are real, powerful and can have actual effects.

Necessary relation   What necessarily forms part of an object or structure, what does it presuppose? Can you abstract these relations?

Contingent relation   What is not necessary to an object or structure but nevertheless may or may not influence it? Can you abstract these relations and how they may interact with necessary ones?

Causation   The realist view of causation is not based on empirical regularities, as in positive social science. It seeks to uncover the mechanism(s) that may activate real relations with emergent powers to operate and produce an outcome. It requires the researcher to consider the necessary and contingent relations which influence outcomes, and to ask what are these relations and how do they interact and influence each other? What kind of alternative mechanism(s) may impede these outcomes?

Recommended reading

After years of teaching research methodology to postgraduate social science students, Norman Blaikie (Policy, 1993) has written an encyclopaedic book entitled *Approaches to Social Enquiry*. It is a useful reading guide to ontological and methodological alternatives, including Critical Realism.

An excellent introduction to realist thinking is provided in Andrew Sayer's *Realism and Social Sciences* (Sage, 2000), especially chapter one. For a comprehensive treatment of Critical Realist concepts see also Sayer (1984), Hartwig (forthcoming), Danermark *et al.* (2001), in the Critical Interventions series.

For those who wish to read pure Critical Realist philosophy a good start is *The Possibility of Naturalism*, written by Roy Bhaskar (1979). A compilation of key philosophical contributions can be found in *Critical Realism: Essential Readings* (1998). Applied texts, dedicated to the application of realist concepts in social science include once again, Sayer's first book on realism, *Method in Social Science: A Realist Approach* (1984) and Danermark *et al.* (2002) as well as Pawson and Tilley's *Realistic Evaluation* (1988) and Tony Lawson's *Economics and Reality* (1997). The field is growing and many more texts are available apart from those mentioned here. It is also worthwhile to refer to the web and participate in internet bulletin boards, for more recent contributions and debates.

Notes

1 Introduction

1 Sayer (2000: 31) refers to these as defeatist postmodernists.
2 Recently, Sayer has argued for the more explicit distinction of the term 'critical' in realist studies. Just as libertarian philosophy provides an underpinning for neo-libertarian policy prescriptions, the left must also find a clear normative standpoint for its claims of 'just' policy (see Sayer, 2000, Chapters 7 and 8).
3 This standpoint could also form the subject of an entire book, but is not the focus here. Susan Fainstein (2000) provides a critical and concise review of recent progress and new developments in normative thinking applied to the field of urban planning.
4 In responding to such claims, the World Bank recently introduced the Poverty Reduction Strategy Process (PRSP) paper inviting local participation in developing national social and economic plans for recipient countries. Yet implementation remains top down and ad-hoc with basic principles for policy prescriptions unchanged.

2 Ontology matters

1 All discussed in Chapter 4 concerning theories of housing provision.

3 Methodology and comparative research

1 The development of this chapter has benefited from comments by participants at the International Workshop on Comparative research, organised by PhD researchers of AME in December 1999 and participants of the Realism Workshop for Planners, Aarlborg University, Denmark, May 2002. It was published in an earlier form in *Housing and the Built Environment*, 2001, 16 (2).
2 Berry (1998) uses the term in a somewhat looser sense, referring to the low-density, home-ownership dominated outcomes of the Australian housing system.
3 Different explanations for Australia's 'solution' of home ownership dominated low-density cities have been provided by various researchers, including Badcock (1984), Berry (1983a, 1994, 1998), Bourassa *et al.* (1995), Burke and Hayward (1990), Castles (1998, 1997, 1994), Dalton (1999), Frost (1991), Frost and Dingle (1995b), Grieg (1999), Halligan and Paris (1984), Hayward (1992, 1997), Kemeny (1978, 1983), Mullins (1981, 1995), Neutze (1978, 1981), Paris (1993), Stretton, (1975, 1986), Troy (1995, 1990, 1974), Yates (1994, 1997a), Wood (1999), Wood and with Bushe-Jones, (1990, 1991). Also, various explanations, with different emphases and foci, of the Dutch 'solution' of social rented dwellings in compact cities and current changes include: Dieleman (1994), Van der Krabben and Lambooy (1993), Needham (1997, 1992), Needham *et al.* (1993), Papa (1992), Prak and Priemus (1992), Priemus (1996,

1992, 1990), Priemus and Smith (1996), Van der Schaar (1987, 1998, 1999), Steiber (1998) and Terhorst and Van de Ven (1997).
4 Contributors to this debate include Ball, 1986, 1988; Ball and Harloe, 1992; Bourne, 1986; Harloe, 1991; Harloe and Martens, 1983; Kemeny, 1987, 1992; Kemeny and Lowe, 1998; Lundqvist, 1989, 1991; Oxley, 1991; Pickvance 1986; Somerville, 1994; and Van Vliet, 1990.
5 Kleinman makes the point more forcefully:

> 'which [countries] have the best policies?'...often seems to lurk around the corner in comparative studies (particularly those funded by national governments) is intellectually a dead-end. Trying to determine which country has the 'best' housing policy is an utterly fruitless exercise.
>
> (1996: 16)

6 Terhorst and Van de Ven, 1997; Boelhouwer and Heijden, 1992; Balchin, 1996; Power, 1993; Van Vliet, 1990; Harloe, 1987, 1995; Kleinman, 1996; Donnison, 1967; Donnison and Ungerson, 1982.

4 Alternative theories for the composition and dynamics of housing provision

1 These social relations may include their investment in ownership (and other assets), the transaction costs associated with moving out of ownership, the implications for the division of domestic labour, the need to replace two (not one) incomes, the relative cost of ownership in the new job locations and the relative value placed on socio-cultural aspects of the living environment (social status of current/proposed location, tenure, kinship and community networks, education of children, etc.).
2 Although it may provide stimulating clues! (See Lawson T, 1998: 149–152.).
3 For example, during a period of economic crisis, a radical shift in thinking about the role of government, excessive housing costs or high mortgage defaults.
4 A useful review of the convergence debate can be found in Kemeny and Lowe, 1998; Kleinman, 1996 and Somerville, 1994.

5 Postulating an explanation for housing divergence

1 Typical indicators measure forms of tenure, standards of quality, occupancy rates and housing costs. Whilst these indicators may alert researchers to changes in the housing system, they cannot explain the reasons for change.
2 Most recently, private, individual land ownership has been viewed as a necessary pre-requisite in 'growing' home ownership. International financial institutions, such as the World Bank, promote the development of freehold land tenure and title registration systems as a means to facilitate and secure investment in individualised housing forms in developing countries. Yet private ownership of land can also bring speculation, as disastrously experienced in the ownership promoting housing programmes in South Africa, ultimately undermining explicit policy intentions of affordable housing for low-income squatter settlers. In contrast, a number of critical housing economists and other commentators (Achtendberg and Marcuse, 1986; Ball, 1983; Berry, 1983) argue that in order to avoid inflationary problems in areas of scarcity, a policy of publicly owned and allocated land is necessary. Indeed, many social housing programmes such as in the Netherlands incorporate a high degree of state intervention in land development and non-market allocation procedures to avoid such problems (Needham *et al.*, 1993).
3 In Australia, for example, company share apartments are difficult to finance in a market dominated by strata titled apartments. The former involves the purchase of the internal space and a share in a building company, which manages the maintenance of the building structure and communal areas. The risk of poor management arrangements to the

ongoing maintenance is considered too high and a threat to the maintenance of value. For this reason few banks are willing to finance the purchase of company share apartments.

4 Kemeny (1981: 20, 1983) has much to say about the desirability of individualistic home purchase, which concentrates costs in the early phases of the family cycle yet relieves mature households capable of paying higher costs.

5 For a review of such developments in the Netherlands and Australia, see Lawson (2005) and Berry *et al.*, 1999.

6 Kemeny (1981) criticises this type of mortgage contract for its mismatch with the family life cycle, housing needs and spending power.

7 In southern European countries, for example, the direct route dominates. Parents transfer their savings to their offspring to assist the process of home purchase. In doing so, parents maintain their influence over the choice and location of their children's residence enabling familial care in old age. In Portugal, for example, the system for registering land title and ownership has been quite undeveloped. Costly legal disputes naturally affect levels of property investment. Together these features erode the financial security for mortgage providers and more secure investments are made elsewhere. Partly, for this reason, the contract savings, deposit finance and mortgage bank routes for housing finance have been less developed in this country. However, rapid change has occurred with the adoption of the Euro and common banking practices.

8 On this point, the work of Bengs and Rönkä (1994) concerning competition and monopoly in Finnish housing provision provides an appropriate illustration.

6 Explaining divergent tenure patterns and urban form:
the Australian case of low-density home ownership

1 The nation's capital Canberra, located inland and midway between the rival cities Melbourne and Sydney, emerged from an exceptional set of property and financial relations. These included a public leasehold system, public rental housing and a strictly planned hierarchy of land uses.

2 In earlier work Berry (1983a) suggested that there have been four stages in Australian capitalism, influencing the development of Australian cities and housing forms. To define the time period for each phase, Berry uses the dominant form of class structure, relations between capital and labour. In contrast, this chapter examines the causality of shifting property rights, savings and investment, and labour and welfare. The phases defined in this chapter emanate from major shifts in housing outcomes, in order to expose their generative social relations and contingent conditions.

3 Butlin, N (1964) *Investment in Australian Economic Development, 1861–1900*, p. 6 and Weber, A (1899) The Growth of Cities in the Nineteenth Century, republished in 1963 by Cornell University Press, New York, in Sandercock, 1975: 7–8.

4 State Year Book, 1891 in Sandercock, 1975: 8.

5 Dalton stresses the fundamental importance of South Australian legislation, which later formed the basis of regulation underpinning growth in private land ownership and investment across Australia. The Real Property Act 1858 (SA) supported the land market by certifying land parcels and listing them in a register.

6 Melbourne and Sydney were both incorporated as municipalities in 1842 and Adelaide in 1840. For Melbournians, incorporation was perceived as a move for independence from convict-burdened New South Wales, whilst Sydney dwellers hopelessly resisted the shifting tax burden from the larger colonial government (Davison and May, 1992: 6).

7 Nevertheless, mortgage payments were usually higher than rents, and in Adelaide absorbed around 31 per cent of average unskilled wages (Frost and Dingle, 1994: 24, sources Adelaide Advertiser, 1881).

8 Williams, P (1984) in reference to Australian Insurance and Banking Record, 1894, Harcus, 1876, Jevons, 1858, Twopenny, 1883, Dingle and Merret, 1972, Kelly, 1978, Robinson, 1873.

 9 Victorian parliamentary debates, 1904, 107: 268 in Williams, 1984: 175.
10 In 1954 the Melbourne Metropolitan Board of works developed plans for the city's expansion, laying out future freeways and growth areas, in easily developable areas, which largely served as speculators' guides for the astute land purchaser.
11 Berry, M, Dalton, T, Engles, B and Whiting, K (1999) *Falling out of Home Ownership: Mortgage Arrears and Defaults in Australia*, AHURI, RMIT, Melbourne, p. 8.
12 The Nationalist Party tried to court voters in an election pamphlet: 'Reasons why you must vote Nationalist Home Lovers, because I am prepared to raise 20,000,000 pounds to ensure that every city and country dweller who desires to own his own house shall have the means to do so', advertisement, 1925. Also, in the Commonwealth parliament, a Nationalist Party member notes that former labour party voters in South Australia, once accommodated by a government home ownership scheme, turned their vote to the Nationalists, Commonwealth Parliamentary Debates, 1927, 116: 602 in Williams, 1984: 179.
13 Makin, Labour member for Hindmarsh speaking in parliament, Commonwealth Parliamentary Debates, 1927, 116: 669 in Williams, 1984: 180.
14 Bethune, 1978: 274 in Williams, 1984: 181.
15 Quoted in Crough, G (1980) Money, Work and Social Responsibility, Trans-national Corporations Research Project, University of Sydney, Sydney, p. 3.
16 During the 1920s Commonwealth Royal Commission in the Basic Wages specifically blamed poor housing conditions for this industrial unrest. It concluded that wage rises were simply being absorbed by rising rents in the exploitative rental sector. At the time, the Labour Daily argued that a healthy, able and happy workforce could not be reproduced under such poor housing conditions. The labour movement raised the concept of a national housing scheme for all workers to secure their *own home*.
17 New suburbs established in areas that had remained 'dormant' since the 1890s land bust.
18 This fiscal crisis of the regional and local state continued to plague the urban development process well into the 1980s and 1990s, leading to radical calls for more dense cities, privatised infrastructure and new principles for raising regional taxes (Briggs, 1992; DPUG, 1990).
19 This situation contrasts with the widespread ownership of 100 years before illustrated in Table 6.4.
20 No longer a ministry on its own, responsibility for housing was submerged in the nebulous Department of Family and Community Services.
21 In 1998, the Director of Planning for the Housing Industry Association stated, 'Government development agencies are enjoying unfair development advantages in competition with the private sector' Building News, 1998, September/October, p. 14.
22 Earlier in 1989, Hayward identified five groups of land developers operating in Melbourne: Urban Land Authority, small unlisted private development companies, subsidiaries of trading banks, credit companies and life offices, subsidiaries of publicly listed property development companies, and land developers connected with private house builders.
23 The Commonwealth Standing Committee for Long Term Strategies (1992) considered the trend towards consolidation and the need to link urban planning more closely with economic policy.
24 The Council of Australian Governments (COAG, 1995) developed a set of principles based around the notion of competition and recommended the review of all urban planning legislation which may impede it.
25 Perkins, J, states in his introduction that the removal of controls has meant that the Australian financial system has been transformed from 'one of the most controlled banking systems in the world to one of the least controlled' in (1989) *The Deregulation*

on the Australian Financial System: The Experience of the 1980s, Melbourne University Press, Melbourne, p. 1.

26 The argument for an economic restructuring was forcefully put by the Crawford Committee.

27 Perkins, J, 'one consequence appeared to be a substantial increase in the relative strength, and probably the profitability, of banks, especially the major banks' in (1989) *The Deregulation on the Australian Financial System: The Experience of the 1980s*, Melbourne University Press, Melbourne, p. 47.

28 Wood, G and Bushe-Jones, S (1990) Financial Deregulation and Access to Home Ownership in Australia, *Urban Studies*, 7.

29 Savings Banks had been rationing home loans in the previous phase.

30 Commonwealth Bank was once a public bank and is one of the largest traditional providers of home finance. It was privatised during the 1990s.

31 In a well-prepared doorstep interview with journalists Commonwealth Treasurer Costello promotes a recent decline in interest rates. 'An interest rate which has got a 6 in front of it...is an interest rate that we haven't seen in Australia since the 1970s. These are historically low interest rates now, and I would say to young home buyers, you now have the opportunity to get a $14,000 grant for the construction of a new home and an interest rate of 6.8 per cent and this is a very good time to go out and to buy your first home.' Senate Alcove Courtyard, Parliament House, 4 April 2001.

32 Figures for each quarter following deregulation in April 1986 to December 1998 for Melbourne reveal percentage increases from 3 per cent in the first quarter of 1986 to a high of 29 per cent in the first quarter of 1988, in Wood, G and Bushe-Jones, S (1990) Financial Deregulation and Access to Home Ownership in Australia, *Urban Studies*, 7.

33 Following their study of interest rate deregulation and access to home ownership Wood and Bushe-Jones (1990) conclude, 'With credit foncier mortgage instruments remaining the predominant loans instrument (Yates, 1988), growth in household incomes must exceed house price inflation if increases in the deposit gap are to be avoided' Wood, G and Bushe-Jones, S (1990). Financial Deregulation and Access to Home Ownership, in Australia, *Urban Studies*, 7.

34 Yates (1994) analyses income, age and tenure unit record files from the 1991 Housing and Location Choice Survey.

35 Yates (1994) draws upon work by Johnson and Kenyon (1993) on the gap between rich and poor, Gregory (1992) on the 'disappearing middle', Probert (1993) and Freeland (1993) on the causalisation of female labour, Chapman (1993) on the job mismatch and the unemployed, EPAC (1993) on the problems for single-income families, and McLelland (1993) on the after housing poverty of elderly tenants.

7 Explaining divergent tenure patterns and urban form: the Dutch case of compact social housing provision

1 An interesting review and critique of Dutch 'geography of housing' has been undertaken by Van Weesep (1986) and Terhorst and Van de Ven (1997), but *housing studies* is the focus here.

2 Municipal housing companies provided an important vehicle for the implementation of local government housing aspirations. Legislation drastically changed their privileged position in 1965.

3 In 1865 the local 'octrois' was abolished and later fiscal centralisation made municipal governments less dependent upon various indirect taxes (see Terhorst and Van de Ven, 1997 for an extensive discussion on the process of fiscal change shifting local dependence upon regressive tax bases).

4 It was argued in municipal chambers that more housing for lower-income groups would permit upward mobility and allow vacated unsanitary dwellings to be disposed of.

5 Known as the Vestingswet, implementation of this law remained subject to influence of important local contingencies, including the power of local military circles that argued for the continued necessity of walls and moats for defence purposes. Few walled cities remain, notably Naarden, where such lobbies successfully posed forceful argumentation (M Wagenaar, 2003).

6 Middle-class families purchased a dwelling and rented single rooms to generate savings and provide a form of old age income security.

7 Mercier report, 1887, Parliamentary Commission, 1886 considers housing and family allowance.

8 Once again, it should be noted that this figure, as with those in the remainder of this chapter, depicts an abstraction from complex, multi-dimensional reality. Abstraction enables key relationships in the mode of provision to be more clearly seen. For this reason wider connections, which exist between mortgage, banks and the capital market and tenants to the labour market, are not shown but are assumed. These interconnections are revealed by the crises this open system is subject to and are discussed in the surrounding text.

9 However, in larger cities such as Amsterdam the social housing continued to play a more significant role. They continued to expand social housing production throughout the 1920s despite the goals of central government and actively replaced slum dwellings (Feddes, 1995; Schaar, 1987; Terhorst and Van de Ven, 1990).

10 '[Land lease] was considered to be the adequate instrument for a better model of urban development; only municipal land lease could eradicate land speculation...all land that was owned by the municipality was to be leased for the yearly payment of a rent. At the end of the 75th year, the lease would expire and full ownership would return to the municipality, including all built premises without right of compensation. By means of laws and covenants attached to land-lease contracts, the city could gain influence on the type and the use of buildings' (Terhorst and Van de Ven, 1997: 256).

11 Reporting on the parliamentary debate over the *Woningwet* some argued that the law 'een aanslag op den particulieren eigendom' [an attack on private ownership], De Ingenieur, 1901, 15 (4): 53.

12 Report on the congress chaired by Goeman Borgesius concerning Public Health Regulation in De Ingenieur, 1906, 20 (38): 727–729.

13 The proportion of home ownership actually rose between 1921 and 1938, possibly due to low purchase prices and relatively low user costs (Feddes, 1995: 347).

14 According to Kersbergen and Becker, 'The Dutch case shows that Christian democratic hegemony can also be a pivotal power resource of labour' (1988: 497).

15 Tenants were to be passive and their initiative limited to the payment of rent and minor maintenance of the dwelling. Indeed, tenants were carefully monitored by the boards of associations and educated by residential schools for adults, teaching desirable standards of behaviour and domestic management in and around the home (Deben, 1993). Women inspectors kept a watchful, helpful eye on household practices and reinforced notions of good tenancy throughout the 1930s (Turpijn, 1987). Families unable to adjust to the desired norms and standards of the housing association were placed in special residential schools for domestic education. Single women were separated in a special residential home, to be protected from falling into disrepute (Meijel *et al.*, 1982). Building related professionals reinforced the family and village ideal, designing and building dwellings with separate bedrooms, internal access to water and toilet facilities (Grinburg, 1977).

16 During this period up to 80 per cent of all land for urban development was made available via the municipality, through its land company (grondbedrijf). Municipalities owned most of the vacant land on their periphery, over which they had land use control (Badcock, 1994 from Lefcoe, 1978 and Needham, 1992).

17 Interview with Ir Jan van der Schaar 1983, Harloe archive, Salford University, Manchester.

18 In 1954 a commission, emanating from Catholic political circles and chaired by Van Helvoort, which was established to examine the relationship between the social housing providers and central and municipal governments, recommended the primacy of associations in delivery, and the role of central government in finance. Later the divided De Roos commission eventually argued in a majority report for the greater financial independence of associations to build and exploit dwellings not just for low-income households but also for sale and higher income renters (Schaar *et al.*, 1996: 126–136).

19 During this period, only the damaged and empty dwellings were demolished, a 1 per cent rent subsidy for slum replacing new dwellings was introduced, but this was completely insufficient to promote investment and a massive housing shortage threatened (Van der Schaar, 1987: 96).

20 Wages and rising interest rates further increased the cost of construction. For a brief period during the early 1970s, the new, left-dominated government proposed that housing be considered a 'merit good', with rents pegged at 10 per cent of taxable income. This was displaced by a mechanism proposing gradual, systematic and regular rent increases (Schaar, 1987: 112–113).

21 Social housing production rose from 28 per cent in 1978 to 54 per cent of total production in 1982, as construction for ownership fell sharply (Boelhouwer *et al.*, 1990: 95).

22 Women's organisations and advice committees portrayed the ideal housewife as efficient domestic manager of a clean living environment, reinforcing the division between paid and unpaid labour and their dependence upon the male income.

23 Between 1974 and 1982 expenditure on rental allowances increased from 112 million to almost 1 billion guilders, with nine times as many recipients (De Jong and Schoonhoven, 1992).

24 Drawing upon royalties from gas deposits in the North Sea, the Dutch welfare state provided a cushioning effect, delaying the imperative to restructure the Dutch economy and invest in technological developments. This cushioning effect is also referred to as the Dutch disease of providing short-term 'exit strategies' in the form of welfare provisions rather than long-term structural solutions to address inherent economic problems (Therborn, 1989).

25 Reporting on Dutch land practices in 1988 Needham exclaimed that

> [t]he high quality of the housing and of the built environment in The Netherlands is undoubtedly attributable to a very large extent to the fact that the municipalities are the suppliers of most of the building land, and that they use this position most positively and creatively; the land cost in housing is not high; housing is built when and where it is desired, not when and where the land market makes it possible; some 'social mix' is achieved within neighbourhoods by not disposing of land for huge one-class housing estates.

> (1988: 73)

26 According to these authors, environmentalists advocated compact urbanisation connected by public transport, the agricultural sector favoured urban containment, pensions funds favoured scarcity created by physical planning and planners orientated to balanced development favoured control over sprawl (Terhorst and Van de Ven, 1997: 319).

27 Indeed, the municipality of Leidsendam experienced a three-fold increase in land prices, from 15 to 45 guilders per square metre in the Leidseveen VINEX location. (Groetelaers, 2000; Meijer, 1996; Needham, 1997). In other cases, private developers simply bought the best plots from farmers just outside VINEX locations, where development gain could be the greatest, and waited.

28 Residential development, once the domain of municipalities and housing associations, now involves multiple often-conflicting partners necessitating lengthy negotiations. This is confirmed by Groetelaers' study of 181 municipal land development companies. Groetelaers writes,

> the risks [for non-municipal players in the land market] decreased because of a flourishing housing market, a good economy and a changing context (policy). The smaller risks in combination with the publishing of VINEX, in which future urban extension areas where marked out on a map, where an 'open invitation' to private developers and building companies to acquire land and to get involved in the urban land development process.

(2000: 3)

29 According to Groetelaers, 'All actors [in the] real estate market have acquired land by negotiating. In the process municipalities often have less financial space than private developers, which results in a weak position during negotiation' (2000: 7).
30 Further, the VINEX policy stipulates a maximum percentage of social housing to be developed, 30 per cent in new areas and 50 per cent in inner cities. 'Fair' allocation has been perceived as the construction of as many non-subsidised home ownership units as possible (Terhorst and Van de Ven, 1997: 320).
31 Bouw, 1998, Ontwikkelaars negeren volkshuisvesting: corporaties en vinex, 53 (12): 8–11.
32 Speaking in an interview in 1983, one substantial and influential constructor of dwellings considered that the social housing budget was cut due the heavy drain it placed on government finances, via loans, object and subject subsides. Harloe Archive, Salford University Manchester.
33 A Parliamentary Inquiry was held in 1987–1988 to investigate accusations of fraud and the role of central government administrating various subsidy rules and regulations affecting municipalities and the building industry (Murie and Priemus, 1994: 113).
34 Whilst between 1934 and the early 1960s market rates were reduced by hidden government subsidies to suppress cost rents.
35 Between 1970 and 1979 real rents actually declined by 0.3 per cent. Between 1980 and 1989 real rents increased by 1 per cent (source: CBS and VROM, in Nota Wonen (2000) table 6.2 Huurprijsontwikkeling 1950–2000).
36 Yet this also had the consequence of pushing better off tenants into home ownership.
37 In 1996 the BNG provided 18 billion USD in loans to housing associations. It is owned by and provides a dividend to central and municipal governments, each holding a 50 per cent share holding. The bank has a supervisory board of Ministers, Mayors, housing associations and economic experts. Efficient payment services, secure electronic banking mechanisms and small overheads (one central office), reduce costs and therefore interest charged. The Banks also have a triple A rating and provide some of the cheapest loans to associations, allowing for a very low return.
38 Interview with Hans Polman, Director Public Housing, BNG, 1999, Lawson interview archive.
39 Cobouw (1994) ING Groep ijzersterk verankerd in de bouw [ING group strongly anchored in construction], 138 (3).
40 Initially established in 1957, this mechanism had been locally administrated with differing conditions and was relatively ineffective nationally.
41 Since 1996 the process of securitisation of home mortgages began to develop and a secondary mortgage market is now firmly established. This market permits the originator of mortgages to hand over legal responsibility to a special purpose vehicle (SPV). A SPV can issue mortgage-backed securities that can be openly traded. This process

improves the balance sheet and cash flow of the mortgage originators and allows them to issue more loans (DNB, 2000a; Mersmann, 2002).

42 The policy mortgage of interest relief is not set in stone. During the 2003 election campaign, the Labour Party floated the reduction of mortgage interest relief for high-income earners and the broadening of relief for lower incomes to promote access to the housing market. Conservative political parties, the Christian Democrats and Liberals, were opposed, and in preference promoted the scrapping of the property tax (of most benefit to those with high value properties).

43 Home loan interest rates are currently declining to the benefit of those with variable rate loans. Yet, many Dutch purchasers prefer the certainty of a fixed rate for up to 10 years. Yet in April 2002, the EU announced that lenders would not be able to issue fixed interest loans after 2005.

44 In the 2003 election the Christian Democrats promoted a doubling of social security premiums and wholesale revision of the system, the Labour party was against the increase and the pace of reforms.

45 These efforts included disassociating changes in minimum income from the changes in the level of subsidy, passing on rent increases to both non- and subsidy receivers, calculation of all incomes in subsidised dwellings, lowering of the maximum subsidised dwelling and implementation of special rules for single-person households (De Jong and Schoonhoven, 1992: 61).

46 Despite targeting almost half of renters remained eligible for the subsidy (De Jong and Schoonhoven, 1992: 80–86). Further, targeting would not control contingent developments affecting demand for the subsidy, such as divorce, structural unemployment, low wage growth in certain sectors and the individualisation of households.

47 Since the late 1980s the government has expressed its commitment to the sale of some (15,000–20,000) social houses with the proceeds returning to the association to fund new or improvements to dwellings (Murie and Priemus, 1994: 120). In recent years, the central government's drive to sell stock has accelerated, with the demand to sell 500,000 rental dwellings to tenants via heavy discounting (DGVH, 2002).

48 However, the number of rental dwellings sold to (future) renters by social landlords increased only very slowly, from 5,687 dwellings (2.5 per 1000) in 1993 to 8,158 (3.5 per 1000) in 1995 (various years, CBS, Maandstatistiek Bouwnijverheid: table 5).

49 The current state secretary for housing (DGVH, 2002) employs the libertarian language of public choice and anti-paternalism to increase sales of social housing and bring more houses onto the private market in cities such as Amsterdam. He has embedded home ownership into a notion of citizenship, and in the context of very low production, this ideal can only be achieved by the sale of many more social rental dwellings.

Appendices

1 The Age, 21 June 1972 and The Herald, 30 June 1972, referred to in Kilmartin, L (1978).

2 Neutze describes this process briefly as follows: 'Raw land is purchased. Land for housing is either developed and sold directly to individuals or through builders, or released as raw land through developers, on freehold title which limits its use to single family housing' (Neutze, 1978:79).

3 'The Committee believes that there are serious implications for the private development industry in the rapid expansion on activities of the public sector, and reaffirms its belief that over a period, the public sector should not supply more than 20 per cent of total requirements.' Report of the committee of Inquiry (1975) Presented to the Premier of Victoria, Recommendation 19, p. 8.

4 The Australian Newspaper, 9 January 1976, quoted in Harrison, 1978: 153.

5 Gowans Report (1978) Report of the Board of Inquiry into Certain Land Purchases by the Housing Commission and Questions Arising Therefrom, Government Printer, Melbourne.

6 Frost Report (1981) Report on the Royal Commission into Certain Housing Commission Land Purchases and Other Matters, Government Printer, Melbourne in Kilmartin, 1988: 177.

7 Named after Caroline Chisholm, colonial philanthropist assisting women to find suitable housing in adverse conditions.

8 A concept Delfin has embedded in marketing Caroline Springs estate and negotiations with infrastructure partners.

Bibliography

6, P (1998) Housing Policy and the Risk Archipelago: Towards Anticipatory, Holistic Government, *Housing Studies*, 13 (3): 347–375

ABF (2000) Onderzoek Volkshuisvesting [Public Housing Research], *ABF Onderzoek Informatie*, Delft 30 November, accessed 24 April 2006, http://www.abo.nl/default.asp?r=13

Abma, R (1981) The Labour Plan and the Social Democratic Workers Party in the Low Countries, *History Year Book, Acta Historicae Neerlandicae, Studies in the History of the Netherlands*, 14 Martinus Nijhoff, The Hague

Achtenberg, E P and Marcuse, P (1986) Toward the Decommodification of Housing Chapter 28, in R Bratt, C Hartman and A Meyerson (eds) *Critical Perspectives on Housing*, Temple University Press, Philadelphia, PA, pp. 474–483

ACTU and AU (1944) Short Film on the Right to Housing, Australian Council of Trade Unions, Melbourne

AEDES (2001) Key figures, AEDES, Hilversum

AEDES (2003) Cijfers, Hilversum

AIHW (1994) *Public Housing in Australia*, Australian Institute of Health and Welfare, Sydney

Allen, C (2000) On the 'Physiological Dope' Problematic Housing and Illness Research: Towards a Critical Realism of Home and Health, *Housing, Theory and Society*, 17 (2): 49–67

Allen, C and Gurney, C (1997) Beyond 'Housing and Social Theory', *European Network for Housing Research Newsletter*, 3 (97): 3–5

Allen, C and Sprigings, N (1999) *Reflexive Winners, Reflexive Losers and Non-runners: Housing, Policy, Housing Management and Tenant Power in the 'Risk Society'*, Housing and Urban Studies Unit, University of Salford, UK

Allen, J and Hamnett, C (eds) (1991) *Housing and Labour Markets: Building the Connections*, Unwin Hyman, London

Allport, C (1983) Women and Suburban Housing: Post War Planning in Sydney, 1943–1961, in J B Mc Loughlin and M Huxley (eds), *Urban Planning in Australia: Critical Readings*, Longman Cheshire, Melbourne, pp. 233–250

Ambrose, P (1991) The Housing Provision Chain as a Comparative Analytical Framework, *Scandinavian Housing and Planning Research*, 8 (2): 91–104

Ambrose, P (1994) *Urban Process and Power*, Routledge, London

Ambrose, P, Danermark, B and Grintchel, B (1998) A Comparative Study of Housing Privatisation in Russia, Sweden and the UK, Draft Report, University of Örebro, Sweden

Ando, A, Guiso L and Visco, I (1994) Savings and the Accumulation of Wealth. Essays on Italian Households and Government Saving Behaviour, Cambridge University Press, Cambridge

Australian Bureau of Statistics (1996) Australian Social Trends – Home Ownership, ABS, AGPS, Canberra

Australian Bureau of Statistics (1999) Australian Social Trends, Cat. 4102.0, ABS, AGPS, Canberra

Australian Bureau of Statistics (2000) Australian Social Trends, Cat. 4102.0, ABS, AGPS, Canberra

Australian Bureau of Statistics (2001) Australian Social Trends, Cat. 4102.0, ABS, AGPS, Canberra

Australian Bureau of Statistics (2002) Australian Social Trends, Cat. 4102.0, ABS, AGPS, Canberra

Australian Bureau of Statistics (various years) Census and Year Books, ABS, Canberra

Australian Council of Trade Unions and Affiliated Unions (1944) Not only the Need (Audio Visual), ACTU/AU

Australian Financial System Inquiry (1981) Australian Financial System: Final Report of the Committee of Inquiry into the Australian Financial System (Mr J K Campbell, Chairman), AGPS, Canberra

Badcock, B (1984) *Unfairly Structured Cities*, Basil Blackwell, Oxford

Badcock, B (1994) The Strategic Implications for the Randstad of the Dutch Property System, *Urban Studies*, 31: 425–445

Badcock, B (1995) Towards More Equitable Cities: A Receding Prospect? in P Troy (ed.) *Australian Cities: Issues, Strategies and Policies for Urban Australia in the 1990s*, Cambridge University Press, Melbourne, pp. 196–219

Baharoglu, D and Lindfield, M (2000) *Housing Finance Guidelines Developed by the Institute for Housing and Urban Development*, Housing Department, Rotterdam

Bakker, P (1978) Interview with Amsterdam City Council Planning Department, Harloe Archive

Balchin, P (1996) *Housing Policy in Europe*, Routledge, London

Ball, M (1983) *Housing Policy and Economic Power: The Political Economy of Owner Occupation*, Methuen, London

Ball, M (1986) Housing Analysis: Time for a Theoretical Refocus? *Housing Studies*, 1 (3): 147–165

Ball, M (1988) Housing Provision and Comparative Housing Research, in M Ball, M Harloe and M Martens (eds) *Housing and Social Change in Europe and the USA*, Routledge, New York

Ball, M (1998) Institutions in British Property Research: A Review, *Urban Studies*, 35: 1501–1517

Ball, M and Harloe, M (1992) Rhetorical Barriers to Understanding Housing Provision: What the 'Provision Thesis' is and is not, *Housing Studies*, 7 (1): 3–15

Ball, M, Harloe, M and Martens, M (1988) *Housing and Social Change in Europe and the USA*, Routledge, New York

Banai, R (1995) Critical Realism and Urban and Regional Studies, *Environment and Planning*, 22 (5): 563–580

Barlow, J and Duncan, S (1988) The Use and Abuse of Tenure, *Housing Studies*, 3 (4): 219–231

Barlow, J and Duncan, S (1994) *Success and Failure in Housing Provision: European Systems Compared*, Pergamon, Oxford

Bassett, K and Short, J (1980) *Housing and Residential Structure*, Routledge, London

Beck, U (1992) *Risk Society: Towards a New Modernity*, Sage, London

Beck, U, Giddens, A and Lash, S (1994/1995) *Reflexive Modernization: Politics, Tradition, and Aesthetics in the Modern Social Order*, Oxford, Polity and Stanford University Press, Oxford

Beer, A (1993) 'A Dream Won, a Crisis Born?' Home Ownership and the Housing Market, in C Paris (ed.) *Housing Australia*, MacMillan, South Melbourne, pp. 147–172

Beer, A (1999) Fast Forward to the Future? A Vision of Home Ownership and Housing Wealth in the Next Century, in J Yates and M Wulff (eds) *Australia's Housing Choices*, Australian Housing and Urban Research Institute, Melbourne

Bengs, C and Rönkä, K (1994) Competition Restrictions in Housing Production: A Model for Analysis, *Economic Modelling*, 11 (2): 125–133

Berg, N van der and Moer, J van der (1983) Interview with Nationale Woningraad, Harloe Archive

Berry, M (1983a) The Australian City in History, in L Sandercock and M Berry (eds) *Urban Political Economy: The Australian Case*, Allen and Unwin, Sydney, pp. 91–115

Berry, M (1983b) Posing the Housing Question, in L Sandercock and M Berry (eds) *Urban Political Economy: The Australian Case*, Allen and Unwin, Sydney, pp. 91–115

Berry, M (1994) The Political Economy of Australian Cities, in L Johnston (ed.) *Suburban Dreaming: An Interdisciplinary Approach to Australian Cities*, Deakin University Press, Geelong

Berry, M (1998) Unravelling the Australian Housing Solution: The Post War Years, Presented to the 8th International Planning History Conference, University of New South Wales, Sydney, Australia, 15–17 July

Berry, M and Dalton, T (2000) Home Ownership into the New Millennium: A View from the Margin, *Urban Policy and Research*, 18 (4): 434–454

Berry, M, Dalton, T, Engels, B and Whiting, K (1999) *Falling Out of Home Ownership: Mortgage Arrears and Defaults in Australia*, Australian Housing and Urban Research Institute, Melbourne

Beusekom, H G van (1955) Getijden der Volkshuisvesting: notities ener geschiedenis van een halve eeuw, Samson, Alphen aan den Rijn

Bhaskar, R (1975) *A Realist Theory of Science*, The Harvester Press, Brighton

Bhaskar, R (1979) *The Possibility of Naturalism: A Philosophical Critique of the Contemporary Human Sciences*, The Harvester Press, Brighton

Bhaskar, R (1993) *Dialectics: The Pulse of Freedom*, Verso, London

Bijlsma, A (1978) Interview with Squatter in New Markets Area of Amsterdam, Harloe Archive

Blaikie, N (1993) *Approaches to Social Enquiry*, Polity Press, Cambridge

Block, F (1987) Social Policy and Accumulation: A Review and Critique of the New Consensus, in M Rein, G Esping-Anderson and L Rainwater (eds) *Stagnation and Renewal in Social Policy*, Armonk, NY and London, M.E Sharp, pp. 13–31

Boelhouwer, P (1993) Housing Finance in Seven European Countries: Financial Instruments and Government Expenditure, *Netherlands Journal of the Built Environment*, 8 (4): 405–420

Boelhouwer, P (1997a) Financing the Non-profit Rented Sector in Western Europe, *Netherlands Journal of the Built Environment*, 12 (4): 445–461

Boelhouwer, P (ed.) (1997b) Financing the Social Rented Sector in Western Europe, *Housing and Urban Policy Studies*, Delft University Press, Delft, 13

Boelhouwer, P and Heijden, H van der (1992) *Housing Systems in Europe Part 1: A Comparative Study of Housing Policy, Housing and Urban Policy Studies*, Delft University Press, Delft

Boelhouwer, P and Heijden, H van der (1993) Methodological Trends in International Comparative Housing Research, *Netherlands Journal of Housing and the Built Environment*, 8 (4): 371–382

Boelhouwer, P, Heijden, H van der and Priemus, H (1990) The Netherlands, in W van Vliet (ed.) *International Handbook of Housing Policies and Practices*, Greenwood Press, New York

Bolan, R (1999) *The Dutch Retreat from the Welfare State and its Implications for Metropolitan Planning*, AME, University of Amsterdam, Amsterdam

Boléat, M (1985) *National Housing Finance Systems: A Comparative Study*, Croom Helm, London

Bontje, M (2001) *The Challenge of Planned Urbanisation: Urbanisation and National Urbanisation Policy in the Netherlands in a Northwest-European Perspective*, AME, University of Amsterdam, Amsterdam

Bourassa, S, Greig, A and Troy, P (1995) The Limits of Housing Policy: Home Ownership in Australia, *Housing Studies*, 10 (1): 83–104

Bourne, L (1986) Urban Policy Research in Comparative Perspective: Some Pitfalls and Potentials, *Tijdschrift voor Economische en Sociale Geografie*, 77 (3): 163–168

Bourne, L (1990) Introduction, in W van Vliet (ed.) *International Handbook of Housing Policies and Practices*, Greenwood Press, Westport, CT

Bouw (1998) Ontwikkelaars Negeren Volkshuisvesting, *Corporaties en Vinex*, 53 (12): 8–11

Boyer, R (1986) *La Théorie de la Régulation: Une Analyse Critique*, La Decouverte, Paris

Brandsen, T (2000) Social Construction of the Housing Market, paper presented to ENHR conference, Gävle, June

Brandsen, T (2001) PhD Dissertation, University of Twente, Department of Sociology, Faculty of Public Policy and Public Administration, Twente

Briassoulis, H (2000) Analysis of Land Use Change: Theoretical and Modeling Approaches PhD, accessed 24 April 2006, http://www.rri.wvu.edu/WebBook/Briassoulis/chapter4 (models5).html

Briene, M, Dieleman, F, Jobse, R and Floor, J (1989) *Beheer en Verhuurbaarheid: Een Empirische Studie van Enkele Naoorlogse Woningcomplexen*, IOP Bouw, Instituut voor Ruimtelijk Onderzoek, Rotterdam en Utrecht

Briggs, S (1992) *The Application of Developer Contributions for Social Infrastructure*, AGPS, Canberra

Bruinsma (1978) Interview with landlord in Amsterdam, Harloe Archive

Bryson, L and Winter, I (1999) *Social Change, Suburban Lives: An Australian Newtown, 1960s to 1990s*, Allen and Unwin, Sydney

Buckley, R (1994) Housing Finance in Developing Countries: The Role of Credible Contracts, *Economic Development and Cultural Change*, 42 (2): 317–332

Bunker, R (1988) Life in the Suburbs, in R Heathcote (ed.) *The Australian Experience: Essays in Australian Land Settlement and Resources Management*, Longman Cheshire, Melbourne, pp. 221–232

Burke, T and Hayward, D (1990) Housing Melburnians for the Next Twenty Years: Problems Prospects and Possibilities, Working Paper 4, Department of Planning and Urban Growth, Melbourne

Burke, T, Hancock, L and Newton P (1984) A Roof Over Their Heads: Housing Issues and Families in Australia, Institute of Family Studies Monograph 4, Melbourne

Burnley, I (1980) *The Australian Urban System: Growth, Change, and Differentiation*, Longman Cheshire, Melbourne

Burns, L and Grebler, L (1977) *The Housing of Nations: Analysis and Policy in a Comparative Framework*, Methuen/MacMillan, London

Butlin, N (1964) *Investment in Australia's Economic Development, 1861–1900*, Cambridge University Press, London

Cadman, D, Austin-Crowe, L, Topping, R and Avis, M (1991) *Property Development*, Third Edition, E and F N Spon, London

Cannon, M (1995) *The Land Boomers: The Complete Illustrated History*, Melbourne University Press, Melbourne

Castells, M (1977) *The Urban Question*, Arnold, London

Castles, F (1994) The Wage Earners' Welfare State Revisited: Refurbishing the Established Mode of Australian Social Protection, 1983–1993, *Australia Journal of Social Issues*, 29 (2): 120–145

Castles, F (1997) Leaving the Australian Labour Force: An Extended Encounter with the State, *Governance: An International Journal of Policy and Administration*, 10 (2): 97–121

Castles, F (1997a) The Institutional Design of the Australian Welfare State, *International Social Security Review*, 50 (2): 25–41

Castles, F (1997b) The Home Ownership Society, unpublished manuscript

Castles, F (1998) In the Old and the New World, *Acta Politica*, 33 (1): 5–19

Castles, F (1998a) The Really Big Trade Off: Home Ownership and the Welfare in the New World and the Old, *Acta Politica*, 33 (1): 5–19

CBS (various years) Financial Monthly Figures, The Hague

CBS/VROM (2000) Rent Price Developments, Table 6.2, The Hague

CDWV (1952) 50 jaar Woningwet 1902–1952: Gedenkboek in Opdracht van de Centrale Directie van de Wederopbouw en de Volkshuisvesting van het Ministerie van Wederopbouw en Volkshuisvesting en het Nederlands Instituut voor Volkshuisvesting en Stedenbouw, Samsom, Alphen aan den Rijn

Chouinard, V (1990) The Uneven Development of Capitalist States Part 2: The Struggle for Co-operative Housing, *Environment and Planning A*, 22: 1291–1308

Coghlan, T (1969) *Labour and Industry in Australian, V 4*, MacMillan, Melbourne

Cobouw (1994) ING Groep ijzersterk verankerd in de bouw, 138 (3)

Collier, A (1994) *Critical Realism: An Introduction to Roy Bhaskar's Philosophy*, Routledge, London

Conijn, J (1995) *Enkele financieel-economische grondslagen van de volkshuisvesting*, Volkshuisvestingsbeleid en bouwmarkt, 25, Delftse Universitaire Pers, Delft

Croft, J (2001) 'A Risk' or 'At Risk': Reconceptualising Housing Debt in a Risk Welfare Society, *Housing Studies*, 16: 757–773

Crough, J (1980) Money, Work and Social Responsibility, Trans-national Corporations Research Project, University of Sydney, Sydney

Daalder, H (1989) The Mould of Dutch Politics: Themes for Comparative Inquiry, in H Daalder and G A Irwin (eds) *Politics in the Netherlands: How Much Change*, London: Cass (also special issue of *West European Politics*, 12: 97–116)

Dalton, T (1999) Making Housing Policy in Australia: Home Ownership and the Disengagement of the State, unpublished PhD Thesis, RMIT, Melbourne

Daly, M (1988) The Australian City: Development in an Open World, in R Heathcote (ed.) *The Australian Experience: Essays in Australian Land Settlement and Resources Management*, Longman Cheshire, Melbourne

Dam, M van (1983) Interview with Member of Parliament Concerning Rented Housing Policy, Harloe Archive

Danermark, B, Ekström, M, Jakobsen, L and Karlsson, J Ch (2002) *Explaining Society: Critical Realism in the Social Sciences*, Routledge, London

Davison, G (1981) *The Rise and Fall of Marvellous Melbourne*, Melbourne University Press, Melbourne

Davison, G and May, A (1992) Melbourne Centre Stage: The Corporation of Melbourne 1842–1992, *Royal Historical Society of Victoria in Association with the City of Melbourne*, 63 (2–3) Issue 240

Deben, L (1988) *Van Onderkomen tot Woning: Een Studie over Woonbeschaving in Nederland 1850–1969*, Institute of Sociology, University of Amsterdam, Amsterdam

Deben, L (1993) Civilizing the Residential Working Class by Regulation and Lease Rules for Tenants: 1850–1980, *Economic and Social History in the Netherlands NEHA*, 5: 129–147

De Ingenieur (1901) De Ingenieur, Vol. 15, 4, The Netherlands

De Ingenieur (1906) De Ingenieur, Vol. 20, The Netherlands

De Jong, M and Schoonhoven, R (1992) *Afscheid van de zorgeloze verzorgingsstaat*, Spectrum/Aula, Utrecht

Department for Reconstruction and Housing (1950) *Housing Associations in The Netherlands*, Governments Information Office, The Hague

Department of Community Services and Health (1988) 1984 *CSHA Background Information and Statistics*, DCSH, Melbourne

Department of National Development (1957) *The Housing Situation*, DNG, Canberra

Department of Planning and Development (1991) *Vacant Residential Lot Report*, DPD, Melbourne

Department of Planning and Development (1993) *Land Release Forecast*, DPD, Melbourne

Department of Planning and Development (1995a) *Land Release Forecast*, DPD, Melbourne

Department of Planning and Development (1995b) *Land Supply Report*, DPD, Melbourne

Department of Planning and Development (1997) *Land Release Forecast*, DPD, Melbourne

Department of Planning and Urban Growth (1990) Development Contributions: a discussion paper, Department of Planning and Urban Growth, November, Melbourne

Department of Urban and Regional Development (1974) *Urban Land: Problems and Policies*, AGPS, Canberra

De Volkskrant Newspaper, September 8, Amsterdam

DGVH (1997) *Volkshuisvesting in Goud*, Directoraat Generaal Volkshuisvesting, The Hague

DGVH (2002) Press Releases, various dates

DGVH/RPD (2001) Woon Milieu Data Base, The Hague

Dickens, P, Duncan, S, Goodwin, M and Gray, F (1985) *Housing, States and Localities*, Methuen, London and New York

Dieleman, F (1994) Social Rented Housing: Valuable Asset or Unsustainable Burden? *Urban Studies*, 31 (3): 447–463

Dieleman, F (1996a) Modeling Housing Choice, *Netherlands Journal of Housing and the Built Environment*, 11: 201–207

Dieleman, F (1996b) The Quiet Revolution in Dutch Housing Policy, paper presented to CECODHAS/OTB Housing Finance Conference, Nunspeet, February

Dieleman, F (1998) The Impact of Housing Policy Changes on Housing Associations: Experiences from the Netherlands, paper ENHR conference, September, Cardiff

Dieleman, F, Burie, J, Stoppelenburg, P, Ijmkers, F and Nederpelt, G (1985) *Toekomstverkenning Volkshuisvesting: bijdrage aan de toekomst van de volkshuisvesting een inventarisatie en programmeringstudie*, Delft University Press, Delft

Dieleman, H (1997) European Housing Market Developments, in H Vestergaard (ed.) *Housing in Europe*, Statens Byggeforskningsinstitute, Hørsholm, 43–56

Dingle, T and Merrett, D (1972) Home Owners and Tenants in Melbourne 1891–1911, *Australian Economic History Review*, 12: 21–35

DNB (2000) Taking Out Second Mortgages: A Statistical Analysis of Spending and Risks, M C J van Rooij en A C J Stokman, The Netherlands Bank, Amsterdam

DNB (2000a) Nederlandsche Bank publishes Statistical Bulletin (Dutch version) December 2000, Amsterdam

Doling, J (1997) *Comparative Housing Policy: Government and Housing in Advanced Industrialized Countries*, Macmillan, Basingstoke/ St. Martin's Press, New York

Donnison, D (1967) *The Government of Housing*, Penguin, Hammondsworth

Donnison, D and Ungerson, C (1982) *Housing Policy*, Penguin, Hammondsworth

DPUG (1990) Development Contributions: A Discussion Paper, Department of Planning and Urban and Urban Growth, Melbourne

Dunleavy, P (1981) *The Politics of Mass Housing in Britain, 1945–1975*, Clarendon Press, Oxford

Economic Commission for Europe (1998) Housing Finance Key Concepts and Terms, ECE/HBP/102, United Nations, New York and Geneva

Elander, I, Strömberg, T, Danermark, B, Söderfeldt B (1991) Locality Research and Comparative Analysis: The Case of Local Housing Policy in Sweden, *Environment and Planning: A*, 23 (2): 179–196

Elias, N (1939) *The Civilizing Process*, Vol. 1, *The History of Manners* (1978), Vol. 2, *State and Civilization* (1982), Blackwell, Oxford

Elster, J (1986) *Foundations in Social Choice Theory*, Cambridge University Press

Elton, B and Assoc. (1991) Background Paper No. 2, The supply of the private rental market, National Housing Strategy, AGPS, Canberra

Esping-Anderson, G (1990) *Three Worlds of Welfare Capitalism*, Cambridge: Polity Press

Esping-Anderson, G (1996) (ed.) *Welfare States in Transition: National Adaptations in Global Economies*, Sage, London

Esping-Anderson, G and Kersbergen, K van (1992) Contemporary Research on Social Democracy, *Annual Review of Sociology*, 19: 187–208

Fainstein, S (2000) New Directions in Planning Theory, *Urban Affairs Review*, 35 (4) (March), 451–478

Fair, R (1972) Disequilibrium in Housing Models, *Journal of Finance*, 27 (2): 207–221

Faludi, A and Van der Valk, A (1994) Rule and Order: Dutch Planning Doctrine in the Twentieth Century, *The Geojournal Library*, 28, Kluwer, Dordcrecht

Fay, B (1975) *Social Theory and Political Practice*, Allen and Unwin, London

Feddes, A (1995) *Woningmarkt, regulering en inflatie: het na-oorlogse volkshuisvestings-beleid van tien Noordwest-Europese landen, Koninklijk Nederlands Aardrijkskundig Genootschap, Faculteit Ruimtelijke Wetenschappen*, Universiteit Utrecht, Utrecht

Feddes, A and Dieleman, F (1997) Development of the Rented Sector Under Financial and Economic Conditions prevailing in North Western Europe between 1950–1985, *Netherlands Journal of Housing and the Built Environment*, 12 (2): 221–235

Fincher, R (1991) Locational Disadvantage: An Appropriate Policy Response to Urban Inequities, *Australian Geographer*, 22 (2):132–135

Fincher, R and Nieuwenhuysen, J (1998) *Australian Poverty: Then and Now*, Melbourne University Press, Melbourne

Fleetwood, S (ed.) (1999a) *Critical Realism: Development and Debate*, Routledge, London

Fleetwood, S (1999b) Situating Critical Realism in Economics, in S Fleetwood (ed.) *Critical Realism: Development and Debate*, Routledge, London

Floor, J (1972) Rents, Subsidies and Dynamic cost, paper presented by Director General of Housing and Building, Ministry of Housing and Physical Planning to the XXVIIIth Congress of the International Institute of Public Finance, New York, September

Florida, R and Feldman, M (1988) Housing in US Fordism, *International Journal of Urban and Regional Research*, 12: 187–210

Ford, J, Burrows, R and Nettleton, S (2001) *Home Ownership in a Risk Society: Analysis of Mortgage Arrears and Possessions*, Policy Press, London

Fornier (1983) Interview with Ministry of Housing on Physical Planning Policy, Harloe Archive

Forrest, R (1983) The Meaning of Home Ownership, *Society and Space*, 15 (1): 205–216

Forrest, R and Murie, A (1988) *Selling the Welfare State: The Privatisation of Public Housing*, Routledge, London and New York

Forster, C. (1999) *Australian Cities. Continuity and Change*, 2nd edn, Oxford University Press, Melbourne

Frost, L (1991) *The New Urban Frontier*, NSW University Press, Sydney

Frost L and Dingle T (1994) Infrastructure, Technology and Change: An Historical Perspective, *Working Paper*, La Trobe-Department of Economics

Frost, L and Dingle, T (1995a) Infrastructure, Technology and Change: A Historical Perspective, in P Troy (ed.) *Technological Change and the City*, Cambridge University Press, Melbourne, pp. 14–31

Frost, L and Dingle, T (1995b) Sustaining Suburbia: An Historical Perspective of Australia's Urban Growth, in P Troy (ed.) *Australia's Cities: Issues, Strategies and Policies for Urban Australia in the 1990s*, Cambridge University Press, Melbourne, pp. 20–38

Fukuyama, F (1995) *Trust: The Social Virtues and the Creation of Prosperity*, Free Press, New York

Fulpen, H van (1982) Maatschappelijke Aspecten van de Financiering van de Volkshuisvesting [Social Aspects of Financing Public Housing], S.C.P.-cahier; 29, Sociaal en Cultureel Planbureau, Rijswijk

Fulpen, H van (1983a) Woonlasten- en inkomensbegrippen in onderzoek en statistiek [Living expenses and income issues in research and statistics], Onderzoeksprojekt woonlasten en woonlastenbeleid, Working Paper 5 Delftse Universitaire Pers, Delft

Fulpen, H van (1983b) *Het kostprijsvraagstuk in de volkshuisvesting* [Costprice Demand in Public Housing], University Press, Delft

Fulpen, H van (1984) Een Internationale Vergelijking van Woonuitgaven [An International Comparison of Living Costs and Policy], Onderzoeksprojekt woonlasten en woonlastenbeleid, Working Paper 13, Delftse Universitaire Pers, Delft

Fulpen, H van (1985) Volkshuisvesting in demografisch en economische perspectief [Public Housing in Demographic and Economic Perspective], Sociale en Culturele Studies – 8, SCP, Government Printer, The Hague

Geelhoed, L (1989) Social Policy-Issues in Economic Planning: Report of a Conference, W 40, 11th Seminar organised by the Netherlands Government Advisory Council for Social Welfare Policy (HRWB) and the Netherlands Scientific Council for Government

Policy (WRR), held at The Hague from 2–4 November 1988, Wetenschappelijke Raad voor het Regeringsbeleid, Distributiecentrum Overheidspublikaties, The Hague

Ghekiere, L (1996) Allocation of Social Housing in Europe, CECODHAS, European Social Housing Observation Unit, Paris

Giddens, A (1976) *New Sociological Method*, Hutchinson, London

Giddens, A (1982) *Profiles and Critiques in Social Theory*, Macmillan, London

Giddens, A (1984) *The Constitution of Society: Outline of the Theory of Structuration*, Polity Press, London

Golland, A (1998) *Systems of Housing Supply and Housing Production in Europe*, Ashgate, Aldershot

Goodwin, M (2001) Regulation as Process: Regulation Theory and Comparative Urban and Regional Research, *Netherlands Journal of Housing and the Built Environment*, 16 (1): 71–87

Goodwin, M, Duncan, S and Halford, S (1993) Regulation Theory, the Local State, and the Transition of Urban Politics, *Environment and Planning: Society and Space*, 11 (1): 67–88

Gourevitch, P (1986) *Politics in Hard Times: Corporative Responses to International Economic Crisis*, Ithaca, NY and London, Cornell University Press

Gowans Report (1978) Report of the Board of Inquiry into Certain Land Purchases by the Housing Commission and Questions Arising Therefrom, Government Printer, Melbourne

Graaf, B van der (1983) Interview with Gemeente Grondbedrijf, Rotterdam, Harloe Archive

Gramsci, A (1971) *Selections from Prison Notebooks*, New Left books, London

Gran, B (1997) Book Review of Kees van Kersbergen: Social Capitalism: A Study of Christian Democracy and the Welfare State, Routledge, London, 1995, *Acta Sociologica*, 40 (3): 304–308

Gregory, B and Sheehan, P (1998) Poverty and the Collapse of Full Employment, in R Fincher and J Nieuwenhuysen (eds) *Australian Poverty: Then and Now*, Melbourne University Press, Melbourne, pp. 103–126

Gregory, D and Urry, J (1985) *Social Relations and Spatial Structures, Critical Human Geography*, Macmillan, London

Gregory, R G (1992) Aspects of Australian Labour Force Living Standards: The Disappointing Decades 1970–1990, *The Copeland Oration*, 21st Conference of Economists, July

Grieg, A (1999) *The Stuff Dreams are Made of: Housing Provision in Australia 1945–1960*, Melbourne University Press, Melbourne

Grinburg, D (1977) *Housing in the Netherlands 1900–1940*, Delft University Press, Delft

Grinburg, D with Bakema, J (1982) *Housing in the Netherlands 1900–1940*, Delft University Press, Delft

Groetelaers, D (2000) *Urban Land Development Process in the Netherlands: Municipalities in Control*, Geodesy, Delft University of Technology

Gruis, V (2002) Portfolio Management in the Social Rented Sector; Valuation, Risk Analysis and Strategy Development, *Housing Studies*, 17: 245–266

Guiso, L, Japelli, T and Terizzese, D (1994) Housing Finance Arrangements, Intergenerational Transfers and Consumption: The Italian Experience, *Economic Modeling*, 11 (2): 145–155

Gurney, C (1997) Wither (sic) Housing Studies? The Defective Housing Imagination and the Problem of Epistemological Emancipation, Paper prepared for Centre for Housing Management and Development seminar series presentation. University of Wales Cardiff, 22 February

Guy, S and Harris, R (1997) Property in a Global Risk Society: Towards Marketing Research in the Office Sector, *Urban Studies*, 34 (1): 125–140

Haan, de (1978) Interview with Ministry of Housing Regarding Rent Policy, Harloe Archive

Haberer, P (1982) Urban Renewal in the Netherlands, Dutch National Committee for the European Urban Renaissance Campaign, July

Habermas, J (1972) *Knowledge and Human Interests*, Heinemann, London

Habermas, J (1976) *Legitimation Crises*, translated by McCarthy, Heinemann, London

Hadjimatheou, I (1976) *Housing and Mortgage Markets: The UK Experience*, Saxon House, Westmead

Haffner, M (1999) Kosten en Uitgaven van eigenaar-bewoners:een fiscal-economische vergelijking tussen west-Europese landen, volkshuisvestingsbeleid en woningmarkt, Delft University Press, Delft

Haffner, M, Turner, B and Whitehead, C (1997) Editorial, *Netherlands Journal of Housing and the Built Environment*, 12 (4): 357–360

Hajer, M and Reijndorp, A (2001) *In Search of New Public Domain: Analysis and Strategy*, Nai Publishers, Rotterdam

Hakford, J and Matysiak, G (1997) Housing Investment in the Netherlands, *Economic Modelling*, 17 (4): 501–516

Halligan, J and Paris, C (1984) *Australian Urban Politics*, Longman and Cheshire, Melbourne

Hamnett, S and Freestone, R (eds) (2000) *The Australian Metropolis: A Planning History*, Allen and Unwin, St Leonards, Australia

Haralambos, M and Holborn, M (1991) *Sociology: Themes and Perspectives*, Harper Collins, London

Harcus, W (1876) *South Australia: Its History, Resources and Productions*, Adelaide

Harloe, M (1987) The Declining Fortunes of Social Housing in Europe, in D Clapham and J English (eds) *Public Housing: Current Trends and Future Developments*, Croom Helm, London

Harloe, M (1991) Short Note: Towards a Theorized Comparative Housing Research, *Scandinavian Housing and Planning Research*, 8: 129–132

Harloe, M (1994) Social Housing in Transition, *Netherlands Journal of Housing and the Built Environment*, 9 (4): 343–355

Harloe, M (1994a) The Social Construction of Social Housing, in B Danermark, and I Elander (eds) *Social Rented Housing in Europe: Policy, Tenure and Design, Housing and Urban Policy Studies*, 9, OTB, Delft

Harloe, M (1995) *The People's Home: Social Rented Housing in Europe and America*, Blackwell, Oxford

Harloe, M and Martens, M (1983) Comparative Housing Research, *Journal of Social Policy*, 13: 255–277

Harloe, M and Martens, M (1985) The Restructuring of Housing Provision in Britain and the Netherlands, *Environment and Planning A*, 17: 1063–1087

Harré, R (1961) *Theories and Things*, Sheed and Ward, London

Harré, R (1970) *The Principles of Scientific Thinking*, Macmillan, London

Harré, R (1976) The Constructive Role of Models, in L Collins (ed.) *The Use of Models in the Social Sciences*, Tavistock, London, 16–33

Harrison, P (1978) City Planning, in P Scott (ed.) *Australian Cities and Public Policy*, Georgian House, Melbourne

Harvey, D (1973) *Social Justice and the City*, Edward Arnold, London

Harvey, D (1978a) Labour Capital and Class Struggle Around the Built Environment, in K Cox (ed.) *Urbanisation and Conflict in Market Societies*, Macroufa Press, Chicago, pp. 9–37

Harvey, D (1978b) The Urban Process under Capitalism: A Framework for Analysis, *International Journal of Urban and Regional Research*, 2: 101–131

Harvey, D (1989) *The Urban Experience*, Blackwell, Oxford

Hayden, D (1981) What Would a Non-sexist City be Like? Speculations of Housing Urban Design, and Human Work, in C R Stimson, E Dixler, M Nelson and K Ytrakil (eds) *Women and the American City*, University of Chicago Press, Chicago, IL

Hayge, W (1978) Interview with Tenant Leaders in Rotterdam, Harloe Archive

Hayward, D (1992) Reconstructing a Dream: An Analysis of Home Ownership in Australia, unpublished PhD thesis, Department of Anthropology and Sociology, Monash University, Melbourne

Hayward, D (1997) The Reluctant Landlords? A History of Public Housing in Australia, *Urban Policy and Research*, 14 (1): 5–35

Heijden, H van der (2000) Theoretical Approaches of Comparative Housing Research: Similarities and Differences, Convergence and Divergence, paper presented to Housing and Social Theory Working Group, ENHR Conference, Gävle, Sweden, 26–29 June

Hemerijk, A and Kersbergen, K van (1997) A Miraculous Model? Explaining the New Politics of the Welfare State in the Netherlands, *Acta Politica: International Journal of Political Science*, 32 (Autumn): 259–280

Hoop, W de (1981) Housing Policy in the Netherlands after World War II – Conflicts in Housing Provision, paper presented to European Workshop Crisis of Housing Policy, Hamburg, October

Hutson, S and Liddiard, M (1994) *Youth Homelessness: The Construction of a Social Issue*, Macmillan, London

Jakubowicz, A (1984) The Green Ban Movement: Urban Struggle and Class Politics, in J Halligan and C Paris (eds) *Australian Urban Politics: Critical Perspectives*, Longman Cheshire, Melbourne, pp. 149–166

Jary, D and Jary, J (1991) *Sociology*, Harper Collins, New York

Jessop, B (1982) *The Capitalist State*, Martin Robertson, London

Jessop, B (1990) *State Theory: Putting Capitalist States in Their Place*, Polity Press, UK

Jessop, B (1995) Towards a Schumpeterian Workfare Regime in Britain? Reflections on Regulation, Governance, and the Welfare State, *Environment and Planning A*, 27: 1613–1526

Jessop, B (1997) A Neo-Gramscian Approach to the Regulation of Urban Regimes: Accumulation Strategies, Hegemonic Projects and Governance, in M Lauria (ed.) *Reconstructing Urban Regime Theory*, Sage, Thousand Oaks, pp. 51–74

Jessop, B (draft 2000) Institutional (Re)Turns and the Strategic-Relational Approach, accessed 24 April 2006, http://www.comp.lancs.ac.uk/sociology/soc046rj.html

Jevons, W (1858) *Remarks on the Social Map of Sydney*, Mitchell Library, Sydney

Johnson, B and Covello, V (1987) The Social and Cultural Construction of Risk: Essays on Risk Selection and Perception, Reidel Publishing, Dordrecht

Johnston, L (ed.) (1994) *Suburban Dreaming: An Interdisciplinary Approach to Australian Cities*, Deakin University Press, Geelong

Jones, M (1972) *Housing and Poverty in Australia, Ch. 7 Home Ownership*, Melbourne University Press, Melbourne

Jurriens, R (1981) The Miner's General Strike in the Dutch Province of Limburg (21 June–2 July 1917), *The Low Countries History Year Book Acta Historiae Neerlandea*, XIV, pp. 124–153

Jyrkämä, J (2000) *Action, Social Practices and 'Human agency' in Old Age*, Department of Social Sciences and Philosophy University of Jyväskylä, Finland, accessed 24 April 2006, http://www.jyu.fi/ liikunta/tervtiede/SGT/abstrakteja.htm#ACTION

Karn, V and Wolman, H (1992) *Comparing Housing Systems: Housing Performance in the United States and Britain*, Clarendon Press, Oxford

Keat, R and Urry, J (1975/1982) *Social Theory as Science*, 2nd edition, Routledge and Keagan Paul, London

Kelly, M (1978) Eight acres: subdivision and the building process. Paddington 1875–1890, in McCarty, J and Schedvin, B (1978) (eds) Australian Capital Cities, Sydney University Press, Sydney

Kemeny, J (1978) Home Ownership and Finance Capital, *Journal of Australian Political Economy*, 3, September, 89–97

Kemeny, J (1981) *The Myth of Home Ownership: Private Versus Public Choices in Housing Tenure*, Routledge Direct Series, London

Kemeny, J (1983) *The Great Australian Nightmare*, Georgian House, Melbourne

Kemeny, J (1986) The Ideology of Home Ownership, in J B Mc Loughlin and M Huxley (eds) *Urban Planning in Australia: Critical Readings*, Longman and Chesire, Melbourne, pp. 251–258

Kemeny, J (1987) Toward a Theorised Housing Studies: A Counter Critique of the Provision thesis, *Housing Studies*, 2 (4): 249–260

Kemeny, J (1988) Defining Housing Reality: Ideology, Hegemony and Power in Housing Research, *Housing Studies*, 4 (3): 205–218

Kemeny, J (1992) *Housing and Social Theory*, Routledge, London

Kemeny, J (1995) *From Public Housing to Social Market: Rental Policy in Comparative Perspective*, Routledge, London

Kemeny, J (2001) Comparative Housing and Welfare: Theorising the Relationship, *Journal of Housing and the Built Environment*, 16 (1): 53–70

Kemeny, J and Lowe, S (1998) Schools of Comparative Research: From Convergence to Divergence, *Housing Studies*, 13 (2): 161–176

Kemp, P (1997) A Comparative Study of Housing Allowances, DSS Research Report, The Stationery Office, London

Kempen, E van (1986) High-rise Housing Estates and the Concentration of Poverty (the Case of the Bijlmermeer), *Netherlands Journal of Housing and Environmental Research*, 1 (1): 5–25

Kempen, R, Schutjens, V and Van Weesep, J (2000) Housing and Social Fragmentation in the Netherlands, *Housing Studies*, 15 (4), 1 July: 505–531

Kersbergen, K van (1991) Social Capitalism: A Study of Christian Democracy and the Post-war Settlement of the Welfare State. PhD Dissertation, European University Institute, Florence, Italy, reprinted in 1995, see Gran

Kersbergen, K van and Becker, U (1988) The Netherlands: A Passive Social Democratic Welfare State in a Christian Ruled Society, *Journal of Social Policy*, 17 (4): 477–499

Kersbergen, K van and Verbeek, B (1997) The Future of National Social Policies in the Context of European Integration, *Sociale Interventie*, 6 (1): 20–35

Kickert, W (1991) Complexiteit, Zelfsturing en Dynamiek, Samson, Alphen aan den Rhijn

Kilmartin, L (1988) The Land Deals, in R Howe (ed.) *New Houses for Old, Fifty years of Public Housing in Victoria 1938–1988*, Ministry of Housing and Construction, Melbourne

King, R (1986) Housing Policy Planning Practice, in J B McLoughlin and M Huxley (ed.) *Urban Planning in Australia: Critical Readings*, Longman and Cheshire, Melbourne

Kleinman, M (1996) *Housing, Welfare and the State in Europe: Comparative Analysis of Britain, France and Germany*, Edward Edgar, Cheltenham

Klien, P (1975) *Depression and Policy in the Thirties, Acta Historicae Neerlandicae, Studies in the History of the Netherlands, VIII, Martin Nijhoff, The Hague*

Klijn, E (1996) Regels en sturing in netwerken: de invloed van netwerkregels op de herstructuring van naoorlogse wijken, Eburon

Klijn, E and Stoppelenburg, A (1991) Machtverschuivingen in het volkhuisvestingsnetwerk, *Openbaar Bestuur*, 1 (9): 24–31

Klijn, E and Teisman, G (1992) Besluitvorming in beleidsnetwerken; een theoretische beschouwing over het analyseren en verbeteren van beleidsprocessen in complexe beleidstelsels, *Beleidswetenschap*, 6 (1): 32–51

Koning (1983) Interview with Director of Wilma Building Company, Harloe Archive

Kooiman, D (1943) De Woningwet, Samson, Alphen aan den Rijn

Koppenjan, J, De Buin, J and Kickert, W (eds) (1993) *Netwerkmanagement in het Openbaar Bestuur; over de mogelijkheden van overheidsturing in beleidsnetwerken*, VUGA, The Hague

Korthals Altes, W and Groetelaers, D (2000) De ontwikkeling van uitbreidingslocaties: context en praktijk, Achtergrondinformatie van de Vereniging van Grondbedrijven, Achttiende jaargang, 1, Maart

Kosareva, N and Struyk, R (1997) Long Term Housing Finance from Scratch: The Russian Case, *Netherlands Journal of the Built Environment*, 12 (4): 361–380

Kosonen, K (1997) The Pricing of Subsidized Housing Loans in Finland, *Netherlands Journal of the Built Environment*, 12 (4): 381–399

Krabben, E van der and Lambooy, J (1993) A Theoretical Framework for the Functioning of the Dutch Property Market, *Urban Studies*, 30 (8): 1381–1397

Kruijt, B and Needham, B (1980) Gronprijsvorming en Grondprijspolitiek: theory and praktijk, Stenfort Kores, Leiden/Antwerpen

Lawson, J (2000) Explaining Divergent Tenure Patterns and Urban Form – The Australian Case of Low Density Home Ownership, YHR Workshop, 25 June 2000 preceding ENHR main conference, Gävle, Sweden

Lawson, J (2001a) Agency, Structure, Risk and Trust in Dutch Housing Provision: A Comment on Brandsen, *Housing Theory and Society*, 18 (3)

Lawson, J (2001b) Approaching Explanation in Housing History – a Review of Dutch Progress. Referred paper published in Housing Studies Association Conference Proceedings, Cardiff, 4–5 September

Lawson, J (2001c) Book Review of Realism and Social Science, by Andrew Sayer, 2000, Sage, London, Tijdschrift voor Economische and Sociale Geografie (3): 22–24

Lawson, J (2001d) Comparing the Causal Mechanisms Underlying Housing Networks Over Time and Space, *Housing and the Built Environment*, 16 (1): 29–52

Lawson, J (2002) Thin Rationality, Weak Social Constructionism and Critical Realism: The Way Forward in Housing Theory: A Comment on Somerville and Bengtsson, *Housing Theory and Society*, 19 (3): 142–144

Lawson, J (2005) *Home Ownership and the Risk Society, Eigen Woningbezit en de 'Risico Maatschappij'*, DGW and Nethur Partnership, Nethur, Utrecht

Lawson, J and Metaal, S (2001) Volkshuisvesting Opnieuw Bezien, *Rooijlijn*, March, 132–138

Lawson, J, Ploeger, R and Bontje, M (2001) Editorial: Challenges for Comparative Urban and Housing Research, *Netherlands Journal of Housing and the Built Environment*, OTB, Delft 16 (1): 4–5

Lawson, T (1997) *Economics and Reality*, Routledge, London

Lawson, T (1998) Economic Science Without Experimentation, in M Archer, R Bhaskar, A Collier, T Lawson and A Norrie (eds) *Critical Realism, Essential Readings*, Routledge, London

Lawson, T (1999a) Critical Issues in Economics as Realist Social Theory, in S Fleetwood (ed.) *Critical Realism: Development and Debate*, Routledge, London

Lawson, T (1999b) Developments in Economics as Realist Social Theory, in S Fleetwood (ed.) *Critical Realism: Development and Debate*, Routledge, London

Legislative Assembly NSW (1994) Select Committee upon Home Fund and FANMAC Report, May, NSW Parliament, Sydney

Leuvensteijn, M and Koning P (2000) The effects of house-ownership on labour mobility in the Netherlands: Oswald's theses revisited, CPB Research Memorandum, No. 173, Hageman Verpakkers, Den Haag

Leuvensteijn, van M and Koning, P (undated @2001) The Effects of Home Ownership in Labour Mobility in the Netherlands, Oswald's Thesis revisited, Research Memoranda, 173, CPB, Netherlands Bureau for Economic Policy Analysis, The Hague

Lewis, M (1999) *Suburban Backlash: The Battle for the World's Most Liveable City*, Bloomings Books, Hawthorn

Lewis, P (1999) Metaphor and Critical Realism, in S Fleetwood (ed.) *Critical Realism: Development and Debate*, Routledge, London

Lijphart, A (1968) *The Politics of Accommodation Pluralism and Democracy in the Netherlands*, Berkeley, CA: University of California Press

Lijphart, A (1976) Verzuiling, Pacificaties en Kentering in the Nederlandse Politiek, Amsterdam (original in English, 1968)

Lipietz, A (1986) Behind the Crisis: The Exhaustion of a Regime of Accumulation. *Review of Radical Political Economics*, 18 (1–2): 13–32

Lomax, J (1994) Market Structure, Institutional Development, and the Provision of Housing Finance: A Comparative Study, *Economic Modelling*, 11 (2): 215–227

Lukes, S (1974) *Power: A Radical View*, Macmillan, London

Lundqvist, L (1989) Economics, Politics, and Housing Finance: What Determines the Choice Between Privatisation and Collective Redistribution, *Scandinavian Housing and Planning Research*, 6: 201–213

Lundqvist, L (1990) Rolling Stones for the Resurrection of Policy as the Focus of Comparative Housing Research, Paper presented to Housing Debates-Urban Challenges Conference, Paris, 3–6 July

Lundqvist, L (1991) The Challenges of Comparative Housing Policy Research, *Scandinavian Housing and Planning Research*, 8: 65–66

Lundqvist, L (1992) Dislodging the Welfare State? Housing and Privatisation in Four European Nations, *Housing and Urban Policy Studies*, 3, Delft University Press, Delft

McClelland, A (1993) Long Term Unemployment: Costs and Responses, *Australian Economic Review*, 2: 26–30

McDowell, L (1997) *Capital Culture: Gender at Work in the City*, Oxford, Blackwell

Maclennan, D (1982) *Housing Economics*, Longman, London

Maclennan, D and Gibb, K (1990) Housing Finance and Subsidies in Britain after a Decade of 'Thatcherism', *Urban Studies*, 27 (6): 905–918

Maclennan, D, Gibb, K and Moore, A (1994) Housing Systems, Regions and the National Economy, *Economic Modelling*, 11 (2): 228–237

Maclennan, D, Munroe, M and Wood, G (1987), Housing Policies and the Structure of Housing Markets, in B Turner, J Kemeny and L Lundvist (eds) *Between the State and Market: Housing in the Post Industrial era*, Almqvist and Wiskell, Stockholm

McLoughlin, J B (1993) *Shaping Melbourne's Future: Town Planning, the State and Civil Society*, Cambridge University Press, Melbourne

McLoughlin, J B and Huxley, M (1986) *Urban Planning in Australia: Critical Readings*, Longman and Cheshire, Melbourne

Macrone, G and Stephens, M (1995) *Housing Policy in Britain and Europe, The Natural and Built Environment Series 5*, UCL Press, London

Malik, K (1996) Universalism and Difference: Race and the Postmodernists, *Race and Class*, 37 (3): 1–18

Malpezzi, S (1990) Urban Housing and Finance Markets: Some International Comparisons, *Urban Studies*, 27 (6): 971–1002

Marcuse, P (1986) Housing Policy and the Myth of the Benevolent State, in R Bratt C Hartman and A Meyerson (eds), *Critical Perspectives on Housing*, Temple Press, Philadelphia, PA, pp. 248–257

Marcuse, P (1994) Privatization, Tenure, and Property Rights: Towards Clarity in Concepts, in B Danermark and I Elander (eds) *Social Rented Housing in Europe – Policy, Tenure and Design*, The Netherlands, Delft University Press, pp. 21–36.

Meen, G (1994) Changes in the Relationships Between Housing and the Rest of the Economy, Housing Research Findings 22, Joseph Rowntree Foundation, York

Meijel, S van, Renou, R, Schendelen, M van, Vehneijer, Y and Verloo, M (1982) *Vrouwen domicilie en mannen dominatie: reader over vrouwen, wonen and the gebouwd omgeving*, Sua, Amsterdam

Mercier, H (1887) *Over arbeiderswoningen*, Haarlem, Tjeenk Willink

Mersman, H (2002) *Foundation Mortgage Guarantee for Home Ownership in the Netherlands*, Zoetermeer, Netherlands

Michael, K and Pile, S (eds) (1993) *Place and the Politics of Identity*, Routledge, New York

Milort, G (1998) *Dutch Housing Policy in Historical Perspective*, Association of Netherlands Municipalities (VNG), The Hague

Ministry of Reconstruction and Housing (1948) *Housing in the Netherlands and the Relevant Acts and Regulations from 1900 Onward*, Information Department, The Hague

MMBW (1954) Melbourne Plan, Melbourne Metropolitan Board of Works

Moorsel, W van (1992) *Contact en Controle: het vrouwbeeld van de Stichting Goede Wonen*, Sua, Amsterdam

Mowbray, M (1996) Local Government in Victoria: Hijacked or Returned to Its Roots? Just Policy, No. 8, November

Mullins, P (1981) Theoretical Perspectives in Australian Urbanisation: Material Components in the Reproduction of Australian Labour Power, *Australian and New Zealand Journal of Sociology*, 1 (1and 3), pp. 65–76

Mullins, P (1995) Households, Consumerism and Metropolitan Development, in P Troy (ed.) *Australian Cities: Issues, Strategies and Policies for Urban Australia in the 1990s*, Cambridge University Press, Melbourne

Muñoz Gielen, D (2002) Schaarste op woning markt wordt structureel in stand gehouden, De Volkskrant, Forum, 19 December, p. 19

Murie, A and Priemus, H (1994) Social Rented Housing in Britain and the Netherlands: Trends, Trajectories, and Divergence, *Netherlands Journal of Housing and the Built Environment*, 9 (2): 107–126

Murie, A, Niner, P and Watson, C (1976) Housing Policy and the Housing System, Urban and Regional Policy, No. 7, George Allen and Unwin, London

Muter and Tan (1983) Interview with Algemeen Verbond Bouwbedrijven, Harloe Archive

Naess, P (2004) Prediciton, Regression and Critical Realism, *Journal of Critical Realism*, 3 (1): 133–132

National Housing Strategy (NHS) (1992) The Efficient Supply of Affordable Land and Housing: The Urban Challenge, Issues paper Number 4, NHS, AGPS, Canberra

Needham, B (1988) The Netherlands, Chapter 4, in G Hallett (ed.) *Land and Housing Policies in Europe and the USA: A Comparative Analysis*, Routledge, New York, pp. 49–75

Needham, B (1992) A Theory of Land Prices when Land is Supplied Publicly, *Urban Studies*, 29: 669–861

Needham, B (1997) Window on the Netherlands: Land Policy in the Netherlands, *Tijdschrift voor Economische en Sociale geography*, 88 (3): 291–296

Needham, B and Kam, G de (1999) Land for Social Housing: Description of a Study Being Carried Out in the Netherlands, prepared for CECODHAS working party meeting Brussels, September

Needham, B, Kruit, B and Koenders, P (1993) *Urban Land and Property Markets in the Netherlands*, University College London Press, London

Neutze, M (1978) Urban Land, in P Scott (ed.) *Australian Cities and Public Policy*, Georgian House, Melbourne

Neutze, M (1981) *Urban Development in Australia: A Descriptive Analysis*, George Allen and Unwin, Sydney

Neutze, M (1988) Planning as Urban Management: A Critical Assessment, Urban Research Unit, Australian National University, Canberra

New, C (1995) Sociology and the Case for Realism, *The Sociological Review*, 43 (4): 808–827

Nooteboom, B (1995) Trust, opportunism and governance, Research report, 95B33, University of Groningen, The Netherlands

NRW (1997) *Social Housing in The Netherlands*, National Housing Council, Almere

Nycolaas, J (1974) Volkshuisvesting: een Bijdrage tot de Geschiedenis van Woningbouw en Woningbouwbeleid in Nederland, met name sedert 1945, Sunschrift, Sun, Nijmegen

Ogilvy, E (1998) City Plan '97 and the Death of Planning Control, in K Shaw (ed.) *Planning Practice 1998: The Best and Worst Examples of City Planning and Development*, Forum Papers, People's Committee for Planning, Melbourne

Olson, M (1965) *The Logic of Collective Action: Public Goods and the Theory of Groups*, Harvard University Press, Cambridge, MA

Ostrom, E (1990) *Governing the Commons: The Evolution of Institution for Collective Action*, Cambridge University Press, New York

Ottens, H (1989) Verstedelijking en Stadsontwikkeling, Van Gorcom, Assen/Maastricht

Outhwaite, W (1987) *New Philosophies of Social Science: Realism, Hermeneutics and Critical Theory*, Macmillan Education, Basingstoke and London

Outhwaite, W (1998) Realism and Social Science, Chapter 10, in M Archer, R Bhaskar, A Collier, T Lawson and A Norrie (eds) *Critical Realism, Essential Readings*, Routledge, London

Oxley, M (1991) The Aims and Methods of Comparative Research, *Scandinavian Housing and Planning Research*, 9: 67–77

Oxley, M (1996) International Comparisons, in R Camstra and J Smith (eds) *Housing: Levels of Perspective*, AME, UVA, Amsterdam

Oxley, M and Smith, J (1996) *Housing Policy and Rented Housing in Europe*, E and FN Spon, London

Pahl, R (1975) *Whose City?* Penguin, Hammondsworth

Pahl, R and Winkler, J (1974) The Coming Corporatism, *New Society*, 10 October: 72–76

Painter, J and Goodwin, M (1995) Local Governance and Concrete Research: Investigating the Uneven Development of Regulation, *Economy and Society*, 24 (3): 334–356

Papa, O (1992) *Housing Systems in Europe, Part II, Housing and Urban Policy Studies*, OTB Research Institute for Policy Sciences, Delft University Press, Delft

Paris, C (1993) *Housing Australia*, Macmillan, Melbourne

Pawson, R and Tilley, N (1998) *Realistic Evaluation*, Sage, London

Peelen (1983) Interview with Federation of Estate Agents – Nederlands Maarkelaarsbond, Harloe Archive

Pejovich, S (1990) *The Economics of Property Rights: Towards a Theory of Comparative Systems*, Kluwer Academic Publishers, Dordrecht, Boston, MA, New York

Perkins, J (1989) *Deregulation of the Australian Financial System: The Experience of the 1980s*, Melbourne University Press, Melbourne

Pickvance, C (1986) Comparative Urban Analysis and Assumptions about Causality, *International Journal of Urban and Regional Research*, 10 (2): 162–184

Pickvance, C (2001) Four Varieties of Comparative Analysis, *Housing and the Built Environment*, 16 (1): 7–28

Pooley, C G (1992) *Housing Strategies in Europe, 1880–1930*, Leicester University Press, London and New York

Power, A (1993) *Hovels to High-rise: State Housing in Europe Since 1850*, Routledge, London

Prak, N and Priemus, H (1992) The Netherlands, Paper prepared for the Working Group on Public and Social Rented Housing Workshop Origins of the Public and Social Sector, held by the European Network for Housing Research, The Hague, 12 April 1994

Pratt, G (1982) Class Analysis and Urban Domestic Property: A Critical Examination, *International Journal of Urban and Regional Research*, 6 (4): 481–501

Pratt, G (1989) Incorporation Theory and the Reproduction of Community fabric, in M Dear and J Wolch (eds) *The Power of Geography*, Unwin Hyman, London

Priemus, H (1978a) Housing in the Private Renting Sector, unpublished mimeo, Harloe Archive

Priemus, H (1978b) Volkshuisvesting, Begrippen, Problemen, Beleid, Alphen aan de Rijn

Priemus, H (1981) Rent and Subsidy Policy in the Netherlands During the Seventies, *Urban Law and Policy*, 1: 299–355

Priemus, H (1983) Volkshuisvesting Systeem en Woningmarkt [Public Housing Systems and Housing Market, Public Housing in Theory and Practice] Volkshuisvesting in theorie en praktijk, Delft University Press, Delft

Priemus, H (1990) Changes in the Social Rented Sector in the Netherlands and the Role of Housing Policy, paper presented to the Housing Debates and Urban Challenges Conference, Paris, July

Priemus, H (1992) Social Rented Housing in the Netherlands: Recent Policy Changes, Financial 'Independence' and the Relation Between Tenants and Housing Associations. Paper prepared for the Working Group On Public and Social Rented Housing for the Workshop Origins of the Public and Social Sector, held by the European Network for Housing Research, The Hague, 12 April, 1994

Priemus, H (1995) Redefining the Welfare State, Impact upon Housing and Housing Policy in the Netherlands, *Netherlands Journal of Housing and the Built Environment*, 10 (2): 141–155

Priemus, H (1996) Dutch Housing Policy in the 80's and 90's: Growing Uncertainties, *Scandinavian Housing and Planning Research*, 13 (4): 205–213

Priemus, H (1996a) Recent Changes in the Social Rented Sector in The Netherlands, *Urban Studies*, 33 (10): 1891–1908

Priemus, H (2000) *Mogelijkheden en Grenzen van Marktwerking in the Volkshuisvesting*, 9, Nethur and DGVH partnership, Utrecht

Priemus, H and Smith, J (1996) Social Housing Investment: Housing Policy Finance in the UK and the Netherlands 1970–1992, *Netherlands Journal of the Built Environment*, 11 (4): 401–420

Proudfoot, H (2000) Founding Cities in Nineteenth-century Australia, in Stephen Hamnett and Robert Freestone (eds) *The Australian Metropolis: A Planning History*. Sydney: Allen and Unwin

Pryke, M and Whitehead, C (1994) The Influence of Private Finance on the Provision of Social Housing in England, *Netherlands Journal of the Built Environment*, 9 (4): 357–380

Pugh, C (1976) Intergovernmental Relations and the Development of Australian Housing Policies, Centre for Research on Federal Financial Relations, Research monograph 15ANU, Canberra

Randolf, B (1991) Housing Markets, Labour Markets and Discontinuity Theory, in Allen, J and Hamnett, C (eds) *Housing and Labour markets: Building the Connections*, Unwin Hyman, Boston

Regt, A de (1984) *Arbeidersgezinnen en Beschavingsarbeid. Ontwikkelingen in Nederland 1870–1940 een historische-sociologisch studie*, Boom, Meppel

Reijden, Van der (1989) Social Policy-issues in Economic Planning: Report of a Conference, W 40, 11th Seminar organised by the Netherlands Government Advisory Council for Social Welfare Policy (HRWB) and the Netherlands Scientific Council for Government Policy (WRR), held at The Hague from 2–4 November 1988, Wetenschappelijke Raad voor het Regeringsbeleid, Distributiecentrum Overheidspublikaties, The Hague

Rein, M and Schon, D (1986), Frame-reflective Policy Discourse, *Beleidsanalyse*, 15 (4): 4–17

Reitsma, A (1998) The Changing Role of the Government in Housing Systems in Relation to the Welfare State in the Netherlands and Flanders, paper presented to ENHR conference, Cardiff, September

Rele, H ter and Steen, G van (2001) Housing Subsidisation in the Netherlands: Measuring its Distortionary and Distributional Effects, CPB Discussion Paper; no. 002, CPB Netherlands Bureau for Economic Policy Analysis, The Hague

Remkes, J (2001) Nota Mensen, Wensen, Wonen [White paper on People, Wishes, Homes]. The Hague VROM

Renaud, B (1999) The Financing of Social Housing in Integrating Financial Markets: A View from Developing Countries, *Urban Studies*, 36 (4): 755–773

Rex, J (1974) *Sociology and the Demystification of the Modern World*, Routledge and Keagan Paul, London

Rex, J and Moore, R (1967) *Race, Community and Conflict: A Study of Sparkbrook*, Oxford University Press, London

RICS (2002) *RICS European Housing Review 2002*, Royal Institute for Chartered Surveyors, Coventry

RIGO (1991) *Foreign Land Policy in a Dutch Perspective, Summary, Urban Renewal and Urbanization*, number 40, DGVH/VROM, The Hague

Roberts, S (1968) *History of Australian Land Settlement*, Macmillan, Melbourne

Robinson, C (1873) *New South Wales: Oldest and Richest of the Australian Colonies*, Sydney

Ruijter, P de with Faludi, A (1987) *Voor volkshuisvesting en stedenbouw: voorgescheidenis oprichting en programma van het Nederlands Instituut voor Volkshuisvesting en Stedenbouw 1850–1940*, Stichting Matrijs, Utrecht

Ruonavaara, H (1993) Types and Forms of Housing Tenure, Towards Solving the Comparison/Translation Problem, *Scandinavian Housing and Planning Research*, 8: 67–77

Salet, W (1987) *Ordening en sturing in het volkshuisvestingsbeleid*, Staatsuitgeverij, Den Haag

Salet, W (1994) *Om recht en staat: een sociologische verkenning van sociale, politieke en rechtsbetrekkingen*, SDU, Den Haag

Salet, W (1999) Regime Shifts in Dutch Housing Policy, *Housing Studies*, 14 (4): 547–557

Samson (1978) Interview with Ministry of Housing Regarding Rent Protecting, Harloe Archive

Sandercock, L (1975) *Cities for Sale: Property, Politics and Urban Planning in Australia*, Melbourne University Press, Melbourne

Saunders, P (1979) *Urban Politics: A Sociological Interpretation*, Hutchinson, London

Saunders, P (1982) Beyond Housing Classes: The Sociological Significance of Private Property Rights in the Means of Consumption, Urban and Regional Studies Working Paper, 33, University of Sussex

Saunders, P (1983) *Social Theory and the Urban Question*, 2nd edn, Hutchinson, London

Saw, P and Whitehead, C (1997) Financing Social Housing without Guarantee: An English case study, *Netherlands Journal of the Built Environment*, 12 (4): 423–443

Sayer, A (1982) Explanation in Economic Geography: Abstraction versus Generalisation, *Progress in Human Geography*, 6: 68–88

Sayer, A (1984) *Method in Social Science: A Realist Approach*, Hutchinson, London

Sayer, A (1985) Realism and Geography, in R Johnston (ed.) *The future of geography*, Methuen, London

Sayer, A (1991) Beyond the Locality Debate: Deconstructing Localities Dualisms, *Society and Space: Environment and Planning D*, 23: 283–308

Sayer, A (1992) *Method in Social Science: A Realist Approach*, 2nd edn, Routledge, London

Sayer, A (1998) Abstraction: A Realist Interpretation, in M Archer, R Bhaskar, A Collier, T Lawson and A Norrie (eds) *Critical Realism: Essential Readings*, Routledge, London, republished from *Radical Philosophy* (1981), 28, pp. 6–15

Sayer, A (2000) *Realism and Social Science*, Sage, London

Sayer, A (draft 2000) Markets, Embeddedness and Trust: Problems of Polysemy and Idealism, Department of Sociology, Lancaster University, accessed 24 April 2006, http://www.comp.lancaster.ac.uk/sociology/soc047as.html

Sayer, A (2003) Restoring the Moral Dimension in Social Scientific Accounts: A Qualified Ethical Naturalist Approach, paper presented to the International Association for Critical Realism Conference, 15–17 August , Amsterdam

Sayer, A and Ray, L (eds) (1999) *Culture and Economy after the Cultural Turn*, Sage, London

Schaar, J van der (1978) Interview notes, Harloe Archive

Schaar, J van der (1987) *Groei en Bloei van het Nederlandse Volkshuivestingsbeleid, Volkshuisvesting in theorie en praktijk*, 7, Delftse Universitaire Pers

Schaar, J van der (1998) *Honderd Jaar Volkshuisvestingbeleid: van gezondheidsvraag tot woonmilieubeleid*, RIGO, Amsterdam

Schaar, J van der (1999) *De Woningvoorzien Tussen Publiek en Privaat: over aardver-schuivingen in het volkshuisvestingbeleid*, RIGO, Amsterdam

Schaar, J van der (2001) *Syllabus Wonen en Bowen – 1, Wonen end woonbelied: markten, instituties, intrumenten*, University of Amsterdam, Amsterdam

Schaar, J van der and Hereigers, M (1991) *Volkshuisvesting een Zaak van Beleid*, Aula, Utrecht

Schaar, J van der, Faber, A, Koffijberg, J and Piemus, H (1996) *Volkshuisvesting in Goud*, Directorate General Social Housing (DGVH), The Hague

Schillmeier, M (1999) Book Review: Ulrich Beck, Democracy without Enemies, *The Sociological Review*, 47 (1): 172–175

Schuyt, K and Van der Veen, R (1986) *De Verdeelde Samenleving: een inleiding in de ontwikkeling van de Nederlandse vorzorgingsstaat*, Stenfert Kroese, Leiden

Searing, H (1971) Housing in Holland and the Amsterdam School, a Dissertation presented to the Faculty of the Graduate School of Yale University in partial fulfilment for the Degree of Doctor of Philosophy

Shaw, K (ed.) (1998) Planning Practice 1998: The Best and Worst Examples of City Planning and Development, Forum Papers, People's Committee for Planning, Melbourne

Simmel, G (1955) *Conflict and the Web of Group Affiliations*, Free Press, Glencoe, IL

Simmie, J (1981) *Property, Power and Corporatism*, Macmillan, London

Smeets, J (1999) Trends in the Netherlands Housing Management: End of the Non-profit Housing Sector? Draft paper presented to Housing Process and Management Working ENHR Group, Lisbon, May

Smit, F (1994) *Van Amsterdamse Huize: ontwikkeling en identitiet van Het Woningbedrijf* Amsterdam

Smith, J (1996) Social Housing Provision and Investment: A European Comparison, in R Camstra and J Smith (eds) *Housing Levels of Perspective*, De Montfort University and Amsterdam Centre for the Metropolitan Environment, Amsterdam

Snepvangers, M (1993) *Onze Woning…meer dan een dak boven uw hoofd: 75 jaar Woningstichting 'Onze Woning', Woonstichting 'Onze Woning'*, Rotterdam

Soja, E (1989) *Postmodern Geographies*, Verso, London

Somerville, P (1994) On Explanation of Housing Policy, *Scandinavian Housing and Planning Research*, 11: 211–230

Somerville, P (1999) Housing, Rationality and Crime, presented to ENHR Housing Management Working Group meeting, June 1999, Lisbon

Somerville, P (2000) Housing Rationality and Crime, paper presented to ENHR conference Gavle, Sweden, 26–30 June

Somerville, P and Bengtsson, B (2002) Constructionism and Realism and Housing Theory, *Housing, Theory and Society*, 19: 121–136

Spaans, M and Golland, A (1996) Land Supply and Housing Development: A Comparative Analysis of Britain and the Netherlands, *International Planning Studies*, October, 1 (3): 291

Steiber, N (1998) Housing Design and Society in Amsterdam: Reconfiguring Urban Order and Identity, 1900–1920, The University of Chicago Press, Chicago, IL

Steinmetz, G (1998) Critical Realism and Historical Sociology. A Review Article *Comparative Studies in Society and History: An International Quarterly*, 40 (1): 170–186

Stephens, M (1993) Housing Finance Deregulation: Britain's Experience, *Netherlands Journal of the Built Environment*, 8 (2): 159–175

Stilwell, F (1986) *The Political Economy of the Labour Government: The Accord and Beyond*, Pluto Press, Sydney and London

Stockman, N (1983) *Anti-Positivist Theories for the Sciences*, Reichel, Dordrecht

Stretton, H (1970/1975) *Ideas for Australian Cities*, Georgian House, Melbourne

Stretton, H (1978) Housing Policy, in P Scott (ed.) *Australian Cities and Public Policy*, Georgian House, Melbourne

Stretton, H (1986) Housing – an Investment for All, in J B Mc Loughlin and M Huxley (eds) *Urban Planning in Australia: Critical Readings*, Longman Cheshire, Melbourne

Stuurman, S (1983) Verzuiling, Kapitalisme en Patriarchaat: aspecten van de ontwikkeling van de moderne staat in Nederland, SUN Socialistiese Uitgeverij Nijmegen

Taylor-Gooby, P (1991) Welfare State Regimes and Welfare Citizenship, *Journal of European Social Policy*, 1 (2): 93–105

Taylor-Gooby, P (1991a) *Social Change, Social Welfare and Social Science*, Harvester Wheat sheaf, Hemel Hempstead

Taylor-Gooby, P, Dean, H, Munro, M and Parker, G (1999) Risk and the Welfare State, *British Journal of Sociology*, 50 (2):177–194

Taylor, J and Jureidini, R (1994) The Implicit Male Norm in Australian Housing Finance, *Journal of Economic Issues*, 28 (2): 543–555

Terhorst, P and Van der Ven, J (1983) Woonlasten en Bouwlokaties: een vergelijking van de woonlasten van premiekoopwoningen in en buiten Amsterdam, CGO, University of Amsterdam

Terhorst, P and Van de Ven, J (1995) The National Urban Growth Coalition in the Netherlands, *Political Geography*, 14 (4): 343–361

Terhorst, P and Van de Ven, J (1997) *Fragmented Brussels and Consolidated Amsterdam: A Comparative Study of the Spatial Organisation of Property Rights*, Nederlandse Geografische Studies, University of Amsterdam, Amsterdam

Therborn, G (1989) 'Pillarization' and 'Popular Movements' Two Variants of Welfare State Capitalism: the Netherlands and Sweden, in F Castles (ed.) *The Comparative History of Public Policy*, Polity Press, Cambridge, pp. 191–241

Tickell, A and Peck, J (1995) Social Regulation after Fordism, *Economy and Society*, 24 (3): 357–386

Tritter J and Archer M (eds) *Rational Choice Theory: A Critique (Critical Realism)*, Routledge

Troy, P (1974) *A Fair Price: the Land Commission Program 1972–1977*, Hale and Iremonger, Sydney

Troy, P (1990) The Evolution of Government Housing Policy: The Case of New South Wales 1901–1941, URU Research Paper, ANU, Canberra

Troy, P (1991) The Benefits of Owner Occupation, Urban Research Program Working Paper 29, ANU, Canberra

Troy, P (ed.) (1995) *Australian Cities: Issues, Strategies and Policies for Urban Australia in the 1990s*, Cambridge University Press, Melbourne

Turpijn, W (1987) In de Schaduw van de Volkshuisvesting: een studie over de zelfwerkzaamheid van bewoners, VUGA, 's-Gravenhage

Twopenny, R (1883) Townlife in Australia, copy edited 1973, Sydney University Press, Sydney

Vereeniging van Huis Eigenaars (1983) Interview with one of the founders of the Vereeniging, Harloe Archive

Verloo, M (1992) *Macht en Gender in Sociale Bewegingen: over de participatie van vrouwen in bewonersorganisaties*, Sua, Amsterdam

Vermaat, J (1996) *The Guarantee Fund for Social Rented Housing*, VUGA, The Hague

Visser, J and Hemerijck, A (1997) *'A Dutch Miracle': Job Growth, Welfare Reform and Corporatism in the Netherlands*, Amsterdam University Press, Amsterdam

Vlek, R (1998) From Welfare to Work: Report II on the Netherlands: With a Special Focus on the Case of Amsterdam, Amsterdamse School voor Sociaal Wetenschappelijk Onderzoek, University of Amsterdam, Amsterdam

Vliet, W van (1990) Cross-National Housing Research: Analytical and Substantive Issues, in W Van Vliet (ed.) *International Handbook of Housing Policies and Practices*, Greenwood Press, Westport, CT

Vliet, W van and Weesep, J van (1990) *Government and Housing: Developments in Seven Countries*, Sage, Newbury Park, CA

VROM (1976a) *Housing in the Netherlands*, Information Department, The Hague

VROM (1976b) *Structura Schema Volkshuisvesting deel a beleidsvormen*, Ministerie van Volkshuisvesting en Ruimtemelijke Ordening, The Hague

VROM (1976c) *Summary Report on Urbanization in the Netherlands*, Ministry of Housing and Physical Planning, The Hague

VROM (1978) *Special Housing Needs in the Netherlands*, Ministry of Housing and Physical Planning, The Hague

VROM (1983) *A Perspective on Government Housing Policies in the Netherlands*, Ministry of Housing and Physical Planning, Department of Information and International Relations, The Hague

VROM (2000) De Nota Wonen [White Paper on Housing] VROM, The Hague

VROM (2001) Cijfers over Wonen, The Hague

VROM/DGVH (1990–1996) Key Data for Social Renters, The Hague

Wagenaar, M (2003) Interview conducted by the author, AME, Amsterdam

Walker, D (1978) The Transformation of Urban Structure in the Nineteenth Century and the Beginning of Urbanisation, in K Cox (ed.) *Urbanisation and Conflict in Market Societies*, Methuen, London

Watling, R (1999) The High Life: The Apartment Boom in Melbourne, in K O'Connor (ed.) *Housing and Jobs in Cities and Regions: Research in Honour of Chris Maher*, AHURI, Melbourne

Watson, S and Austerberry, H (1986) *Housing and Homelessness: A Feminist Perspective*, Routledge and Kegan Paul, London

Watson, S and Gibson, K (eds) (1995) *Post-modern Cities and Spaces*, Blackwell, Cambridge

WBO (1990) Housing Need Research, CBS/VROM

WBO (1994) Housing Need Research, CBS/VROM

Weber, M (1968) *Economy and Society*, Bedminster Press, New York

Weesep, J van (1982) Production and Allocation of Housing: The Case of the Netherlands, Geografische en Planologische Notities, No. 11

Weesep, J van (1986) *Condominium: A New Housing Sector in The Netherlands*, Geography Institute, Utrecht University, Utrecht

Weesep, J van and van Kempen, R (1993) Low Income and Housing in the Dutch Welfare State, in G Hallet (ed.) *The New Housing Shortage: Housing Affordability in Europe and the USA*, Routledge, London, 179–206

Weicher, J (1994) Housing Finance Fiefdoms the Mortgage Market: The Privileged Positions of Fannie Mae and Freddie Mac, *American Enterprises*, September–October: 62–66

Whipple, R (1974) Land Reform and the Real Estate Market: A Review of Proposals by the Commission of Inquiry into Land Tenure, Presented to a Conference on the First Report to the Commission, 30 March, Sydney

Whitehead, C (1974) *The UK Housing Market*, Saxon House, Farnsborough

Wilenski, H, Luebert, G and Hahn, J (1987) *Comparative Housing Research*, Gower, Berlin

Williams, P (1984) The Politics of Property: Home Ownership in Australia, in J Halligan and C Paris (eds) *Australian Urban Politics: Critical Perspectives*, Longman Cheshire, Melbourne

Winter, I (1994) *The Radical Homeowner: Housing Tenure and Social Change*, Gordon and Breach, Australia

Winter, I and Stone, W (1998) *Social Polarisation and Housing Careers: Exploring the Interrelationship of Labour and Housing Markets in Australia*, AIFS, Melbourne

Wollmann, H and Jaedicke, W (1989) The Rise and Fall of Public and Social Housing, *Tijdschrift voor Economische and Sociale Geografie*, 80 (2): 82–88

Wood, G (1990) The Tax Treatment of Housing: Economic Issues and Reform Measures, *Urban Studies*, 27 (6): 809–830

Wood, G (1990a) Housing Finance and Subsidy Systems in Australia, *Urban Studies*, 29 (6): 847–876

Wood, G (1999) Tax Home Owner Residential Property Taxes and their Burden on Net Personal Wealth: An Empirical Study for Australia, *Urban Studies*, 36 (2): 239–254

Wood, G and Bushe-Jones, S (1990) Financial Deregulation and Access to Home Ownership in Australia, *Urban Studies*, 7: 583–590

Wood, G and Bushe-Jones, S (1991) *Housing Affordability: An International Context*, National Housing Strategy, AGPS, Canberra

World Bank (1993) Enabling Markets to Work, World Bank Policy Paper, Washington, DC

Wright, E (1978) *Class, Crises and the State*, New Left Books: London.

Wright Mills, C (1959/1976) *The Sociological Imagination*, Oxford University Press, New York

Wulff, M (1992) Low Income Home Ownership: The Privatisation of Squalor or the Great Australian Dream, *Housing Studies*, 5 (4): 229–241

Wulff, M and Maher, C (1998) Long Term Renters in the Australian Renters Market, *Housing Studies*, 13: 83–98

Wulff, M and Yates, J (1999) *Australia's Housing Choices: Changing Opportunities and Constraints*, AHURI, Melbourne

Yates, J (1994) Home Ownership and Australia's Housing Finance System, *Urban Policy and Research*, 12 (1): 27–39

Yates, J (1997) *Trends in Home Ownership*, Report to NSW Department of Urban Affairs, Sydney

Yates, J (1997a) Changing Directions in Australian Housing Policies: The End of Muddling Through? *Housing Studies*, 12 (2): 265–277

Yates, J (1997b) *Trends in Home Ownership*, Department of Urban Affairs and Planning, Sydney

Yates, J and Wulff, M (1999a) *Australia's Housing Choices*, AHURI, Melbourne

Yates, J and Wulff, M (1999b) Housing Markets and Household Income Polarisation: A Metropolitan and Regional Analysis, ARC-SPIRT Housing Choices Project, AHRF Rental Housing Project, Presentation

Yates, J and Wulff, J (1999c) Recent Developments in the Analysis of Australia's Private Rental Market, in K O'Conner (ed.) *Houses and Jobs in Cities and Regions: Research in Honour of Chris Maher*, AHURI, Melbourne

Young, T (1991) Change and Chaos Theory, *Social Science Journal*, Fall, 28: 3
Young, T (1992) Chaos Theory and Human Agency, *Humanity and Society*, 16 (4): 441–460
Zanden, J-L van (1997) Een Klein land in de 20e eeuw: economische geschiedenis van Nederland 1914–1995 [A small country in the 20th century: an economic history of the Netherlands], Het Spectrum, Utrecht

Index

6, P 34

abduction process: abduction mode of inference 22; and retroduction process 19, 30–31
agency and risk concept 82–84
Allen, C 14
Allen, J 75
Ambrose, P 25–26, 46–47, 77, 85, 239; Ambrose's state – market – citizen relations and the chain of provision 239–241
Amsterdam 1, 7, 150, 156, 162, 168, 171–172, 175, 180–181, 203, 270, 273, 276–280, 288–289, 292–294
Australian case of low-density home ownership 93–149
Australian households: versus Dutch households 225–227; home purchase during 1990s 227–229
Australian housing solution 248–249; core of 98–106; critical evaluation of explanatory progress 104–106; as a dynamic outcome of social relations in a contingent context 101–102; existing explanations for 99–104; first phase (emergence) 109, 114–121, *see also separate entry*; fourth phase (towards dismantling and reconfiguration) 110, 133–140, *see also separate entry*; observable outcomes 96–98; phases 108–110; phases, analysis and contrast 111–140; policy analysis, political power and normative critique 103–104; postulated model of causal mechanisms 106–111; retroductive analysis 141–148; second phase (establishment and acceleration) 109, 121–128, *see also separate entry*; significant

relations underpinning 102; state role in 102–103; state role in, theorising 110–113; third phase (intermediate period of deceleration and decline) 109–110, 128–132, *see also separate entry*, urban development and housing tenure 99–100

Ball, M 26–27, 53, 56, 64, 66, 74, 85, 101, 106, 243
Barlow, J 26, 58
Beck, U 37, 55
Becker, U 170, 270 n.14
Bengs, C 48, 267 n.8 (chap.5)
Bengtsson, B 14, 35
Berry, M 57, 99–101, 106–107, 111, 265 n.2 (chap.2), 267 n.2
betterment tax 67
Beusekom, H G van 153
Bhaskar, R 8, 20, 31, 264
Blaikie, N 8, 14, 16, 31, 263
Block, F 158
Boelhouwer, P 26, 157–158
Bourassa, S 101
Brutering process/agreement 200, 258–259
Bunker, R 104
Burnley, I 101
Bushe-Jones, S 33
Butlin, N 117

capital accumulation process 86–87
capital markets, in housing investment 72
Castles, F 58, 102
causal clusters mechanisms, in realist concepts 29–31
causal explanatory approaches, critical review 59–62